Nationalism and the Moral Psychology of Community

Nationalism and the Moral Psychology of Community

BERNARD YACK

THE UNIVERSITY OF CHICAGO PRESS   CHICAGO AND LONDON

BERNARD YACK is the Lerman-Neubauer Professor of Democracy in the Department of Politics at Brandeis University. He is the author of several books, including *The Problems of a Political Animal* and *Liberalism without Illusions*.

The University of Chicago Press, Chicago 60637
The University of Chicago Press, Ltd., London

Printed in the United States of America

21 20 19 18 17 16 15 14 13 12   1 2 3 4 5

ISBN-13: 978-0-226-94466-1 (cloth)
ISBN-13: 978-0-226-94467-8 (paper)
ISBN-10: 0-226-94466-2 (cloth)
ISBN-10: 0-226-94467-0 (paper)

Library of Congress Cataloging-in-Publication Data
Yack, Bernard, 1952–
Nationalism and the moral psychology of community / Bernard Yack.
p. cm.
Includes bibliographical references and index.
ISBN-13: 978-0-226-94466-1 (cloth: alkaline paper)
ISBN-10: 0-226-94466-2 (cloth: alkaline paper)
ISBN-13: 978-0-226-94467-8 (paperback: alkaline paper)
ISBN-10: 0-226-94467-0 (paperback: alkaline paper) 1. Nationalism. 2. Nation-state. 3. Nationalism—Moral and ethical aspects. I. Title.
JC311.Y23 2012
320.54—dc23

2011030920

♾ This paper meets the requirements of ANSI/NISO Z39.48-1992 (Permanence of Paper).

FOR MARION

Contents

Preface

General studies of nationalism usually take one of two forms: the short, sharp theoretical essay and the long, exhaustive comparative study. This book, I am afraid, falls somewhere between the two. It is a rather long—though I hope not exhausting—theoretical study of the subject.

As such, the book is relatively unusual. We political theorists have finally begun to pay serious attention to nationalism. But we still rarely devote anything like the sustained analysis to the subject that we devote to other key concepts, such as liberty or justice or the state. Perhaps that is because with nationalism we have few canonical examples to follow. No Marx, no Mill, no Machiavelli. Only minor texts by first-rate thinkers, like Fichte, or major texts by second-rate thinkers, like Mazzini. Or perhaps it is because the success of nationalism has proved such an embarrassment for virtually every major modern school of political thought, from liberalism and Marxism to conservatism and communitarianism. The fact that fascism is the only major modern political ideology that seems unembarrassed by its association with nationalism does not exactly enhance its attractiveness. Whatever the reason, the short, pointed essay—most often directed at our colleagues' delusions about the subject—seems to be the form in which social and political theorists feel most comfortable dealing with nationalism.

That is the kind of book I set out to write as well. I was astonished by the way in which moral and political philosophers in the 1980s seemed to be ignoring the importance of nationalism, even as they threw themselves into a series of intense debates about the role of community in modern society. As a Canadian living and teaching in the United States in the 1980s, I found it very difficult to connect these debates to my experience of everyday life in this country. How could anyone think of the individuals chanting "U.S.A., U.S.A." at the Los Angeles Olympics of 1984 as "unencumbered selves," to use the expression Michael Sandel made popular? (The Russians and East Germans boycotted the games that year, so American spectators got to celebrate their "encumbrances" even more than they usually do on such occasions.) How could social and political theorists talk so much about whether or not American individualists could live without community and yet show no interest in Americans' intense and noisy attachment to their nation?

I tried to answer these questions in a pair of essays, "Does Liberal Practice 'Live Down' to Liberal Theory?" and "The Myth of the Civic Nation." But having explained why many of my colleagues were ignoring the national elephant in the room, I still found it difficult to say what it was doing there or even to give a coherent account of its characteristics as a species. I had, it seems, cleared a construction site rather than an unobstructed view of a previously hidden subject. Rather than return to more familiar and less daunting subjects, I decided to get to work on that site and write the book you have before you.

The key claim of this book—and the primary reason for its length—is that it is the inadequacy of our understanding of the phenomenon of community that has made it so difficult to explain and evaluate our reliance on national loyalties. In other words, it is our misunderstanding of the genus, community, that has created so much confusion and uncertainty in the study of its surprisingly powerful species, the nation. In order to correct this misunderstanding, the book proposes an alternative theory of community, one that develops a broader and more flexible understanding of the moral psychology that animates this form of human association. ("Moral psychology" here and throughout the book refers to the ways in which we imagine others as objects of our concern and obligation. As such, it is an essential, if often underappreciated, phenomenon for political theorists like myself.) The book argues that we need to replace models of community shaped by images of solidarity or collective identity with a model shaped by the relations of mutual concern and loyalty characteristic of what I call "social friendship." It then shows how this alternative understanding of community can help us make better sense of nations and nationalism and the problems that they create for us.

I suspect that many students of nationalism, tired as they are of the seemingly endless and circular attempts to define the nation, may think that the last thing we need is a step back to an even higher level of abstraction. But I hope to show that it is precisely our failure to take this step and rework our understanding of community that has made our efforts to make sense of nations and nationalism so frustrating. Theoretical studies of nationalism have so far shown little of what Hegel liked to call "the patience of the concept." I hope that this study will prove that such patience will be rewarded.

Acknowledgments

This project has been supported over the years by a number of institutions: the American Council of Learned Societies (ACLS), the Swedish Collegium for Advanced Studies in the Social Sciences (SCASSS) at Uppsala, the Center for European Studies at Harvard, the University of Wisconsin at Madison, and Brandeis University. I am very grateful to them all for their interest in my work and for their generosity. I would especially like to thank Mark Beissinger, Crawford Young, and the rest of my former colleagues at Madison's Research Circle on Nationalism and Cultural Pluralism for the encouragement they gave me at the start of this project, as well Johann Arnason, John Hall, Hans Joas, and Björn Wittrock for their intellectual fellowship during my year at Uppsala. My thanks also to Julie Seeger for help preparing the final version of the text.

:::

I have benefited tremendously from the responses I have received over the years to my ideas about nationalism—much more, I suspect, than I can remember. I would, however, like to take the opportunity to thank a few individuals whose comments were particularly important to the development of my book: Jens Bartelson, Sam Beer, Ron Beiner, Margaret Canovan, Ingrid Creppell, John Hall, Stephen Holmes, John Hutchinson, Margaret Moore, Gary Shiffman, Rogers Smith, and Kamila Stullerova. My greatest debt, as ever, is to Marion Smiley, my co-conspirator in life. I could never have begun—let alone completed—this book if her insight and generosity had not lit the way.

: : :

Portions of this book have appeared in earlier forms, though all have been extensively revised for their publication here. Chapter 1 first appeared as "The Myth of the Civic Nation," *Critical Review* 10 (Spring 1996): 193–212, and then in a revised form in Ronald Beiner, ed., *Theorizing Nationalism* (Albany, NY: SUNY Press, 1998), 103–18. Portions of chapter 6 first appeared as "Popular Sovereignty and Nationalism," *Political Theory* 29 (4): 517–36. © 2001 Sage Publications. One section of chapter 8 draws on material that appeared in "Birthright, Birthwrongs: Contingency, Choice and Community in Recent Political Thought," *Political Theory* 39 (3): 406–16. © 2011 Sage Publications. And some sections of chapter 9 first appeared as "You Don't Have to Be a Fanatic to Act Like One," *Studi Veneziani* 59 (2010): 27–43.

Introduction

Nationhood and Community

The rise of nationalism is one of modern history's greatest surprises. Our classic theories of modern society have taught us to associate modern times with the weakening of inherited loyalties, with a shift from intergenerational communities to voluntary associations of individuals. But the near universal spread of nationalism tells a different story. For it suggests that at least one form of intergenerational community has not just survived, but flourished in the modern world. The nation, it seems, has shared the individual's rise to prominence in modern political life.

When historical developments surprise us in this way, it usually means that there is something wrong with either our assumptions about what should have happened or our interpretations of what actually did happen. With regard to the triumph of nationalism, most scholars seem to have concluded that it is our interpretations of events that need correction. For they have worked very hard at developing accounts of nationalism that bring the phenomenon back into line with the conceptual dichotomies—gemeinschaft versus gesellschaft, tradition versus modernity—that ground our most influential theories of modern society and development. Some argue that despite its bad manners and country dress nationalism is really quite at home, even indispensable, in the modern world of contract and commerce. Others teach us that nationalism is an intruder from the premodern world of blood and soil, an outburst of the primitive passions that modern society has tried so hard to repress. Still others contend that nationalism appears in both forms, as a liberal devotion to shared political principles in "civic" nations and as an illiberal passion for ancestor worship in their "ethnic" counterparts.

But if nations and nationalism have become so commonplace in the modern world, then perhaps it is our theoretical assumptions about intergenerational community that cry out for revision, rather than our interpretations of nations and nationalism. If national community plays so large a role in modern societies, then perhaps we were wrong to identify modern life so completely with a shift from the contingencies of intergenerational loyalty to the purposiveness of individual choice and contract. If large and impersonal national forms of community appear in traditional societies, then perhaps we were wrong to identify the premodern world so strongly with kin- and village-centered communities. The nation, with its passionate appeals to inherited loyalties, certainly looks like an anomaly in the modern world when it is viewed through the lens of our most influential theories of history and social development. But if it has nevertheless risen to unprecedented political importance in that world, then perhaps it is time to have our eyes checked and get some new glasses.

This book grinds the lenses for these glasses and shows how to use them in the study of nations and nationalism. It proposes a broader and more flexible theory of community, one that treats community as a generic component of human association, rather than as a special product of traditional family and village life. And it then shows how this theory can help us solve old puzzles and generate new insights into the role of nations and nationalism in modern political life. Part 1 addresses explanatory issues, such as how to understand nations and nationalism as social phenomena and how to account for their unexpected rise to political prominence. Part 2 addresses normative and practical issues, focusing, in particular, on what I call the moral problem with nationalism. Both parts, however, try to show that we can dispel much of the confusion surrounding the study of nationalism once we free our understanding of community from the grip of the dichotomies that shape our most influential social theories.

Benedict Anderson's account of nations as "imagined communities" takes an important step toward this goal.[1] Indeed, I suspect that this famous argument owes much of its influence to the way in which it loosens the conceptual straitjacket that modern social theories have placed on thinking about national community. The concept of imagined communities helps us cross the divide that separates gemeinschaft from gesell-

1. B. Anderson, *Imagined Communities*, 5–7.

schaft and begin to think more creatively about the forms of community that bind large and relatively impersonal groups like the nation.

Nevertheless, Anderson's concept provides us with only a first step in the right direction. For the triumph of nationalism in the modern world challenges us to rethink our understanding of communal membership itself, not just our understanding of how far such membership can be extended. In particular, it challenges us to improve our understanding of the moral psychology of community, by which I mean the way in which we imagine ourselves connected to the concerns of people with whom we share things. If community plays such a powerful role in large, impersonal forms of association like the nation, then it cannot be defined in terms of familiarity, kinship, frequent interaction, or any of the other factors that unite the small face-to-face forms of association with which it is usually identified. Anderson's concept of imagined community helps us account for the strong connections we feel to people with whom we never interact. But in doing so it raises new questions about what it means to be connected to others in a distinctly communal way.[2]

In gemeinschaft models, it is the subordination of individuals to the group that makes a community. Communities connect us by submerging our differences in a collective will or identity and are contrasted with forms of association that we construct to serve our interests as discrete individuals.[3] Nations, from this point of view, must fall into one category or the other. They must either subordinate individuals or be subordinated to individual needs and interests, hence the familiar contrast between so-called primordialist and instrumentalist (or modernist) theories of nationalism that shapes so much scholarly analysis of the subject.[4]

2. Craig Calhoun (*Nations Matter*, 110) also notes the incongruity of the invocation of the specific conception of community, rooted as it is in the study of face-to-face associations, to make sense of the impersonal forms of belonging promoted by national and cosmopolitan forms of association.

3. Tönnies (*Community and Society*, 177–78), e.g., talks of "of two diametrically opposed systems of law: one in which human beings are related to each other as natural members (or parts) of a whole, and another where they come into relation with each other as independent individuals, merely by virtue of their own rational wills."

4. Primordialism is a position that scholars today tend to ascribe to others, rather than endorse themselves. For a rare, serious defense of the approach in recent scholarship, see Grosby, *Nationalism*, and "The Verdict of History." I should note, however, that Grosby, like myself, believes that we need to get beyond the gemeinschaft/gesellschaft dichotomy if we want to make sense of nationalism. See Grosby, "Nationalism and Social Theory."

In my alternative model, it is a moral relationship between individuals, which I call social friendship, that makes a community.[5] Communities connect us by means of our disposition to show special concern and loyalty to people with whom we share things, rather than through our subordination to or merging with the group. These feelings of mutual concern and loyalty, unlike the submergence of individuals in the group, are a common feature of everyday life, though they vary in depth and intensity from one form of community to another. For the members of some communities we are disposed to sacrifice a minute of our time; for the members of others, our lives. But every form of community relies on these moral sentiments to establish connections among individuals.

Community, I shall argue, has taken so many different forms because human beings share so many different things—from places and practices to beliefs, choices, and lineages—that can be imagined as sources of mutual connection. From this perspective, the relatively small and tightly integrated groups that our theoretical vocabulary associates with the term represent a particular species of community, one that has less prominence in our lives now than it once had. The nation represents a different species of community, an intergenerational community whose members are connected by feelings of mutual concern and loyalty for people with whom they share a heritage of cultural symbols and stories.[6]

Since this alternative model of community does not demand the surrender of individual will or identity associated with older and more familiar models, it does not compel us to choose between nation and individual as the focus of analysis, between primordialist theories of nationalism that exaggerate our loss of individuality and modernist theories that underestimate the depth and genuineness of our communal attachments. We have every reason to unmask the efforts that nations often make to extend their reach deep into the past, all the way back to the kind of small, tightly integrated communities associated with the concept of gemeinschaft. But we need to be careful not to throw the baby out with the bathwater. The fact that nations falsely claim one form of intergenerational community should not lead us to ignore the kind of intergenerational community that they actually do possess. Unfortu-

5. I present this theory of community in chapter 2, "The Moral Psychology of Community."

6. I defend this understanding of national community in chapter 3, "What Then Is a Nation?"

nately, as long as we continue to employ conceptual dichotomies that oppose community to voluntary, impersonal, and distinctly modern forms of association, we will probably continue to do so.

The rise of nationalism does not represent the return of some repressed desire to surrender ourselves to the group. But it does draw on and intensify our disposition to show special concern and loyalty toward people with whom we share things. That is why I believe that we cannot make sense of the place of nations and nationalism in our lives until we develop a better understanding of the moral psychology of community and its role in everyday life.

Nationalism and Liberal Individualism

The prominence of nations and nationalism in modern political life poses special problems for liberals, since they generally welcome the loosening of intergenerational ties as a measure of moral and political progress. In the liberal vision of history, increasingly cosmopolitan individuals were supposed to inherit the earth from authoritarian patriarchs and religious moralists. As things have turned out, however, they have had to share that inheritance with nations. For the age of liberal individualism has been the great age of nationalism as well, at least so far. Every major landmark in the spread of liberal democracy since the end of the seventeenth century—the Glorious Revolution of 1688, the French Revolution of 1789, the revolutions of 1848, the American Civil War, the collapse of the European empires at the end of World War I, decolonization after World War II, and the dissolution of the Soviet Empire in 1989—is also a landmark in the spread of nationalist sentiments. The modern enhancement of individual rights and autonomy seems to be connected in some way to the spread of a new and immensely powerful expression of communal loyalty.

Most liberal theorists find this development rather perplexing, since inherited community "is not, we are repeatedly told, the approach favored in our modern world of free and autonomous individuals."[7] Marxists, Ernest Gellner once joked, felt compelled to come up with a "wrong address" theory in order to explain why the message that history had prepared for the workers of the world had been delivered instead to na-

7. Shachar, *The Birthright Lottery*, 115.

tions.[8] Liberals, it seems, face a similar challenge, although they are only now beginning to address it. Some, like John Dunn, suggest that there has been a massive betrayal of liberal principles, "a habit of accommodation of which we feel the moral shabbiness readily enough ourselves."[9] Others, like Yael Tamir, suggest that we must have access to a distinctly liberal form of nationalism, one that allows us "to translate nationalist arguments into [the] liberal language" of individual rights and voluntary association.[10] Both groups agree, however, that the task is to bring liberal practice into line with the familiar image of a modern world of free and autonomous individuals. They disagree merely about whether we need to abandon nations and nationalism in order to do so.

Yet if national loyalties play such a prominent role in our world of relatively free and autonomous individuals, then might that not suggest that there is something wrong with what we are repeatedly told about it? I think so. It appears that there is much more room in that world for communal loyalty and intergenerational connection than we have been led to believe. Imagining nation and state as voluntary associations of independent individuals may have helped us win the fight against patriarchy, paternalism, and aristocratic privilege. But it prepares us poorly for dealing with the communal loyalties that continue to inform our moral life and the forms of membership that most of us enter involuntarily, by means of the contingencies of birth. Whether it is the explanation or the evaluation of nationalism that we seek, we need to broaden the understanding of human association that informs the most familiar pictures of the liberal political world.

If you believe that inherited communal loyalties are an anomaly in the modern political world, then the connections between nationalism and liberal individualism can only be explained if one of these ideologies has triumphed over the other: either liberals have been seduced by nationalist passions or they have found a means of remaking nationalism over in their own image. But if we revise and loosen our understanding of community in the ways in which I have recommended, we open the door to other and better ways of accounting for these connections. For while the tight-knit, tradition-bound, and patriarchal forms of community that we associate with the concept of gemeinschaft leave little room

8. Gellner, *Nations and Nationalism*, 129.

9. Dunn, *Western Political Theory in the Face of the Future*, 57–59.

10. Tamir, *Liberal Nationalism*, 14.

for the individual self-assertion that liberals prize, that tells us little about liberalism's relationship to the more diffuse and impersonal form of intergenerational community actually introduced by the nation. If national community does not demand the subordination of individuals to the group, then we need not invoke liberalism's betrayal or nationalism's liberal makeover in order to explain the surprisingly close connections between nationalism and liberal individualism. We can look, instead, for points of contact between these two ideologies that sustain them both at the same time.

This book zeroes in on what seems to me to be the most important of these links between nationalism and liberal individualism: the new, more indirect conception of popular sovereignty introduced by seventeenth- and eighteenth-century European thinkers. This conception of the people as constituent sovereign, the source—not the exerciser—of all legitimate authority, has steadily displaced its rivals as the foundation of a state's legitimacy. In doing so, I shall argue, it provided the catalyst that has transformed the old and familiar phenomenon of national loyalty into that powerful new social force that we call nationalism, a development that helps explain why nationalism usually follows so closely on the heels of new triumphs of liberal democracy.[11] At the same time, liberals have repeatedly found themselves turning to the nation's intergenerational sense of mutual concern and loyalty to deepen and stabilize the conception of the people upon which they rely for political legitimacy. That is why, I shall try to show, even such distinctively liberal practices as representative government and the constitutional protection of individual rights coexist so comfortably with the sense of intergenerational loyalty and continuity that national community provides.[12] In other words, nationalism and liberal democracy rise to prominence together for two reasons: liberal understandings of political legitimacy make an important, if unintended, contribution to the rise of nationalism; and national loyalties help liberals strengthen the principle of legitimacy that supports their political goals.

This explanation of the relationship between these two ideologies, I shall argue, is not only more plausible than its competitors, it serves us better in dealing with the problems that nationalism creates for liberal ideals and institutions. Standing firm against any political accommoda-

11. See especially chapter 6, "Popular Sovereignty and the Rise of Nationalism."

12. See chapter 8, "National Loyalty and Liberal Principles."

tion with the contingencies of birth and cultural inheritance may give us the satisfaction of feeling superior to the moral shabbiness of political reality. But it does little to help us address the problems that national ties create for liberal politics if key liberal practices are sustained by the intergenerational loyalties that they provide. For, in that case, national loyalties will sometimes be an ally as well as an enemy in the struggle with the moral shabbiness of the world. Insisting, instead, that we should translate nationalist arguments into the liberal language of individual rights and voluntary association may give us hope for a relatively safe and domesticated form of nationalism. But it will not help us much in taming nationalism, if, as I shall argue, visions of a purely civic nation or an apolitical cultural nationalism rest upon myths about liberal practice and wishful thinking about the origins of nationalism.[13] For, in that case, intergenerational loyalties and cultural legacies will play a strong role in whatever forms of nationalism are confronted by liberal ideals and institutions.

Liberalism was never meant to be a utopian doctrine. It was developed to identify and justify practical reforms, taking "men as they are and laws as they might be."[14] But by insisting that we live up to a vision of the polity as a voluntary association for the expression of shared interests and principles, many contemporary liberal theorists revert to a kind of utopianism. We enter the world helpless and in need of a very long period of care. If we survive to become fully formed members of our species, it is only because we receive care from people who have entered life before us, care that inevitably establishes important connections between our world and theirs. Instead of chasing false promises of a way round this fact of human existence, promises of a purely principled and voluntary basis for political identity, we need to spend more of our time figuring out what kinds of accommodations with the contingencies of birth and cultural inheritance—and with what moral advantages and disadvantages—are available to us at any particular time and place. And in order to do that, we need to develop ways of talking about how choice and the contingencies of birth work together in the formation of community in modern political life in general, and in liberal societies in particular.

Liberal theorists have generally resisted doing so in the name of a worthy goal: protecting us from the cruel forms of violence and exclusion

13. See chapter 1, "The Myth of the Civic Nation."

14. Rousseau, *The Social Contract*, book 1, chap. 1.

that have often followed in nationalism's wake. But they do not serve that goal very well by proceeding in this way. The search for an intrinsically liberal nationalism promotes the illusion that we have nothing to fear from the forms of nationalism that thrive in liberal polities. And the blanket rejection of contingent and inherited communal loyalties not only blinds us to the positive role that such loyalties play in our moral lives,[15] it misleads us about what makes nationalism such a powerful and potentially dangerous force in our lives. For nationalism, I shall argue, blends feelings of social friendship with beliefs about political justice in a way that tends to turn others into wrongdoers and loosen the moral restraints on the actions we are inclined to take against them. It is this explosive combination of feeling and belief that poses a serious threat to liberal ideals and institutions, not our mere inclination to display special concern and loyalty toward the members of our nation.[16] Ironically, the translation of nationalism into the liberal language of individual rights and voluntary association may end up enflaming the passions it was designed to tame. For it not only misrepresents the threat that nationalism poses to liberal ideals and institutions; it deepens that threat by encouraging the members of national communities to assert themselves in the liberal language of fundamental rights.[17]

Moral Shabbiness and Moral Complexity

If, however, we make room for partial, inherited loyalties in our vision of liberal politics, are we not, as John Dunn suggests, indulging in a kind of "moral shabbiness"?[18] It is hard to see things any other way as long as we cling to a Kantian or neo-Kantian view of morality, a view that locates the sole source of morality in the will of the good and rational individual. From this point of view, our reliance on national loyalties confronts us with a question about our moral flexibility: how far should we be willing to compromise our moral principles in the face of recalcitrant social conditions, or, in other words, how much moral shabbiness

15. See chapter 7, "The Moral Value of Contingent Communities."

16. See chapter 9, "The Moral Problem with Nationalism."

17. See chapter 10, "What's Wrong with National Rights to Self-Determination," and chapter 12, "Learning to Live with Nationalism."

18. Dunn, *Western Political Theory in the Face of the Future*, 57–59.

should we tolerate? But if we reject, as I believe we should, this overly monistic understanding of morality and treat mutual loyalty and concern as one of a number of sources of moral behavior, then it is our *moral complexity* that the prominence of national communities in liberal politics compels us to confront, rather than our moral shabbiness. We need to ask ourselves how to check and balance the different and competing sources of moral behavior available to us in our world, rather than how much we should be willing to bend our moral principles to make them effective in the world.

Insofar as the contingencies of birth and history shape the extent and character of the sentiments of mutual concern, friendship, and loyalty that people express toward each other, they contribute significantly to the moral resources we draw on when we ask people to behave in other-regarding ways. A world in which our connections to friends, family, and compatriots were the only source of moral behavior upon which to draw would indeed be an especially dangerous and violent world. But then so would a world in which moral principle were the only basis for judging what to do for each other, as even the most casual glance at history confirms. For reckless confidence in our moral righteousness has inspired no less violence than mindless solidarity with our own. That is why every society, including our own, has mined the moral resources in loyalty as well as obligation, in friendship as well as justice, and in contingency as well as choice.

In seeking some kind of accommodation with national loyalties, we must be prepared then to seek a balance between competing sources of morality rather than a compromise between moral principle and a recalcitrant world. Some ways of balancing these two aspects of our moral life will undoubtedly deserve our strongest condemnation. But the goal, from this perspective, is to find the best balance of competing moral concerns—remembering that even the best balance will include things to regret and fear—rather than to agonize about how far and fast we should relax our strict moral standards in order to be effective in an imperfect world.

Certainly, any commitments that lead us to ignore—let alone participate in—the wholesale murder and persecution of members of other ethnic and cultural communities deserve to be described as morally shabby and worse. But for many contemporary liberals it is the very idea of acknowledging contingencies of birth and cultural inheritance in our political arrangements, not just the violence that may be encouraged by doing so, that is perceived as morally shabby. As a result, they are sympathetic to arguments that *any* political accommodation with contingencies of birth, such as the privileges of birthright citizenship accorded to children of citizens or to individuals born within a particular state's territory, is morally indefensible, a violation of liberalism's commitment to "a radical critique of all ascriptive privileges."[19] "Citizenship in Western liberal democracies," according to these arguments, "is the modern equivalent of feudal privilege—an inherited status that greatly enhances one's life chances."[20] From this point of view, liberals can make no accommodation with national community without betraying their most fundamental moral principles. The majority of contemporary liberals do not go this far, but most tend to share Dunn's sense that such arrangements are morally questionable, if often unavoidable.

There is, however, something odd about their moral rigor in this matter. Even Plato, whose name is synonymous with excessive rationalism for most contemporary liberals, recognized that we cannot undo the contingencies of birth and cultural inheritance that ground communal boundaries, however nobly we may lie about them. Accordingly, Plato acknowledged that even the most rational understanding of justice must find a place for the principle of "doing good to friends and harm to enemies," even though our enemies often include as many virtuous individuals as our friends.[21] Why then do so many contemporary liberals seem so willing to go beyond even Plato's faith in reason's ability to transform the underlying conditions of political life?

The reason, it seems, is that accommodation with the contingencies of birth and inherited loyalties appears to threaten a principle that liberals, unlike Plato, hold dear: that human beings are all born free and equal. If, as Figaro eloquently put it, no one should have the power to control another's fate simply because he or she "took the trouble to be born" the son of a duke or the daughter of a slave-owner, why should anyone de-

19. Bader, "Citizenship and Exclusion," 214. See Shachar, *The Birthright Lottery*, and Stevens, *States without Nations*, for powerful explorations of this theme.

20. Carens, "Aliens and Citizens," 230.

21. Plato, *Republic*, 332a–333e. Although Socrates rejects this definition of justice when first introduced by Polemarchus, he reinstates it later in the dialogue with his insistence that even a just regime must be based on a "noble lie" that portrays all citizens as a single family born of the earth on which the city stands.

serve our special concern and attention, not to mention unequal privileges and resources, simply because he or she was lucky enough to be born to a member of our relatively wealthy and fortunate political community? Liberals have always prided themselves on their resistance to ascription, from eighteenth-century assaults on royal patriarchy and aristocratic privilege to twentieth-century attacks on gender and racial discrimination. As a result, many liberals condemn any accommodation with the contingencies of birth that ground national loyalties as a moral lapse, a shameful admission of failure or cowardice in the face of the resistance of the world to our moral ideals.

We are born free and yet we are also born helpless and dependent on others in ways that make the contingencies of birth and cultural inheritance extremely important in our lives. How can we put these two descriptions of the human condition together? Kantians do so by erecting a wall between these two characterizations of human life: they portray the first as a normative claim and the second as an empirical description whose details can do nothing to prove or disprove the existence of our freedom. They then proceed to ground moral and political judgments on the rational faith in our freedom that this wall protects from empirical challenge. Contemporary neo-Kantians, such as Rawls and Habermas, no longer accept the distinction between phenomenon and noumenon that Kant used to erect this wall. But they continue to derive moral and political principles from the special moral point of view that we gain when we abstract from the contingencies that divide human beings up into different and competing communities.

But this general abstraction from contingency to a distinctive moral point of view was not part of the meaning behind early liberal claims that we are born free and equal. For early liberals, like Locke and many English and French revolutionaries, being born free meant being born free of anything that might naturally *subordinate* us to the political authority of others, in the way that we are naturally subordinated to the domestic authority of our parents or whoever it is that takes care of us at birth.[22] Pre-Kantian liberals were concerned about the use of the contingencies of birth to establish special rights and privileges *within* political communities. Their attack on the celebration of these contingencies was part of a battle against caste and patriarchy. It is clear that they as-

22. This point is brought out very well in Samuel Beer's book *To Make a Nation*.

sumed that the shape and boundaries of these communities would continue to be informed by the contingencies that had always shaped them in the past.

Their failure to explore this assumption—as well as their overly optimistic expectations about the relatively peaceful quality of commercial societies—has left a large gap in most liberal theories. Neo-Kantian liberals urge us to fill this gap by generalizing the early liberals' resistance to contingency. In doing so, I shall argue, they fail to understand the special requirements and difficulties of liberal politics. Pre-Kantian liberals did not feel compelled to choose between contingency and choice in forming their view of political morality and neither should we.[23] But we need to understand the special problems created for us by the reliance of liberal practice on a balance between these two sources of political morality.

Facing Up to Contingency

As should be clear by now, my arguments in this book reflect two recent trends in liberal political thought: its increased awareness of nations and nationalism as moral phenomena;[24] and its growing attachment to moral pluralism as a way of understanding and justifying our practical judgments.[25] Where my approach to these issues is most distinctive is in its focus on the concept of contingency, in particular, those contingencies that surround the conditions of our birth and help sustain intergenerational communities. Yael Tamir is certainly right to insist that any satisfactory theory of nationalism must try to "structure itself independently of all contingencies."[26] But any satisfactory theory of nationalism will also have to be, among other things, a theory *about contingency* and its role

23. See Kymlicka, *Multicultural Citizenship*, 50, 68, for examples.

24. As in books by David Miller (*On Nationality*), Yael Tamir (*Liberal Nationalism*), Paul Gilbert (*Philosophy of Nationalism*), Margaret Moore (*The Ethics of Nationalism*), Will Kymlicka (*Multicultural Citizenship* and *Politics in the Vernacular*), and Wayne Norman (*Negotiating Nationalism*).

25. As in work by Isaiah Berlin, Michael Walzer, and Bernard Williams, among others. See, e.g., the symposium on liberalism and moral pluralism in *Social Research*, December 1999.

26. Tamir, "Theoretical Difficulties in the Study of Nationalism," 82.

in our lives. If such a theory draws its conceptual vocabulary and conclusions from the contingencies of a particular national history or ethnic struggle, it will severely limit its value. But if it fails to examine the role of contingency in our moral and political life, it will have missed its target entirely. For all nations, even those that sustain liberal practices and ideals, rely on the contingencies of birth and history that sustain intergenerational loyalties. Without a good understanding of the concept of contingency and its role in our lives, there will be a great hole in the center of even a relatively liberal account of nations and nationalism.

Contingency is one of those concepts that derives its meaning from the way in which it is contrasted with other concepts and phenomena. The two concepts with which it is most commonly contrasted are necessity, in one direction, and choice or purpose, in the other. When we are thinking about necessity, we tend to associate the contingent with the accidental, with whatever could easily have been otherwise, a category broad enough to include both random events and voluntary acts. From this point of view, our choices seem contingent unless they can be treated as inevitable consequences of a preceding set of causes. When we are thinking about choice and purpose, however, we tend to associate the contingent with the purposeless, a category broad enough to include mindless necessity, as well as random events. From this point of view, natural necessities seem contingent, unless we believe that nature itself was constructed to serve the aims of some superior being.

I shall, accordingly, use the term contingency to refer to things that are neither chosen nor necessary. Contingencies lack the regularity and purposiveness that come from either causal necessity or conscious design. They are things that impose themselves on us, but could easily be otherwise.

By the contingencies of birth I mean the connections to particular groups of people and their ways of doing things that are established by our being born in a particular place and time, rather than the particular set of events that led to our birth. Obviously, we do not choose the particular range of social relationships into which we are thrust by the conditions of our birth. And even if we choose eventually to reject some or most of these relationships and replace them with others, they still shape our lives, if only by giving us particular and distinctive models of what to avoid in human associations. At the same time, the particular set of social relationships into which we are thrown by our birth are not necessary because they could easily have been otherwise. A different choice of royal marriage partner, a slight shift of events in a battle, a timely display of eloquence at just the right moment—small changes in the course of events such as these could easily have rearranged the pattern of social relationships that greet us at our birth.[27]

Three distinctive characteristics of our species magnify the importance of the contingencies of birth for human beings. First of all, the fact that we are born helpless and take such an unusually long time to develop our mental and physical faculties makes us especially dependent on those who come before us into the world. If we were born fully mature, the contingencies of birth might only function as background constraints on the choices we make. But since we must rely on others for so long for our survival and development, these contingencies shape the very faculties we use in making our choices.

Second, the fact that human beings are social animals means that the people on whom we come to depend when we enter into the world are ranged in a complex and overlapping pattern of social groups. As a result, a vastly greater range of possible conditions confront us at our birth than there would be if human beings lacked this capacity to form different communities. What we become as we develop our faculties is bound to reflect the particular pattern of association into which we enter at birth, not just the particular qualities of the individual or individuals who take the primary responsibility for raising us.

Finally, the fact that human beings are (or have become) cultural animals, creatures capable of preserving and passing on cultural artifacts to later generations, greatly increases and deepens the consequences of our being born at one place and time rather than another. For it means that human societies develop and differentiate themselves from each other at an incomparably faster rate than those of other species.[28] The people on whom we depend for our development thus are not only arrayed in particular patterns of association, they express themselves in very distinctive

27. A historical contingency is something that could easily have been otherwise, given small and easily imaginable changes in preceding conditions, rather than something that cannot be traced back through a chain of external causes. For an excellent discussion of the distinction between contingency and necessity in historical explanation, see Ben Menahem, "Historical Contingency."

28. By speed I mean here the number of generations, rather than the passing of time. Insect and plant species may evolve through natural selection in fewer years than humans do through the invention and dispersal of cultural artifacts. But it takes them many more generations to do so.

and constantly changing cultural idioms. In sum, then, contingencies of birth have a much greater impact on human beings than other creatures because we are so dependent for so long on our predecessors and because our social and cultural capacities create such a tremendous and constantly changing variety of conditions into which we are born.

National communities, I shall argue, grow out of the way in which we imagine these contingencies as sources of intergenerational friendship and loyalty. Nevertheless, contingency as such often disappears from normative discussions of nationalism. Conservatives tend to exaggerate the degree of order and necessity in our historical inheritance, as if the past were handed down to us in neatly ordered bundles that we can open whenever problems arise. Liberals, in contrast, tend to exaggerate our ability to transform received institutions and loyalties into real or at least hypothetical objects of choice so that they can continue to employ consent as the final arbiter of political morality. Each group ridicules the other's naïveté. Liberals criticize conservatives for their belief that the past comes down to us in prepackaged and usable portions, while conservatives laugh at liberals for their belief that we can impose that kind of order on our historical inheritance by means of conscious choice and design. But both groups are disposed to wish or argue away historical contingency when they advance their own arguments.

Liberal students of nationalism have been happy to expose the way in which more conservative and ethnic models of nationhood hide the contingencies and inconsistencies of our historical inheritance behind a mask of fixed and inevitable characteristics. That is why they remind us so often that nations are imagined or constructed or invented, rather than simply handed to us by our ancestors. But communities are imagined, invented, or constructed by people trying to sort out the meaning of the many overlapping and often inconsistent forms of sharing that they discover among themselves, rather than by detached or independent individuals. And prominent among these forms of sharing are the intergenerational connections introduced by the contingencies of birth. We need therefore to be wary when unmasking conservative myths about the roots of national difference, lest we fall back on liberal myths about our ability to reorder our communities to fit our goals and principles. The conservative myths do indeed conceal the contingent selections that turn a mass of overlapping and inconsistent ways of connecting to each other into communities. But the liberal myths conceal the contingent connections without which we would not be coming together to construct communities in the first place.

Although this book aims at correcting both sets of myths, it devotes much more of its attention to the liberal variety. It does so because while the conservative myths continue to play an important role in nationalist politics, it is the liberal myths about community and nationhood that thrive among contemporary students of nationalism.[29] Moreover, while the conservative myths mislead us about the character of intergenerational communities, the liberal myths encourage us to ignore them altogether, except as obstacles to be overcome. For these reasons we need to clear the air of the liberal myths before attempting to reconstruct our concepts of community, nationhood, and nationalism. To that end, the book begins with a critique of what I call the myth of the civic nation, the widespread belief that liberal democratic nations represent freely chosen communities of principle, rather than a form of cultural inheritance.

In the end, the contingencies of birth that contribute to sentiments of mutual concern and loyalty are not only restraints on the application of liberal principles, they are among the means by which these principles have been realized within liberal communities. Indeed, liberal democratic communities have far less room for choice in the shape of their boundaries than the aristocratic and patriarchal communities that they seek to supplant. Patriarchal monarchs, for example, regularly altered the extent of their realms by the choices they made of marriage partners for themselves and their heirs. These choices ran roughshod over the contingencies of shared identity among their subjects. In communities of subjects, where political authority was seen as a distant and alien power, they did not necessarily cause much disruption—except through the dynastic wars that they sometimes occasioned. But communities of free and equal citizens cannot live so easily with continual adjustments of their boundaries. For these communities need to know exactly whom the state is serving and where the limits of its authority lie. Without sharp and relatively settled boundaries the liberal project of rendering coercive authority accountable to the people who created it is impossible.[30]

29. The exceptions, scholarship drawing on the myths of ethnic nationalism, tend, like Samuel Huntington's recent book, *Who Are We? The Challenges to America's National Identity*, to address larger political audiences beyond the scholarly community.

30. See Moore, *The Ethics of Nationalism*, 198.

For this reason, the contingencies that establish communities of mutual concern and loyalty, arbitrary as they may seem, tend to play a larger role in liberal polities than in the polities that they replace. Liberal theory may place most of its emphasis on choice; but liberal practice, at least in this case, relies more heavily on historical contingencies than many of its predecessors. Hence, if we want to enhance the best of liberal practice, we need to take these historical contingencies and the boundaries they sustain more seriously.

Stoic cosmopolitans, to take an example much discussed in contemporary debates about globalization,[31] could ignore contingent forms of solidarity because they were concerned merely with persuading us to live according to the common laws of reason, something that they believed it is always within our power to do.[32] Liberals, in contrast, cannot afford to ignore these contingencies because they seek to *reorder* the world, rather than merely follow the natural laws that govern it. The liberal order, unlike the Stoic cosmos, has to be constructed by human agents who can recognize and trust each other as participants in a shared project of mutual accountability. Contingent sentiments of mutual concern and loyalty thus provide means, as well as obstacles, to the establishment of liberal practices and institutions.

Explanation and Evaluation

One final introductory note. The combination of *explanatory* and normative argument in this book is relatively unusual, at least in the literature on nationalism. Political and moral philosophers have generally steered clear of the former, while social theorists and students of comparative politics and history have been reluctant to address the latter. I believe, however, that we need to bring explanation and evaluation together when thinking about the impact of nationalism on modern political life.

The need to do so is probably clearest when pursuing normative and practical issues. Since there is nothing remotely resembling a scholarly

31. See, e.g., Nussbaum et al., *For Love of Country*.

32. The Stoic cosmopolis "in which all human beings live need not be created; it *is* the world. The cosmic 'city' is not an ideal; it is a reality." It is "the cosmos" within which all rational creatures live. Vogt, *Law, Reason, and the Cosmic City*, 4, 66.

consensus on the nature of nationhood and nationalism, any normative discussion of the subject rests on potentially controversial explanatory claims—even if these claims are hidden away in innocuous-sounding definitions. Failure to consider the assumptions packed into definitions of the nation and nationalism encourages normative recommendations that are often beside the point, since they ignore or obscure the practical problems that we actually face.[33] The normative study of nationalism therefore cries out for something like the more realistic approach to political morality recently advocated by Bernard Williams and others.[34] That approach, which I follow throughout this book, insists that we derive our understanding of the problems of political morality from an analysis of the unique social relations that structure political life, rather than from the application to political life of independently derived moral principles.[35]

But the need to integrate explanatory and normative analysis is just as great when we are trying to make sense of nationalism as when we are trying to figure out what to do about it. Explanatory theories that fail to consider the normative assumptions built into empirical categories, like the dichotomy between civic and ethnic nations, encourage the spread of inaccurate and, occasionally, self-serving impressions of the way the world works. In addition, explanatory theories of nationalism need to maintain contact with normative analysis in order to identify the social forces that interest them in the first place. For, as I try to show in part 1, we need a good understanding of the ways in which people come to be concerned about each other's well-being if we want to understand what makes nationalism such a powerful force in our lives. Nationalism, I suggest there, is in large part a product of moral dispositions, and a particularly complex product at that. We cannot adequately explain its emergence and impact on modern politics unless we are willing to go

33. For similar arguments, see Gilbert, *Philosophy of Nationalism*, 1, and Poole, *Nation and Identity*, 7.

34. Williams, *In the Beginning Was the Deed*, 1–3. For an account of the various ways in which recent political theorists have invoked the notion of realism, see Galston, "Realism in Political Theory," 385–411.

35. Although Williams distinguishes between "realism" and "moralism" in political theory, he is clearly advocating a particular approach to understanding political morality, rather than the discounting of morality's importance to politics, as pursued in more familiar understandings of political realism. The problem with political moralism, from his point of view, is not that it asks moral questions, but that it asks the wrong moral questions.

beyond the individual psychology of interest, identity, and belonging and consider the moral psychology of mutual concern and loyalty associated with communal relations.

That said, I should note that even in the second part of the book my approach is more diagnostic than prescriptive. The continuing violence associated with ethnic hatreds and nationalist conflicts makes the search for solutions to our problems a matter of considerable urgency. But figuring out exactly what problems we face is more than half the battle in any good moral or political theorizing. For solutions that fail to address the real problems before us are not, in the end, much help at all. To those who rightly point to the urgency of solving these problems I can only say, take your time, they are not going to go away soon.

PART I

CHAPTER ONE

The Myth of the Civic Nation

Nationalism's students have devoted a lot of time and energy to debunking myths that exaggerate the special virtues and antiquity of nations. But in debunking one set of myths, they have inadvertently breathed new life into another: myths that exaggerate our independence from the contingencies of birth and cultural heritage. One of these myths, which I call the myth of the civic nation, is shared by many Western intellectuals and policy makers. It suggests that in liberal democratic nations freely chosen principles have replaced cultural heritage as the basis of political solidarity. If only, so the argument goes, we could persuade Serbians—or Kosovars or Hindus or the Quebecois—to replace their visions of ethnic or cultural unity with our visions of civic solidarity, then nationalism need no longer promote ethnic violence and intolerance.

There are, however, three major problems with this portrait of liberal democracies as purely civic communities. First of all, it gets the history wrong. Liberal democratic nations like France, Canada, and the United States may have become relatively open societies that offer citizenship rights to all peoples, but they did not start out that way. In each case, they began with restricted core communities—be they white or Catholic or British or European—and expanded outward.[1] Second, and more important, the celebration of civic nationalism misrepresents liberal democratic communities as they are now, not just as they were in the bad

1. As a result, when we urge nationalists, say in Bosnia or Iraq, to follow our example and *found* nations solely on the basis of shared political principles, we are in fact urging them to do something that we never did ourselves. See Marx, *Faith in Nation*, 114, 167–68, passim, for an account of the exclusionary origins of so-called civic nations.

old days of the past. However much their citizens may associate these communities with a set of political principles, each of these nations derives its identity from a heritage associated with their peculiar histories. Finally, even if contemporary liberal democratic communities were to transform themselves into purely civic nations, the transformation would introduce different forms of exclusion and intolerance just as powerful as those that they were trying to eliminate. The myth of the civic nation thus misrepresents the *value* as well as the existence of the form of community that it celebrates.

The persistence of such myths makes it difficult to appreciate the role that intergenerational community plays in modern political life. I therefore begin this book by subjecting the myth of the civic nation to a thoroughgoing critique.

The Civic Nation and Its Myth

The distinction between the ethnic and civic nations is the latest in a long line of more or less parallel distinctions that scholars have used to conceptualize the different forms of nationhood: Eastern versus Western nationalism,[2] "ethnos" versus "demos,"[3] cultural versus political or "state nations,"[4] and German versus French understandings of nationhood.[5] These conceptual distinctions were developed to help make sense of a number of easily observable facts about nations and nationalism. Some national communities, like the United States, Canada, and most of the African nations, owe their origin to the establishment of states, while others, such as the German or Czech nations, can plausibly claim to precede the states with which they are now associated. Some nations, like France or Canada, derive more of their character from political ideals, practices, and symbols than others, such as Japan or Italy. Some nations, like Germany, rely more on descent from previous members of the community than others, like France or the United States, that ex-

2. Kohn, *The Idea of Nationalism*, 574ff. For a subtler version of this distinction, see Plamenatz, "Two Types of Nationalism."

3. Francis, *Ethnos und Demos*, 60–122.

4. Meinecke, *Cosmopolitanism and the National State*, 9–12. This distinction has been revived recently by Chaim Gans in *The Limits of Nationalism*.

5. See Renan, "What Is a Nation?," and Dumont, *German Ideology*.

tend membership to those who are born within the national territory as well as to those born to members of the community. Finally, these distinctions mirror the two ways in which the term nation is used in everyday language: to point to culturally distinctive intergenerational communities and to characterize the political communities that correspond to modern states (as in expressions like the "United Nations").

But the distinction between ethnic and civic nations, like all of its predecessors, was developed to serve normative as well as descriptive goals. In other words, it was developed to help distinguish the more valuable or acceptable forms of nationalism from their less appealing counterparts. Nationalism is associated with some of the best and worst features of modern politics, the assault on tyranny and imperialism as well as some of the greatest cruelties to which human beings have ever been subjected. It would make things much simpler if we could attribute all the good things to one form of nationalism and the bad things to another. Some earlier scholars, such as Friedrich Meinecke, distinguished cultural from political nationalism in order to celebrate the superior depth of the former.[6] Today, however, most scholars tend to favor the political or civic side of these dichotomies. They distinguish civic from ethnic understandings of nationhood in order to bring national solidarity into line with the liberal ideals and institutions that they associate with a decent political order.

Michael Ignatieff's *Blood and Belonging* provides an excellent illustration of this dual use of the distinction between civic and ethnic nations. Ignatieff is a self-professed cosmopolitan—how else, he asks, to describe someone "whose father was born in Russia, whose mother was born in England, whose education was in America, and whose working life has been spent in Canada, Great Britain, and France."[7] But he recognizes that cosmopolitanism is only a viable option for a rather privileged subset of citizens of wealthy industrial societies. And even their security rests upon their being able to take nationally defended citizenship rights for granted.

Accordingly, Ignatieff admits that the Enlightenment vision of a cosmopolitan world society of rational individuals, a vision that he shares,

6. Meinecke, *Cosmopolitanism and the National State*, 9–12.

7. Ignatieff, *Blood and Belonging*, 11. These words were written before Ignatieff went on to become the leader of the Canadian Liberal Party.

cannot be realized in the modern political world, at least in the foreseeable future. Modern individuals, he argues, seem to need a sense of belonging to a national community to support the very rights and freedom from fear that Enlightenment cosmopolitans strove to create.[8] But the Enlightenment's political legacy can only be preserved in a civic nation, which Ignatieff conceives of as "a community of equal, rights-bearing citizens, united in patriotic attachment to a shared set of political practices and values." The civic nation, Ignatieff argues, is a community created by the choice of individuals to honor a particular political creed. As such, it is relatively compatible with the Enlightenment legacy of rationalism and individualism, since it turns "national belonging [into] a form of rational attachment." Ethnic nationalism, in contrast, abandons that legacy because it insists "that an individual's deepest attachments are inherited, not chosen," that "it is the national community that defines the individual, not the individuals who define the national community."[9] Or, as Hans Kohn put it, one form of nationalism "looks to the future" and expresses "a rational and universal conception of liberty," while the other looks to "history, monuments and graveyards," and expresses a kind of "tribal solidarity."[10]

It is hard for anyone with relatively liberal, relatively cosmopolitan sympathies to reject such arguments. Nevertheless, I am very skeptical about this characterization of the difference between civic and ethnic nationalism. When the rational, voluntary, and good way of doing things just happens to be *ours*, and the emotive, inherited, and bad way of doing things just happens to be *theirs*, we ought to proceed with great caution. It all seems a little too good to be true, a little too close to what we would like to believe about the world. Although it was invented to protect us from the dangers of ethnocentric politics, this vision of civic na-

8. Ibid., 11–13.

9. Ibid., 7–8. In a similar vein, Liah Greenfeld describes Anglo-American nationalism as a form of principled individualism. See Greenfeld, *Nationalism*, 31.

10. Kohn, *The Idea of Nationalism*, 574. For similar arguments, see Bogdan Denitch's defense of civic nationalism in *Ethnic Nationalism: The Tragic Death of Yugoslavia*, Liah Greenfeld's distinction between Anglo-American and continental European forms of nationalism in *Nationalism*, and Dominique Schnapper's defense of the idea of the civic nation, in which she attempts to prove that the "very notion of an ethnic nation is a contradiction in terms," in *La communauté des citoyens: Sur l'idée moderne de la nation*, 24–30, 95, 178.

tionalism seems rather ethnocentric itself, since it seems blind to the fact that political identities like French and American are also culturally inherited artifacts.[11] In the end, I suggest, it represents little more than a combination of self-congratulation and wishful thinking.

Civic identities, like Canadian, are no less inherited cultural artifacts than supposedly ethnic identities, like Quebecois.[12] Residents of Quebec who think of Canada rather than Quebec as their political community are choosing one inherited location of identity over another. They may make that choice because they believe that the Canadian government will better defend certain political principles, but those political principles do not in themselves define Canada. Canada is a contingent location for these principles, a location that comes with all kinds of inherited cultural baggage: the connection to Great Britain and British political culture, the history of tension and cooperation between French speakers and English speakers, the ambivalent relationship to Canada's powerful neighbor to the south, and so on.

The same is true for the United States and France as objects of identification. However much they may have come to stand for certain political principles each comes loaded with inherited cultural baggage that is contingent upon their peculiar histories. That does not mean that we must accept the image of a "true" France or United States that some seek in the historical record. Shared identities are ever in the process of development and interpretation. Claims about our authentic or original identity most often represent ways of silencing debate about the interpretation of our complex and often contradictory cultural legacies.[13] But even

11. Indeed, the idea of the civic nation, with its portrayal of community as a shared and rational choice of universally valid principles, is itself a cultural inheritance in nations like France and the United States. One aspect of distinctly French and American political ideologies is to portray their own cultural inheritance as a universally valid object of rational choice. See Dumont, *German Ideology*, 3–4, 199–201.

12. See Kymlicka, "Misunderstanding Nationalism," for a similar critique of Ignatieff's use of the idea of civic nationalism. For other recent criticisms of the idea of civic nationalism, see B. C. J. Singer, "Cultural versus Contractual Nations," and Spencer and Wollman, "Good and Bad Nationalisms."

13. See Lebovics, *True France*, and R. Smith, *Stories of Peoplehood*. An appeal to original political principles, by the way, functions just as well as an appeal to cultural origins in shutting down debate about the meaning of one's political community. Opponents of multiculturalism, such as Arthur Schlesinger (*The Disuniting of America*), often use the appeal to original principles like *e pluribus unum* in this way.

if shared identities such as French and American are little more than sites for controversy and construction, these sites themselves are cultural artifacts that we inherit from preceding generations.

Liberal theorists sometimes talk as if the state should take as great a distance from competing cultures as it does from competing religions. The liberal state, from this perspective, is "not to subscribe to, let alone to enforce, a specific body of moral, religious or cultural beliefs, save those such as the rule of law which are inherent in its structure. Its job is to provide a framework of authority and a body of laws within which individuals are at liberty to live the way that they [want]."[14] But liberal states cannot distance themselves from culture in the way that they sometimes step back from religion, if only because they must use cultural tools and symbols to organize, exercise, and communicate political authority.[15] States therefore cannot provide us with culture-free sites for the construction of political identity. Political identities, even when they center on states, are bound, to a certain extent, to take on the form of inherited cultural artifacts.

The political identity of French, Canadian, or American citizens is not based on a set of rationally chosen political principles. No matter how much residents of the United States might sympathize with political principles favored by most French or Canadian citizens, it would not occur to them to think of themselves as French or Canadian. An attachment to certain political principles may be a necessary condition of loyalty to the national community for many citizens of contemporary liberal democracies; it is very far from a sufficient condition for that loyalty.

It may be reasonable to contrast nations whose distinctive cultural inheritance centers on political symbols and stories with nations whose cultural inheritance centers on language and stories about ethnic origins. But it is unreasonable and unrealistic to interpret this contrast as a distinction between rational attachment to principle and emotional celebration of inherited culture. In order to characterize "national belonging [as] a form of rational attachment,"[16] one must ignore the contingent inheritance of distinctive experiences and cultural memories that is an inseparable part of every national political identity. And one must pretend

14. Parekh, "The 'New Right' and the Politics of Nationhood," 39.

15. Kymlicka, "Sources of Nationalism," 58. See also Francis, *Ethnos und Demos*, 104, who argues that the nation-state is necessarily also a cultural state.

16. Ignatieff, *Blood and Belonging*, 7–8.

that it makes sense to characterize nations such as France, Canada, and the United States as voluntary associations for the expression of shared political principles. Such is the myth of the civic nation.

The Myth of Consent and the Myth of Descent

Defenders of this myth often cite Ernest Renan's famous description of the nation as "a daily plebiscite," a phrase that seems to point to individual consent as the source of national identity. But they rarely note that this phrase represents only one half of Renan's own definition of the nation. "Two things," Renan insists, constitute the nation.

> One lies in the past, the other in the present. One is the possession in common of a rich legacy of memories, the other is present-day consent, the desire to live together, the will to perpetuate the value of the heritage that one has received in an undivided form. . . . The nation, like the individual, is the culmination of a long past of endeavors, sacrifice, and devotion.[17]

The nation may be a daily plebiscite for Renan, but the issue on the ballot is what to do with the mix of competing symbols and stories that make up our cultural inheritance. Without "a rich legacy of memories" there would be no communal loyalties to be put to a vote.[18]

Renan is not telling us that there are two kinds of nation: one that depends on the subjective affirmation of its members and another that depends on more objective criteria. He is telling us, instead, that *every* nation relies on *both* subjective affirmation and cultural heritage, whether or not they recognize that they do so. From this point of view, the civic vision of the nation, according to which national community is a form of rational attachment to freely chosen principles, is no less a misrepresentation than the ethnic or German idea of the nation, according to which nationhood is an objective characteristic of speech or descent no matter what identity one subjectively affirms.[19] The members of every nation,

17. Renan, "What Is a Nation?," 19.

18. Margaret Canovan (*Nationhood and Political Theory*, 55) notes this misuse of Renan as well. See also Emerson, *From Empire to Nation*, 148. On Renan's fixation on "ancestor worship," see Thom, "Tribes within Nations," 23.

19. Renan's complaint about the "German" understanding of nationhood, according to which Alsatians owed allegiance to Germany in spite of their explicit identification with

Renan is saying, conduct a daily plebiscite in which they selectively affirm particular parts of their cultural heritage.

If Renan is right, as I believe he is, then the strict dichotomy between ethnic and civic nations corresponds to two *myths* or one-sided views of nationhood rather than two ways in which actual communities have been organized. The myth of the ethnic nation suggests that you have no choice at all in the making of your national identity: you are what you inherited from previous generations and nothing else. The myth of the civic nation, in contrast, suggests that your national identity is nothing but your choice: you are the political principles you share with other like-minded individuals. Real nations, in contrast, combine choice and cultural heritage.

The myth of the civic nation is a myth of consent. It misrepresents the selective affirmation of inherited political principles and symbols as a shared choice about how best to govern ourselves. In other words, it suggests that what brings us to together in civic nations is our agreement to organize our political lives in a particular way as opposed to our affirmation of inherited political ideals and institutions. In doing so, it transforms the nation's intergenerational community into a voluntary association for the expression of shared political principles. For even nations founded by explicit agreement, say, in a Declaration of Independence or an Oath of Federation, persist through later generations' affirmation of the heritage that they receive from the nations' founders.

The myth of the ethnic nation, in contrast, is a myth of descent. It misrepresents the shared affirmation of some part of our shared cultural inheritance as a fact of birth. In doing so, it ignores the selectivity that leads us to affirm shared descent, rather than one of the many other things we share with people around us, as a source of mutual connections with others. Moreover, it ignores the way in which even the assertion of our shared ancestry involves the selective affirmation of one part of our cultural heritage rather than another.

After all, how do we determine which of the many people who precede us should count as our ancestors? For example, who are the an-

---

France, is that it eliminates choice from nationhood, not that it refers to cultural inheritance as a source of nationhood. This view of nationhood does not allow the Alsatians to focus on the legacy of French traditions that, like the German language, is part of their cultural inheritance. For Renan, a nation grows out of the choices we make within our cultural inheritance.

cestors of the Quebecois, imagined as a community of shared descent? The Francophone settlers who came to Quebec before the British conquest or the French or Breton communities from which those settlers themselves descended? Similarly, who are the ancestors of the Germans imagined as a purely ethnic nation? The inhabitants of the first Reich, the Germanized Holy Roman Empire? The peoples that overwhelmed the western Roman Empire (and who are also the ancestors of many a Frenchman, Italian, or Spaniard)? The German tribes that Tacitus described? Some purer, original Aryan community that migrated from northwestern India? Each could be imagined as the ancestors of present-day Germans. For we all have more possible ancestors than we know what to do with. If we choose to designate one group rather than another as our ancestors, it is probably because we want to emphasize some trait or experience associated with that group. If some Quebecois describe themselves as descendants of the original settlers of their land, rather than as descendants of their French or Breton ancestors, it is because they are inclined to emphasize their shared experience in the New World and the British conquest as their cultural heritage, rather than some connection to Old World ways and culture. If some Germans describe themselves as descendants of original Aryan tribes rather than the sons of Hermann or the heirs to the first Reich, it is because they seek to emphasize imagined racial purity as their most precious heritage, rather than the battle against the Roman Empire or the attempt to create a universal Christian empire in medieval Europe. Identifying ancestral communities thus requires much more than the climbing of family trees. It demands a choice among the range of competing ancestors available to us, each with their own distinctive characteristics.

Correcting the myths of consent and descent should not keep us from drawing more limited and plausible distinctions between ethnic and civic nations. It makes sense, for example, to describe as civic or political nations those communities that emphasize distinctly political symbols or practices or boundaries as the core of their national heritage. Similarly, it makes sense to describe as ethnic nations those communities that require descent from previous members as a condition of membership. The mistake is to treat the difference between the two as a dichotomy between choice and cultural heritage as the source of national community. For civic nations, understood in this way, rely on intergenerational heritage no less than ethnic nations, even if that heritage is more political in character. And ethnic nations, as we have seen, also involve choice, in both the emphasis on descent as a source of community and the designation of a particular group as the ancestral community.

Understood in this way, the characterization of a community as a civic or ethnic nation requires a more-or-less, rather than an either-or judgment. For even the most explicitly political principles and symbols, such as the American Constitution or the French Revolution, are passed on in distinctive cultural idioms that also become a source of national community. And while ethnic nations may make shared descent a necessary condition of membership, that does not mean that descent has no role in establishing membership in civic nations. All nations, including those that place the greatest emphasis on political heritage, offer membership to descendants of previous members. What makes ethnic nations distinct is that they make descent from previous members a *necessary*, rather than merely a *sufficient*, condition of membership. Making such a distinction no doubt has significant consequences, especially with regard to immigration and naturalization policies. But it hardly eliminates the contingencies of birth from the granting of membership in civic nations. It only insists on opening additional avenues to membership. Moreover, the commonest of these routes to citizenship, the offering of membership to those born within the nation's territorial boundaries (the so-called jus soli), relies no less on the contingencies of birth than the principle of descent (the so-called jus sanguinis).[20]

Once we scale back the ethnic/civic distinction in this way, it should be clear that there are nations that fit into both categories or neither. After all, we can easily make descent from an original group that established a set of political practices or carved out a new polity a requirement of membership in the national community. For example, American nativists, like the Daughters of the American Revolution, sometimes see themselves as the exclusive heirs to American principles, rather than some explicitly nonpolitical legacy. And many African nations restrict citizenship to second- or third-generation residents of its territories, despite the fact that the national territory was itself a purely political creation of the recent division of Africa into states.[21] In addition, there are all the nations that celebrate less political forms of cultural heritage, such as a shared language, but do not make shared descent a necessary requirement of entry in the national community. In the end, the distinc-

20. As Ayelet Shachar emphasizes in *The Birthright Lottery*, 7, 127.

21. See Herbst, *State and Power in Africa*, 239–46.

tion between civic and ethnic nations amounts to a distinction between communities linked by especially political forms of national heritage and communities that claim to pass their heritage on exclusively by descent from previous members. When the distinction is understood in this way, there will be nations that are neither political nor ethnic, as well as nations that are both.

It is tempting to conclude that the real difference between civic and ethnic nations is belief in one or the other of these two myths: that civic nations are distinguished by the false belief that they are united solely by means of consciously chosen principles, while ethnic nations are distinguished by the false belief that they are simply communities of descent. But we should resist this temptation. For while there are many examples of nations that imagine themselves as—or try to turn themselves into—nothing but the descendants of some noteworthy group of ancestors, there are no nations, at least that I am aware of, that actually portray themselves as nothing but voluntary associations for the expression of shared political principles. In practice, the rhetoric of so-called civic nations like France and the United States resounds with the invocation of illustrious ancestors and grateful heirs.

The myth of the civic nation is the ideal of liberal democratic theorists, not liberal democratic nations. For the idea of a purely political and principled basis for mutual concern and solidarity has been very attractive to Western scholars, most of whom rightly disdain the myths that sustain ethnonationalist theories of political community. It is particularly attractive to many American thinkers, whose peculiar national heritage—a constitutional founding and successive waves of immigration—fosters the illusion that their mutual association is based solely on consciously chosen principles. But this idea misrepresents political reality as surely as the ethnonationalist myths it is designed to combat. And propagating a new political myth, it seems to me, is an especially inappropriate way of defending the legacy of Enlightenment liberalism from the dangers posed by the growth of nationalist political passions.

Nationalism and Liberal Democratic Theory

The problems with this purely civic understanding of national community are manifest in the most influential of recent versions of civic nationalist thinking: Jürgen Habermas's defense of the idea of "constitutional patriotism."[22] Habermas uses this idea to combat the resurgence of ethnic chauvinism in the wake of German reunification.[23] He proposes loyalty to the liberal democratic principles of the postwar constitution as an alternative focus for German identity. Accordingly, he contrasts two ways of characterizing the incorporation of the East German states into the Federal Republic: on the one hand, as the restoration of "the prepolitical unity of a community with a shared historical destiny"; on the other hand, as the restoration of "democracy and a constitutional state in a territory where civil rights had been suspended . . . since 1933."[24] Habermas's defense of constitutional patriotism is to a great extent a defense of the second, purely civic description of German reunification.

Given the terrible history of German nationalism, it is understandable that one would seek to downplay the existence of a prepolitical German identity. But Habermas's civic interpretation of German reunification merely justifies or legitimates a change of political regime, from communism to liberal democracy, in East Germany; it says nothing to explain or justify reunification with the Federal Republic. It may have been easier to establish a liberal democratic regime in East Germany by integrating it into an already functioning, not to mention wealthy, liberal democracy such as the Federal Republic. But this option was not offered—or even contemplated—by the Federal Republic to the inhabitants of Czechoslovakia or Poland or any other former communist state. How can one explain the existence of this possibility for a soft landing from communism without invoking the prepolitical community of shared memory and history that tied West to East Germans, a sense of community that led the

22. Habermas, "Citizenship and National Identity." See also Habermas, *The New Conservatism*, 256–62, and "The European Nation-State." For sympathetic discussion and criticism of Habermas's conception of constitutional patriotism, see Booth, "Communities of Memory"; Markell, "Making Affect Safe for Democracy"; and Mueller, *Constitutional Patriotism*. Markell argues that although a large part of Habermas's argument for constitutional patriotism falls prey to the myth of civic nationalism, its "minor theme" (39) presents a suggestive alternative that promotes political solidarity without assuming either a given set of principles or closed national horizons.

23. Habermas is one of the contemporary theorists who misinterpret Renan in the way described in the previous section. He suggests that Renan could counter German claims to Alsace only "because he could conceive of the 'nation' as a nation of citizens." "Renan's famous saying, 'the existence of a nation is . . . a daily plebiscite,' is already directed against nationalism," according to Habermas. Habermas, "Citizenship and National Identity," 258–59.

24. Ibid., 256.

former to single out the latter for special support and attention? Habermas's civic interpretation of reunification begs this question.

Habermas tacitly admits as much when stating that constitutional patriotism represents a way of situating universalistic principles "in the horizon of the history of a nation."[25] This statement clearly implies that the audience for arguments about the focus of political loyalty is not some random association of individuals united only by allegiance to shared principles, but a prepolitical community with its own cultural horizon of shared memories and historical experiences. It is only the existence of such cultural horizons that turns a particular collection of individuals, that is, Germans, into an audience for his arguments about the interpretation of German political history.[26]

Habermas's plea for a constitutionally focused patriotism makes a great deal of sense *within* these cultural horizons.[27] It is precisely because they share terrible memories of racist and militarist violence that it makes sense for Germans to cling to the Basic Law of the postwar constitution as their most valuable historical legacy. Habermas's argument works best as part of a struggle to interpret the significance of a particular community's legacy of shared memories. But as such it assumes the existence of the very prepolitical community that he, like most defenders

25. Ibid., 264. See also *The New Conservatism*, 233, where Habermas speaks of the connections "with our parents and grandparents through a web of familial, local, political, and intellectual traditions . . . that made us what and who we are today," as a way of insisting on Germans' special obligations with regard to remembering and resisting genocide and anti-Semitism.

26. Some of Habermas's defenders, such as Anna Stilz (*Liberal Loyalty*, 153–60) and Patchen Markell ("Making Affect Safe for Democracy," 38–39), suggest Habermas is actually trying to redirect our attention away from shared political inheritance to ongoing democratic practice as the source of the principles that inspire constitutional patriotism. (See also Mueller, *Constitutional Patriotism*, 34ff.) But even if we accept this interpretation, there remain two significant problems with his conception of constitutional patriotism. First of all, it is not at all clear that democratic practice generates shared principles and loyalties of the sort that he is invoking. Disagreements are central to democratic practice, which may explain why more genuinely participatory democracies, as in Athens, tend to inspire more violent forms of disunity than our own. Second, even if it is the shared projects associated with democratic practice that generate the ideals that inspire constitutional patriotism, that does not answer the question why we end up practicing democracy with one group of individuals rather than another, and how our preceding ties to that group shape the projects that we pursue together.

27. In other words, his argument assumes the existence of something like a national community. See Canovan, *Nationhood and Political Theory*, 87–88.

of the civic idea of the nation, reject in the name of a community based on rational consent and political principle.[28]

The existence of such a community is a tacit but usually unexamined assumption in the contractarian and neo-Kantian forms of political theory that Habermas, like many contemporary liberals, favors. Social contract arguments serve to legitimate, through actual or implied consent, different ways of ordering the social and political relationships within a predefined group of individuals. For these arguments assume that there is sufficient reason for individuals deliberating about justice and the social contract to pay attention to each other's proposals and decisions, rather than those made by other individuals outside of this group. Since the whole point of these theories is to determine the proper order *within* a given group of individuals, this assumption of a prepolitical community can be safely tucked away out of sight in most of the debates about the meaning of liberal democratic principles. It is only in situations in which the boundaries of such groups are in question, as when considering the possibility of German reunification, that the assumption of prepolitical communal loyalties comes to light.

Liberal critics of nationalism like to characterize the invocation of prepolitical national identities as part of the Romantic and irrationalism rebellion against the Enlightenment and modern political culture. But these familiar criticisms ignore the extent to which liberal democratic culture *itself* inspires people to think of themselves as members of prepolitical communities. This is especially true of the rhetoric of popular sovereignty. Popular sovereignty arguments encourage modern citizens to think of themselves as organized into groups that are logically and historically prior to the communities created by their shared political institutions. To the extent that one condemns our tendency to look for prepolitical sources of political identity, modern democratic political culture is part of the problem, not the solution.[29]

Habermas deals with this difficulty by putting a Kantian gloss on popular sovereignty arguments. He portrays popular sovereignty as an

28. As Jeff Spinner-Halev ("Democracy, Solidarity, and Post-Nationalism," 14–15) notes, there is a contradiction between Habermas's desire to move us beyond national communities based on shared prepolitical sentiments and his insistence that Germans think of themselves as bound by the memories of their predecessors' crimes.

29. I develop this point at much greater length in chapters 4 and 6 below.

"abstract model" of individual self-legislation in which "consensus is achieved in the course of argument . . . from an identically applied procedure recognized by all."[30] Whatever its philosophic merits,[31] this interpretation of popular sovereignty has little historical value. The contemporary political cultures that Habermas invokes as the basis for constitutional patriotism were, after all, established and defended in the name of the people and *la nation*, not in the name of the original position or the ideal speech situation. Moreover, the procedures for locating consensus that Habermas invokes as the basis for popular sovereignty themselves assume that individuals know beforehand *with whom*—that is, with which group of individuals—they are seeking to achieve consensus. The abstractness of Habermas's understanding of communal consensus does nothing to eliminate this assumption, even if it makes it harder to locate. As long as there is little controversy about the historical referent for rhetorical invocations of the people, as in the English, American, and French Revolutions, this assumption tends to remain in the background. But disagreements about the historical identity of the people bring the assumption into question, creating severe difficulties for popular sovereignty arguments. We need to face up to the implications of our reliance on such assumptions, even if doing so makes us uneasy by showing how individual rights and political freedoms depend to a certain extent on the contingencies of shared memory and identity.

What If the Myth Came True?

But what if the myth of the civic nation came true? What if liberal polities could be turned into the kind of voluntary associations for the expression of shared political principles that the myth portrays them to be? Would they provide the optimal environment for the spread of toleration and diversity, as supporters of civic nationalism clearly assume to be the case? If so, then we might want to preserve the civic nation as a moral and political *ideal*, even if we reject it as a description of existing liberal polities.

30. Habermas, "Citizenship and National Identity," 259–60. See also "Popular Sovereignty as Procedure," in Habermas, *Between Facts and Norms*, 600–31.

31. For a critique, see Yack, "Democracy and the Love of Truth."

I believe, however, that the myth of civic nationalism provides us with a flawed political ideal, not just an inaccurate description of liberal democratic politics. Indeed, I suspect that it is only because so few of us really take the idea of a community of shared principle seriously that we find it easy to think of it as an antidote to exclusion and intolerance. For even the briefest glance at the history of social conflict teaches us that shared commitments can inspire just as much violence and intolerance as mindless ethnocentrism.

After all, American citizens have been denounced and persecuted for clinging to un-American political principles as well as for their foreign backgrounds. The House Un-American Activities Committee searched for hidden subversion rather than illegal immigrants during the McCarthyite witch hunts. And the Jacobin reign of terror, itself "a heavily moralized political variant of ethnic cleansing,"[32] was inspired by civic principles rather than ethnic solidarity. Indeed, as George Mosse reminds us, it was the emphatically civic nation of the French Jacobins that invented many of the techniques of persecution and mass paranoia exploited by twentieth-century fascists and xenophobic nationalists.[33]

Focusing on political principles as the basis of collective allegiance can, it seems, make us more suspicious of each other, not less. It is easy to see why this might happen. If the sole reason we trust each other is our commitment to certain political principles, then we will probably be much more concerned than we are now to discover whether each other's commitments are genuine or not. And since there is no way that we can definitively refute challenges to our sincerity, increased inspection of each other's political commitments is bound to lead to increased distrust. That is one reason why revolutions so often collapse in mutual suspicion and accusations of treason.[34] Revolutionaries demand strong and principled commitments from each other, the sincerity of which is easily questioned in troubled and uncertain times. Similarly, were Americans to make citizenship contingent upon commitment to political principles instead of the mere accident of birth (to citizen parents or on American territory), they might become considerably more suspicious of their fellow citizens' declarations of political loyalty. Birthright citizenship

32. Hont, "Permanent Crisis of a Divided Mankind," 205.

33. See Mosse, *Confronting the Nation*, 65–72.

34. The classic study is Francois Furet's *Interpreting the French Revolution*.

can promote toleration precisely by removing the question of communal membership from the realm of choice and contention about political principles.[35]

What makes shared principle seem like a more inclusive source of community than cultural heritage is that everyone can, at least in theory, choose his or her political principles, while no one can choose when or where to be born. But shared principles are among the most powerful sources of factionalism. For, as Hume notes, "such is the human mind, that it always lays hold on every mind that approaches it; and as it is wonderfully fortified by an unanimity of sentiments, so is it shocked and disturbed by any contrariety."[36] Focusing on shared heritage encourages us to search each other's *background* and *customs* for disturbing signs of contrariety. Focusing on shared principles encourages us instead to search each other's *minds* for evidence of contrariety. It seems far more sensible to make use of each form of community to temper the exclusionary tendencies of the other, rather than to fool ourselves into believing that the sharing of principles can eliminate the problem of exclusion and distrust of otherness. After all, one reason that shared cultural heritage has become so prominent a feature of the modern political landscape is that it provided a way of countering the suspicion and hatred of others sown by some of the most successful communities of principle in human history, Christian religious sects.[37]

Similar problems beset proposals to eliminate social exclusion and distrust by replacing nationalism with republican patriotism as the focus of political solidarity.[38] The problem with this proposal is not the lack of any real distinction between nationalism and patriotism. Although it of-

35. Those, like Ayelet Shachar (*The Birthright Lottery*) and Peter Shuck and Rogers Smith (*Citizenship without Consent*), who complain about birthright citizenship as an anomaly in American political culture, tend to underestimate the value of its contribution to toleration. In his later work, Smith acknowledges that the pure consensualist view of citizenship has, for the most part, been advanced in support of exclusive and intolerant views of political community. See R. Smith, *Civic Ideals*, 507n41, and *Stories of Peoplehood*.

36. Hume, "Of Parties in General," 60–61.

37. For this reason Hume (ibid., 60–63) is quite anxious therefore to dampen our enthusiasm for "parties of principle." See also Holmes, "The Secret History of Self-Interest."

38. The most fully developed version of this argument is presented in Viroli, *For Love of Country*. See also Viroli, "Reply to Xenos and Yack," and Yack, "Can Patriotism Save Us from Nationalism?."

ten seems that nationalism is nothing but patriotism misliked,[39] there are substantive distinctions to be made between them, distinctions that go beyond our preference for the sound of one word rather than another. Republican patriotism is grounded in the "love of the political institutions and the way of life that sustain the common liberty of a people."[40] It differs from ethnic nationalism in its focus on the political values of citizenship. And it differs from civic nationalism in its enthusiastic embrace of a collective passion, the love of the republican *patria*. The question is rather whether it is any more likely to deliver on its promises were we to adopt it in place of the myth of civic nationalism.

Is it really true, as some have claimed, that "unlike nationalism, patriotism has virtually never had the effect of an aggressive political force"?[41] Those who offer patriotism as an antidote to nationalism seem to believe that this is the case. But I am afraid that they have been seduced by the rhetoric of republican patriotism into ignoring its reality.

Dressed up in the language of its most eloquent partisans, from Cicero to Shaftesbury to Robespierre, republican patriotism looks like a generous love of one's compatriots that "sustains liberty instead of fomenting exclusion or aggression" against outsiders.[42] Republican love of country, insists Benedetto Croce, is as different from nationalism as a "gentle love for another human being" and a "bestial lust, diseased luxury, and selfish whim."[43] In short, republican patriotism provides us, in theory at least, with the solidarity of particularism without its nasty side effects, for "the love of common liberty *easily* extends beyond national borders and is translated into solidarity."[44]

Unfortunately, this antidote to nationalism is merely a form of discourse, that is, a way of *talking* about our shared sentiments and identities. Republican patriots may have inspired many memorable and useful virtues over the centuries, but gentleness and sympathy toward outsiders are not prominent among them. Cicero, a founder and central figure in the republican tradition, may characterize patriotism as a form of compassion and respect. But does the history of the Roman Republic give us

39. See Breuilly, "Nationalism and the State," 19.

40. Viroli, *For Love of Country*, 1, 2–6.

41. Alter, *Nationalism*, 3.

42. Viroli, *For Love of Country*, 8–9, 59.

43. Benedetto Croce, quoted in ibid., 168.

44. Ibid., 12, emphasis added.

much reason to think of patriotism as a love that "sustains liberty instead of fomenting exclusion or aggression"? I think not, unless you are willing to believe that the Roman Republic conquered the Western world in response to a never-ending series of unjust and unprovoked attacks by their neighbors. Shaftesbury may urge us to follow the gentle and generous example of ancient Greek patriots who "were yet so far from a conceited, selfish, and ridiculous contempt of others, that they were even, in a contrary extreme, admirers of whatever was in the least degree ingenious or curious in foreign nations."[45] But he ignores the extraordinary cruelty of the Greeks' never-ending wars with both neighbors and strangers. The patriots of the French Revolution may describe their love of country as a generous sentiment that they wished to share with the world. But when the world resisted their embrace they were ready, as recommended by the ferocious chorus of the *Marseillaise*, to "water their fields" with their enemies' "impure blood."[46] Wherever republican patriotism has risen to the level of a shared passion, generosity to outsiders has not been its hallmark.[47]

The problem with nationalism is not its lack of a positive vision of national loyalties, a vision that connects love of one's own to respect and admiration for others. Like republican patriotism, nationalism has had many partisans who describe it in this way. Herder, for example, urges us to cherish each nation as a unique facet of humanity,[48] just as republican patriots teach us to cherish the liberty of each community. And Mazzini argues that a commitment to one's own nation's freedom entails a commitment to the freedom of all nations.[49] The problem in both cases lies in the actual sentiments that their followers express, not in the way that they describe these sentiments. Republican patriotism cannot inoculate

45. Earl of Shaftesbury, quoted in ibid., 59.

46. These words follow the famous call "aux armes, citoyens," in the chorus of the *Marseillaise*. On the development of Jacobin nationalism, see Hont, "Permanent Crisis."

47. This is not to say that republican patriotism has, any more than nationalism, always expressed itself in violent and intolerant ways. See, e.g., Mary Dietz's account of the distinctly nonnationalist meaning of patriotism in eighteenth-century English and American political discourse. Dietz, "Patriotism."

48. This is the theme of Herder's magnum opus, *Ideas*. See also West, *Black Lamb, Grey Falcon*, 843.

49. See the writings collected and translated in Mazzini, *A Cosmopolitanism of Nations*.

us against nationalist intolerance because it seems, in practice, to promote the same kind of irritable pride and hostility toward others that we associate with nationalism. A strong dose of it might make us juster and more conscientious citizens, but I doubt that it would make the world a more peaceful or generous place.

Conclusion

The myth of the civic nation reflects one strategy for protecting liberal politics from the threats posed by nationalist passions: find a form of national solidarity based on shared principles rather than shared heritage. If there were such a form of national community, then the growth of national identity need not undermine social diversity and universal human rights. Nationalism would no longer threaten the liberal vision of progress, since history's message could still be delivered to individuals, by way of the civic nation.

But wishing won't make it so. The myth of the civic nation defends the Enlightenment's liberal political legacy against nationalism by employing the very concept—political community as voluntary association—whose plausibility has been undermined by the success of nationalism. The liberal legacy of individual rights and political rationality has developed within political communities that impart a kind of inherited cultural identity quite unforeseen by Enlightenment liberals. The battle to preserve that legacy is taking place *within* the framework provided by such communities, not between ethnocultural and civic forms of the modern nation. Within that framework we have every reason to construct and defend distinctions between more or less inclusive forms of national community. But in doing so we should not fool ourselves into thinking that what we are constructing is a freely chosen and purely civic form of national identity.

In the end, I believe that Renan got it right. Two things make a nation: subjective affirmation and a rich cultural inheritance of shared memories and practices. Without consent our legacy of shared memories and identity would be our destiny, rather than a set of background constraints on our activities. But without such a legacy there would be no consent at all, since there would be no reason for people to seek agreement with any one group of individuals rather than another. Focusing exclusively on one or the other components of national identity inspires the contrasting myths of ethnonationalist and civic nationalist theories of political community, myths that exaggerate, on the one side, our inability to alter or improve on the communal ties we have inherited and, on the other, our capacity to recreate ourselves in the image of liberal theories.

CHAPTER TWO

The Moral Psychology of Community

Nation and Community

Renan may point us in the right direction when he insists that two things, cultural heritage and subjective affirmation, make a nation. But it is hard to blend those two things into a coherent understanding of nationhood as long as we continue to rely upon the conceptual dichotomies that shape most contemporary conceptions of community. For these dichotomies encourage us to divvy up these two components of nationhood between two mutually exclusive models of association. Cultural heritage is identified with the affective ties and celebration of ancestors associated with models of gemeinschaft and traditional society. Subjective affirmation is identified with the contracts and instrumental reasoning associated with models of gesellschaft and modernity. Viewed in light of these dichotomies, the nation is bound to look like some sort of anomaly: a large, impersonal society masquerading as a small intergenerational community or two distinct forms of association, ethnic and civic communities, mistakenly treated as one.

But once we correct this perspective, the nation becomes much less difficult to understand. For it then becomes clear, I argue, that the combination of objective and subjective factors that has made it so hard to conceptualize nationhood is characteristic of community in all its forms, rather than a peculiarity of nations. In the end, one reason that our conceptions of nationhood are so controversial may be that our conceptions of community have not been controversial enough. In others words, we need to challenge familiar conceptions of the genus, community, if we want to make sense of its most hotly contested species, the nation.

This chapter presents the results of such a challenge. Hopefully, my alternative understanding of community will aid in the analysis of a variety of social phenomena. But I offer it here primarily as a first step toward a better understanding of the role that nations and nationalism play in modern political life.

Sharing and Social Friendship

Let us begin with ordinary language. We use the word "community" to refer to a tremendous variety of social groups. We speak of everything from the business or academic community to the ethnic or international community, from gay or Jewish communities to urban or rural communities.

There are two ways of bringing some order into the use of a concept that we rely on to characterize such a wide range of social groups. We can try to narrow its use to a smaller and more coherent set of associations, or we can look for some common phenomena that might justify our using the same concept to characterize such a wide range of social groups. Social and political theorists have usually pursued the first of these two options when trying to make sense of community, most often inspired by the belief that the modern world has been moving away from the relatively small and tightly integrated structures that they associate with the concept.[1] In this chapter I pursue the second option. I try to make sense of community as a generic concept rather than as a term of distinction that helps us characterize the world we have lost in modern times. I pursue this course because while the identification of community with relatively small and tightly knit forms of association has helped us focus attention on some of the distinctive features of modern and premodern society, it has obscured the much more common form of human connectedness that I shall try to conceptualize here.

In taking this generic approach to the concept of community I am inspired, in part, by the way in which Aristotle deals with the subject. Aristotle, unlike modern social theorists, was not confronted with the problem of how to explain the new and unusually individualistic forms of

1. Their choice is not surprising, since it is either curiosity or despair about the way in which modern societies have departed from earlier forms of society that has inspired most studies of community as a social phenomenon. See Yack, *The Problems of a Political Animal*, 43–50.

association that were emerging in modern Europe and North America. As a result, he was comfortable beginning with a single generic concept of human association, *koinonia* (which is best translated as "community"), rather than with the kind of conceptual dichotomies that ground most modern social theories.[2] Of course, this generic conception is not the only useful way of characterizing community. But it is especially helpful in dealing with social phenomena, such as the nation, that seem to defy the conceptual dichotomies upon which most modern social and political theories rely.

Clearly, there are at least some things that the variety of social groups we describe as communities have in common. First of all, they all consist of groups of individuals who share something, be it a belief, a territory, a purpose, an activity, or merely the lack of a quality that some other group is thought to possess. When we speak of the human community we are referring to all the individuals who share membership in the human species. When we speak of the gay community, we are referring to all the individuals who share a particular sexual orientation. When we speak of an urban community, we are referring to people who share a densely inhabited area, and so on.[3]

In addition to sharing something, however, the members of each of these groups are connected by feelings of social friendship that dispose them to devote special attention to each other's well-being. Human beings always share their species' characteristics with every other human, but the sense of belonging to a single human community comes and goes. Heterosexuals may share a sexual orientation; but they lack the sense of connection to each other as objects of special concern that leads us to talk about a gay community.[4] And city-dwellers may share a common space and certain forms of interdependence; but it makes little sense to

2. See ibid., especially chap. 1. Not much attention has been devoted to Aristotle's theory of community because most readers fail to distinguish between his understanding of the polis, or political community, and the broader genus, community (*koinonia*), to which it belongs.

3. I am speaking here of sharing in all its senses: common usage, division into parts, taking turns, etc. They all can provide the foundation of community when we imagine that they connect us as objects of mutual concern and loyalty.

4. Of course, when they begin to imagine themselves as threatened by the spread of gay rights and culture, heterosexuals easily start thinking in terms of a heterosexual community.

talk of an urban community if they close themselves off to each other in a cloak of mutual indifference or hostility.

Sharing something with others, I am suggesting, does not make you a member of their community unless you imagine and affirm it as a source of mutual connection. Conversely, feeling connected to the members of a community does not make you a member if, like the proverbial "white Negro," you cannot share the things that generate the sense of community in the first place.[5] Of course, others may treat you as a member of a community even when you lack this sense of social connection. But that is likely because you share something with the members of the community—religious beliefs, social customs, or skin color, for example—that is widely treated by *them* as a focus of mutual loyalty and concern.

It is tempting to add a third feature, a sense of exclusion or awareness of boundaries that divide us from others, to this list of defining features of community.[6] After all, opposing ourselves to others is one of the most powerful ways of establishing social connections. Focusing on the qualities that distinguish other groups from ourselves allows us to ignore or discount the qualities that distinguish us from each other. For example, most of the obstacles that keep us from imagining the whole of humanity as a single community would probably melt away were we ever to be confronted by extraterrestrials—especially if they were hostile.

Nevertheless, while opposition or differentiation certainly can help transform sharing into a sense of connectedness and mutual concern, it is not required to do so.[7] Shared purposes and activities often promote a sense of community regardless of whether or not one is competing with the purposes and activities of others. Even a universal human commu-

5. Anyone can choose to identify with the tastes and values of the members of a particular community. But if it is a shared experience that is not available to that individual that makes that community what it is, then that individual will remain outside of it. The "white Negro" can become a member of a community connected by, say, a love of jazz, Harlem nightclubs, and African American culture. He cannot, however, become a member of a community that grows out of the shared experience of being an oppressed racial minority in America.

6. This approach is especially popular among anthropologists, the classic work being Frederick Barth's introduction to his edited volume *Ethnic Groups and Boundaries*. For an interesting application of it to the study of ethnicity and nationalism, see Eriksen, *Ethnicity and Nationalism*.

7. On this point, see Brewer, "The Psychology of Prejudice."

nity could be generated in response some equally shared purpose or danger, such as an imminent threat to the earth's atmosphere or drinking water. So rather than treat a sense of exclusion as a third component of community, I treat it as a particular form of sharing, that is, the sharing of a sense of being distinguished from some group of others. This form of sharing often reinforces other sources of community where they exist and sometimes creates new sources where they do not exist.

Community, as I understand it, thus has two key features: sharing and a sense of social connection or friendship derived therefrom. A community is a group of individuals who imagine themselves connected to each other as objects of special concern and loyalty by something that they share.

As such, communities rest on a combination of objective and subjective factors, something shared and something felt. You can argue that the members of a group do not really share the things that make them think of themselves as having a special connection to each other—for example, that they are not really being persecuted by their neighbors or that they are not really descended from the same distinguished ancestors. But you cannot argue that they do not really feel connected to each other, if they say that they are. For although there are objective ways of measuring whether people actually share things, the only measure of social friendship is subjective.[8]

All communities therefore rest on something like the daily plebiscite that Renan associates with nations. For they all draw their strength from the affirmation of some form of sharing as a source of mutual connection, rather than from the mere existence of shared ancestors, beliefs, places, and the like. That said, the subjective affirmation that makes communities rarely takes the form of an explicit and self-conscious choice among a range of options, as suggested by Renan's expressive metaphor. Most often, instead, it merely registers our acceptance of the salience or prominence in our lives of particular forms of sharing. As with personal friendships, we tend to make self-conscious decisions about which social

8. Of course, the things that members of a community share need not themselves be objective, like a territory or a set of institutions. They can also be subjective, like a set of beliefs or a sense of being excluded by others. When I describe the sharing that constitutes community as objective, I mean to say that it is based on a claim about some objective condition, that a group of people actually share something, and that such claims can, unlike the sense of being connected to others by the things that we share with them, be challenged as inaccurate by outside observers.

friendship to endorse only when forced to resolve questions of conflicting loyalties.

Communities come in so many different forms because human beings can share and have shared so many different things: descent, territorial proximity, beliefs, purposes, rituals, forms of expression, to cite just some of the commonest among them. And they are quite variable, not just because old forms of sharing disappear and new forms are always emerging, but because of the way in which familiar forms of sharing gain or lose significance in new circumstances. A slightly different outcome in a battle or a different choice of royal marriage partner hundreds of years ago might have preserved old forms of sharing that have disappeared in our day. And new communities, even intergenerational communities like nations, can emerge quite suddenly as contingent events—a bloody riot or a successful invasion, for example—focus our attention on one rather than another form of sharing.[9]

I speak of sharing in my characterization of community rather than identity in order to emphasize the heterogeneity that is an essential part of communal life. Community, I suggest, involves awareness of difference as well as commonality. In other words, communities are composed of individuals who focus their attention on something that bridges, rather than erases, their differences. Erase these differences in the pursuit of unity or identity, and, as Aristotle argues in his critique of Plato's *Republic*, you erase community itself.[10] Plato, hoping to promote the kind of unity associated with family life, suggests that we try to turn the just city into a single family. But if you make unity or identity the defining feature of community, Aristotle asks, why stop at a family? Why not a single individual as the model for community? Indeed, Plato accepts the point, for he suggests that his ideal society would share "a community of pain and pleasure,"[11] a community so unified that when my neighbor is poked with a sword, I would feel its point. A single organism, however, is not a community, except in an analogical sense, just as a community is an organism only in an analogical or metaphorical sense.[12] Both possess

9. See Beissinger, "Nations That Bark and Nations That Bite," 173.

10. Aristotle, *Politics*, 1261–62.

11. Plato, *Republic*, 464a.

12. It is easy to lose sight of these distinctions when employing organic metaphors. It would be easier to keep them in mind if, like Aristotle, we occasionally used political metaphors to characterize the unity we find in organisms. When he suggests that internal organization of an animal "resembles that of a city well-governed by laws" (Aristotle, *Motion*

internal differentiation and common purposes or activities. But a community, unlike an organism, is made up of individual members who can survive and experience life apart from others. Its members ordinarily experience their connection to others as the bridging of difference rather than identity or unity.

We need to emphasize this aspect of communal life in order to counter the influence of communitarian rhetoric and its insistence on the need for unity and collective identity. No doubt, the submergence of individual identities into a collective identity can be a powerful force in human life, particularly in conflicts between communities. But it is a relatively rare and transient social phenomenon, what Hans Schmalenbach calls "communion (*bund*)" as opposed to community.[13] Communion is that intense experience of the loss of self in the collective that orators so often seek to induce and the disenchanted so often recall with nostalgia. It can occur in all walks of life, among members of a bowling team sharing an exciting victory no less than among soldiers sharing the adversities of life in the trenches.[14] It is a powerful experience that can inspire high levels of self-sacrifice and greatly enhance the collective power of communities, which is why orators so often seek to promote it. But it is hard to maintain for any length of time, which is why I do not include it in my definition of community. Shared *memories* of a moment of communion, as recalled by, say, participants in revolutionary struggles, the trench battles of World War I, or even athletic triumphs and tragedies, can become the basis of communal attachments.[15] But communion itself,

---

of Animals, 703a28), no one doubts that he is talking about the way in which animals resemble political communities. But when he suggests that citizens resemble parts of a body, he is often interpreted as saying that the political community *is* an organism, rather than it resembles one in some interesting way. See Yack, *The Problems of a Political Animal*, 92–94.

13. Schmalenbach, "Communion—a Social Category."

14. Schmalenbach (ibid.) rightly emphasizes that we make a mistake when we identify the experience of communion with living in the kind of small communities that Tönnies associates with his concept of gemeinschaft. One can lose oneself just as well in a voluntary association, such as a bowling team or an ashram, as you can in an inherited form of community. The key is that in both cases the experience of communion or loss of self is relatively fleeting. It is a by-product of a shared way of life rather than one of its constituent elements.

15. Remembered communions can also disrupt an existing community by raising expectations of unity higher than is possible in normal circumstances. See Musil, "'Nation' as Ideal and Reality," 120–21.

the loss of individual identity in the collective, is too transitory and unreliable a phenomenon to provide the cement that ordinarily holds communities together.

As for social friendship, I use that term to characterize the communal bond because it captures the peculiar kind of mutual commitment that community inspires.[16] Friends, as Aristotle suggests, do what they *can* for each other, rather than what they are *obliged* to do.[17] That means they mark each other out as objects of special concern and loyalty. If they can, they will do somewhat more than they are obliged to do for each other—though if they are not in a good position to help each other, they will want each other to do less than they are obliged to do. The disposition of friends to do what they can is most visible in its most familiar forms, family ties and personal intimacy. But it can also be found, I would argue, in much less personal and familiar forms of community. How far we are willing to go to do what we can for each other will depend very much on the source of friendship in any particular community. Our lives are lived within a rich patchwork of more or less intense social friendships.

The term solidarity is much more commonly used than friendship to conceptualize the sense of mutual connectedness that constitutes communities. But solidarity is too suggestive of social unity to capture the complexity and flexibility of communal ties. At any given time we are connected to others in a complex pattern of overlapping and often competing ties. We sort out these connections by weighing and balancing their tugs on our sentiments—just as we do with the conflicting loyalties generated by personal friendships—rather than by standing in solidarity first with one group, then the other. It is much easier to talk about our friendship with two competing groups, because friendship involves mutual concern rather than the fusion or solidification of identities. For this reason I believe that the complex pattern of communal attachments is therefore much better captured by the concept of social friendship than by the concept of solidarity.

Having characterized social friendship or a sense of mutual concern

16. I am following here the rather broad scope associated with the Greek word for friendship, *philia*, which refers to family, social, and political ties, as well as nonsexual intimacy. See Fraisse, *Philia*. Aristotle makes especially interesting use of the breadth of the Greek term in his moral and political philosophy. See Yack, *The Problems of a Political Animal*, 35–39, 109–26.

17. Aristotle, *Eudemian Ethics* 1244a21, and *Nichomachean Ethics*, 1163b15.

and loyalty as one of community's two basic elements, let me emphasize that I am not suggesting community is grounded in the mutual affection characteristic of personal friendships. As in family relations, we need not have any special affection for the other members of our community in order to express special concern for their well-being. Nor am I suggesting community is an especially harmonious form of association. Special feelings of mutual concern and loyalty generate their own distinctive and nasty forms of conflict, since they often raise expectations of solicitude that we are in no position to meet.[18] Moreover, expressions of special concern are often annoying and unwanted, as anyone who has had to deal with unsolicited advice from friends, family, and acquaintances will no doubt attest. Social friendship is one of the primary means by which we maintain our associations with each other. But it is very far from a guarantee of agreement or harmony.

Friendship, Justice, and Self-Interest

Understood in this way, community is a basic element of what Jon Elster calls "the cement of society,"[19] rather than a special product of traditional village and family life. Human society, I suggest, is bound together by a mixture of self-interest, norms of justice, and social friendship. In other words, three motives inspire us to cooperate with each other: calculations about what will serve our own interests, beliefs about what we owe each other, and feelings of special concern for the well-being of people with whom we share things.

Of these three motives, social friendship is the most often overlooked. Self-interest is impossible to ignore and is easily extended as an explanatory tool. And beliefs about justice, whatever their origins, play a role in countering and channeling self-interest that seems no less difficult to set aside. But social friendship, doing "what we can" for people to whom we feel connected, seems to establish much vaguer and less reliable standards than doing the right thing or what is prudent. It lacks the specificity that comes from either the calculation of means to a self-interested end or the measurement of a particular action against a general rule or prin-

18. This is a major theme of my book *The Problems of a Political Animal.* See especially 1–5, chap. 4, and chap. 7.

19. Elster, *The Cement of Society.*

ciple. But while that makes social friendship harder to track, it should not keep us from recognizing that it provides a third motive, alongside the calculations of self-interest and beliefs about justice, for the creation and maintenance of social ties among human beings. As researchers in social psychology have often demonstrated, even the most arbitrary and trivial forms of sharing seem to be capable of generating strong feelings of connection to one's group.[20] Even when nothing much is at stake or there is little reason to believe that we owe others special attention we tend, it seems, to develop feelings of special concern and loyalty to the people with whom we are aware of sharing things.

There are good reasons for treating this disposition to social friendship as natural to human beings.[21] For one thing, it seems to be one of the rare features of human experience that seems to be universal. More significantly, modern biological studies suggest that this disposition to social friendship is an evolutionary acquisition, one that our species shares with most other primates.[22] These studies set out to show how altruistic dispositions could emerge in our species by means of a mechanism, natural selection, which ordinarily rewards behavior that enhances one's own chances for survival. They focus, for the most part, on two ways in which such dispositions could develop: through selection for traits that might help the survival of individuals, our close kin, who share a significant part of our genetic inheritance; and by selection for traits that promote expectations of reciprocity and punishment of those who fail to provide it.[23]

These two dispositions, concern for close kin and expectations of rec-

20. Baumeister, *Cultural Animal*, 377–79. See the discussion of these studies in Appiah, *The Ethics of Identity*, 62.

21. See, e.g., Brewer, "The Psychology of Prejudice," and Stern, "Why Do People Sacrifice for Their Nation," 109.

22. See especially Franz de Waal's *Good-Natured: The Origins of Right and Wrong in Humans and Other Animals*. De Waal's book is a very useful corrective to the overly enthusiastic and uncritical account of these arguments in popular books such as Robert Wright's *The Moral Animal* and Matt Ridley's *The Origins of Virtue*.

23. Both evolutionary paths to altruism are widely accepted. But the former is easier to defend than the latter, since it corresponds to forms of self-sacrifice found throughout the animal kingdom. The latter depends on the assumption that in repeated encounters survival benefits are greatest among those who are prepared to cooperate and punish those who do not. The classic study is the famous article, "The Evolution of Cooperation in Biological Systems," coauthored by Robert Axelord and William Hamilton, in Axelrod, *The Evolution of Cooperation*, 85–105.

iprocity, clearly correspond to feelings of social friendship and norms of justice, the two other-regarding components of what I described as the cement of society. This is not to suggest that every time we express concern for a member of a group or indignation at an injustice we are acting on instinct. It is merely to suggest that our concern for others and our demands for justice are no less natural, no less deeply rooted in human psychology, than our calculations of self-interest. Thrown by our material and cultural evolution into immensely larger and more complex forms of society than those that gave birth to these dispositions, we still make use of all of them to make sense of our world. Once it is clear that we are disposed to look for something like justice, even if in the simplest form of reciprocity, then it should not be surprising that we have become attached to such an elaborate and bewildering variety of justice norms in our infinitely more complex world. And once it is clear that we are disposed to develop feelings of mutual concern and loyalty to those closest to us, it should not be surprising that our imagination extends such feelings in so many different directions in a world in which there are so many competing and overlapping forms of sharing.

The fact that these other-regarding dispositions ultimately promote the survival of our own "selfish" genes has led to some confusion about their character.[24] The use of game theory and other rational choice models to determine the results of genetic competition should not mislead us into treating the practice of social friendship as a form of selfish or self-serving behavior.[25] For it is precisely because genetic competition has produced in human beings other-regarding dispositions that we do *not* need to explain the evolution of social cooperation solely in terms of an aggregation of self-serving individual choices. If human beings have developed a certain limited disposition toward altruistic or cooperative behavior, then that means that the calculation of self-interest has to compete with—or balance or reinforce—a very different source of social connectedness among human beings.

The conflation of genes and individual organisms as objects of natural

24. The predominant interpretation among evolutionary biologists, presented most famously and emphatically by Richard Dawkins in *The Selfish Gene*, is that the gene is the unit of selection. Group selection still has important defenders, however, such as Sober and Wilson, *Unto Others: The Evolutionary Psychology of Unselfish Behavior*.

25. A classic example is Axelrod and Hamilton's article, "The Evolution of Cooperation in Biological Systems." For the development of evolutionary game theory, see Wright, *The Moral Animal*, 189–209.

selection often obscures this point, especially among social scientists.[26] Theories of kin selection and reciprocal altruism sometimes explain the other-regarding dispositions of individual organisms by focusing on the "selfish" interests of the genes that shape them. In other words, these theories show us that "selfish genes sometimes produce selfless individuals to achieve their ends."[27] But if this is so, then it cannot possibly be true that people "inevitably and always pursue what is best for themselves" and that "good things are done for bad motives."[28] For it is precisely the existence of our *good* motives, our disposition to do things for the good of others rather than ourselves, which these theories explain.

When biologists and social scientists move back and forth in this way between self-seeking genes and self-seeking individuals—and, thereby, between evolutionary game theory and rational choice theory—they ignore this distinction. They forget that "the evolutionary *causes* of our motives cannot be judged as if they *are* our motives."[29] The evolution of our genes may not itself rely on "altruistic" motives (i.e., a disposition to aid the replication of other genes). But the individual organisms that they produce do display such motives. And that means that any attempt to explain social cooperation solely in terms of rational calculation of needs and interests is extremely unrealistic.[30]

What distinguishes social friendship as a source of human connection is that it is a sentiment of concern for others rather than a calculation of means to selfish ends or the imposition of a belief about what

26. See de Waal, *Good-Natured*, 15.

27. Ridley, *The Origins of Virtue*, 20.

28. Ibid., 27, 46.

29. Steven Pinker, quoted in de Waal, *Good-Natured*, 237n18. De Waal's criticism of this conflation of genetic and individual selfishness (ibid., 14–17, 116–17) is especially useful.

30. This lack of realism is usually justified, among sociobiologists and social scientists alike, by an appeal to the principle of theoretical parsimony. But as Sober and Wilson demonstrate (*Unto Others*, 291), the appeal to self-interest as the ultimate motive for individual behavior is anything but parsimonious in application. In order to reinterpret all of the seemingly obvious examples of other-regarding behavior as self-seeking, these theorists have to invoke such a wealth of questionable subsidiary hypotheses about human needs and interests that their theories, when viewed as a whole, begin to display the absurd complexity of a Rube Goldberg device. In the end, it is much simpler, much more parsimonious, to accept that there may be two or three ultimate sources of human cooperation than to entertain the seemingly endless series of hypotheses needed to derive all other-regarding behavior from a single self-serving source.

we owe each other. As such, it is, like love or spontaneity, a by-product of our choices and experience, rather than the object of our choices. In other words, while you can choose to share things with others, you cannot choose to feel connected to them by ties of social friendship. Of course, some objects of sharing, such as a home, ancestors, or religious beliefs, for example, are much more likely than others to inspire a sense of connection to others. But even in these cases ties of social friendship do not necessarily follow from sharing things, as the expression "strangers under the same roof" vividly suggests. Moreover, even those who, like modern nation-builders, consciously set out to expand and intensify a particular form of communal friendship, generally do so indirectly. Rather than try to persuade people, say, that France rather than Brittany provides an appropriate focus for communal loyalty, they try to change the habits of language, education, and custom that promote as its by-product a sense of national community.[31]

I emphasize this point in order to clarify the relationship between community and rationality as well as the complexity of our moral dispositions. The bonds of social friendship that connect us to each other in communal life are not irrational in the sense of a primitive force of instinct that blinds and overwhelms reason. They are, however, a-rational, in the sense that they do not owe their origin to calculation and choice. Some rational choice theorists have argued otherwise, suggesting that we should see our attachments to particular communities, to local sports teams as well as competing nations, as rational solutions to the problem of coordination. If individuals, these theorists argue, seek a good like the thrill of cheering with thousands of others for a home team, it is quite rational for them to accept conventions that allow them to settle on a particular shared object of loyalty.[32] But it is the motives rather than the products of human action that are at issue here. In other words, it is the source of human connectedness, rather than its accomplishments, that we are trying to identify. Even if common objects of loyalty solve problems of coordination, the question we are asking now is how do people come to focus on such objects: through an aggregation of individual choices to pursue that end or as a sentimental by-product of the experience of sharing a location, afternoons at the stadium, and stories about

31. The classic account is E. Weber, *Peasants into Frenchmen*.

32. Hardin, *One for All*, 27–33; Goodin, "Conventions and Conversion, or Why Is Nationalism Sometimes So Nasty," 91.

past greatness? The fact that shared sentiments can sometimes provide us with rational solutions to our problems should not blind us to their independence from rational calculation as a force in our lives.

Community and Organization

Members of a community, I have argued, are connected by feelings of mutual concern and loyalty. But that is hardly the only way in which individuals imagine themselves connected and develop a sense of shared membership. Membership, after all, is a metaphor that likens the social relationship between individual and group to the organic relationship between the body and its individual parts or members. Its significance therefore varies with the different resemblances that we find between our social relations and the parts of an organism.

Membership in communities stands in contrast to an even commoner form of membership: our membership in organizations, groups that connect us by combining and coordinating our activities. At their best, organizations, like a team or a club or a symphony orchestra, integrate individual actions so smoothly that we find it difficult to distinguish the contribution that each individual makes to the final product. At their worst, they function with all the cruelty of a slave gang and all the efficiency of a congressional ethics committee. Whatever their quality, however, organizations connect us by giving us a share in the benefits and burdens of coordinated activity, rather than by the mutual feelings that they inspire. Communities make their demands by means of the depth and intensity of the special concern for others that they inspire; organizations make their demands by means of the level of obligation that they impose as the price of the benefits produced by collective action. Parents sacrifice themselves for their children because they feel more concern for their children's welfare than their own. Members of organizations, like a team or a state, sacrifice themselves when they think that the shared or collective good that the organization can provide is more important than their own.[33]

Of course, the same group may be both a community and an organi-

33. I save discussion of a third form of group membership, in a network or web, for later chapters. The distinctive form of connection here is interdependence, rather than either mutual concern or group coordination.

zation—for example, think of fraternal lodges and secret societies—and thus draw on both sorts of connections to others. But there is no necessary connection between them. We are often indifferent or even hostile to the other members of organizations to which we belong. And we sometimes lack or eschew any coordinated means of promoting the well-being of the members of the communities with which we identify. It is thus important to keep these two forms of membership distinct, especially if one is interested in the rise of nationalism in the modern world. For nationalism, as we shall see, grows out of the relationship between a community and an organization: the relatively old form of community manifested in nations and the relatively new and extraordinarily powerful form of political organization that we call the modern state. In particular, it grows out of efforts, on the one hand, to harness communal loyalties to increase the power of states and, on the other, to legitimate and control that power by imagining the state as the servant of the nation's prepolitical community.

Membership in organizations and communities is often confused with our membership in a set or species, thus inspiring the misimpression that organization and community are present or, at least, latent wherever people share some feature important enough to attract our attention. But membership in sets or species refers simply to likeness or commonality, the possession of some characteristic significant enough to serve as a means of categorizing a group of human beings. In itself, such membership demands no sense of social connection. You can share in a culture, say, by speaking a language, without working together with or feeling any special concern for its other members. Finnish and Hungarian speakers, for example, are regularly classified as members of the same language—and thus, to a certain extent, cultural—group. But no one would suggest, at least so far, that they are members of the same cultural community. Similarly, the members of the set of all French speakers or all relatively dark-skinned people need not feel any more sense of community than the members of the set of all prime numbers.

The conflation of these three forms of membership, sets, organizations, and communities, has contributed mightily to what Rogers Brubaker and others call the "reification" of groups.[34] In particular, the confusion of organizations and communities with sets makes social groups

34. Brubaker, *Ethnicity without Groups*, 7–15.

seem much more solid, stable, and continuous than they really are. Organizations that spread erratically and unevenly among a group of individuals seem much steadier and more uniform when we focus on some common characteristic that leads us to categorize them as a set or species. Similarly, partial, overlapping, and evanescent feelings of social friendship seem much more permanent and integrated when we keep our eyes on the commonality that marks a group of individuals as members of a single set. The expectation that we should be able to discover distinctive organizations whose membership corresponds to those of communities leads us to exaggerate the extent and strength of both. This is a particular problem in the study of the nation where, as we shall see, the expectation that the nation should refer to an organization as well as a community has led to the exaggeration of both its solidity and its modernity.

How Community Is Imagined

If communities are constituted by our sense of being connected to other human beings as objects of special concern and loyalty, then they are all, to appropriate Benedict Anderson's famous expression, "imagined communities." In other words, every community, small face-to-face groups no less than large and impersonal societies like modern nations, relies on human imagination to connect its members to each other as objects of special concern and loyalty.

After all, shared ancestors, let alone shared genes, do not make a family. A family is a group of individuals who imagine themselves connected by shared ancestors and descendents. Accordingly, there are as many forms of family community as there are ways of imagining ancestry, marriage, and descent. Similarly, it takes more than shared space and frequent interaction to make a village community, since familiarity can breed contempt and diffidence as easily as a sense of connection. In a village community shared space and daily interaction often inspire a sense of connection that, on the one hand, bridges the differences that could easily provide the focus for smaller communities and, on the other, distracts attention from the broader forms of sharing that could inspire larger ones. For even the smallest communities contain differences—of age, gender, and social status, for example—that cannot be ignored or erased. If a sense of community emerges despite these differences, it is because we are capable of imagining the things we share as a source of connection that transcends them.

Anderson coined the expression "imagined communities" in order to characterize forms of community, like the nation, that connect people who never meet or interact with each other. He wanted to remind us that in many communities we have nothing but a mental image of most of our fellow members, since these communities connect us over space and time to distant individuals, as well as to past and future generations.[35] This point is well worth emphasizing. But it is, in the end, a point about *imagined compatriots*, rather than imagined community. In other words, it helps us distinguish communities in which fellow members are present and familiar from those in which we must conjure them up by an act of imagination. If we want to talk instead about *imagined community*, then we need to look more closely at the way in which we imagine the connections that bridge our manifest differences.

How then do we imagine community? In two different ways, each of which can provide the starting point for the other. On the one hand, we picture some of the things that we share as sources of connection that make particular individuals objects of special concern and loyalty. On the other hand, we sometimes wonder what it is that we share with the people to whom we feel connected by a sense of social friendship. In the first case, the what leads to the who: the sense of sharing some good or practice or purpose leads us to imagine ourselves connected to a particular group of individuals. In the second case, the who leads to the what: the sense of connection to others leads us to try to specify what it is that we share with them. In other words, community involves imagining connections to those with whom we share things as well as imagining the things that we share with those to whom we feel connected. The first process creates communities as objects of imagination; the second leads to their development.

Promoters of a global community, for example, often start from a new

35. Despite his emphasis on imagined forms of community, there remains a trace of the gemeinschaft/gesellschaft dichotomy in Anderson's approach to community since the key distinction seems to be between face-to-face community based on familiarity and interaction and impersonal community based on the exercise of imagination. I believe, however, that it is the recognition of the role that imagination plays in all forms of community life that helps account for the extraordinary influence of Anderson's concept of "imagined community." In any case, that is what I have taken from it.

form of sharing that they strive to bring to our attention: the interdependence that they believe is being created by new forms of technology, commerce, and communication. In moving from shared interdependence to talk of a global community, however, they picture this new form of interdependence as a source of connection that bridges the differences that have previously divided the peoples of the world. Promoters of a European community, in contrast, start with the sense of connection among Europeans and then try to picture what it is that Europeans share as a community. The older forms of sharing that originally established this sense of connection among the different communities within Europe—the sense of being the center of Christendom or the origins of civilization or the home of the world's superior race—are not acceptable bases of community in present circumstances. That leaves the members of the European community with a sense of connection to each other, but considerable uncertainty about what they share as a community. Similarly, Japan's devastating defeat in World War II left the Japanese searching for a new understanding of what they shared. The disasters of the war had discredited the old leadership and old values, but left intact a strong sense of connection to each other among most Japanese, the meaning of which they were eager to explain to themselves, even to the point of talking about a "community of remorse."[36]

Each of these two ways of imagining community can provide the starting point for the other. For the specification of new or even slightly altered objects of sharing can significantly alter our sense of the range of people to whom we are connected, which in turn can lead us to wonder what it is that connects us, and so on. The founding of the United States, for example, established a new nation, a new political object of sharing that eventually inspired the former colonists and their descendants with a sense of connection to each other. But having established that sense of connection, it leaves Americans wondering about what it is that connects them, what it means to be an American.[37] Those who answer this question by referring to the Constitution or a set of political principles and examples or a kind of rugged individualism might find themselves expanding the range of individuals to whom they feel connected. Those

36. See Dower, *Embracing Defeat*, 234–39.

37. For examples of the large body of literature that reasons in this way, see Walzer, *What It Means to Be an American*; R. Smith, *Civic Ideals*, 80–81; and Huntington, *Who Are We?*.

who cite European origins or Anglo-Protestant culture will probably contract the range of people with whom they feel associated. There is, however, no reason for the process to stop there. People who believe that commitment to popular sovereignty makes an American may come to the conclusion that people of African descent are incapable of exercising that commitment. And people who believe that it is Protestant morality that makes an American may come to the conclusion that such a morality requires them to emphasize what all people, whatever their race or religion, have in common. The process of imagining community never stops, as Americans move from a sense of what they share to who they are and back again.

And this process goes on even in communities, like the family, that lack a public forum for debate and self-examination. Families may start with a particular sense of shared ancestry and descent. But in establishing connections of mutual concern and loyalty to a particular group of individuals, families also open us up to things that we might ordinarily reject as foreign. Loyalty and concern for a gay son, an atheistic grandchild, or a sister who enters an interracial marriage can broaden our understanding of what we share with people who otherwise seem alien to us.[38]

The process by which people move back and forth between questions about who is connected to whom to what it is that actually connects us helps explain the continuity of communal identities in spite of wholesale transformations and even inventions of their understanding of what they have in common. An invented tradition, such as the adoption of Highland cultural symbols by Lowland Scots, represents a new answer to the question of what constitutes the cultural heritage shared by members of a national community. The fact that Lowlanders now adorn themselves with symbolic attire that their ancestors would have despised as "the dress of a thief" does not mean that they lack a genuine sense of community.[39] It merely means that there has been a revision in the sense of just what it is that ties "we" Scotsmen and -women to each other. Highland symbols and rituals, often reshaped and inflated, provided a con-

38. Of course, I do not want to suggest that such reflections always lead to greater inclusiveness. Our connections to others just as easily and as often lead us to exclude people that we otherwise would have included within our sense of community.

39. Devine, *A History of the Scottish Nation*, 231–35. See also Trevor-Roper, "The Highland Tradition in Scotland."

veniently striking and colorful way of distinguishing the Scots from the English, even though they only became attractive when the power of the clans had been broken. The elevation of these symbols and traditions to a prominent role in the Scottish national heritage changes the sense of what connects members of the national community to each other. But this process of change and development goes on throughout the lifetime of every community.

Community then is indeed imagined or constructed, as we are so often reminded today. But it is imagined or constructed by people who share things and/or feel connected to each other, not by independent and disconnected individuals.[40] This does not mean that we are bound to reproduce the communities that have been handed to us. We could not do so, even if we were so inclined. For events and changing circumstances are constantly undermining old forms of sharing and bringing new ones to the fore, as well as compelling us to confront tensions and inconsistencies within the patterns of communal attachments that we receive. Moreover, as we have seen, the very existence of a sense of loyalty and concern for others can promote a changing image of community by leading us to reconsider what it is that we share with them. It does mean, however, that the contingencies of birth and history provide us with much of the material from which we construct our images of community. For we construct these images by focusing our attention on one or another form of sharing that we find in our world or by changing our minds about exactly what it is that sustains the connections among a particular group of people.

Natural Necessity, Choice, and Contingency

The things that we share in different forms of community can be divided into three broad categories: the natural or necessary, the chosen, and the contingent. Nations, as we shall see in the following chapter, clearly fall

40. Indeed, it would make sense to talk of "imagined individuals" when talking of the rational actors in rational choice and social contract theories. They exist only to the extent to which we use our imagination to strip away their connections to others. One could even talk of a community of imagined individuals, the sense of connection to others that we would expect from the disconnected rational individuals whom we have conjured up in our imagination. Civil society, as Hegel conceives of it in *The Philosophy of Right*, would be a good example of such a community.

into the last of these categories, for neither natural necessity nor conscious design creates categories like Basques, Britons, and Bretons.[41] That makes it quite difficult to justify our divisions into national communities, which is one reason why the proponents of the myths of ethnic and civic nationalism strive so hard to make nationhood look like something that is either natural or chosen.

We share a few things by nature and necessity: for example, our species. Regardless of whether they recognize or affirm it as something positive, human beings apparently share all but a tiny portion of the human genome, which opens considerable ground upon which to build a sense of a universal human community. Race is another example of a form of sharing that has at least been treated as natural. Of course, in the light of modern studies of genetic variation it does not seem like an especially important form of sharing, since racial differentiation does not seem to go beyond the surface of skin tone, hair colors, and facial configuration. But shared surfaces can, like any other form of sharing, become the basis of a strong sense of community—even if the proponents of racial community have almost always insisted that racial differences go much deeper than that. If sexual orientation is, as often suggested, a natural or genetically programmed disposition, then one could argue that homosexuals and heterosexuals each share something that is natural and necessary. And parents and their biological children clearly share, among other things, a natural connection, usually symbolized by the metaphor of blood—though that metaphor of common blood has to be stretched pretty thin to cover the wide range of ancestors and descendants included in images of an extended family.

A number of factors make the things we share by nature an attractive foundation for community. First of all, there is the prestige and positive connotation still attached to the idea of nature, despite generations of complaint about the "naturalistic fallacy" that equates the natural with the good. It is also favored as a basis for community because of the assumption that natural forms of sharing are promoted or accompanied by natural dispositions toward social friendship. The model here is clearly the friendship that connects children and parents, though some are inclined to talk about a natural philanthropy that emerges when we eliminate the influence of the conventional boundaries that divide human be-

41. See the second last section of the introduction where I treat contingency as a quality of things that are neither necessary nor chosen.

ings from each other. Most important, natural bases for community have the advantage of necessity or inevitability, which means, in principle at least, we do not have to force, persuade, or habituate people into accepting them.

A much larger and more diverse group of communities is based on forms of sharing that are created by human choice rather than natural necessity. These communities range from business partnerships and bowling leagues to ashrams and self-help groups. As the mention of an ascetic religious community like an ashram should make clear, chosen forms of sharing do not all produce the kind of cold detachment of the contractual groups associated with the concepts of gesellschaft and voluntary association. Some of the most intensely communal groups, such as ascetic sects or utopian settlements, owe their origins and continued existence to the decision that some people make to share their lives with each other.[42] In fact, the commonest and most tightly integrated of affective communities, the family, owes its origins to such decisions. For although families link ancestors and descendants, they begin with a marriage contract, an agreement to live together.[43] (Whether this agreement is made by the marriage partners themselves or is made for them is irrelevant in this context.) This combination of choice and descent makes the family much more complex than it is ordinarily thought to be,[44] since marrying and being born into a family would seem to promote two very different senses of belonging. Melding them into a single form of community takes considerable cultural ingenuity, as witnessed by the variety of customs and laws that have developed to give force to the expression "marrying into a family."

The things that we share by choice provide an attractive basis for community for at least two reasons. Willingness to share or, more precisely, the absence of compulsion to share, makes chosen community much

42. For a study that makes choice a key component of community, see Catlin, "The Meaning of Community," 126–27, 133.

43. That is why Hegel, for one, describes marriage as a contract to transcend the standpoint of contract. Hegel, *Philosophy of Right*, ¶163.

44. One indication of this complexity is that everyone has ancestors that his or her parents lack. Because of the way in which marriage brings together otherwise unrelated people, the passing of time leads families to enlarge their pools of ancestors as well as their pools of descendants. The identification of a family line requires selection from among the ancestors according to some principle, such matrilineal or patrilineal descent, rather than the mere collection of birth certificates.

easier to justify. In addition, when we choose the forms of sharing that inspire communal ties, we can measure their value in terms of the purposes that they serve. Was that purpose reasonable to choose? Is it reasonably pursued by the means chosen? By allowing us to raise such questions, communities based on chosen forms of sharing make it easier to justify some of our feelings of social friendship and reject others.

Finally, there are the communities based on forms of sharing that owe their existence to the contingencies of history and human development rather than natural necessity or human choice. This is the largest category of community, because all of the various forms of cultural community grow out of forms of sharing that are neither necessary nor chosen. One could argue that human beings are by nature or necessity culture-producing animals. But no one could reasonably maintain that the French language or the Hindu caste system or Aztec court ritual is a necessary product of human development. Small and easily imaginable alterations in the course of events, a death here or a military victory there, could easily have prevented such cultural artifacts from ever emerging, let alone serving to connect millions of people in intergenerational communities.[45] Moreover, we are always capable of shedding our share in any of these artifacts in a way that we cannot shed our species or biological ancestry. Similarly, one could argue that each of these cultural artifacts is a by-product of human choice and purposive action. But no one could reasonably maintain that they were created as such by the choice of people to establish them. For while there are certainly people who choose to promote or impose a shared sense of cultural heritage or language among others, in doing so, they ordinarily take up and repackage an already existing form of sharing, rather than urge people to choose to create a new one in the way that a club or self-help group or any other purposive association is established.

Nations belong to this category of community since they grow out of our affirmation of the shared cultural legacies that we inherit from previous generations. Although we can withhold our affirmation and thus reject membership in national communities, we cannot choose or undo our cultural inheritance. What's done is done. Where we were thrown by the contingencies of birth determines what materials we have to work with in establishing any kind of national community. At the same time, cultural inheritance lacks the necessity of biological descent as a focus

45. On historical contingency, see Ben Menahem, "Historical Contingency."

for mutual concern and loyalty. I cannot be me, I cannot be the creature I am without being the biological descendant of my parents, since that fact was fixed at conception and revealed at birth. My cultural inheritance, in contrast, could easily have been otherwise, if, for example, my parents moved shortly before or after my birth.

Communities that grow out of contingent forms of sharing are much harder to justify than those that owe their origins to nature or choice. For they lack both the sense of necessity of the former and the sense of rational purpose of the latter. That is one reason for the popularity of the myths of ethnic and civic nationalism. The myths of ethnic nationalism assimilate national community to natural community, making nationhood something that is inevitable and inescapable for us. They represent new versions of Plato's noble lie, false images designed to mislead us into treating our cultural and political divisions as natural and necessary, as if each nation represented a distinct species, sprung from the earth on which its people dwell. The myths of civic nationalism, in contrast, assimilate national community to chosen community, making nationhood something that we construct according to our own purposes. They are designed to make it seem as if we could measure the friendships that connect us to others in national communities solely in terms of the political purposes that we choose to share with them.

Both myths, as we have seen, seriously misrepresent nations and nationalism. In order to evaluate our membership in nations we must squarely address the question about the value of contingent communities, as I shall attempt to do in part 2. In order to make sense of the role that nations and nationalism play in modern political life we have to keep in focus the combination of subjective affirmation and contingent forms of sharing that inform them.

CHAPTER THREE

What Then Is a Nation?

Conceptualizing National Community

What then is a nation? What distinguishes this form of association that has risen to such prominence in modern times that we have felt compelled to coin the term nationalism to describe its role in our lives?

First of all, a nation is a community. In other words, a nation is a group of people who imagine themselves connected to each other as objects of special concern and loyalty by something that they share. As such, a nation is more than a set or a species and less than an organization. The mere sharing of some characteristic or practice, such as skin color or a language, may make individuals members of a set; but until they affirm what they share as a source of mutual concern and loyalty these individuals do not form a community. And while the members of nations may aspire to organize their lives to achieve certain shared ends—for example, as states—nations can and have existed without organized means of coordinating their members' activities toward common ends.

Second, and most important of all, a nation is an intergenerational community. The members of a nation share something that connects them back in time to a particular point of origin and forward into an indefinite future.[1] As such, they share predecessors and successors who

1. Hence definitions, like Rupert Emerson's, that characterize the nation "as a community of people who feel they belong together in the double sense that they share deeply significant elements of a common heritage and have a common destiny for the future" (Emerson *From Empire to Nation*, 95).

are regularly invoked to deepen the ties that bind the living and extend their sense of obligation to past and future generations.

Third, the nation is a cultural heritage community. In other words, it is the affirmation of a shared inheritance of cultural artifacts, such as language, relics, symbols, stories of origin, memories of traumatic experiences, and so on, that links the members of nations to past and future generations. People inherit a vast array of cultural artifacts from previous generations, much of which they ignore or take for granted. But it is their affirmation of particular lines of cultural heritage as a source of mutual concern and loyalty that establishes the kind of intergenerational community characteristic of nations.

Let me emphasize that it is shared cultural *inheritance*, rather than shared cultural practice, belief, or expression that characterizes the nation as I understand it. That is why I describe the nation as a cultural *heritage* community, rather than more simply as a cultural community. You do not need to speak Gaelic, or even like it, in order to be a member of the Irish nation; you need merely to imagine yourself connected by ties of special concern and loyalty to those with whom you share a cultural heritage that includes somewhere in past and present the speaking of Gaelic.[2] Similarly, you do not need to practice Judaism, or even like it, in order to be a member of the Jewish nation (as opposed to a member of the Jewish religious community); you need merely imagine yourself connected by ties of social friendship to those who share the inheritance of cultural artifacts that reflect Jewish practice and history.

Fourth, a nation is a singular or irreproducible community, hence the proper name that it bears. In imagining a cultural inheritance as a source of social friendship, the members of nations affirm the slicing up of human experience into units that reflect the irreproducible contingencies of history—that *x* followed *y* in one case and something else in another—rather than either natural necessity or conscious design. Like individuals, each of these units is known by a proper name that marks the singularity of the combination of experiences that constitutes it. Moreover, like individuals, each of these units is identified by their unique combination and arrangement of inherited artifacts, no matter how many things that they may hold in common with each other. National commu-

2. Like the early Irish nationalist leader, Daniel O'Connell, who "dismissed the Irish language robustly, as a drawback in the modern world." See Foster, *Modern Ireland*, 300.

nity thus helps situate individuals in time by associating them with contingently divided lines of cultural inheritance.

Fifth, the cultural heritage affirmed by nations is associated with particular territories, an association that gives these territories special value for their members. As we shall see, national attachments to particular territories become especially problematic when, in the wake of the spread of popular sovereignty theories, nations claim the right to have the final say over what goes on in their "own" lands.

Sixth, a nation is, to use Craig Calhoun's expression, a "categorical" community: it links people directly and equally rather than by means of hierarchical subcommunities.[3] Nationality is not received indirectly through one's relationship to a social superior. Accordingly, every member of a nation is as much a member as any other. That does not mean that nations cannot coexist with caste and other forms of status hierarchy. It merely means that nationality cuts across and competes with these status hierarchies. A deep attachment to caste and other status hierarchies is bound to make nationhood, something we share equally with slaves, untouchables, and outcasts, less attractive and significant. Conversely, the rejection of such hierarchies is bound, all other things being equal, to make nationhood look more important and attractive, which, we shall see, is one of the reasons why nation and individual have risen to prominence together in modern political life.

A nation, then, is a categorical community in which the sharing of a singular and contingent cultural heritage inspires individuals to imagine themselves connected to each other—and to certain territories—through time by ties of mutual concern and loyalty.

The rest of the chapter develops and defends this characterization of national community. Here I shall merely point out that there is nothing new or distinctly modern about the nation conceived in this way. This way of imagining community has a long history, back to the ancient Greek world and beyond. It is nationalism, not national community, which is relatively new or temporally modern. In other words, it is our attitude toward national community, especially our political attitude, which has changed in the modern world, rather than nationhood itself. The failure to distinguish between national community and nationalism is a major limitation of many otherwise insightful modernist theories of national-

3. Calhoun, *Nationalism*, 39.

ism.[4] We need, I shall argue, to be able to speak about "nations before nationalism," if we are to make sense of nationalism as a social phenomenon.[5] For we need to able to ask how and why did an old and familiar form of community, the nation, come to take on such striking political importance in the modern age. If, as many theorists insist, we insert the demand for sovereignty into our very definition of national community,[6] then it becomes impossible to pose such questions.

The semantic history of the term nation is often depicted as a wild ride that careens from one new meaning to another.[7] The story usually begins with something similar to the meaning I have just advanced. It shifts to the much narrower and more idiosyncratic conception of nationhood applied to church and university associations in the Middle Ages, turns to the focus on communities that share a common government in the early modern period, and finally ends with the romantic ideal of a unique cultural community at the beginning of the nineteenth century.

The problem with such semantic histories, however, is that they focus so much attention on new ways of using terms that they tend to obscure continuities, even when older meanings continue to inform common usage. There can be no doubt that the term nation has accumulated an unusually diverse set of meanings over the millennia. But that does not mean that the original meaning or the phenomenon it characterized ever disappeared. As Susan Reynolds and other students of medieval European history have made clear, "there is no foundation at all for the belief, common among students of modern nationalism, that the word *natio* was seldom used in the middle ages except to describe *nationes* into which university students were divided. It was used much more widely than that, often as a synonym for *gens* . . . and was thought of as a community of custom, descent, and government."[8]

As for the common belief in an early modern or Enlightenment transformation of the term nation into a culturally neutral community merely

4. On this point, see O'Leary "Ernest Gellner's Diagnoses of Nationalism," 54–55.

5. As suggested by John Armstrong in *Nations before Nationalism*.

6. As in Benedict Anderson's famous definition of the nation as a community imagined as bounded and sovereign (*Imagined Communities*, 6–7).

7. Liah Greenfeld (*Nationalism*, 5–7), e.g., speaks of "the zigzag pattern of semantic change" that characterizes the nation.

8. Reynolds, *Kingdoms and Communities in Western Europe*, 255–56.

sharing a common government,[9] one telling example should suffice to bring it into question. Accounts of this transformation usually invoke the definition of term nation in that great monument of the French Enlightenment, the *Encyclopédie*.[10] That definition does indeed begin by describing nation as a "collective word used to characterize a considerable number of people who inhabit a certain stretch of territory, bounded by certain limits, and obey the same government." But it immediately goes on to suggest that "each nation has its own character," as illustrated by the familiar proverb, "glib as a Frenchman, jealous as an Italian, naughty as an Englishman, proud as a Scot, and drunk as a German."[11] Since three of his five examples, the Italians, Scots, and Germans, lacked a common government during the eighteenth century, the author of this entry clearly does not deem a shared government a necessary condition of nationhood—nor, for that matter, is he reluctant to associate nations with distinctive cultural traits.

It is certainly true that the term nation starts to be used in new ways in the seventeenth and eighteenth centuries, as a synonym for the people, the group from which states were increasingly seen as deriving their authority. Indeed, I shall argue that the key to understanding the rise of nationalism in modern political life lies in the effect of this new way of thinking about political authority on an old way of imagining community, that is, the intergenerational ties of the nation. But in order to understand this effect we need first to distinguish clearly between the two ways of imagining groups that they represent, regardless of the terms used to express these images. To that end, the next chapter outlines the differences between these two images of group membership, which I describe as the people and the nation, and then shows how they support two very different images of the nation-state.

Nevertheless, while my definition of the nation reflects common usage for more than two thousand years, my primary aim in this chapter is to identify a social phenomenon, a form of association that has taken on unprecedented political importance in the last three hundred years, rather than to clarify our use of terms. The semantic history of the term nation

9. See, e.g., Cobban, *The Nation-State and National Self-Determination*, 30: "by the eighteenth century, in fact, most of the cultural and linguistic significance had been emptied out of the word nation."

10. See, e.g., Fehrenbach, "Nation," 76–77, and Nora, "Nation," 743.

11. Diderot et al., *L'Encyclopédie*, 11:36.

and its equivalents in other languages is quite complex. But it is the slipperiness of the phenomenon itself that has made the definition of national community so frustrating, not just the ambiguity of the words we use to describe it. For even after we have cleaned up our use of language, we still have to figure out what to make of a form of community that seems to draw on almost every source of distinctiveness, from language and territorial boundaries to religious belief and political organization.

At this point many scholars simply throw up their hands and conclude that a nation "is a group that thinks it is a nation."[12] In doing so, they fall back on the need for subjective affirmation that the nation shares with every other form of human community. It is not clear, however, that one learns anything of importance about the distinctive character of national community from emphasizing its subjective element in this way. If a nation is a group of people who think that they form a nation, to what kind of social group do they imagine that they belong? A nation, which, in turn, is a group that thinks of itself as a nation.[13] If this kind of circularity were unavoidable, then we might have to grit our teeth and make the best of it. But it is not. Although we must rely on subjective affirmation to confirm the existence of nations, that does not mean that a nation is whatever people say it is. It merely means that whatever shape nations take, we should look for it in the imagination rather than in any particular form of social organization.

Intergenerational Community and Temporal Depth

The different forms of community reflect the many different objects of sharing that we imagine as sources of connection: ancestors, beliefs, rituals, languages, institutions, territories, and so on. One reason we have had such difficulty in defining the nation is that it seems to draw in one place or another on all of these different objects of sharing.

The three forms of sharing most commonly cited in definitions of the nation are language, kinship, and demands for self-government. But

12. Hobsbawm, *Nations and Nationalism since 1780*, 8. Or, similarly, a nation "exists where a significant number of people consider themselves to be nation or behave as if they formed one" (Seton-Watson, *Nations and States*, 5).

13. See Nathanson, "Nationalism and the Limits of Global Humanism," 177, for a discussion of this infinite regress. See also Gilbert, *Philosophy of Nationalism*, 12–13, for a good critique of this approach.

there are a sufficient number of examples of multilingual nations—as well as nations divided by a common language—to bring into doubt the association of nations with linguistic communities. The reliance on a shared sense of kinship to identify nations unduly narrows the range of communities we can call nations, unless we are willing to inflate metaphorical invocations of founding fathers and motherlands into assertions of genuine kinship. And the definition of nations in terms of assertions of sovereignty leaves us with the problem of what to do about communities that look like nations, but do not seek the right to political self-determination. (Are they "proto-nations" or perhaps ethnic communities lacking in self-consciousness, a familiar position that ahistorically assumes that self-awareness of ethnic community leads inevitably to demands for self-rule?) In order to distinguish the nation from other forms of community it seems that we have to choose between an overly narrow focus on one or the other of these objects of sharing and a more inclusive focus so broad as to lack much analytic value.

We can, however, escape this unhappy choice once we recognize that it is the shared *inheritance* of cultural artifacts and memories that distinguishes the nation, rather than the sharing of the artifacts themselves. In other words, it is the affirmation of a shared cultural heritage as a source of mutual concern and loyalty that makes a national community, rather than the sharing of any particular beliefs, practices, or institutions. In a nation we share, to use Renan's expression, a "rich *legacy* of memories" and other cultural artifacts,[14] regardless of whether or not we are inclined to employ or celebrate the contents of that legacy. We become members of a linguistic or political or religious community when we imagine ourselves connected to people who believe or practice some of the same things that we do. We become members of a national community when we imagine ourselves connected to people who inherit some of the same cultural artifacts and memories that we do. Some of these artifacts we use, some we ignore, while others we put in storage where later generations often discover them and put them to new and unexpected use.

Affirming a shared line of cultural inheritance often leads the members of nations to celebrate and perfect its contents. Disdained vernaculars are transformed into literary languages, monuments are raised to forgotten heroes, and intellectuals go to the people to learn how to practice the national virtues that they preach. But the affirmation of a na-

14. Renan, "What Is a Nation?," 19.

tional heritage need not lead to this kind of cultural revival. Often it merely directs individuals to new groups as objects of their special concern and loyalty. That helps explain why, as Ernest Gellner and others have often pointed out,[15] national self-assertion so often leads to the homogenization of cultural difference rather than to its accentuation. It is often the intellectuals and city-dwellers, precisely the individuals who have left behind the distinctive practices associated with a particular cultural heritage, who insist most strongly on affirming communal ties with the people who share it.

Of course, some people feel so strongly about a particular piece of their national heritage that they cannot imagine their nation without it. Such people often complain bitterly about the way in which their nation is "losing its soul" with the abandonment of its mother tongue or its ancestral constitution or its inherited religious beliefs and rituals.[16] And they may be right. But nations often survive the loss of their souls. The Jewish people survived the loss of its homeland, its independence, and its religious center; the Irish people, the loss or subordination of its mother tongue; the German people, the collapse of imperial, liberal democratic, and fascist regimes; and the Japanese people, the divinization and dedivinization of its emperor, among the many extraordinary transformations of character it has undergone in the last century and a half. As long as the members of succeeding generations continue to imagine themselves connected by their shared cultural heritage, the nation lives on, even if its members no longer employ the language or the laws or the rituals of their predecessors. It makes a tremendous difference to the character of life in a particular national community which elements of its heritage it celebrates. But the measure of a nation's survival is its temporal continuity, not its fidelity to a particular way of life. Just as a single family has room for both Constantine the Great and Julian the Apostate, both Wilfred the Hairy and Charles the Bald, so a single nation can encompass both the creator and destroyers of any particular practice or belief with which it has been associated. However strongly its members may disapprove of the direction their national community has taken, they remain members of it as long as they imagine themselves connected to the people who inherit the consequences of moving in this direction.

15. Gellner, *Nations and Nationalism*, 57–58.

16. For example, see Samuel Huntington's recent warning, in *Who Are We?*, about what will happen to America if it loses the Anglo-Protestant culture that gave it its value.

For, in the end, "what unites co-nationals is less the characteristics that they possess as individuals than the inheritance that they share."[17]

Metaphorical invocations of national community, as in celebrations of a "queer nation,"[18] can be distinguished from the original by their lack of this kind of intergenerational community. The object of sharing affirmed by the members of a queer nation as a source of mutual concern and loyalty is a set of sexual inclinations, as well as the experiences of those who have lived with them, rather than a cultural inheritance. Disinterest or disdain for homosexual inclinations would spell the end of such a community, but not of a nation that might, among other things, include a number of distinctively gay cultural artifacts as part of its shared heritage. For in the metaphorical nation it is the affirmation of shared beliefs and practices that creates community, while in the nation itself it is the shared inheritance of such beliefs and practices that inspires feelings of mutual concern and loyalty.

This sense of intergenerational connection gives the nation what Steven Grosby aptly describes as its "temporal depth,"[19] that sense of sharing a place in a line stretching from past to future that is probably the most distinctive characteristic of national community. In nations we situate ourselves within a shared sequence of predecessors and successors, the affirmation of whom deepens our feelings of mutual concern and loyalty by invoking the memory of past generations and responsibility for future ones. In other words, our shared heritage, our shared connection to a temporal line that transcends our own lifespan, lends a special poignancy to our feelings of social friendship for each other. It is as if we imagine that we share a particular path through time, a named highway on some imagined time map,[20] rather than just the course of years allotted to our own lives.

This sense of intergenerational community is no less prominent among so-called civic nations than among their ethnic counterparts. A national holiday in France or the United States calls up just as vivid a sense of the connection to generations past as do national holidays in Serbia or Japan. Indeed, given the greater continuity of American his-

17. Canovan, *Nationhood and Political Theory*, 72.

18. See Walker, "Social Movements as Nationalisms, or The Very Idea of a Queer Nation."

19. Grosby, *Nationalism*, 8.

20. For the concept of time maps, see Eviatar Zerubavel's insightful little book, *Time Maps*.

tory over the last two hundred years, such holidays probably call up more of a sense of intergenerational connection in America.[21] The difference between the two sets of cases lies in how far back that community goes and what kind of events and memories are celebrated at its origins. No one would call a nation that affirms the heritage of a well-documented constitutional founding a primordial community. But it is a mistake to identify intergenerational community with primordiality. The fact that one has witnessed or can present reliable evidence about the beginnings of a nation does not necessarily undermine its cohesion. In fact, remembering the beginnings, even when they are quite close and familiar, often serves to bind a nation together. "Four score and seven years ago," Lincoln reminds Americans in the Gettysburg Address, "our fathers brought forth a new nation, conceived in liberty and dedicated to the proposition that all men are created equal." As his generational metaphors should make clear, Lincoln, like most Americans, imagines his countrymen and women as *heirs* to the founders' political ideas and institutions, rather than merely proponents of their principles.[22]

At this point, it is important to emphasize that the nation's temporal depth involves something more than a common history. Every group, once recognized as such, can construct for itself a shared history of its actions and experiences. States, religious communities, military organizations, even commercial societies—"he was the greatest salesman ever to grace a used car lot!"—they all generate their own histories and invoke the example of revered forerunners. But nations are part of a much smaller set of communities in which the group's sense of mutual connection is *itself* established by sharing in a line of inheritance from some notable predecessors. In these communities our horizontal connections, so to speak, are established by our vertical connections, that is, our ties to other living individuals are established by our shared inheritance from those who have preceded us.

The family is the most familiar and obvious example of this kind of

21. On this point, see Yack, *Fetishism of Modernities*, 101, where I argue that it is high time to abandon the picture of the United States as the nation without history. As Oscar Wilde said already at the end of the nineteenth century, the eternal youth of Americans "is their oldest tradition." Quoted in Woodward, *The Old World's New World*, 68.

22. On the use of generational language by liberal democratic states, see Stevens, *Reproducing the State*. Stevens suggests that "the difference between the United States and elsewhere is simply that here the conventions [of ancestral connection] are more recent, from the point of view of contemporary history" (148).

community. For "descent 'connects' us not only to ancestors but to numerous contemporaries as well."[23] People recognize each other as members of the same family by noting or tracing back their connections through successive generations to some common ancestor. It is this temporal connection that makes it possible to identify the members of the family whose history someone makes the effort to record. Take away the vertical connection, the common ancestor, and the horizontal connection among family members loses its raison d'être. That is one reason why distant ancestors are so often venerated: they provide the glue that binds their present-day descendants to each other.

> If we think of descent as a tree with the founding ancestor as the trunk . . . we can also visualize the disastrous effect on that tree when the trunk died—the branches would all fall apart as there was nothing left to hold them together. If the tree were to be kept whole, a way of preserving the trunk had to be found; and this in effect is what ancestor worship did, it preserved the founding ancestor without whom there was no connection between the various lines of his descendants.[24]

The nation, I am suggesting, has a similar structure. We recognize each other as members of the same nation by the shared inheritance that we trace back to some monumentalized predecessors.[25] Take away that vertical connection, the sense of sharing something that can be traced back in a line to a common point of origin, and our horizontal connection to each other falls apart. Unfortunately, our familiarity with the family has made it very difficult to articulate the distinctive form of intergenerational community that the nation inspires. Most scholars who recognize the importance of intergenerational inheritance in national communities tend to conceptualize it as an extended or fictive form of kinship that relies in some way on the mystique of biological descent. And most scholars who recognize the limitations of kinship as the model for national community tend to downplay the importance of intergen-

23. Zerubavel, *Time Maps*, 63.

24. Hugh Baker (discussing Chinese family and kinship ties), quoted in ibid., 63.

25. It is important to note here that monumentalized ancestors need not be revered ancestors. It may be some great wrong or mistake that marks out particular ancestors as the beginning of a new line of descent.

erational ties in the construction of national communities.[26] In order to get a better sense of the distinctiveness of national community we need therefore to bring its form of intergenerational ties out of the shadow cast by our familiarity with the family.

The Family and the Nation as Forms of Intergenerational Community

Human beings come into this world weak and helpless, completely dependent for their own survival and development on those who have preceded them. This dependence inevitably establishes connections to members of preceding generations, most obviously through our parents and whoever else takes a hand in raising us. But because human beings are cultural and social animals, we inherit a very particular mix of cultural artifacts and social constructions, not just a particular set of genes when we take the trouble to be born in one place and time rather than another. This inheritance, no less than our descent from our parents, establishes a sense of connection to those who have come before us.

Intergenerational communities develop out of the affirmation of our inherited connections to previous generations as a focus of mutual concern and loyalty. They celebrate or, at least, affirm the importance of shared conditions of nativity, even though we had no role in choosing or shaping these contingencies of birth. We are inclined to notice and, often, affirm these conditions for a simple reason: they "bear, protect, and transmit life."[27] Since we do not come into the world equipped to make it on our own, we are inclined to affirm the importance of the connections to others that allow us to survive and fully develop our faculties.

As the most familiar form of intergenerational community, the family has come to dominate both the rhetoric as well as the study of intergenerational community. That is hardly surprising. When national communities are not inventing eponymous ancestors from whom to trace their descent they are, like Lincoln, invoking "fathers" from whom we have received our most precious legacies. But biological descent is not the

26. Benedict Anderson in (*Imagined Communities*) and Rupert Emerson (in *From Empire to Nation*) are important exceptions.

27. Grosby, "The Verdict of History," 169; see also Grosby, *Nationalism*, 12–13.

only shared inheritance we receive from previous generations. "Nations, like individuals, are products of heredity and environment, although in this case heredity is to be sought not in the genes but in the social heritage that flows from generation to generation to give some real content to men's minds."[28] Of course, much of our cultural inheritance is passed on from parent to child. But that does not make any group that affirms such a heritage a kinship community. For even when we ignore all the other nonparental sources from which we receive our cultural inheritance, it is clear that the group with whom we share that inheritance almost always extends well beyond the range of people with whom we share a single line of descent. Eponymous ancestors are almost always invented post hoc, often to make up for this very insufficiency. If national communities share an intergenerational line of succession, then they must represent something more than a line of descent.

Walker Connor is probably the most forceful defender of the association of national community with the family. He goes so far as to define the nation as "the fully extended family," "the largest group of people that can command a person's loyalty because of felt kinship."[29] But does the power of Bismarckian appeals "to think with your blood" really rest, as Connor suggests, on the assumption that "there existed in some hazy, pre-recorded era a . . . German Adam and Eve, and that the couple's progeny has evolved in essentially unadulterated form down to the present?"[30] I think not. Even Connor himself acknowledges that the nation works its magic through "familial *metaphors*," rather than through the drawing of family trees. If so, then we need to ask ourselves what these metaphors communicate, that is, what makes the nation seem *like* a family, rather than ask ourselves what kind of family it forms. Kinship metaphors can indeed "transform the mundanely tangible into emotion-laden phantasma."[31] But they do so precisely by investing connections that are not based on kinship with the emotional intensity and sense of intergenerational continuity that we associate with family descent.[32]

28. Emerson, *From Empire to Nation*, 60.

29. Connor, *Ethnonationalism*, 202.

30. Ibid., 94.

31. Ibid.

32. Race metaphors work in a similar way when applied to national communities, but with one important difference: the sinister inventiveness of scientific racism provided a means of transforming the metaphor of shared blood into an actual description of the

They resonate so strongly in nationalist rhetoric because, like families, nations are built on the sharing of links between generations.

Families can be represented simply by tracing blood lines. We recognize sisters or cousins or the children of cousins as members of our family because they share with us common ancestors one or two or three generations back. But to represent nations you need something more: the memory of coming from a particular place, the celebration of some special deeds, the familiarity with a received language, or the contrast with traditional rivals. In other words, it is the affirmation of some shared heritage as our own, rather than the simple image of descent from some ancestor, that makes a nation. Similarly, shared affinities for particular ways of expressing oneself are quite sufficient to create cultural communities. But to create nations, you need something more: the sense that one is part of a group that affirms a shared cultural inheritance as a source of connection and passes it on to future generations. An English skinhead and an Oxford don, for example, do not share many cultural tastes or inclinations, let alone much of a sense of common descent. But they can share in a national community if they affirm a common heritage of symbols and stories as a source of mutual concern and loyalty.[33]

The contingencies of birth clearly play a key role in the construction of national communities, as is suggested by the Latin roots (*natio*, *nasci*) of our word "nation." But birth does not determine cultural heritage in the way that it determines biological descent. For while birth fixes our biological descent, it merely places us in a position to inherit different collections of cultural artifacts, a position that itself can change if, for example, our parents take us to another part of the world. In other words, while descendants are born, cultural heirs are made by a social process of transmission that follows our birth.[34] The initiation of this process by the birth and growth of children makes it seem much more natural than

---

world. Nothing similar has happened to create the illusion that family genealogy is a plausible way of identifying the character of nations.

33. See Canovan, *Nationhood and Political Theory*, 72.

34. Citizens, individuals with the rights and duties of members of a political organization, are also born in a way that members of nations are not. For in almost every state the children of citizens automatically receive citizenship upon their birth. It is ironic, given the way in which civic nationalism is portrayed as a way of raising politics above the contingencies of birth, that civic membership should, at least in this regard, take descent more seriously than national membership.

social processes initiated by agreement or decree—hence the celebration of the naturalness of national communities in some formulations. Nevertheless, it remains a social rather than a natural process of reproduction.

That said, nations generally have little difficulty in reproducing themselves. When children receive from their parents and neighbors and teachers a cultural heritage already associated with strong feelings of mutual concern and loyalty, it usually takes much more of an effort to reject than to reproduce these feelings and the intergenerational community that they maintain. It is much harder, however, to see how new nations emerge in the first place. Indeed, if national community grows out of the affirmation of a shared inheritance from previous generations, then the very idea of a *new* nation is bound to seem a little paradoxical.

In order to resolve this paradox we need to keep reminding ourselves that national community grows out of a mix of two elements: a shared cultural inheritance and its affirmation as a source of mutual concern and loyalty. Only a small part of the extraordinarily diverse and overlapping range of inherited cultural artifacts that we share with each other is ever affirmed as a source of communal loyalty. Moreover, new cultural artifacts are almost always being created and spread. As a result, we almost always have within reach the material out of which to create new nations. French, Breton, Celt, Aryan, European—the alternatives are finite and contingent, but always multiple. The never-ending activity of nation-building, with its none-too-gentle programs of cultural consolidation and integration, aims at eliminating or at least diminishing the threat that these other cultural inheritances pose to national ties.

So new nations emerge, first of all, when a previously ignored or downplayed or suppressed cultural inheritance, such as a spoken language or a common homeland or a long-dead political tradition, comes to take on new significance as a focus for mutual concern and loyalty. A good example is the Turkish national community that emerged out of the decay and collapse of the Ottoman Empire. Turkish language and stories about Turkish heroes continued to be passed on through the years of the Ottoman Empire. But they did not become a major focus of mutual concern and loyalty until the ties of shared religion and imperial rule began to lose their importance as the focus of communal life.

New nations are also formed when new cultural artifacts are forged and affirmed as a source of connection by the later generations that inherit them. This is plainly the case with immigrant nations, like the

United States, which was "brought forth," as Lincoln says, by its Founding Fathers. It is also the case with African and Asian nations struggling to turn relatively recent political boundaries into a cultural heritage that might override the competing ethnocultural loyalties contained within them. This connection with assertions of political will can make the intergenerational character of such nations seem rather shallow. It is therefore important to remember that some of the oldest and most seemingly ethnic nations, such as the Han Chinese, were formed in this way—in this case, by the consolidation of an extensive empire more than two thousand years ago.

Contingency, Choice, and the Construction of National Communities

The preceding account of nationhood has, I hope, confirmed Renan's assertion that "two things" make a nation: the desire to live together and "a rich legacy" of shared memories and cultural artifacts.[35] We need, however, to be a little more precise about the role of choice and contingency in the making of nations, since Renan's irresistible description of the nation as "a daily plebiscite" has encouraged many scholars to misread the nation as a kind of voluntary association for political and cultural expression.

The choice or consent involved in the making of nations is the same that we find in all forms of community: the subjective affirmation of one particular form of sharing rather than another as the focus of mutual concern and loyalty among a particular group of individuals. The ties that bind a family, no less than a nation, grow out of the affirmation of some of the things that we share rather than others as sources of mutual connection. And the process by which we affirm these connections is indeed continuous, in that community cannot persist without this affirmation. But the phrase "daily plebiscite" is misleading, since it suggests we regularly and explicitly ask ourselves which forms of sharing we ought to affirm as sources of mutual concern and loyalty. Such explicit and self-conscious choices are the exception rather than the rule. We tend to make them only when we are pressed by circumstances to re-

35. Renan, "What Is a Nation?," 19.

solve the tensions between competing allegiances, as were the Alsatians under Prussian rule, the group whose plight inspired so much of Renan's thinking about nationhood.

Moreover, and this is a crucial point, with national community we affirm as a source of mutual connection something that we have *received* from others, rather than chosen for ourselves. An American in Paris may know more about French history than a particular native, she may even speak a purer French; but that does not make her a member of the French nation if she developed her facility in French culture in the courses she chose to take at American universities. It is the sharing of a heritage, rather than any special knowledge of what that heritage contains, that qualifies us as members of the nation's intergenerational community of past glories and future prospects.

Even when we have to make an explicit and self-conscious choice about our national ties in a real plebiscite, we make a decision about which of two shared legacies to affirm. In the recent referenda on secession, Francophone citizens of Quebec found themselves compelled to decide whether to continue to affirm the Canadian political culture that they had inherited as a source of mutual connection with other Canadians. Similarly, Renan's Alsatians found themselves in a situation that compelled them to choose as the focus of mutual concern and loyalty between the political heritage they shared with the French and the linguistic heritage they shared with the Germans. National plebiscites, real or metaphorical, ask us to affirm sets of connections we have received from others rather than choose the kind of people with whom we would like to associate.

It is this emphasis on shared heritage that makes it hard to imagine immigrant citizens as full members of the nations whose polities they join. "Naturalization," the granting of citizenship status to those who did not receive citizenship rights at birth, cannot "naturalize" the immigrants' cultural heritage, since it cannot replay the conditions of their birth and education. As a result, even though immigrants have often made a much more self-conscious choice to become a member of their new community than the people who simply took the trouble to be born there, they do not share the intergenerational connections that members of their new nation affirm as the focus of mutual concern and loyalty. There is no reason, contrary to immigration's nativist critics, that their children cannot come to share that heritage. Indeed, in most nations it takes a self-conscious effort to keep them from doing so. But because distinct nations are grounded in forms of sharing that are inherited rather than chosen, the first generation of immigrants will always stand a little outside of the national community.[36]

Nations that encourage immigration, like the United States or France, tend to encourage other ways of imagining community that are more open to the naturalized citizen. In the United States the emphasis is on political community and the affirmation of shared political principles and practices, the so-called American creed, as a source of mutual connection. In France the emphasis, in contrast, is on cultural community, the acquisition of fluency in key French cultural practices, as the immigrant's entry ticket. In both cases, something that can only be inherited is replaced with something that can be chosen, thus encouraging ideas about an alternative understanding of the nation as a voluntary association for shared political or cultural expression.

These alternative images of community have many advantages, not the least of which is the way that they facilitate the integration of immigrant citizens into political life and civil society. But they should not be confused with the mutual connections established by nations, which grow out of our affirmation of shared cultural heritage. The nation (or whatever term you use to characterize the form of community described in this chapter) works its effects by affirming our shared place in a line of heirs and predecessors. These other images of community are much more present oriented, focusing on shared political beliefs or cultural practice, rather than past glories and future prospects. The nation need not invoke shared blood or descent to inspire its members. But it cannot do without shared heritage and the "mystic chords of memory" that it sounds. Sooner or later, even the most liberal defenders of the nation find themselves strumming these chords as an accompaniment to their invocations of political principle.

That said, clearly our choices play a very large role in the never-ending process by which we construct national heritages out of the raw material of shared cultural legacies and memories. The neat boundaries that allow us to distinguish one line of cultural inheritance from another

36. Ironically, this is a quality that they share with the founders or founding generation of a nation. Like immigrants or new Americans, the first Americans chose rather than inherited America. They do not share the experience of inheriting a place in a lineage. Even when they are self-consciously engaged in the founding of a new nation, as most founders are not, they cannot be sure, after all, that the lineage that they are trying to establish will ever take hold and be affirmed by next generations.

are the product of organized intervention as well tradition and habit. For very different groups of people can trace their own line of connection back to the same historic achievements and experiences. As a result, they often find themselves competing for the same inheritance, like present-day Macedonians and Greeks squabbling over the right to invoke the legacy of Alexander the Great. And a single group of people can find some place in many different lines of cultural inheritance, which means that the process of nation-building usually relies on self-conscious efforts to integrate and stabilize singular lines of cultural succession. Consequently, organizations with special interests in nation-building, like cultural societies and modern states, often take the lead in trying to turn the fuzzy lines of our cultural inheritance into distinct and easily recognized patterns.[37]

A cultural heritage inevitably includes different and inconsistent elements, since it has been assembled by a contingent process of accretion over time. The monumentalization of first generations inevitably gives the advantage in any argument about, say, the true France or authentic India to those who urge us to honor or return to our roots. But much as these people tend to associate the existence of their nation with some supposed founding practice, they have to admit, if they are honest, that the loss of their nation's original character means the end of the nation that *they* know and love, rather than the end of the nation itself. For nations have no constitution, no original organizing principle that determines the conditions of their existence. They are thus the site of never-ending debates about what to honor or emphasize—and what to ignore—within a given line of inheritance, debates that inevitably expand and contract the shape of that line.

I will not go into detail about these debates about how to construct the content of national heritages, since they are the focus of so much excellent scholarship these days. But I would like to draw attention here to the way in which these debates are often driven by moves back and forth between the two ways of imagining community discussed in the previous chapter: focusing on particular forms of sharing as ways of connecting to others and asking ourselves what it is that we really share with the people to whom we feel connected. Having identified ourselves as Americans or

37. See Roshwald, *The Endurance of Nationalism*, 58, for an interesting discussion of the need to fill in temporal gaps in a national heritage in order to maintain a sense of continuity.

Germans or Iranians, we often find ourselves asking what it is that really connects us to other members of the community. At such times we often start rummaging around in the relatively new or previously ignored parts of our collection of inherited artifacts and memories, looking for something that might make better sense of our current situation. If we find it, we may come to introduce new images of national community to compete with old and familiar ones. Or, as sometimes happens, it may lead us to try to change our conception of community altogether, to argue that what *really* connects us is not a shared inheritance of particular practices and memories, but, say, our shared racial makeup or our shared religious beliefs or our shared political principles.[38] Arguments about what constitutes a national community thus can inspire assertions that transform a national community into a racial community or a religious community or a political community.

Among the most important choices that influence the shape of nations is the identification of individuals, groups, and experiences that we treat as the beginning of new lines of cultural inheritance. Like all intergenerational communities, nations emphasize temporal continuity, the passing of one generation's experience and achievements on to the other. But like all intergenerational communities smaller than the human race, the "birth" of nations demands new beginnings, breaks with past generations, as well as the establishment and maintenance of intergenerational connections. And since every person or generation possesses some connections to preceding generations, we have to construct these temporal discontinuities, rather than simply uncover them in the historical record.[39] We usually construct these breaks in temporal continuity by focusing on the importance of some particularly noteworthy actions or experiences in the lives of the members of groups who precede us. Conquests and defeats, immigration and expulsions, unifications and secession, political foundings and collapses, these are the kind of shared experiences that we most often rely on—and monumentalize—to mark the beginnings of new lines of cultural heritage. Only by treating such experiences as the site of breaks with the past can we clearly distinguish between these different lineages. Thus there is a sense in which we choose our national ancestors.

38. For some interesting examples drawn from Chinese and German history, see Duara, *Rescuing History from the Nation*, 37.

39. Zerubavel, *Time Maps*, 8, 93.

Choosing our ancestors, despite its paradoxical sound, is not in itself all that unusual or outlandish an exercise of our freedom. For we make such choices all the time in the construction of families. After all, if common descent were a sufficient indication of family membership, we would have to conclude we are all members of the group of families that left Africa one hundred thousand years ago and spawned the various branches of the human race. Families are made up of individuals who claim common descent from someone whom they have pulled out of the succession of generations to treat as the founder of a new family line.[40] Sometimes the identification of such individuals merely reflects the limits of our knowledge; we have simply lost all trace of, say, the parents of our grandparents. But just as often, it reflects our association of matriarchs and patriarchs with especially noteworthy virtues or experiences—not to mention the traditions and organized efforts that enforce particular ways of constructing descent, patrilineality versus matrilineality, for example.

The identification and commemoration of individuals and groups as national ancestors encourages us, anachronistically, to impute to them our own sense of national community. We project on them our own affirmation of the cultural inheritance that their actions helped get started, even though they often displayed indifference or even hostility to the national group with whom it now connects us. In this way Prince Lazar's death in battle against the Turks comes to be seen as a sacrifice for the Serbian nation and the Qin emperor's ruthless imperialism as an expression of the Chinese struggle for national unity.

Indeed, if my argument in this chapter is correct, it will always be anachronistic to impute consciousness of nationality to the groups imagined as the founding generation of new nations. For even if these first generations self-consciously set out to found new nations, the one thing that they cannot share is the *reception* of the new line of inheritance that their efforts make possible. In any case, rather than seek to found such a community, most were trying to do something completely different: take over neighboring lands, escape from local persecution, establish new religious sects, unite warring tribes, and so on. Whatever they did to inspire later generations to treat them as the founders of new nations, it was not the product of their affirmation of a national heritage—unless,

40. Ibid., 63–64.

of course, they were affirming their shared heritage of an earlier and different nation than the one their actions inspired. Often these groups did not take the form of communities at all, let alone national communities. They sometimes make their impact, for example, as the introducers of new forms of political or religious organization, the representatives of new churches or monarchs, rather than the providers of new forms of community. Whatever they were, however, they were not members of the new national community that, in hindsight, their actions have inspired. The construction of national community inevitably involves the identification and monumentalizing of groups of founders who owe their fame and head at the place of national lineages to something that often has little to do with the nations associated with them. Bound by one set of communal or organizational ties, to empires, sects, older nations, and the like, their achievements and experiences give rise to a very different set of communal ties when recalled as a shared inheritance by later generations.

By speaking of our ability to choose even our national ancestors, it might seem that I am, after all, treating the shape of the nation as an object of choice. It is therefore important to note that we rarely find ourselves in the position to make effective choices about how to construct cultural lineages. Almost all cultural artifacts and experiences come down to us attached to the names of particular communities and organizations, national or otherwise, names that we learn as guides to temporal as well as spatial geography. No doubt, we are always in the position to deconstruct the way in which these names have divvied up human experience and monumentalized insignificant or unworthy ancestors. But since national communities, like all other communities, rely on some degree of *mutual* concern and loyalty, it is not enough to point out the arbitrariness of national divisions, if we are interested in reconstructing them; we have to find alternatives that fit well enough with the experience of others for them to recognize it as a shared basis for social friendship. That is why the struggles over the construction of national community usually focus on what to emphasize *within* existing lines of national heritage or how to choose *between* the different lines to which we currently have access, rather than on the destruction of old lines and the creation of new ones. So nations are indeed constructed or imagined; but they are constructed or imagined by people trying to make sense of shared intergenerational connections that they have received rather than chosen.

Territorial Attachments

Most scholars agree that some connection to specific territories should be part of our understanding of national community. The few cases that might make us doubt their claims, such as the pre-Zionist Jewish nation, usually prove the rule by compelling us to come up with subtler understandings of the relationship between nations and territories. Pre-Zionist Jews neither lived in the land that they thought of as their own nor sought to take possession of this land. But they still felt connected to the land of Israel, as the sacred site of the most important stories and events in the history of Judaism and the Jewish religion.[41]

The question is what form does this connection to territory take. The classic, primordial view roots national identity in the connection between blood and soil. *La terre et les morts*: there is *la patrie*, Maurice Barrès famously proclaimed.[42] From this perspective, it is familiarity and continuous dwelling in a place, generation after generation, which connects nations to particular territories. The roots of the nation are nurtured with the blood of the sons and daughters buried in its soil, so that particular places become figuratively—and sometimes literally—sacred to its members.

There are two problems with this classic primordial view of the connection between nations and territory. First of all, while quite common, it is far from universal among nations. Many national communities remain as or even more attached to the territories from which they came as they are to the territories in which they dwell. Some nations are more attached to the territories in which they displayed recent greatness than to ones in which they used to dwell. New nations can and have developed very strong attachments to particular territories without the sense of timeless dwelling (although in their rhetoric they often invoke such a sense).[43] And there is nothing at all inconsistent about the idea of nomadic nations. Strong attachments to territory can develop without the sense of rootedness so central to the primordialist vision of blood and

41. See Emerson, *From Empire to Nation*, 105–6.

42. Barrès, *Scènes et doctrines du nationalisme*, 8–13.

43. Consider the French words that begin the original, French version of the Canadian national anthem: "O Canada, terre de nos aieux," which suggests that their ancestral territory is in North America rather than Normandy or Brittany.

soil. This vision of timeless dwelling is thus too specific to characterize national connection to territory per se.

Second, this understanding of the connection between nation and territory emphasizes the local and the familiar, an emphasis that seems out of keeping with the large, impersonal form most nations take. We need here to distinguish between what Frederick Hertz calls "home feeling" and "national feeling" about territory.

> It is often assumed that the national spirit is nothing else but attachment to the native soil. Yet national feeling and home feeling are not the same, and the national territory . . . is not identical with the home country in the narrower sense, that is the place where we have been born or which is nearest to our heart through long residence and many cherished memories. This narrow territory has a psychological significance quite other than that of the fatherland. It means the remembrance of childhood and youth, of family life, relatives and early friends. Its woods and meadows, its valleys and rivers, its villages and historic monuments are much more familiar to us than those of other parts of fatherland, many of which we have only seen as passing visitors, if at all. . . . Affection for the national territory [in contrast] is implanted in our mind by a common history, by the force of public opinion, by education, by means of literature, the press, national songs, monuments, and in many other ways.[44]

The members of nations, I would suggest, are connected to particular territories by the way that these lands figure in their cultural heritage. Stories about dwelling in a particular place may take pride of place in some national cultures; but such stories do not necessarily drown out tales of origins or past greatness. As Anthony Smith suggests, nations territorialize memory. They turn the places of great drama and achievement into homelands.[45]

Understood in this way, the same or overlapping lands can belong to more than one nation, since the members of national communities not only dwell frequently side by side in the same territories, but can also recall the same sites of past greatness and trauma. It is only with the rise of beliefs about the right to national self-determination that people begin

44. Hertz, *Nationality in History and Politics*, 149

45. A. Smith, *The Antiquity of Nations*, 75.

to assume that a given territory must belong to one and only one nation. For the idea of national sovereignty introduces a new and different sense of possession of territory: control or the extension of authority evenly throughout some given space. One reason nationalist disputes over territory are so acute is the tension between these two different ways of describing territory as our own. National communities come, in the age of nationalism, to demand the right to exercise control over "their" lands; but they identify particular lands as "theirs" by means of a loose understanding of national territory that allows multiple nations to develop strong claims on the same territory. National conflicts in the Balkans, for example, were greatly increased and intensified by the fact that each community had memories of past greatness that extended well beyond its present dwelling places. If it were just a matter of sorting out the boundaries currently containing different linguistic and cultural groups, the tensions between them would be much less difficult to resolve.[46]

Nationality and Ethnicity

If we accept the preceding characterization of national community, how should we understand ethnicity and its relationship to nationality? Judging by the way in which we commonly use the term, ethnicity closely resembles nationality in its evocation of intergenerational connections, but seems older, less subjective, and more reliant on biological descent. Does that mean that nationality and ethnicity manifest distinct and different forms of community? Clearly, many scholars seem to think so. However, their efforts to construct a distinction between ethnic and national community have run into numerous difficulties—not the least of which is the lack of an ordinary English word to represent the ethnic side of the dichotomy. The most elaborate of these efforts, Anthony Smith's influential account of the ethnic origins of nations, borrows the French word *ethnie* to make up for this lack.[47] But the fact that scholars have to turn to cognates of a Greek word, *ethnos*, that has long been translated as "nation" or "people" in order to draw contrasts with our concept of national community gives us a good sense of the conceptual difficulties that they face.

46. See Bibo, "The Distress of East European Small States," 22–23.

47. A. Smith, *The Ethnic Origins of Nations*, 15, 22–23, and *The Antiquity of Nations*, 184–90.

Indeed, close examination of the communities designated as examples of the *ethnos* usually reveals that they share the nation's distinctive form of intergenerational community. In particular, they turn out to be no more primordial, objective, and necessary than national communities. Like nations, they depend on the subjective affirmation of a shared heritage,[48] even if that heritage often includes myths of common descent. And they have the same tendency to divide and fuse in response to the contingencies of war and politics, religious strife and cultural innovation,[49] which probably explains why Max Weber ends up confessing that "the concept of the ethnic group, which dissolves if we define the term exactly, corresponds in this regard to one of the most vexing, since emotionally charged, concepts: the nation."[50] Our need to borrow an ancient Greek term in order to distinguish these two forms of community may be telling us something about the world, not just about the poverty of our vocabulary.

The surest sign that the concepts of nation and *ethnos* refer to the same communal phenomena is the fact that students of the latter often end up throwing up their hands in frustration in exactly the same manner as the former, declaring that an ethnic group is a collection of people who believe they form an ethnic group.[51] As Thomas Eriksen notes, there has recently been a convergence between anthropologists studying ethnic groups and theorists of nationalism, though the latter have been slow to recognize it. The anthropologists have come to see that ethnic groups are also constructions based on "talk about culture," rather than objective cultural differences.[52] In the end, nation and *ethnos* (or *ethnie*) are two words for a single form of association: an intergenerational community based on the affirmation of a shared cultural inheritance.

There is, however, another, more objective characteristic of individuals that we often use the terms ethnicity and nationality to describe. When we say that someone is half Polish and half Italian—let alone when we start dividing them up into quarters and eighths—we are not-

48. See Zubaida, "Nations, Old and New," 329–31; J. M. Hall, *Ethnic Identity in Greek Antiquity*, xiii, 19–23, 32–33; Tambiah, "Ethnic Conflict in the World Today," 335.

49. For an exhaustive study see Armstrong, *Nations before Nationalism*. See also Horowitz, *Ethnic Groups in Conflict*, 115–18; J. M. Hall, *Ethnic Identity in Greek Antiquity*, 28–29; Tambiah, "Ethnic Conflict in the World Today," 335–36.

50. M. Weber, *Economy and Society*, 389, 395.

51. See Eriksen, *Ethnicity and Nationalism*, 12.

52. Ibid., 99.

ing the fact that they had one Polish and one Italian parent, rather than measuring their degree of commitment to other Poles and Italians. We are referring, as it were, to the stamp that their parentage has left on them, Polish on one side, Italian on the other, rather than to any subjective feelings that they may have about being stamped in this way.[53] This use of the term ethnicity—or, for that matter, the term nationality, as in the passports once issued by the Soviet Union—distinguishes among us by drawing attention to our parents' communal attachments, rather than to our own. From this perspective someone like Daniel Deronda, the hero of George Eliot's last novel, is no less Jewish before he discovers his previously hidden Jewish parentage than after it becomes known to him. And he retains this Jewish ethnicity regardless of whether he chooses to embrace or abandon his newly discovered connections to the Jewish community.[54] For ethnicity, as an objective marker, tells us something about where we come from rather than about what we know about ourselves or feel about others.[55]

As such, ethnicity manifests membership in a set, as opposed to the more demanding forms of membership associated with communities and organizations. Many members of an ethnic group will probably imagine themselves connected as objects of mutual concern and loyalty by their shared parentage. Others may try to coordinate their activities and thereby establish organizations devoted to mutual aid and cultural preservation. Indeed, it was the persistence of such ethnic organizations and communities in large polities like the United States that drew attention to ethnicity as a distinct social phenomenon. But sharing ethnicity or nationality in this sense demands neither empathy nor organization from its members.

Returning to ethnicity as a manifestation of intergenerational community, the desire to distinguish it from nationality reflects the same interest in distinguishing intergenerational inheritance and political principles that we saw in the dichotomy between ethnic and civic nations. Some nations, usually older ones, make a great deal of their stories of common descent, the sharing of which is commonly cited as the defining

53. Stevens, *Reproducing the State*, 11.

54. The great irony in Deronda's affirmation of his Jewish heritage is that it is motivated to a large extent by a sense of honor—for example, that it would be ungentlemanly to refuse an inheritance from one's parents—that he derived from his English heritage.

55. Ethnicity, understood in this manner, is a broader concept than race or racial inheritance, since it refers to a parent's affiliations as well as their biological marks of distinction.

trait of an *ethnos*. Others, usually more recent examples, make a great deal of their efforts to take control of their political life, the assertion of which is in many theories what distinguishes the nation from an *ethnos*.[56] Thus it seems as if we should distinguish between these groups and the two forms of community that they represent. But when we do so, we tend to exaggerate their differences and downplay the important and poorly understood form of intergenerational community that they share.

It is not the nature of national community that has changed in the modern world, but rather the use, and especially the political use, to which this form of intergenerational community has been put. The communities that Smith and others are inclined to characterize as *ethnies* emerged in periods and places when the predominant forms of political organization—empires, dynasties, tribal federations, cities—usually cut across communal boundaries. The communities that they are inclined to describe as nations rose to prominence in periods when there are pressures to coordinate intergenerational community and political organization. No doubt, this drive introduces many changes into the life of nations. But it is a mistake to assume that this drive itself is inspired by the emergence of a new and distinct form of community. As I shall try to show in the following chapters, it is instead the product of the confrontation of an old and familiar form of community with a new and unprecedented form of political organization, the modern state.

56. See A. Smith, *The Ethnic Origins of Nations*, 15, 22–23, and *National Identity*, 21, 42. Smith, as noted, develops the most extensive distinctions between nations and what he calls "*ethnies*." He distinguishes the nation from the *ethnie* by adding political organization to the list of features that characterize the former. Both forms of community share a common name, historical territory, shared myths, feelings of solidarity, and a sense of a shared fate.

CHAPTER FOUR

The People, the Nation, and the Nation-State

Many well-known students of nationalism place great emphasis on something in their conceptions of nationhood that is missing in mine: a connection to the modern state and political self-determination. Benedict Anderson, for example, defines the nation as a community imagined as "bounded and sovereign." And Eric Hobsbawm insists that it is "pointless to talk about nations apart from the state."[1] Common sense and historical sensitivity would both seem to support them in doing so. For we regularly use the term nation to refer to the community that corresponds to state, as when we talk about organizations like the United Nations. And even a minimal acquaintance with the course of modern history makes it clear that the state has played a crucial role in the spread and politicization of national community.

Why then persist in omitting any reference to state or sovereignty in my conceptualization of national community? Three reasons. First, the preceding chapter has shown, I hope, that it is far from "pointless to talk about nations apart from the state," that there is a distinctive form of intergenerational community associated with the nation, one that does not depend on the state for its existence. Second, I hope to show in this chapter that while there is indeed a new and distinctive way of imagining group membership that is connected to the modern state, that group is the people, rather than the nation. In other words, it is the group for

1. Hobsbawm, *Nations and Nationalism since 1780*, 9; B. Anderson, *Imagined Communities*, 6–7.

whom modern theorists have constructed the notion of constituent sovereignty that is inconceivable without reference to the modern state, rather than the intergenerational cultural community discussed in the previous chapter.

Finally, I insist on distinguishing between nation and people in this way because I believe that the interaction between these two ways of imagining group membership provides the key to understanding nationalism and the unruly social forces it has unleashed on the modern world.[2] It is the modern state's undeniable contribution to the rise of nationalism that encourages scholars to define national community with reference to state and sovereignty. But it is precisely in order to make sense of that contribution that we need to exclude such references from our conceptions of national community and develop a clear distinction between the nation and the people. For the need to control and limit the unprecedented powers of the modern state has inspired a new way of imagining group membership, one that, as we shall see, helps transform national loyalty into nationalism. Define the nation in terms of the state and popular sovereignty and you lose sight of the meeting between these two independent sources of the modern social imagination: one inspired by new beliefs about political legitimacy; the other, by sentiments associated with a relatively old and familiar form of intergenerational loyalty.

I should note at the outset that this chapter presents a conceptual distinction between the nation and the people, rather than a semantic distinction. In other words, it does not suggest that ordinary usage in English or any other language with which I am familiar regularly employs the distinction between the people and the nation developed here.[3] Instead, it suggests that we use these two terms as convenient reference points for two different ways of conceiving of membership. The fact that we have come to use the words "nation" and "people" interchangeably

2. As Istvan Hont suggests in his important article on "The Permanent Crisis of a Divided Mankind" (171), "without a historically informed understanding of the theory of popular sovereignty, no clarification of the modern language of nation-state and nationalism is possible."

3. Quite the contrary, in most languages the two terms or their equivalents are used interchangeably. In English the term nation tends to have more of a cultural connotation, the people more of a political connotation. In German it is the other way round, though as Emmerich Francis points out, that is the result of a long evolution that reversed the use of the terms. See Francis, *Ethnos und Demos*, 61.

to describe these two forms of group membership should not prevent us from distinguishing between them—even if we have to strain ordinary language a bit in order to do so.

The People as Constituent Sovereign

Like the term nation, the people has come to stand for a variety of ways of imagining group membership, including the kind of intergenerational community identified with nations in the previous chapter. It is especially familiar as a way of characterizing nonelite groups within any political community—the plebs, the many, or the common folk. Call this the populist image of the people. At the same time, the term is regularly used to designate the whole community that exercises its will by means of political institutions. Call this the republican or democratic image of the people. The ambivalence between these two images of the people goes back to the ancient Athenians, who regularly invoked both images when they talked about the demos. And it is clearly invoked in modern political rhetoric, such as Lincoln's famous celebration of "government of the people, by the people, and for the people."

But it is a relatively new image of the people, one that emerges in response to the modern state's extraordinary concentration of power, which plays the crucial role in the rise of nationalism and is regularly confused with national community. This is the image of the people as the group from which all legitimate political authority is derived and to which it returns with the dissolution of government. While this image of the people is easy to confuse with the older republican or democratic image of the people as the body that determines the will of a political community, it is in fact an invention of early modern political thought. It envisions the people as the ultimate source of political authority and judge of how it has been used, rather than as its wielder, as the constituent rather than the governmental sovereign.[4] The state, according to this view, is a hierarchically organized structure of institutions and offices, each of which has specific and limited powers. Only the power to establish or dissolve

4. On the theory of constituent sovereignty, see Franklin, *John Locke and the Theory of Sovereignty*; Hont, "Permanent Crisis," 201; Forsyth, "Thomas Hobbes and the Constituent Power of the People," 191; Béaud, *La puissance de l'état*, 208–27; Beer, *To Make a Nation*, 312–21; and Pasquino, *Sieyes et l'invention de la constitution en France*.

such a structure is unlimited, and that power is reserved for the people as a whole and denied to any individual or group that claims to represent them. The traditional understanding of popular sovereignty was much simpler: the exercise of political authority by the many or the majority rather than by a single individual or a relatively small group of "better" individuals. The new understanding constructs, in contrast, a vision of indirect sovereignty with which to temper the struggles for political power among the one, the few, and the many. In doing so, it "undercuts the traditional notion of popular sovereignty as much as the traditional notion of a princely state."[5]

Among the first to develop this understanding of the people systematically was George Lawson in his *Politica Sacra and Civilis* (1660).[6] Lawson distinguishes there between "community" and "commonwealth," a distinction that Locke echoes in the closing paragraph of the *Second Treatise*.[7] "A community," Lawson suggests, "is a society of persons immediately capable of a commonwealth; or it is a society fit to receive a form of public government."[8] Understood in this way, a community precedes the establishment and survives the dissolution of government and at such times "hath a liberty and right to determine upon what form [of government] they please." As such, the community retains what Lawson calls "real majesty," which he defines as "the power to constitute, abolish, alter, reform forms of government," a power "greater than personal [majesty,] which is the power of a commonwealth already constituted."[9]

Locke, in a similar fashion, builds his famous defense of the right to revolution on a distinction "between the *Dissolution of the Society* and the *Dissolution of the Government*." With the dissolution of government,

5. Hont, "Permanent Crisis," 172, 184–85.

6. Lawson, *Political Sacra et Civilis*. On Lawson's version of the constituent sovereignty argument, see Franklin, *John Locke and the Theory of Sovereignty*, 53–86, and Morgan, *Inventing the People*, 87–89.

7. Locke, *Two Treatises of Government*, 2:§243.

8. Lawson, *Politica*, 24, 22.

9. Ibid., 30, 46–47. Echoing Aristotle's *Politics*, Lawson describes the community as the matter and the constitution as the form of the commonwealth (22). In doing so, however, he reverses Aristotle's formulation in a telling way. For Aristotle gives priority to the constitution or form of the polis, arguing that the citizens (or matter) of a polis depend on the constitution (or form) for their existence and distinctive character. See Aristotle, *Politics*, 1276a–b. Lawson, in contrast, gives priority to the matter or community of the commonwealth, since he insists that it preexists and establishes the constitution that gives the commonwealth its form.

he argues, supreme power "reverts to the Society, and the People have a Right to act as Supreme, and continue the legislative in themselves, or erect a new form, or under the old form place it in new hands, as they think good."[10] Article III of the French Revolution's "Declaration of the Rights of Man and Citizen," presents an even more resounding statement of the new doctrine. "The principle of all sovereignty resides essentially in the nation. Nor can any individual, or group of individuals, be entitled to any authority which is not expressly derived from it." "Sovereignty," as Thomas Paine interprets this right, "appertains to the Nation only, and not to any individual; and a Nation has at all times an inherent indefeasible right to abolish any form of Government it finds inconvenient, and establish such as accords with its interest, disposition, and happiness."[11]

No matter what term is used—people, nation, community, society—the same image of group membership is being invoked: the whole body of a political association as the ultimate source of the structure of political authority that shall direct its public affairs. As Paine makes clear, the terms people and nation are used interchangeably to refer to the bearer of constituent sovereignty. "In America constitutions are established by the people. In France the word nation is used instead of the people; but in both cases, a constitution is a thing antecedent to the government."[12] And even Sieyès, who eloquently celebrates the nation as the site of popular sovereignty, notes that in "a political society, a people, a nation are synonymous terms."[13] Political authority, he suggests "comes from the people, that is to say, the nation."[14]

"Since the revolutionary period," Murray Forsyth suggests, "this idea of the people as the constituent power has gradually become a reality throughout the Western world." Increasingly, "the people" has come to be seen as "the 'subject' of the constitution," the ultimate source from

10. Locke, *Two Treatises*, 2:§211, §243. Note that throughout these passages Locke uses the terms "people," "society," and "community" interchangeably, contrasting them all with the "commonwealth," the community established by a particular form of government.

11. Paine, *The Rights of Man*, 165, 207.

12. Ibid., 213. There is thus no reason to conclude, as does Yeoshua Arieli (*Individualism and Nationalism in American Ideology*, 95), that the two terms referred to two different conceptions of community, "'the people' . . . to men freely associated; 'nation' to an indivisible unity of society."

13. Sieyès, "Contre la ré-totale," 175.

14. Sieyès, *Écrits Politiques*, 200.

which all legitimate authority is derived.[15] "In some form or other this principle is now accepted in all constitutional systems" and even in many dictatorships. Indeed, "it may even appear obvious."[16]

Perhaps. But it is still a rather strange idea, in some ways stranger and more abstract than the absolutist doctrines it was designed to replace. After all,

> a king, however dubious his divinity might seem, did not have to be imagined. He was a visible presence, wearing his crown and carrying his scepter. The people, on the other hand, are never visible as such. Before we ascribe sovereignty to the people we have to imagine there is such a thing, something we personify as though it were a single body.[17]

And the mystery does not disappear when liberals become liberal democrats. For in liberal democracies the people, like a medieval monarch, has two bodies: the institutionally defined majority that rules in the government and the much more inclusive, but formless group that establishes the limited institutional powers of majority rule.

What makes this way of thinking seem especially mysterious is that it asks us to think of the people as a singular collective actor *prior* to the establishment of any of the institutions of government that ordinarily allow us to distinguish one collectivity's voice from another's. It is relatively easy to imagine the people as a community of all individuals subject to the same political authority or as a community of all individuals who share in the exercise of that authority themselves. But what distinguishes one people from another in the absence of the organized coordination of individual wills established by existing structures of political authority? Nothing, answer absolutists like Hobbes. Government may be established by and for the needs and purposes of ordinary people, Hobbes argues. But without a sovereign to represent them, a group of individuals is incapable of speaking and acting as a collective actor. "The people," he insists, "are not in being before the constitution of government as not being any person, but a multitude of persons."[18] And "a multitude of men

15. Forsyth, "Thomas Hobbes and the Constituent Power of the People," 191.

16. Franklin, *John Locke and the Theory of Sovereignty*, 124.

17. Morgan, *Inventing the People*, 153.

18. Hobbes, *De Cive*, 110. It follows, for Hobbes, that "the *People* rules in all governments, for even in *Monarchies* the people commands; for the *People* wills by the will of one

are made *one* person when they are by one man, or one person, represented; . . . For it is the *unity* of the *representer*, not the *unity* of the represented, that maketh the person *one*."[19] If, despite Hobbes's powerful objections, the principle of the constituent sovereignty of the people has become obvious, then it is only because we have grown accustomed to imagining ourselves as members of this odd and loosely defined group. That means that liberal ideals of limited government rest on appeals to our social imagination as much as on the construction of institutional mechanisms like the separation of powers.

How then does the principle of constituent sovereignty lead us to imagine our membership in the people? What kind of group does the people, so imagined, represent? Despite—or perhaps because of—its familiarity as the foundation of almost all contemporary claims to political legitimacy, little effort has been made to give precise answers to these questions.[20]

Should we think of the people as a form of community, that is, as a group of individuals who imagine themselves connected to each other by ties of mutual concern and loyalty? I think not. The people of a given state retain the power to establish and dissolve government regardless of how its members feel about each other. As Kant said, legitimate political authority could be established by a "nation of devils" as long as they were rational.[21] Mutual goodwill is not what makes a people, understood in this sense.

Perhaps then we should think of the people as a kind of organization, a way of coordinating the wills of a group of individuals to meet a shared

---

man . . . And in a *Monarchy*, the subjects are the *Multitude*, and (however it seems a *paradox*) the King is the People" (ibid., 154).

19. Hobbes, *Leviathan*, chap. 16.

20. The idea of the people is such a commonplace of liberal democratic theory and practice that you would think that almost everything that could be said about it has already been said. In fact, the idea of the people has received nothing like the scholarly attention social and political theorists have devoted to the nation. That is starting to change recently, with works like Margaret Canovan's *The People*. See also R. Smith, "Citizenship and the Politics of People-Building"; Frank, *Constituent Moments*; and Nässtrom, "The Legitimacy of the People." Still, some of the most interesting insights into this concept have been presented in studies of the nation, which is not all that surprising given the way the two concepts have come to be identified with each other. See, e.g., Beer, *To Make a Nation* and the first chapters of Greenfeld's *Nationalism*. For a good historical account of the origins of the concept of the people, see Morgan, *Inventing the People*.

21. Kant, "Perpetual Peace," 112.

purpose, in this case, the establishment and control of the state's powers. Locke, for one, encourages us to do so with his theory of a double contract, the first to establish the people as constituent sovereign and the second to establish a form of government. "That which makes the Community, and brings Men out of the loose State of Nature, into *one* Politick Society, is the Agreement which every one has with the rest to incorporate as one Body, and so be one distinct Commonwealth."[22] But following Locke's lead raises the question of who, and with what authority, organizes a group of individuals to form a people in the first place, which suggests that there might be another authority behind that of the people. That is why Sieyès, who claims for France the honor of discovering the distinction between constituent and legislative sovereignty, insists that "it is the government, not the nation which is constituted."[23] A constituted nation or people, he notes, would be a contradiction in terms, since only a nation or a people possess the constituent power.[24] In other words, it would take a nation to constitute a nation, which means that the search for the contractual origins of a nation leads us into an infinite regress.

I suggest, therefore, that the people imagined as constituent sovereign is best understood as a set, rather than as an organization or community. In other words, membership in the people comes from the mere sharing of a particular trait or situation, rather than the kind of connectedness that comes from the feelings of goodwill created by communities or the coordinated activities created by organizations. The group to which this new understanding of political legitimacy grants sovereignty is the set of all permanent subjects of a particular state's authority imagined in abstraction from the way in which political authority is organized there. The characteristic that members of this group share is subjection to the authority of a particular state. The theory of constituent sovereignty at-

22. Locke, *Two Treatises*, 2:§211. Even Locke, however, cannot conceal the implausibility of this assertion and admits that "those, who like one another so well as to join into Society, cannot but be supposed to have some Acquaintance and Friendship together, and some Trust one in another; they could not but have greater Apprehensions of others, than of one another." "Twas natural," he acknowledges, for such individuals "to put themselves under a Frame of Government" (ibid., 2:§107). For a full account of the extent to which "Locke takes for granted that a political society rests on social affinities" rather than voluntary association, see Rabkin, "Grotius, Vattel, and Locke."

23. Pasquino, "The Constitutional Republicanism of Emmanuel Sieyes," 111.

24. Sieyès, *What Is the Third Estate?*, 126–28. See Hont, "Permanent Crisis," 193n46.

tributes the ultimate and unlimited power to establish and dissolve government to this group, which is then imagined as prior to or abstracted from any particular structure of political organization.

The people, imagined in this way, is a decidedly abstract group, as political theorists have often complained. Hegel, for example, ridicules this "wild idea of the people" as "a formless mass and no longer a state. It lacks every one of those determinate characteristics—sovereignty, government, judges, magistrates, class-divisions, etc.—[by which] a people cease to be that indeterminate abstraction."[25] Yet it is precisely this abstract and formless conception of the people that has displaced all of its rivals as the source of the modern state's political legitimacy.[26] The populist image of the people as the commons, the mass of humble, ordinary citizens, certainly survives in modern politics; it is always available to fuel appeals against the advantages of the rich and powerful. And the older image of the people as demos certainly survives to sustain demands for greater democracy. But it is this newer image of the people, which allows all of a territory's inhabitants to be spoken of as the collective source of the state's authority, that has had the broadest impact on modern political theory and practice.

What makes this image of group membership especially abstract is that it calls on our social imagination to *dissolve* social connections, rather than establish them. In a community we imagine things that we share as sources of mutual concern and loyalty. In an organization we imagine shared practices and institutions as the means of making many individuals act as one. With the people as constituent sovereign, in contrast, we use our imagination to *strip away* something that we currently possess: a set of mutual connections created by the state's authoritative means of coordinating our individual actions. This negative or deconstructive use of social imagination is familiar from political philosophers' thought experiments about a state of nature or an original position. Its use there is to fix our minds on the needs and interests of what we might call "imagined individuals" and their reasons for entering into political connections with each other. With the people, in contrast, the dissolu-

25. Hegel, *Philosophy of Right*, ¶279. On this passage, see Stevens, *Reproducing the State*, 79–80.

26. Franklin, *John Locke and the Theory of Sovereignty*, 124. See also Hont, "Permanent Crisis," 201, and Forsyth, "Thomas Hobbes and the Constituent Power of the People," 191.

tion of established political connections is supposed to focus our attention on what we share as members of a particular group.

Such an image of group membership has many problems, not least of which that it seems to suggest that the people exists *prior* to the state, even though it is shared subjection to a particular state's authority that distinguishes one people from another. But it does make some sense of our social situation in the midst of a revolution, when our organizational connections have indeed dissolved and yet our shared membership in a group defined by subjection to the old state's authority is still quite significant for us. When protestors gather to shout that "*we* are the people," as in the East German revolution of 1989, they are declaring the political priority of the population to the organizations constructed to represent them.[27] Indeed, it is to justify collective action taken in such conditions, or the contemplation of creating such a revolutionary situation, that the theory of constituent sovereignty was developed, not to explain the historical origins of government. The theory suggests that all governmental authority is derived from the voice of the people, but the voice of the *disorganized* people, not from the people's voice as structured by any particular set of procedures and institutions.[28]

Liberal defenders of constituent sovereignty wanted to make sure that no individual or group of individuals can claim a sovereign's authority. To that end, they divided our image of political membership in two. On one side, there is our membership in the state, an organization in which we are connected by means of a hierarchically ordered set of institutions and procedures that clearly define the limited authority that particular individuals, groups, and assemblies can legitimately claim. On the other side, there is our membership in the people—or the nation or society or civil society—the group that is given the power to establish and disestablish the state and its institution, a group in which we are connected by much more subjective and indeterminate ties than those that bind us in the state. Joseph de Maistre ridiculed this understanding of the people as a "sovereign who cannot exercise sovereignty."[29] But, in a way, that is precisely what it was intended to be. For the liberal constituent sovereign

27. See Canovan, *The People*, 1, 104.

28. Ibid., 4–5. Sheldon Wolin, for one, identifies democracy explicitly with the actions of a disorganized people, rather than with the organized people who speak through representatives and various forms of majority rule. See especially Wolin, "Norm and Form."

29. Maistre, "On the Sovereignty of the People," 45.

is imagined as the source of political legitimacy and a check on the ambitions of office-holders, rather than as the holder of the final and highest power within a state. Turning this group into an organization defined by a shared procedure or decision rule, such as majority or supermajority rule, might satisfy critics like Hobbes, but it would undermine the purpose for which this image of membership was invented: to keep absolute and unlimited power out of the hands of any group of individuals, no matter how large or democratic.

Liberal critics of nationalism often insist that the "modern state is historically unique in that, unlike its predecessors, its unity is located in its structure rather than . . . on an illusory prepolitical foundation."[30] Whether or not this claim is true for the modern state in general, it is highly questionable for the liberal state in particular. When James Wilson complained in 1794 that it "is not *politically correct*" to toast the United States, as opposed to "the people of the United States," he may have been a little extreme, but he was only speaking like a good liberal republican.[31] For liberal constitutionalists the state is indeed a relatively neutral instrument that requires "nothing more and nothing less of its members than to acknowledge the legitimacy of the prevailing structure of authority."[32] But its purposes and limits are determined by a group that is imagined as prior to and independent of the state.

The People and the Nation

Having outlined the distinctive features of the people imagined as constituent sovereign, it is important to highlight a number of ways in which this image of group membership differs from that which I have associated with the nation.

First of all, the people, unlike the nation, is a relatively new or modern image of group membership. It is called into being by new ways of thinking about political legitimacy, ways of thinking that were designed to focus and limit the extraordinary concentration of power in

30. Parekh, "The Incoherence of Nationalism," 320–22.

31. Quoted in R. Smith, *Civic Ideals*, 137, 151, emphasis added. The quote is from Wilson's opinion in Chisholm v. Georgia, a case that, according to Wilson, raised the question, "do the people of the United States form a nation?"

32. Parekh, "The Incoherence of Nationalism," 321–22.

the modern state. The nation, in contrast, is a relatively old image of community—even though it is regularly evoked by new nations as well as old ones. Second, the people, unlike the nation, is always juxtaposed to a state. More precisely, it is imagined as corresponding to, yet preexisting a particular state. "Bounded and sovereign," Anderson's description of a nation, is a good definition of the people, as long as we recognize that its boundaries are provided by the borders at which a particular state's authority ends. The nation, in contrast, does not take its boundaries from states, no mater how closely they may be associated with them. And since the shared cultural heritage from which it does take its boundaries often has roots in events and practices that preexist particular states, national loyalties can be used to challenge the boundaries of a state in ways that images of the people cannot—which is one reason why state leaders often work so hard to reshape nations into forms that correspond to their political borders.

This difference with regard to the state leads to a third important difference between the nation and the people. The people is a territorial group in a way that the nation is not. The limit of membership in the people is the territorial boundary that separates the extent of one state's authority from another's. Within that line all permanent residents—or all adult, or all male adult permanent residents, depending on one's way of thinking—are part of the people. Beyond it, they are not, unless their absence is temporary. The limit of national membership, in contrast, is not defined by territorial boundaries, despite the importance of particular territories to national community. What makes one a member of a nation is the sharing of a heritage associated with a particular territory, not residence within its boundaries. That makes it possible for more than one national community to share the same territory, but only so long as they do not seek to exercise exclusive control, that is, sovereignty, over it in the manner of the people.

Fourth, the people does not depend on subjective feelings of mutual concern and loyalty in the way that the nation does. For the people is a set or a species, rather than a community. As a result, while national community may be present or absent, thriving or dying, the people is imagined as always in place, always available to be invoked in one's struggles with political authority or in one's competition for political power. For the people exists by right, rather than by custom or consciousness-raising. To assert or deny its existence is a matter of principle rather than a matter of sociology. It exists as long as one believes in a particular theory of political legitimacy. Those who deny its existence are guilty of an injustice rather than a misdescription. Perhaps that is why there is so much less talk of "people-building" than "nation-building."[33] A nation needs time and effort to establish a legacy of memories and symbols salient enough to link one generation to another. Indeed, one cannot really be sure about the existence of a nation until one has given it sufficient time to grow—or collapse.[34] The people, in contrast, needs no nurturing. It is available as soon as individuals accept the principles of legitimacy that assert its existence.

Fifth, the people, unlike the nation, is a relatively static, present-focused image of group membership. Unlike nations, which evolve over time, the people neither ages nor changes in any other fundamental way.[35] Nor does it change in character from one instance to another. The people invoked as the ultimate source of the Swedish state's authority is no different in character than the people invoked as the source of the authority of the Chinese or Canadian state. In every case the people is the same: the whole body of a territory's inhabitants imagined as the final judge of how the state's authority should be constructed. Of course, those whom we include in our image of the people—property-holders, all adult men, all adult men and women, and so on—change over time with the evolution of political beliefs. But once we accept such changes we tend to see them as corrections of mistakes that our predecessors made about the composition of the people, rather than as a further evolution of the people itself. In other words, it is our interpretations of the people, rather than the people itself that we view as changing.[36] Once we come, say, to include women in our image of the people, then our image of every people, not just our own, is sexually integrated.

Finally, membership in the people elevates the status of nonelite individuals in the way that membership in the nation need not. Both people

33. See, however, R. Smith, "Citizenship and the Politics of People-Building," and *Stories of Peoplehood.*

34. Emerson, *From Empire to Nation*, 90–91.

35. As Yeoshua Arieli (*Individualism and Nationalism in American Ideology*, 41) suggests with regard to the American founders' conception, "'the people' were timeless, beyond the contingencies of history."

36. I should also add that our view of the people as governmental, as opposed to constituent, sovereign is constantly evolving as we contract or broaden the franchise, the qualifications for office, and the powers granted to one institution or another. Such a view supports changing rules of citizenship, as in studies like Rogers Smith's *Civic Ideals.*

and nation are "categorical" groups,[37] that is, they grant equal membership directly to individuals rather than through the mediation of other groups; no one is more a member of the people or the nation than any other member. But, as Liah Greenfeld emphasizes, moving from an image of the people as plebs or commoners to an image of the people as the source of a state's authority lends ordinary individuals a source of status previously denied them, even if it leaves many other sources of inequality in place.[38] That means that the invocation of the people inspires forms of pride and vanity that the nation does not—at least until people start attributing to national community the kind of sovereignty originally designed for the people—wherein, I shall argue, lies a large part of the tale about the nature and origins of nationalism.

Add up these differences between the people and the nation and what have you got? On the one side, a relatively new, static, territorially bounded image of group membership, an image focused on the status-raising activity of establishing and controlling the powers of the modern state; on the other side, an older intergenerational image focused on shared cultural heritage rather than political control of a state. It might seem then that my distinction between the two has simply revived in different language the dichotomy between civic and ethnic nationhood. But that is not the case, even though the idea of the civic nation draws much of its inspiration from the image of the people as constituent sovereign.

The civic nation is, in Michael Ignatieff's words, "a community of equal, rights-bearing citizens, united in patriotic attachment to a shared set of political practices and values."[39] As such, it represents a kind of synthesis of the images of the people and the nation. It combines the former's purely political character with the latter's feelings of mutual concern and loyalty. Its defenders want the members of the peoples associated with liberal democratic states to imagine themselves connected to each other by forms of social friendship derived from purely political forms of sharing, such as shared belief in foundational political principles. The fact that we already tend to imagine ourselves members of groups that hold the power to constitute and dissolve government leads them to assume that we already form such communities. That is where their mistake lies, as I have tried to show in chapter 1.

37. Calhoun, *Nationalism*, 39.

38. Greenfeld, *Nationalism*, 6–7, 487.

39. Ignatieff, *Blood and Belonging*, 7–8.

The people and the nation, as described in this chapter, represent two of the essential building blocks of the modern social and political imagination. Our imagined membership in the former sustains the theories of popular sovereignty that have gradually edged out almost all competitors as sources of political legitimacy for the modern state. And our imagined membership in the latter shapes our sense of who we are and where we belong in the contingent unfolding of human history. The civic nation, in contrast, is something that many liberal students of nationalism wish for, a synthesis of popular sovereignty and social friendship that promises us—falsely, I have argued—something like nationalism's sense of belonging and mutual goodwill without its potential for violence and exclusiveness. The dichotomy between civic and ethnic nationalism thus represents a flawed corrective to the modern social imagination rather than the empirical guide that it usually purports to be.

The Nation-State

If, as I have argued, a connection to the state is not a distinguishing feature of national community, what kind of social phenomenon do we have in mind when we speak of the nation-state, a term most people think of as the predominant form of polity in the contemporary world? First of all, the nation-state refers to a form of the state, that is, to a particular form of political organization. When we combine the terms nation and state we are qualifying our understanding of the kind of political organization that we are talking about, rather than our understanding of the kind of nation or community before us. Moreover, since the term state has come to refer to a particular form of political organization, one in which all political authority within a territory is organized in a single hierarchically ordered structure, a nation-state represents a form of political organization in which such a structure of political authority is related in some way to a national community.

There are two major sources of ambiguity with regard to the term nation-state. The first arises from the different understandings of association that have come to be connected with the term nation. The second arises from confusion about the nature of the relationship between political organization and national community that the term nation-state is designed to express. Since the second of these two sources of ambiguity is less obvious, I shall deal with it first.

The simplest understanding of the relationship between community and political organization that makes a nation-state is overlapping membership. In this understanding a nation-state is a political organization all of whose members are also members of the same national community, however such community is understood. This understanding of the nation-state is encouraged by the familiar definition of nationalism as the ideology that insists that boundaries of states match the boundaries of nations.[40]

I suggest, however, that our use of the term nation-state to characterize the predominant form of political organization among us is inspired by a more specifically political relationship between community and political organization than mere congruence of membership. When we talk about the nation-state supplanting the dynastic state or the imperial state, we have in mind changes in the way we think about political legitimacy, not just the way in which we draw political boundaries. The term nation-state, I suggest, thus refers to the kind of state that draws its legitimacy in some way from the nation whose servant it is imagined to be, rather than to a state whose members are also members of the same national community. In other words, a nation-state is a state whose legitimacy is drawn in some way from the approval of the members of a national group. From this point of view, dynastic or patrimonial states cannot be nation-states, even if most of their subjects are members of the same national community, since they derive their authority from sources independent of the needs and will of the communities they serve. Dynastic states begin to turn into nation-states when they alter their understanding of the relationship between political authority and the community they serve, as when Louis-Philippe declared himself "the king of the French," rather than the ruler of France. The nation-state thus brings together two forms of membership, membership in a political organization and membership in a set or a community, but makes the former subordinate in crucial ways to the latter. In a nation-state, we are members of an organization governed by a single hierarchically ordered structure of political authority that we expect to act as the voice and servant of our national group.

What kind of group does the state serve in the nation-state? It all depends, of course, on how we think of the nation. In the expression "nation-state," I would suggest that the term nation is generally used to rep-

40. See, e.g., Gellner, *Nations and Nationalism*, 1.

resent the two distinct images of associations discussed in the previous section, the people and the nation. In other words, we generally use the term nation-state to refer to the form of state that derives its legitimacy from either the approval of people who share the same singular structure of state authority or the approval of people who feel connected by an intergenerational cultural heritage. When, as in expressions like the "United Nations," we assume that all states are connected with nations, we are invoking the first of these two uses of the term. In doing so, we are not, as some complain, simply confusing the nation with the state.[41] We are, instead, expressing our expectation that any legitimate state will derive its authority in some way from the nation or people within its boundaries. When, however, we talk about the nation-state as a term of distinction among legitimate states, then we are usually invoking the second of these two uses of the term nation-state and referring to those states that derive their authority from the approval of distinct intergenerational communities. It is sometimes argued that there are few if any true nation-states in this sense of the term since almost every contemporary state contains significant cultural minorities within their boundaries.[42] But if, as I have argued, it is the demand for sovereignty over states rather than common membership rosters in nation and state that defines this version of a nation-state, these objections to their existence disappear. For the existence of cultural minorities does not preclude the claim of a majority to retain the final say over the structure and basic aims of their political institutions.

Nationalism, needless to say, is associated with the second, culturally distinctive form of nation-state. But it is the general acceptance of the first form of nation-state, the form which simply gives expression to the principle of popular sovereignty, that, I shall argue, provides the catalyst for the emergence of these demands and thus for nationalism's rise to prominence in the modern world.

41. See especially, Connor, *Ethnonationalism*, 89–92.

42. Ibid., 29–30.

CHAPTER FIVE

Legitimacy and Loyalty: Making Sense of Nationalism

What Then Is Nationalism?

Nationalism, of course, has proved no easier to define than the nation. Indeed, in one sense our disagreements about the concept of nationalism run considerably deeper than those associated with the concept of the nation. At least with regard to the nation there is a general consensus about the kind of social phenomenon—namely, a community—that we are considering. Disagreement begins when we start asking ourselves just what kind of community makes a nation: the sharing of culture or the sharing of political principles, a sense of kinship or a sense of impersonal association, age-old customs or newly minted rituals? With nationalism, however, we lack even this minimal consensus about what kind of social phenomenon we are discussing. Is nationalism a sentiment or an ideology, a new form of political contention or a distinctly modern form of social ritual and mobilization? It has been defined as each of these things, and with considerable plausibility, since nationalism clearly manifests itself in all of these ways and more.

Students of nationalism have not expressed all that much interest in sorting out this confusion.[1] The great debates about nationalism tend to be inspired by why, whence, and whither questions rather than the what question that stands at the center of so much work on the nation. Some scholars, like Craig Calhoun, have more or less thrown in the towel on

1. For an interesting exception, see Gilbert, *Philosophy of Nationalism*, 4–5.

the latter question by concluding that nationalism represents nothing more than a "discursive formation," a diverse and inconsistent bundle of rhetorical references and strategies surrounding the term nation, rather than any more specific kind of social phenomenon.[2] Most scholars, however, simply stipulate a definition of nationalism—most often, as the ideology that demands that we bring the boundaries of states into line with those of nations—that allows them to circumscribe the phenomenon in a way that focuses attention on the issues that most interest them. They rarely worry about what is left out by these definitions.

While I appreciate the pragmatic sensibility that encourages scholars to concentrate their efforts on the questions that they can best answer, I worry about the relatively one-sided definitions of nationalism upon which most contemporary scholarship rests. For these narrow definitions of nationalism not only promote confusion about the subject; they discourage us from trying to capture the distinctive character of the surprising and powerful phenomenon that has caught our attention in the first place. We may have to conclude in the end that nationalism represents a set of distinct phenomena that share little but a common name. But we should not begin with such a conclusion and simply assume that our efforts to come up with a fuller, more integrated conception of nationalism are bound to be fruitless.

This chapter presents such an effort. It argues that what distinguishes nationalism as a social phenomenon is the way in which it combines beliefs and sentiments, rather than a particular set of ideas or feelings alone. More specifically, it tries to show that nationalism represents a mixture of beliefs that elevate the importance of national community with feelings of special concern and loyalty for one's nation and its members. And it suggests that one form of this mixture, an explosive blend of beliefs about political legitimacy and feelings of national loyalty, has spread to every corner of the modern world and thus represents an appropriate focus for our attempts to account for the rise and spread of nationalism in modern life.

Nationalists, I am suggesting, are people who seek sovereignty—or cultural preservation or some other good—for the members of their *own* community, rather than people who believe that nations in general should be granted sovereignty or the means of preserving their culture. And they seek to enhance the well-being of the community members to

2. Calhoun, *Nationalism*, 2–5.

whom they feel connected by granting them sovereignty—or some other good they believe national communities have coming to them—rather than merely expressing a strong attachment to their nation and its members. Some nationalists will probably recognize the validity of other nations' claim to these goods; others will not. Some will loudly demand that we sacrifice everything for the good of the nation; others will make much more moderate demands on us. But it is neither by their commitments to general principles nor the intensity of their expressions of national loyalty that we recognize them as nationalists, according to my account. It is rather the way in which a combination of beliefs and sentiments motivate them to seek a particular good for the members of their own nation that marks them as nationalists.

Such a definition of nationalism may seem no less narrow than the ones that it seeks to replace. After all, we surely have occasion to describe as nationalists people who merely express powerful attachments to their nation or deep commitments to principles like the right to national self-determination. But by limiting the concept of nationalism to the combination of such convictions and sentiments, I am trying to identify the phenomenon that has made nationalism such an object of attention in the first place. No doubt, people have expressed strong attachments to their nations before the emergence of the beliefs about the nation's importance that I make part of the definition of nationalism. But we only call them nationalists now, I shall argue, because their sentiments resemble the strong attachments to the nation that have become commonplace as a result of the blending of belief and feeling that I identify with nationalism.

Indeed, this understanding of nationalism helps us see that the intensification of national loyalties in modern politics is in large part a product of the rise and spread of nationalism, rather than its cause. In other words, we have come to express much deeper and more intense attachments to the members of our national communities because we have come to seek political sovereignty for our nations rather than the other way round. Ernest Gellner went too far when he insisted that nationalism produces nations, rather than the other way round.[3] But his inversion of the relationship between nations and nationalism makes sense when thinking about the intensification of national loyalties in the modern world. For while the desire for national sovereignty has greatly deep-

3. Gellner, *Nations and Nationalism*, 55.

ened national loyalties, you do not need especially strong attachments to the nation for that desire to emerge and spread.

Blending Belief and Sentiment

Since most "ism" terms refer to sets of beliefs, it is not surprising that nationalism is most commonly defined as an ideology—whether elaborately, as in Anthony Smith's list of nationalism's seven core commitments,[4] or more simply as the ideology that demands that we bring the boundaries of states into line with nations.[5] Some "isms," however, clearly refer to the feelings that connect people to each other as well as the beliefs that they may hold about these connections. Racism, for example, refers to both the special concern and loyalty that some people express toward members of their race and beliefs about the existence and hierarchical ranking of different races.

We use the term nationalism in a similarly ambivalent way. When we speak of nationalists, sometimes we refer to people who draw attention to the strength of their attachment to their national communities, rather than to people who express a commitment to principles that elevate the importance of the nation. Many nationalists, of course, fit both of these descriptions. Like Giuseppe Mazzini, these nationalists are known for both their vigorous defense of the right to national self-determination and for their passionate celebration of their own nation's virtues. Others, however, fit only one of these descriptions. When we characterize Woodrow Wilson as a nationalist, it is because of his insistence on the principle of national self-determination rather than for the way in which he expressed his loyalty to America and Americans. When, in contrast, we characterize Benito Mussolini as a nationalist, it is because of the violence and aggressiveness with which he expressed his loyalty to Italy and Italians; the rights of other nations were hardly a priority for him.

This ambivalent usage would not be all that troubling if the two meanings of nationalism mirrored each other, as they do in the case of terms like ethnocentrism or patriotism. As an ideology, ethnocentrism refers to a set of beliefs that encourages and justifies ethnocentric loyalties, just

4 Smith, *Theories of Nationalism*, 20–21.

5 See, e.g., Gellner, *Nations and Nationalism*, 1; MacNeil, *Polyethnicity and National Unity*, 7; Alter, *Nationalism*, 92; Hechter, *Containing Nationalism*, 7.

as patriotism refers to a set of beliefs that encourages and justifies the love of country. In other words, ethnocentric and patriotic ideologies tell us why we should be ethnocentric and patriotic. But our different uses of the term nationalism do not mirror each other in this way. As an ideology nationalism most often refers to principles of political legitimacy, such as the right to national self-determination, rather than to principles that would justify our giving special care and attention to the members of our national community.

It might seem, at first, that our ambivalent use of the term suggests that we really have two very different phenomena in mind when we speak of nationalism: that is, a particular set of convictions about the world, on the one hand, and a particular form of group loyalty or social friendship, on the other. But does it really make much sense to talk about nationalism apart from feelings of special concern and loyalty toward our nation and its members? I think not. Ask yourself who are the nationalists in a conflict over a disputed territory: the people who defend their own nation's claim to the territory or the people who distance themselves from competing claims in order to satisfy each nation's right to self-determination? The German demanding the destruction of Czechoslovakia in order to get the Sudetenland? Or the rare Czech who might be willing to part with it in the name of the principle of national self-determination? Insist on a purely ideological definition of nationalism and you will find yourself in the absurd position of identifying the self-effacing Czech rather than the self-aggrandizing German as the nationalist.[6] Clearly, we do not ordinarily describe people who abandon their own national loyalties in the name of principle as nationalists, even when the principle is a belief in the nation's right to self-determination.[7] And that suggests that special concern for the well-being of one's nation and its members is an indispensable component of nationalism, rather than the foundation of one of two distinct phenomena that are hidden by a common term.

6. Anthony Smith seems to be boxed in on this point by his ideological definition of nationalism. Because Smith defines nationalism in terms of a commitment to a universal principle of self-determination, he is compelled to deny that the Nazis and Italian Fascists were really nationalists, since they did not respect their neighbors' right to self-determination. See A. Smith, *Theories of Nationalism*, 4–5, 262.

7. As Aviel Roshwald suggests (*The Endurance of Nationalism*, 12), while it is true that nineteenth-century Italian nationalists like Mazzini and Garibaldi took up the cause of oppressed peoples other than their own, "it is in their capacity as fighters for their own nation's unity and independence that we refer to them as nationalists."

Perhaps then our ambivalent use of the term nationalism reflects the complexity of the phenomenon itself. If so, then nationalists would be people who both *feel* a sense of connection to members of a national community and *believe* that nations have a special role to play in human life.[8] And nationalism would draw its strength and distinctive character from the mixture of two different sources: convictions that elevate the nation's importance and feelings of social friendship that bind its members to each other.

I believe that this is the best way to conceptualize the social phenomenon that has caught our attention under the name of nationalism. The relative novelty of the convictions that elevate the importance of national community, such as beliefs about the sovereignty or cultural creativity of nations, makes nationalism seem relatively new or modern. The old and familiar character of national loyalties—not to mention the way in which they focus our attention on what we receive from previous generations—makes nationalism seem like some kind of primordial passion. But it is the combination of the two, the mixture of a particular form of social friendship with beliefs about its special importance in our lives, which gives nationalism its distinctive character. New beliefs about the importance of national community focus and energize shared loyalties that in the past rarely ranked very high in the balance of human passions. And sentiments of group loyalty and collective self-preference provide nationalist principles with the kind of emotional force, the power to mobilize and engage masses of people, that Marx sought so much less successfully for socialism from working-class solidarity.

The most plausible instances of nationalism before the modern era involve national communities, such as the ancient Hebrews or the Czech Hussites, whose group loyalties were intensified by the belief that their nation has been specially chosen to serve a divine mission.[9] One reason that nationalism is so much more common in the modern world is that nations need not claim such special missions—though they often dis-

8. One might save the definition of nationalism as an ideology by describing it as an ideology with two distinct principles: one that justifies a view of political legitimacy and the other that justifies a particular view of group loyalty. But while the *justification* of nationalism may require a commitment to these two principles, the *expression* of nationalism does not.

9. On the Hussites, see Sayer, *The Coasts of Bohemia*, 41–42. On ancient Hebrew nationalism, see Mendel, *The Rise and Fall of Jewish Nationalism*, and Grosby, *Biblical Ideas of Nationality*.

cover them—in order to claim a special role in our lives. General beliefs about political sovereignty and cultural creativity elevate the importance of nations even in the absence of any special role that God or history calls on a particular nation to play.

Conceptualizing nationalism as a mixture of ideology and group loyalty, conviction and sentiment brings us closer to the actual experience of nationalism than a definition that focuses on either ideology or sentiment alone. One of the things about nationalism that repeatedly startles its students is the way in which such strong social forces can be generated from such seemingly shallow group sentiments or relatively inchoate and unpersuasive ideologies. By focusing attention on the way in which nationalism mixes conviction and sentiment, my account of the phenomenon can help us understand why this happens. Relatively shallow or weak national loyalties can quickly become a powerful force when combined with a belief that one's own nation is being denied its rights. Conversely, relatively inchoate and unimpressive beliefs about the importance of nations can be energized by even a minimal sense of mutual concern and loyalty toward one's co-nationals. If it is the interaction of convictions and group loyalties that produces nationalism, then the rise and near universal spread of nationalism in the modern world can be explained without the universal dissemination of either especially strong beliefs about national communities or especially passionate commitments to them.

The Nationalist Principle of Political Legitimacy

A great variety of beliefs about the significance of national community have emerged in the last two centuries, even leaving aside those ideologies—such as the "great idea" of Greek nationalism or the victimology of Serbian nationalism—that celebrate the unique heritage of particular nations. The variety of these beliefs might make nationalism seem sometimes to be little more than a discursive formation, a bundle of inconsistent ways of invoking national community.[10] But some of these ways of invoking nations have been vastly more influential than others. And one, which involves the assertion of beliefs about political legitimacy, can be found almost everywhere in the modern world. It is

10. See Calhoun, *Nationalism*, 2–5.

this form of nationalism that demands our attention if we want to account for the extraordinary rise of nationalism to prominence in modern social life.

Of course, the modern age has also seen the emergence of a distinctively cultural form of nationalism, one rooted in the belief, most powerfully expressed by Herder,[11] that the cultural heritage of nations is an indispensable source of human creativity.[12] The troops of intellectuals who go to the hills, notepads and tape-recorders in hand, in order to preserve the remaining elements of the folk cultures with which they identify are undoubtedly nationalists.[13] Their sense of intergenerational loyalty is energized by the conviction that people ought to preserve and enhance their national heritage, rather than by the belief that nations have any special political role to play in our lives. Indeed, cultural nationalism can inspire opposition to political nationalism, as Neal Ascheron reminds us with a wonderful anecdote about his mother, who voted against the establishment of a Scottish parliament because it would make Scotland more like England![14] But while cultural nationalism is hardly rare, it is nowhere near as widespread as the political form of nationalism. Moreover, cultural nationalism rarely inspires the intense and violent expressions of national loyalties that have drawn our attention to nationalism as a social phenomenon. Accordingly, when people are seeking to understand the rise and spread of nationalism, it is the association of national community with beliefs about political legitimacy that they usually have in mind.[15]

11. See Herder, *Another Philosophy of History.*

12. "Cultural nationalism," as John Hutchinson declares (*The Dynamics of Cultural Nationalism*, 14), "is a movement of moral regeneration which seeks to re-unite the different aspects of the nation . . . by returning to the creative life-principle of the nation." See also A. Smith, *Nationalism and Modernism*, 177–80, and Gans, *The Limits of Nationalism*, 2.

13. Or at least those who imagine themselves connected by the cultural heritage they went to study are cultural nationalists. Cultural nationalism, like political nationalism, requires a combination of ideological commitment and group loyalty. The American ethnographer who dedicates her career to saving Serbian epics is not a cultural nationalist, though a Serbian ethnographer who does the same most likely is.

14. Ascheron, *Stone Voices*, 113.

15. There is some confusion in this matter due to the fact that so many theories of nationalism draw their materials primarily from Central and Eastern Europe, areas where Herder's ideas about the cultural creativity of nations played an important role in the revival and invention of national loyalties. This disproportionate emphasis on Central and

I therefore join with the majority of contemporary scholars in focusing most of my attention on the political form of nationalism. Nevertheless, I believe that the most familiar formulation of the nationalist principle of political legitimacy, as the demand that we bring the boundaries of states into line with the boundaries of nations, needs to be revised. It is, first of all, too narrow a formulation of this principle, since it denies the title nationalist to people who seek for their nation something more or less than its own state. Does it really make sense, for example, to say that the Nazis were nationalists when they worked to bring the German speakers of Austria and the Sudetenland into one German Reich, but *not* when they worked so ruthlessly to impose a German national character on all of the Reich's institutions and inhabitants?[16] Similarly, does it really make sense to suggest Quebecois or Catalan activists cease being nationalists the moment they settle for anything less than a state of their own? Surely, it makes much more sense to describe these activities as different expressions of political nationalism than to reserve the term nationalism for attempts to bring the borders of states into line with those of nations.

Moreover, if we define nationalism as the ideology that demands we bring states into line with national boundaries, then it follows that nationalism should disappear once nations get their own states.[17] For once state boundaries have been made legitimate in this way, nationalist mobilization and self-assertion should, according to this definition, have lost its reason for existence. Historical experience, however, suggests that this is not the case and thus raises further doubts about this definition of the nationalist principle of legitimacy. Consider, once again, German nationalism under the Nazis. It certainly aimed at integrating German nationals from the Sudetenland, Danzig, and other parts of Eastern Europe into a single national state. But it also aimed at defeating the internal and external enemies that, so it was believed, were preventing the German nation from controlling its own destiny. Had the Nazis been

---

Eastern Europe has led some students of nationalism either to exaggerate the importance of cultural nationalism in other parts of the world or to unduly narrow their understanding of nationalism itself and deny its existence in places where cultural nationalism is absent or unimportant.

16. See Rogers Brubaker's discussion (*Nationalism Reframed*, 9) of the relative neglect of what he calls "nationalizing states" in favor of "state-seeking nations."

17. Breuilly, *Nationalism and the State*, 390–91. See also Hechter, *Containing Nationalism*, 26.

granted truly national borders for an expanded German state, it would not have ended their nationalist agitation. For the Nazis and their followers believed that the German nation was having its political destiny, not just its boundaries, imposed on them.

Finally, if we accept the definition of nationalism as the "idea that a government rightfully rules only over citizens of a single *ethnos*,"[18] we are immediately confronted with a paradox. Despite the purported triumph of nationalism in the modern world, there are very few contemporary states that come close to meeting this standard of legitimacy. The great majority of modern states contain a variety of large cultural minorities within their borders and thus violate the principle of cultural and political congruence.[19] Why then do citizens of these states accept them as legitimate? If nationalism is "the legitimating principle of politics today,"[20] then it must demand something less than the "perfect congruence between political and ethno-cultural community."[21] We must then either reject the idea of nationalism as one of the legitimating principles of modern politics or revise our understanding of its core commitments.

I recommend the second option. Matching the boundaries of states with those of nations represents a specific interpretation of a broader and more widely accepted principle of political legitimacy: that nations should have the final say over the adequacy of the political arrangements that govern them. In other words, it is some form of national sovereignty that is sanctioned by the most widely shared nationalist principle, rather than cultural homogeneity. In even the most brutal cases of genocide and ethnic cleansing, it is the perceived—and often absurdly exaggerated—threat of subversion of the national will by minorities that inspires their persecution by nation-states, not their mere presence within national boundaries. It is thus the introduction of the belief that states should be the servants of their national communities, rather than an unprecedented intensification of distaste for cultural heterogeneity,

18. MacNeil, *Polyethnicity and National Unity*, 7.

19. Walker Connor, in an influential series of articles, "The Politics of Ethnonationalism," "A Nation Is a Nation, Is a State, Is an Ethnic Group, Is a . . . ," and "Nation-Building or Nation-Destroying" (all collected in Connor, *Ethnonationalism*), complains that less than 10 percent of the members of the United Nations are appropriately described as nation-states, if a nation-state is a political unit whose boundaries roughly correspond to the boundaries of one ethnic or cultural group.

20. A. Smith, *The Ethnic Origins of Nations*, 129.

21. Alter, *Nationalism*, 92.

that has made it so much harder for different nations to live under the same political arrangements.

The difference between these two formulations of the nationalist principle of political legitimacy may seem rather slight, but it is very significant. For one delegitimates cultural heterogeneity within a state; the other, the imposition on nations of political goals and institutions. One is inspired by a demand for cultural homogeneity; the other, by the demand to be, as Quebecois nationalists proclaim, *maîtres chez nous*. No doubt, there are some nationalists who dream of cultural homogeneity. But the insistence on being "masters in our own house" rings loud and clear everywhere nationalist rhetoric is heard. Nationalists usually want a state that they can call their own. But that desire reflects a belief that a nation should *own* or control the political arrangements by which it is governed rather than a belief that nations should share political arrangements *only* with their own kind.

Formulating the nationalist principle of political legitimacy in terms of national sovereignty rather than the congruence of national and state boundaries better captures the full range of beliefs and activities associated with nationalist politics. Nationalists often stop short of demanding their own state if they believe that federal or some other special institutional arrangements will best make the state serve their national communities. For it is the imposition of such arrangements on minority nations within larger states, rather than federalism per se, that they categorically reject. And nationalists regularly go well beyond gaining a state for their nation, since there is always the possibility of internal and external enemies who might undermine their efforts to make that state into the nation's servant.

Focusing on national sovereignty as the nationalist principle of political legitimacy thus helps make sense of the elasticity of nationalist politics. Nationalist political goals range from seeking some say in determining the arrangements that govern nations, through seeking their own national states, to stifling all of the nation's internal and external enemies. It all depends on how broadly one interprets the nation's right to have the final say over the arrangements that govern them. A narrow interpretation of this principle requires only some process of consent or consultation; the broadest interpretation, the elimination of all the obstacles that prevent nations from taking control of their political destiny. All violations of this principle can be represented by nationalists as illegitimate impositions on the life of nations. But the narrow interpretation focuses on the obstacles to consent and consultation, while the broader interpretation can make mere opposition to a nation's efforts to shape its political life seem illegitimate.

Consider, in this regard, the moral outrage expressed by so many Americans toward friends and allies opposed to the Bush administration's decision to invade Iraq. That outburst of American nationalism was inspired by resistance to American efforts to determine the best way of pursuing its national interest, not by opposition to efforts to bring all American nationals under the same political roof. If you interpret national sovereignty in the broadest fashion, then not only will your nationalism continue past the point your nation gains its own state, it is likely to persist as long as there remain any obstacles to achieving your nation's goals—in other words, it is bound to last forever. The principle of nation/state congruence lacks this openness and flexibility and therefore cannot account for the full range of nationalist politics nearly as well as the principle of national sovereignty.

Focusing on national sovereignty also helps explain how culturally heterogenous states persist despite the widespread acceptance of nationalist principles of political legitimacy. If it is the recognition of national sovereignty that is required by the nationalist principle of legitimacy, then there is nothing illegitimate in itself about cultural heterogeneity within the boundaries of a state. What makes such heterogeneity questionable is the challenge that it poses to national communities having the final say about the adequacy of their political arrangements. From this point of view, a multinational state can satisfy the nationalist principle of political legitimacy as long as its component communities believe that such a state reflects their understanding of their needs. Similarly, the presence of cultural minorities within the boundaries of a nation-state can satisfy this principle as long as the minority communities find the arrangement acceptable and the majority community does not feel control of its political fate is threatened by their presence. Indeed, far from treating culturally heterogenous states as illegitimate, the international community generally encourages efforts to sustain them, as long they are not being imposed against the will of their constituent national communities.

The problem, of course, is that it is much harder to see the state as the servant of your nation when you share its political institutions with equal or even minority partners, let alone with culturally distinctive majorities. This is the case even with a relatively narrow interpretation of national sovereignty, let alone the infinitely expansive interpretation that some nationalists are tempted to adopt. Relatively equal partners in multinational states can readily imagine how much easier it would be to reach their goals without the need for constant negotiation. Majority communities find convenient targets in cultural minorities when their political aims are blocked in some way. And cultural minorities, the most vulnerable groups, can only ease the perceived illegitimacy of the political institutions under which they live by seeking their own state, winning some special accommodations from the majority, or finding some common ground on which to build a broader, more inclusive understanding of the national community. As a result, belief in national sovereignty tends to destabilize culturally heterogenous states, even if it does not necessarily delegitimate them.

Nevertheless, the tendency toward more culturally homogenous states is a consequence of the most widely accepted nationalist principle of political legitimacy, rather than its goal. If mere congruence between national and state boundaries were the nationalist measure of political legitimacy, then it would be hard to see why so-called ethnic cleansing inspires such universal condemnation these days, since it represents one means of achieving that goal. I would suggest that ethnic cleansing is generally rejected today because it represents a particularly brutal way—expulsion and murder!—of imposing political arrangements on cultural minorities, not because it is seen as a bad means to a relatively good end.

National Sovereignty and the Intensification of National Loyalties

The depth and intensity of competing group loyalties reflect a variety of factors, such as the duration, extent, and relative significance of the things that people share. National loyalties, like national community itself, have been with us long before nationalism's rise to prominence. But until the last two or three hundred years, they have tended to be overshadowed by other, more intensely felt forms of group loyalty associated with sect, clan, and caste, and thus rarely played much of a role in political life.

The emergence of a number of beliefs that elevate the significance of national communities has changed all that. For these beliefs, especially the invocation of the nationalist principle of political legitimacy discussed in the previous section, have deepened and intensified the feelings of special concern and loyalty that connect members of national communities to each other. If we talk about nationalism today, it is largely because these deeper and more intense expressions of national loyalty have become relatively commonplace.

The belief that nations should have the final say over the political arrangements that govern them intensifies national loyalties by connecting them to some of the most powerful human passions. First, and perhaps most important, it connects the feelings of social friendship to a fundamental principle of political justice, and thus to feelings of moral indignation when we see that principle violated. As victims of injustice, the subjects of illegitimate political authority, our co-nationals become much more prominent as objects of our special concern and loyalty. We begin to take much more seriously forms of suffering and blows to their pride that would not have previously drawn much of our attention. And our efforts to help them begin to take on a much tougher edge when we begin to interpret their distress as the result of political oppression and exploitation. As Karl Marx, among others, knew very well, there are few more potent social forces in this world than the combination of moral indignation and group loyalty. Marx looked for that force in a mixture of egalitarian principles of justice and working-class solidarity. But his world and ours found that force instead in the combination of national loyalty and the principle of national sovereignty.

Second, the belief in the principle of national sovereignty deepens the significance of national loyalties by linking them to one of the most important collective responsibilities we can imagine: the establishment and control of our political institutions. In doing so, it connects national loyalty to the pride we feel in controlling the world around us and to the resentment we feel when our attempts to do so are stifled.[22] Of course, we tend to express pride in most things that we share, simply because they are our own. But beliefs in national sovereignty fuse the pride we take in a shared heritage that connects us to the pride that we feel in asserting our control over the external world, thereby encouraging us to treat any restriction of national autonomy as a sign of disrespect for our national heritage and any insult to our national heritage as a threat to our abil-

22. See Stokes, "Cognition and the Function of Nationalism," 539.

ity to master our political fate. Why, nationalists ask, should we have any less control over our political institutions than other nations? Our nation deserves no less respect than yours; so why treat us as if we lack the maturity or seriousness to become masters of our own house? It is this explosive combination of the assertion of autonomy and national loyalties that makes wounded pride and resentment so powerful and prominent a nationalist passion.[23]

Belief in the principle of national sovereignty also intensifies national loyalties by opening up vast new opportunities for the expression of shared and collective vanity. By making a political organization, the state, the servant of the nation, this principle gives the nation a collective subject it never had before, an actor whose ups and downs, compliments and slights, are felt by all members of the nation. In doing so, it allows for a kind of group identity, the identification with a collective subject that acts and reacts to the world, that members of nations rarely had in the past. It is this kind of group identity that infuses group loyalties with the force of personal vanity. Community members regularly take pride in the achievements of those to whom they feel connected. But it is only when we associate these achievements with an organization, a collective subject, that serves or represents our community—a team or a state, for example—that we begin to brag about these achievements as our own or complain that "our" achievements have not been sufficiently recognized.[24]

Finally, the belief in national sovereignty deepens and intensifies national loyalties by giving us much greater reason to fear those who do not share them. The state is an immensely powerful instrument of self-government. If people believe that the state should serve as the means by which nations rule themselves, then our foreign neighbors begin to loom in our eyes as a source of danger to us, either as the wielders of this powerful political instrument against us or as the subverters of our efforts to make it serve our nation. Indeed, it would be irrational for national minorities or small nations next to large ones not to fear their neighbors in such situations—especially given the ambiguous, infinitely inflatable character of the demand that nations be masters in their own house. And

23. Liah Greenfeld's discussion of pride and *ressentiment* in nationalism (*Nationalism*, especially 487–88) is particularly helpful.

24. See Vincent, *Nationalism and Particularity*, 34, for a good discussion of this point.

cultural majorities come to fear cultural minorities, especially those with some wealth, power, or international connections, as obstacles to their efforts to take control of their political fate. Such fears, whether rational or paranoid, do much to deepen and intensify our sense of connection to members of our national communities.

The commonest way of characterizing nationalism's intensification of national loyalties is to describe nationalism as the sentiment that makes the nation the supreme object of our loyalty. According to this view, nationalists are people who are ready to sacrifice all other commitments and ties of friendship when they come into conflict with those connected to their national communities.[25] But this common view greatly exaggerates nationalism's single-minded intensity and obscures its elasticity. Anyone who shares E. M. Forster's hope that he will always choose his friends over his country is no nationalist.[26] But anyone who *always* sacrificed her friends and family in the name of the nation would probably strike all but the greatest extremists as a monster, no matter how often nationalist ideologues might encourage such fanaticism. Does it really make sense, for example, to deny that W. B. Yeats was an Irish nationalist because he thought of nationalists as people who are "ready to give up a great deal," rather than "everything," for their nation?[27] At least one Irish nationalist thought so, but we would be foolish to agree with him. Were we to do so, we would end up with a definition of nationalism that would exclude all but its most fanatic practitioners.[28]

Friends "do what they can" for each other, rather than just what they are obliged to do.[29] Nationalists are people who will go to considerable lengths, including significant self-sacrifice, to do what they can for the members of their national communities, rather than the much more limited number of people who are ready to sacrifice everything for their nation. Those who struggle with how to balance national and other loyalties may appear less nationalistic than the extremists who demand total

25. See, e.g., Alter, *Nationalism*, 4–5; A. Smith, *Theories of Nationalism*, 21; and Berlin, "Nationalism," 338.

26. Forster, *Two Cheers for Democracy*, 76–77.

27. Yeats, *Explorations*, 118.

28. See the discussion of the affair in Gilbert, *Philosophy of Nationalism*, 50. Gilbert sensibly concludes that no definition of nationalism that would exclude the greatest of Irish nationalist poets deserves serious consideration.

29. Aristotle, *Eudemian Ethics*, 1244a21, and *Nichomachean Ethics*, 1163b15.

self-sacrifice to the nation. But the fact that they struggle at all tells us that they do indeed feel strong sentiments of national loyalty. The measurement of nationalist sentiments, as with all forms of group loyalty, requires more-or-less rather than either-or judgments.

Besides, it is often nothing more than a high degree of confidence and security that separates the relatively quiet or banal nationalists from their louder and more aggressive counterparts. The banal nationalists' loyalties are so safe and familiar that they tend to be taken for granted, even though they are flagged everyday by inherited rituals like the singing of national anthems and pledges of allegiance.[30] But scratch a banal nationalist or, more precisely, threaten the security of his or her compatriots and he or she often starts behaving in anything but banal ways. Americans, for example, may seem relatively quiet in their everyday expressions of loyalty to a shared culture—or at least they often seem that way to other Americans. But once their security is threatened, say, by terrorism or subversion, they can become quite aggressive in their expressions of national loyalty, to the point where we find them demanding that french fries be given a more American name.

In the end, it is important to remember that nationalism is a partial, rather than a total ideology. Nationalist principles tell us who should have the final say over a state's instruments of authority, not what tunes to play on them. That is one reason why nationalism combines so easily with other ideologies, from liberalism and conservatism to fascism and even socialism. It demands adjustments from our other ideological commitments rather than their abandonment. Nationalism does not dissolve all other ideological conflicts in utopian dreams of "ruritanian independence."[31] It provides, instead, some common ground on which to conduct them. Although nationalist ideologues sometimes talk as if national independence will bring an end to all present problems, nationalism does not draw its strength primarily from a utopian vision of social harmony. It draws its strength instead from a combination of loyalty toward those with whom we share a cultural heritage and resentment against those whom we believe are imposing values and institutions on our national communities.

30. See Billig, *Banal Nationalism*.

31. Hobsbawm, "Some Reflections on 'The Break-Up of Britain,'" 11–12; Beiner, "Introduction," 13–14.

Nationalism's Common Denominator

The most easily recognized forms of political nationalism are those that seek to separate nations from larger political units and those that seek to bring together divided nations into a single political unit. (They are usually characterized as separatist and integral nationalism.) But scholars also talk about the rise of nationalism in early modern states like the United Kingdom and France, where there was little need to alter the shape of the political unit. They talk about the emergence of what Benedict Anderson calls "creole nationalism," the nationalism of settler communities that reject the rule of the mother country.[32] They analyze the "official nationalism" promoted by imperial elites or their successors seeking to bolster their political legitimacy, [33] as well as the anticolonial nationalism of the subject peoples of European empires in Africa and Asia. And they wonder whether the Fascist or Nazi extremism should be identified with nationalism at all.[34]

Do all of these social phenomena share a sufficiently significant common denominator to justify treating them as species of a single genus called nationalism? Clearly, they do not if you define nationalism in terms of efforts to bring the boundaries of states into line with those of nations. But if you rely on the understanding of political nationalism developed in this chapter, as a mixture of beliefs about national sovereignty with feelings of national loyalty, then it is quite reasonable to continue to discuss them as if they represent different forms of a single social phenomenon. Since separatist and integral nationalism obviously combine national loyalties with efforts to establish national sovereignty over a state, I shall not discuss them further here. Instead, I shall begin with the earlier state-centered nationalisms that scholars identify in eighteenth-century Britain and France.

Neither of these two cases involves a battle for national independence or unity. Indeed, national independence struggles in Britain and France emerge *against* these nation-states in the name of their component or subordinated units. Moreover, in neither case is there, at least at first, much concern for the enhancement and preservation of national cultures. As a result, some scholars are inclined to treat eighteenth-century

32. B. Anderson, *Imagined Communities*, 47–66

33. Ibid., 83–112.

34. See A. Smith, *Theories of Nationalism*, 4–5, 262.

British and French nationalism as a very different kind of phenomenon, the expression of shared fidelity to civic principles rather than the expression of any kind of intergenerational loyalty.

This characterization of British and French nationalism represents another example of that form of liberal wishful thinking I have criticized as the myth of the civic nation. Linda Colley's book *Britons* should allow us, finally, to retire the familiar image of a purely civic, rationalist image of eighteenth-century British nationalism that continues to show up in contemporary scholarship. As she shows, the discovery of the British people's right to self-rule was accompanied by an increasingly touchy assertiveness about all the things that made Britons think of themselves as superior to the papists and garlic-eaters across the Channel.[35] The British and then the French, in the midst of the Revolution, were among the first to experience the combination of beliefs about national sovereignty and feelings of national sovereignty that I have argued give rise to nationalism.[36] The lack of intense or stifled sentiments about national culture in these cases does not mean that nationalism here lacks a sense of intergenerational loyalty. It only means that in these cases nationalism begins with a commitment to the sovereign people, a group that quickly comes to be imagined, given the contingencies of cultural and political history, as a nation, that is as a cultural heritage community.[37]

Creole nationalism is even more difficult to fit into most general conceptions of nationalism. For in the New World revolutions political legitimacy and group loyalty seem to be at odds with each other. Widely accepted principles of political legitimacy in these colonies led, one might argue, to demands for a kind of self-rule that the mother country refused to grant. In order to pursue self-rule the colonists, it might seem, had to abandon their loyalty to their national community and its members. Thus

35. See Colley, *Britons*. See Liah Greenfeld's *Nationalism* for the continued influence of this picture of Anglo-Saxon exceptionalism. For a critique of Greenfeld on this point, see my review essay "Reconciling Liberalism and Nationalism," 177–79.

36. John Breuilly (*Nationalism and the State*, 81–95) presents a useful account of the emergence of British and French nationalism.

37. The only real question was which cultural loyalty—English, Scots, Welsh vs. the British in Great Britain; Breton, Provencal, Catalan vs. the French in France—would fill out assertions about the people's right to rule itself. There was no reason to assume that British or French ties would win this test of cultural loyalties, especially since in many cases it did not and does not. But British and French loyalties had the advantage of making a closer fit with the already existing states.

if the British and Spanish American rebels are properly characterized as nationalists, their nationalism looks like a triumph of political principle over national loyalty, rather than the product of some kind of interaction between the two. After independence was won there may have been a lot of talk about new nations with their own distinctive cultures. But prior to independence cultural loyalty seemed to point in one direction, back to the mother country, and political convictions in another.

This conclusion, however, reflects a far too simplistic picture of cultural loyalties among Creole nationalists. Undoubtedly, for many of them the struggle for independence involved agonizing choices between cultural loyalty and political principle. But we should not forget that for the rebellious settlers it was the mother country that had betrayed them by treating them as if they were, like the indigenous inhabitants of the colonies, inferior others to be ruled from abroad rather than equal heirs to the same culture. By denying North Americans representation in Parliament, the British government was, in the settlers' eyes, denying them their rights as Englishmen, that is, denying them the hard-won rights of their English heritage, not just violating a set of abstract moral or political principles. By reserving the greatest political rights in the colonies for individuals born in Spain, the Spanish government was treating Creole settlers as if they were not really Spanish. The rebellious settlers in both cases shared a cultural identity, as betrayed Englishmen or insulted Spaniards, that inspired much of their loyalty to each other and helped give them a sense of exactly what people they were fighting to liberate.

Creole nationalism, unlike anticolonial nationalism, grows out of a disappointed expectation of cultural loyalty. Creole settlers see themselves, unlike the indigenous inhabitants of the territories that they occupy, as an extension of the mother country's cultural community. They expect, accordingly, special attention and respect from the mother country. They may treat the indigenous inhabitants of their colonies as naturally foreign and inferior to the people back home, but they certainly do not expect to be treated that way themselves. So when they are treated in this way, as if they, like the indigenous peoples, must be ruled in a different way than the people back home, they believe that they are being denied what they see as their cultural heritage. It is in the name of this cultural heritage and the loyalties it creates among them, as well as in the name of political principles, that they rebel. The act of doing so often creates a new national community whose fiery moment of birth is remembered by later generations. But even the initial act of rebellion expresses the mixture of legitimacy and loyalty that I have associated with political nationalism.[38]

Anticolonial nationalism is the clearest manifestation of a nationalism that begins with a conviction about the illegitimacy of foreign rule. Indeed, it might seem, at first, that it ends there as well, with people rising up against their distant rulers to claim their right to rule themselves. But, as in the case of Creole nationalism, this initial impression is mistaken. Anticolonial nationalism draws on sentiments of cultural loyalty as well as on convictions about political legitimacy.

The question, as in all other manifestations of nationalism, is precisely who, which people, deserves to rule itself. Creole nationalists answer this question by saying it is we settlers, we whom the mother country has betrayed by treating as others, fit only for subordination, who deserve to rule ourselves. Anticolonial nationalists, in contrast, have no expectations of cultural loyalty to be betrayed by their imperial rulers. They have been told by their imperial masters directly and unapologetically that they are being ruled precisely because of their racial and cultural inferiority. Mutual loyalty among those who have shared and inherited this experience of cultural subordination, as well as convictions about political legitimacy, inspires their rebellion. Sentiments of cultural loyalty and convictions about political legitimacy feed off of each other in anticolonial nationalism because of the way in which claims of racial and cultural inferiority were used to justify colonial rule. As Crawford Young suggests with regard to African peoples, "in time, the subject populations internalized their classification as other, fused it to the emergent doctrines of nation and self-determination, and fashioned an ultimately invincible weapon of liberation."[39]

The problem with fitting official nationalism into general conceptions of nationalism is the opposite of that created by Creole and anticolonial nationalism. Official nationalism looks like a way of tapping national loyalties to shore up the legitimacy of imperial or postimperial elites. As such, it seems to have little to do with commitments to national sovereignty. In the successor regimes to collapsed empires, as in Atatürk's Turkey, leaders may be genuinely convinced that they are ruling as the

38. Other forms of settler nationalism, as among the Boers or Israelis, lack the complicating factor of continued cultural ties to a mother country and are therefore much easier to explain in the framework provided in this chapter.

39. Young, *The African Colonial State in Comparative Perspective*, 44.

representative of the sovereign nation they work so hard to create. But in waning or reviving empires, such as czarist Russia, Ottoman Turkey, or Meiji Japan, the appeal to national loyalties seems designed precisely to preserve dynastic legitimacy from appeals to one version or another of popular sovereignty. So it looks like we have found at least one form of political nationalism that does not rest on a commitment to national sovereignty.

I believe, however, that official nationalism is not quite so straightforwardly opposed to national sovereignty as it may first appear to be. For the appeals to national loyalties made by imperial dynasts are rarely successful unless the dynasties can recreate themselves as symbols or representatives of the nation and its intergenerational community. But to do so is more or less to acknowledge that the nation rather than the dynasty is the source of political legitimacy—which is why most official nationalists are quite ambivalent about the appeal to national loyalties. The trick is to pull off this transformation into the symbol of the nation without losing power to other groups that can make a better claim to represent the nation. Few imperial nationalists have fully succeeded in doing so.

The most successful case, Meiji Japan, is sui generis, and shows clearly what was lacking in the attempts of most other empires to use nationalism to legitimate their authority. The supporters of the Meiji restoration succeeded in transforming the emperor into the object of a national cult that made him the ultimate source of both Japanese national identity and the state's authority.[40] As such, the emperor was both the ultimate representative of the nation and the object of dynastic or hereditary loyalty. But this solution to the problems of official nationalism is so dependent on the peculiarities of Japanese religious and political history that it has proved almost impossible to imitate elsewhere. The fascist cult of the leader (*il Duce*, *der Führer*) aimed at a similar goal,[41] but lacked the independent, dynastic source of legitimacy that Japanese emperors could call upon. Fascist leaders, in the end, owed their authority to their supposed ability to divine and give voice to the higher needs and interests of the nation, and thus presented themselves as means of achieving na-

40. See Bix, *Hirohito and the Making of Modern Japan*, 107, 280.

41. Indeed, some Italian Fascists consciously aimed, with mixed results, to recreate something like the Japanese emperor cult. See ibid., 280, and Gentile, *The Sacralization of Politics in Fascist Italy*, 14.

tional sovereignty. Even Hitler proudly declared that his "conscience has but one single commander—our *Volk*."[42]

Finally, doubts have been expressed about whether we should think of fascism, and especially Nazism, as an expression of nationalist beliefs and sentiments. The problem here is clearly not a lack of strong assertions of national loyalty. Rather it is the suspicion that nationalist principles of political legitimacy play no role in promoting these assertions of national loyalty, since Mussolini, let alone Hitler, was hardly inclined to respect the right of others to national self-determination. But, as I have argued, it is the combination of loyalty and legitimacy, of special concern for one's own nation and belief in national sovereignty that defines political nationalism. In other words, political nationalism arises when people believe that it is illegitimate to interfere with their nation's efforts to become masters in their own political house. This is a belief that someone like Hitler pushed to undreamed of extremes. Accordingly, it makes sense to place his political movement at the far end of the nationalist continuum, the end that displays the most expansive vision of national sovereignty and the least concern for the rights of others, rather than as an example of another social phenomenon altogether.

Indeed, it is important to remind ourselves again that nationalist demands expand and contract according to the breadth of one's understanding of the meaning of national sovereignty. For Hitler, any obstacles to the German nation's attempts to control its internal or external environment were illegitimate impositions on its right to be master in its own house and had to be eliminated. For many others, it is only the failure to seek the approval of national communities for their basic political institutions that violates the nationalist principle of political legitimacy. There is both good and bad news in the elasticity of nationalism for those who seek to restrain the violence and instability that it often inspires. The good news is that the most common of nationalist principles does not rule out compromises that fall short of the unachievable goal of giving every nation its own state. The bad news is that even if we could give every nation its own state, that would not necessarily tame nationalism, since nationalism is inspired by the infinitely expansible desire to take control of our political fate, rather than the much more limited and specific desire to correct the boundaries of states.

42. Quoted in Koonz, *The Nazi Conscience*, 4.

CHAPTER SIX

Popular Sovereignty and the Rise of Nationalism

If the nation is relatively old and nationalism relatively new or modern, then the rise and spread of nationalism confronts us with a fairly straightforward question: what has changed in the last two or three hundred years to make the nation an object of such powerful feelings and political importance? In this chapter I suggest that a distinctly liberal innovation, the new understanding of popular sovereignty discussed in chapter 4, plays the pivotal role in politicizing and thus intensifying our attachments to national communities. Nationalism, I argue, emerged first in early modern Europe because that is where this new principle of political legitimacy was invented and first appropriated by people who imagined themselves members of national communities. And it has spread so widely because this new principle has displaced its rivals in one part of the world after another, encountering different expressions of national loyalty wherever it has gone.

Even a brief glance at modern history suggests that there is an important connection between popular sovereignty and the rise of nationalism. For wherever popular sovereignty leads, from the French Revolution in 1789 to the collapse of the Soviet Empire in 1989, nationalism seems quickly to follow. Chart the path taken by the new conception of popular sovereignty as it displaces rival principles of political legitimacy and you get a pretty good sense of nationalism's march across the globe. Of course, I am not suggesting that a commitment to this new understanding of the people as constituent sovereign is a necessary condition for the expression of nationalism. Other paths have led to the same result in the past and will probably continue to do so in the future. I do, however, make the following claims: (1) the combination of feelings of national loyalty with commitments to the new idea of popular sovereignty is sufficient to produce nationalist attitudes and behavior; (2) these conditions were met first in early modern Europe and then spread to the rest of the world with the dissemination of this new understanding of popular sovereignty; (3) and, as a result, the spread of nationalism follows the increasing acceptance of this new principle of political legitimacy more than any other feature of modern social and political life.

My reliance on the spread of a particular belief about popular sovereignty to explain the rise and spread of nationalism is bound to inspire at least two kinds of objections. First of all, it might make it seem as if I am trying to reduce an extremely complex social phenomenon to the influence of a single factor. Second, the single factor to which I may seem to be reducing nationalism is a set of beliefs or ideas, which will probably make my approach seem far too idealist, as well as monistic, to suit the tastes of many students of the subject.

In answer to the first objection let me emphasize that my account of nationalism focuses on the interaction of *two* distinct factors, convictions about political legitimacy and sentiments of group loyalty, not just on a single cause and its consequences. Students of nationalism have done an excellent job of explaining why national loyalties persist and become commonplace in the modern age, despite widespread expectations that the spread of commerce and industrial society would lead to their disappearance. They have identified a large number of different factors that can help us account for this surprising development. But because most theorists are inclined to explain nationalism in terms of whatever it is that they believe inspires national loyalties, they tend to treat these different factors as the foundations for mutually exclusive theories of nationalism. My approach, in contrast, allows us to make use of *all* of these different insights in our theories of nationalism because I focus on the politicization of national loyalties in my account of the rise and spread of nationalism, rather than on the emergence of national loyalties themselves. Far from denying the variety and complexity of nationalism as a social phenomenon, I hope that my approach will make room for a greater variety of sources of national loyalty than its rivals.

As for concerns about the idealism of my approach, I think I can diminish them to a certain extent by noting that I do not treat the new ideas about popular sovereignty as an independent phenomenon, as a kind of unmoved mover in history. These ideas develop in response to a variety of independent historical developments, the most important of which is the emergence of the modern state as a distinctive form of political organization. The image of the people as a prepolitical source of legitimate authority only makes sense as a response to problems posed by that distinctive form of political organization. Moreover, as already indicated, I believe that we need to draw on all sorts of nonidealist insights to explain the persistence and growth of national loyalties in the modern world.

Nevertheless, I do not want to hide the fact that I am making the spread of a certain way of thinking the key factor in my account of the rise and spread of nationalism. Doing so does not reflect any more general commitment to idealist explanations in history. It merely reflects my conclusion that in this particular case a new way of thinking about politics was the catalyst for the production of a powerful new social force, one that its inventors certainly were not seeking to create. Ideas, I believe, do matter very much at certain points in history, but rarely in the ways that they were intended to matter.

Explaining the Phenomenon

The previous chapter argued that nationalism, at least in its most common and powerful form, represents an explosive mixture of beliefs about national sovereignty and feelings of mutual concern and loyalty for the members of one's national community. If this characterization of nationalism is accurate, then we need to account for the emergence and near universal dissemination of both in order to explain the rise and spread of nationalism.

Nationalism's students, as already noted, have done a splendid job of identifying reasons for the surprising strength of national loyalties in modern times. The impact of state centralization and competition, the Romantic celebration of folk culture, the social stress created by modernization, industrial society's need for greater cultural homogeneity, secular society's need for an undying collective subject with which to identify—these are just some of the most important factors that scholars have identified as sources of the persistence and spread of national loyalties in the modern age. All of them should have a place in any satisfactory theory of nationalism. But while these factors help us explain the unexpected expansion and persistence of national loyalties in the modern world, they do not necessarily explain their politicization. If we want to explain the rise of nationalism, we need to figure out why national community has taken on such unprecedented political importance in the modern world, not just why it has survived in conditions that were expected to lead to its disappearance.

The simplest way of accounting for the rise of commitments to national sovereignty would be to identify an ideological movement that succeeded in persuading (or indoctrinating) people to commit themselves to its core principles. Few scholars, however, have attempted to explain the rise of nationalism in this way.[1] No doubt, their reluctance to do so reflects a general disinclination to rely on the diffusion of ideas to explain large-scale social changes. But it also reflects a general lack of evidence to support this relatively simple and direct approach to accounting for the rise of nationalism. The great ideological campaigns in the history of nationalism have tended to focus on convincing people of one vision or another of their national heritage and destiny, rather than on convincing people to think of nations as sovereign. Moreover, the most influential philosophy of nationalism, Herder's celebration of national folk cultures, does not even make the achievement of national sovereignty one of its goals.[2] National sovereignty, I suggest, is something that people tend to take for granted, a by-product of other beliefs or sentiments that they share, rather than the central focus of ideological battles. For this reason most theories of nationalism offer more indirect explanations of its emergence and dissemination around the world.

The great majority of these theories treat the assertion of national sovereignty as a product of the intensification of national loyalties in recent times. In other words, they assume that people demand national self-determination because they have come to feel so strongly about their national communities that nothing but some form of national sovereignty will satisfy them. Where these theories differ is in their accounts of what leads to the intensification of national loyalties in modern societies. Many nationalists, like Mazzini, believe that people are naturally disposed to identify with their national communities as a focus for

1. The major exception is Elie Kedourie in his influential critique of nationalism. Kedourie, *Nationalism*. Kedourie's argument is subjected to a withering critique by Ernest Gellner (*Nations and Nationalism*, 39–40, 123–30), among others.

2. At least, not directly. See F. M. Barnard's insightful comparative study of Rousseau and Herder, *Self-Direction and Political Legitimacy*.

self-government. They tend, accordingly, to treat the modern intensification of national loyalties as a product of our liberation from the forms of domination and repression that have suppressed national feeling in the past. Some critics of nationalism share this inclination and treat the rise of nationalism as the return of primitive expressions of group loyalty that modern societies have unsuccessfully tried to repress.[3] "Modernist" theorists of nationalism, like Ernest Gellner, tend to ridicule such "sleeping beauty" and "dark god" theories of nationalism.[4] But they too explain the assertion of national sovereignty in terms of the intensification of national loyalties in the modern age. They merely identify other, distinctly modern factors, such as industrial society's need for a homogenous high culture within political units, in order to explain why national loyalties have deepened and intensified to the point where modern individuals demand political sovereignty for their nations.

The modernists' arguments seem plausible because both nationalism and the processes associated with modernization have followed a similar route in their march from western Europe in the eighteenth and nineteenth centuries to the rest of the world. Moreover, they are supported by the fact that the nation-state has provided a relatively stable platform upon which to develop these processes, such as the new forms of production that distinguish what Gellner calls industrial society. But these arguments are undermined by the fact that the emergence of nationalism often *precedes* rather than follows the processes of modernization in their march across the globe. This is the case with the first stirrings of nationalism in seventeenth-century England and eighteenth-century France, with the so-called Creole nationalisms of North and South America, and with many of the separatist nationalisms of Central and Eastern Europe. Liah Greenfeld goes too far when she reverses the causal arrow and describes modernization as a product of nationalism rather than the other way round. But she is certainly right that "the emergence of nationalism predated the development of every significant component of modernization."[5]

How should we sort out this conflicting evidence about the relationship between nationalism and modernization? Modernist theorists of nationalism do so by either denying the existence of the earlier instances

3. For example, Isaacs, *Idols of the Tribe*.

4. Gellner, *Nations and Nationalism*, 48, 130.

5. Greenfeld, *Nationalism*, 20–21. See also J. A. Hall, "Nationalisms, Classified and Explained," 129.

of nationalism or expanding their understanding of modernity to include earlier developments, like the emergence of the modern state. I suggest, instead, that we distinguish between the factors that help explain nationalism's initial emergence and dissemination from those that help explain its strength and persistence. The unexpected affinities between national community and industrial society uncovered by social theorists like Gellner help us understand why nations have put down such strong roots in a world that was expected to be hostile to them. But these affinities cannot account for the emergence of nationalism in places where they had not yet made themselves felt. As a result, they can help us explain why nationalism thrives in modern conditions, but not its origins nor its path of dissemination around the world.

Of course, if one extends one's conception of modernity to include earlier political innovations, like the consolidation of the modern state, then modernization begins to look much more plausible as an explanation for the rise of nationalism. But extending the concept of modernity in this way dilutes its substance by arguing as if all new or temporally modern social developments share a common, distinctively modern character.[6] The modern state eventually proved compatible with the new forms of production and association identified with modernization; but there is no necessary connection between the two. Since the modern state represents a new or temporally modern form of political organization as well as, in my view, a necessary condition for the rise and spread of nationalism, it is tempting to lump it together with other modern social innovations and insist that nationalism is a product of something called modernization. But in doing so, all one would really be saying is that nationalism is a new or temporally modern development, a development made possible by a number of distinct and disconnected innovations in social organization, rather than that nationalism is a product of a substantive process called modernization.

Most theories of nationalism seem to assume that if you can explain why national community has become or remained popular in the modern age, then you will have explained why it has become politicized as well.[7] I believe, however, that this assumption is mistaken. The persis-

6. My earlier book, *The Fetishism of Modernities*, identifies and criticizes this common fallacy, in which the temporal and substantive senses of the concept of modernity are conflated.

7. For an important exception, see Breuilly, *Nationalism and the State*.

tence and the politicization of national loyalties in the modern age are two distinct phenomena; they require different explanations. The wide range of insights into the former needs to be supplemented by a better account of the latter, an account that requires us to look more closely at the principle of popular sovereignty and its impact on the modern social imagination.

Popular Sovereignty and Democracy

This connection between nationalism and popular sovereignty has not gone unnoticed. But despite repeated claims that "nationalism is incoherent without popular sovereignty" or that nationalism is nothing more than "the application to national community of the Enlightenment doctrine of popular sovereignty,"[8] there has not been much of a sustained effort at explaining why this is true.[9] Those who make this claim often seem to assume that the meaning of popular sovereignty and its application to the nation is self-evident or at least fairly easy to grasp. In doing so, I shall argue, they are mistaken on both fronts. For the new popular sovereignty doctrine has altered our understanding of political community in ways that are anything but self-evident, and it is by means of this altered understanding of political community that it has made its greatest contribution to the rise and spread of nationalism.

The commonest explanation of the parallels between popular and national sovereignty is also the simplest: share power with the people and you free them to assert their nationality. Democratizing government, according to this argument, is bound to nationalize it. "Bring the people into political life" and "they arrive marching in tribal ranks and orders, carrying with them their own language, historical memories, customs, beliefs, and commitments."[10]

There is much to be said in favor of this explanation of popular sovereignty's contribution to the politicization of national loyalties. Nevertheless, it has serious limitations. First of all, the history of democratic republics does not support the claim that when you free ordinary people to

8. Kohn, *The Idea of Nationalism*, 3; Seton-Watson, *Nations and States*, 445.

9. For interesting exceptions, see Greenfeld, *Nationalism*, 25–26; Canovan, *Nationhood and Political Theory*; and above all, Hont, "Permanent Crisis."

10. Walzer, "The New Tribalism," 206.

enter politics they will assert their national loyalties. The citizens of ancient and Renaissance city-states knew what it meant to think of themselves as Greeks and Italians. But they rarely connected that sense of national community to political life.[11] That suggests that something more than liberation from the constraints of undemocratic forms of government must lie behind the politicization of national loyalties in modern democracies. Second, the spread of popular sovereignty doctrines often works to promote the discovery and intensification of national loyalties, rather than merely remove constraints on their expression. That too suggests that the connection between popular sovereignty and nationalism involves something more than democratization. Finally, a focus on democratization unduly narrows the scope of popular sovereignty's influence on nationalism. For even authoritarian and totalitarian nationalists invoke popular sovereignty to justify their demands for extreme forms of national self-assertion.[12] In doing so, they insist that a free and wise people would invest their authority in a party or a leader that best embodies their nation's will. Recall Hitler's declaration that his "conscience has but one single commander—our *Volk*."[13] That suggests that illiberal and antidemocratic interpretations of popular sovereignty may also contribute to the politicization of national loyalties.

It is a mistake, in any case, to identify the modern doctrine of popular sovereignty with a commitment to democratic forms of government. The doctrine of popular sovereignty popularized by the English, American, and French Revolutions definitely promotes a more egalitarian picture of political order, since it denies that any individual or group can claim political authority as a proprietary right. And it provides the starting point for justifications for more democratic forms of government, as one extends the doctrine from constituent to governmental conceptions of sovereignty. But, as we have seen, this new doctrine of popular sovereignty invests final authority in an *imagined* association, the set of all of a territory's permanent inhabitants imagined in abstraction from their current form of political organization, rather than in any institutionally defined, flesh and blood majority. Alongside images of the people who make the decisions in a democratic government and the ordinary or

11. See Finley, "The Ancient Greeks and Their Nation," and Yack, "The Myth of the Civic Nation," 111–14.

12. See Mann, *Fascists*, and Emerson, *From Empire to Nation*, 214.

13. Quoted in Koonz, *The Nazi Conscience*, 4.

common people, it constructs a new image of the people as the prepolitical group that establishes and dissolves the political arrangements that organize our lives.

It is the growing commitment to this new understanding of popular sovereignty that plays a crucial role in the rise and spread of the belief in national sovereignty, rather than a commitment to democracy. For this new image of the people tends to nationalize our understanding of politics and politicize our understanding of nationality. On the one hand, it encourages people who imagine themselves members of the group that shares the final authority over a particular state to think of themselves as members of an intergenerational or national community as well. On the other hand, it encourages people who imagine themselves connected to each other by a shared cultural heritage of some sort or other to think of their national community as sovereign as well. The first path is most common among nationalists who discover old nations or invent new ones in the wake of the collapse of larger political structures such as multinational or overseas empires. The second path is the most common among nationalists who seek to integrate a politically divided cultural community into a new national state or who seek to separate from a larger multinational state or empire. And in states that are already associated with a core national community, such as seventeenth-century England or late eighteenth-century France, the introduction of this new idea of the sovereign people opens up both paths to the emergence of nationalism.

These two distinct paths to the emergence of nationalism might, at first, seem to lend credence to the kind of dichotomies between ethnic and civic nationalism that I rejected in the first chapter. For they might suggest to some that the term nationalism refers to two kinds of social force mistakenly treated as one: intergenerational cultural loyalties seeking political expression and political loyalties seeking some form of cultural expression. But this suggestion is misleading. For no matter which of these two paths you start out on, you end up in the same place: with a social force that blends convictions about political legitimacy with sentiments of intergenerational loyalty. And you end up there regardless of whether the national community that you come to think of as sovereign is imagined as an age-old community or as a new one grounded in a constitutional founding. The discovery or invention of an age-old community as the bearer of sovereignty will, no doubt, inspire different and probably more exclusive feelings than the invention of a new community with a celebrated act of political founding. But in both cases beliefs about sovereignty come to be connected to a sense of belonging to an intergenerational community. And it is this connection between conviction and sentiment, between political legitimacy and intergenerational loyalty, which gives nationalism its distinctive character as a social phenomenon.

The Nationalization of Political Community

Let us begin with the nationalization of political community. Defenders of the new doctrine of popular sovereignty argue that monarchs and aristocrats usurp an inalienable right of the people when they claim the right to make unlimited and arbitrary use of the state's authority over persons and territory. But, as we have seen, they do not counter these claims to personal sovereignty by insisting that the people, rather than the monarch or aristocrats, possess this right to make unlimited use of the state's authority. Instead, they argue that whatever form the political regime may take, it derives its authority from a territory's inhabitants, imagined as a collective body.

Understood in this way, the people represents a new way of imagining political association. In earlier conceptions what binds the political community is sharing either subjection to a particular kind of political authority or the opportunity to take turns in exercising that authority.[14] But the people, as imagined by the defenders of popular sovereignty, represents neither the absolutist's community of subjects nor the republican's community of sharers in ruling. Instead, it is the body of citizens from which political authority arises and to which it reverts when that authority no longer serves its proper function. Since popular sovereignty, in this new conception, is indirect or mediated sovereignty, something other than the structure of political institutions or the exercise of ruling and being ruled must define the people who exercises it. For if the people precede the establishment and survive the dissolution of political authority, then they must share something beyond a relationship to that authority.

But what is that common, prepolitical characteristic? The lack of a

14. The classic statement of the traditional, activist understanding of citizenship is found in Aristotle's *Politics* (1275a23), that the citizen is someone who shares in "ruling and adjudicating" and takes turns in ruling and being ruled.

consistent answer to this question opens the door to the identification of political with national community. For the nation provides precisely what is lacking in the concept of the people: a sense of where to look for the prepolitical basis of political community that the latter evokes. By encouraging us to think of political community as distinct from and prior to the establishment of political authority, the new popular sovereignty doctrine brings our image of political community much closer to national community than it had been in the past.

Of course, the nationalization or culturalization of political community is an unintended consequence of the widespread acceptance of the doctrine of popular sovereignty. The doctrine's defenders certainly did not intend to transform our image of political community in this way. They were attempting, instead, to solve the problem of legitimacy and limited government. But the way in which they solved this problem introduces a new one: the identification of political with cultural community. For in order to conjure up an image of the people as standing apart from and prior to the establishment of political authority, you have to think of its members as sharing something more than political relationships. And the pre- or extra-political community that most resembles the form of the people is the intergenerational community celebrated by nations. The problem is thus not just that the doctrine of popular sovereignty ignores the prepolitical foundations of political community. It is rather that this doctrine encourages us to look for those prepolitical foundations in the places where national loyalties lurk. The new doctrine of popular sovereignty does not just lack the means of resisting the nationalistic sentiments of the people it brings into politics. It positively invites the nationalization or culturalization of politics by the way in which it transforms our image of political community.

One can see this process underway in early modern England, the site where, many would agree, both the new doctrine of popular sovereignty was invented and nationalism first emerges. English or British nationalism has been frequently portrayed as a prime example of a purely civic or political nationalism—most emphatically by Liah Greenfeld in her book *Nationalism: Five Roads to Modernity*.[15] As already noted, the disdain shown by British patriots for the character of their French rivals

15. I discuss the strengths and weaknesses of Greenfeld's argument in "Reconciling Liberalism and Nationalism," 175–80.

makes this portrait hard to accept.[16] More interesting here, however, is how the assertion of particular cultural loyalties follows directly on the heels of the assertion of popular sovereignty, a development apparent in many of the very passages that Greenfeld cites to defend her claim that Anglo-American visions of nationhood lack the emphasis on "unique characteristics" celebrated by ethnic nationalists in Germany and other points eastward.[17]

When John Milton, for example, brags that it is their new and unprecedented civil liberties that give the English "the honour to precede other nations," he is certainly identifying the English community with a form of civil liberty rather than any kind of cultural heritage. But when he goes on to talk about why Englishmen deserve these liberties, he makes it clear that he has a very different understanding of community in mind. "Consider what Nation," he asks Parliament, "it is whereof ye are the governours: a Nation not slow and dull, but of a quick, ingenious, and piercing, spirit, acute to invent, suttle and sinewy to discourse." These shared characteristics, this shared heritage, help Milton explain why the English are the "nation chos'n before any other" to receive from God his epoch-making revelation of liberty.[18] Indeed, the very claim that England has "the honour to precede other Nations" makes it absolutely clear that Milton does *not* view nationhood as nothing more than a container for popular sovereignty and civil liberties. For it is precisely the achievement of these things that distinguishes England from other nations.

One might complain that what is happening here is that two different images of national community are being superimposed on each other: one of the nation as a body of citizens and the other as a cultural community with unique historical characteristics. Nationalism, from this point of view, involves "a sleight of hand" whereby one uses the same word for the two different images of community without acknowledging their opposition.[19] But such a complaint misses the fact that both of these

16. See especially Colley, *Britons*. Indeed, an eighteenth-century Swiss writer (quoted by David Bell in *The Cult of the Nation in France*, 44–45) complained that "no people hates more than the English hate the French."

17. Greenfeld, *Nationalism*, 3–14, 76–77.

18. Quoted in ibid., 76–77. The quotations are mostly from Milton's most famous and influential political essay, *Areopagitica*.

19. This argument is presented most effectively by Breuilly, *Nationalism and the State*, 62, 390.

images of community, the demos as a body of citizens and the nation as a prepolitical cultural community, provide ways of representing a *third* image of group membership, the people of the new doctrine of popular sovereignty. Each captures one aspect of that image of community—the demos its inclusiveness, the nation its prepolitical character—while missing other aspects. It is not surprising then that they should be asserted together. As we have seen, the people constructed by the new popular sovereignty doctrine is an especially abstract group. It invites representation in more concrete images in order, so to speak, to put some flesh on the body politic. It would indeed involve a "sleight of hand" to represent an institutionally defined body of citizens as a nation or unique cultural community. But in order to represent the *preinstitutional* people of popular sovereignty theory as a nation all that one needs is imagination and some cultural heritage of shared symbols and memories to call upon.

The Politicization of National Community

Let me turn now to the second half of my argument, the way in which popular sovereignty doctrines tend to politicize our image of nationality. Popular sovereignty's vision of indirect sovereignty nationalizes our image of political community by encouraging us to look for the prepolitical and cultural roots that bind the people into a community. It politicizes our image of national community, in contrast, by introducing a principle that effectively delegitimates foreign rule. The principle of popular sovereignty does not endorse demands that nations should have the final say in how they are to be ruled. But by denying the legitimacy of foreign rule in the name of a group that, as we have seen, parallels the nation in important and unprecedented ways, it gives national loyalties a political importance that they never had before.

The new doctrine of popular sovereignty introduces a principle by which we can measure the legitimacy of governments: legitimate governments derive their authority in some way from the people, from the permanent residents of the territories that they control. In doing so, it clearly rules out forms of political authority justified solely by claims of family inheritance, personal privilege, divine right, or superior worth. But it also rejects forms of political authority that are derived from foreign sources, including foreign peoples, since it insists that legitimate authority must be derived in some way from the people over whom it is exercised. As a result, the new principle of popular sovereignty challenges imperial rule, rule over groups explicitly defined as other, as well as monarchic and aristocratic rule.[20]

Popular sovereignty doctrines teach us to think of states as masters of territory and peoples as masters of states. Or to put it another way, they teach us that states are the means by which people establish their mastery over given territories. Such mastery, based as it is on the use of the state's singular structure of authority, is exclusive by its very definition. No more than one people can be master of a given territory, since the state, with its exclusive claim to authority, is the means by which it is exercised.

The assertion of this new kind of communal mastery of territory leaves little room for the vaguer and less exclusive connections to territory that have so long characterized national communities. No longer can we think of the same territory as belonging to different nations. How can we continue to talk about a territory as "our own" when another group—moreover a group that, as we have seen, almost inevitably expresses itself in national terms—claims exclusive mastery over it? Pride, fear, envy, or just a strong sense of justice and injustice makes anything less than such mastery seem dangerous or degrading to those who lack it. In this way, the dissemination of ideas about popular sovereignty politicizes national loyalties, as the leaders of one national group after another demand that they be *maîtres chez nous*. "We do not ask Austria be humane and liberal in Italy," proclaimed Daniele Manin, leader of the ill-fated Venetian revolt in 1848, "we ask her to get out. We have no concern with her humanity and liberalism we wish to be masters in our own house."[21]

Of course, popular sovereignty doctrines insist that it is the people, the collective body of a territory's inhabitants, rather than a national community, that should exercise such mastery. Nevertheless, these doctrines open the door to assertions of national sovereignty by justifying the right of peoples to disestablish and reconstruct the authority of the state. For when popular sovereignty doctrines arrive on the scene they find people living not only with the injustices that flow from absolutism, feudal privilege, and other abuses of authority within states, but with all

20. I discuss the emergence of the anti-imperial consequences of the new doctrine of popular sovereignty below, in chapter 10, "What's Wrong with National Rights to Self-Determination."

21. Quoted in Emerson, *From Empire to Nation*, 43.

of the injustices that come from the history of conquest, royal marriages, sales of territory, and just plain bad luck that defines the boundaries of states and empires. When introduced to the new doctrine of popular sovereignty, some people find themselves ruled from distant and alien capitals from which they can expect little understanding or sympathy for distinctive local conditions. Others find themselves subject to the authority of imperial rulers who treat them as inferior races incapable of civilized forms of self-government. Still others find themselves dangerously exposed minorities within larger communities that share a sense of belonging to a national community. The establishment of legitimate and humane forms of government might ease many concerns about injustice for these groups of people. But it would be foolish or naive to say that it could erase all of the potential for injustice that is created by the history of force, fraud, and chance that has led to the current boundaries among states.

Defenders of popular sovereignty often proclaim that human beings are capable "of establishing good government from reflection and choice," rather than "destined to depend, for their political constitutions, on accident and force."[22] But why should exposed minorities, subordinated peoples, and those at the periphery of large indifferent states simply accept state boundaries as given when they begin to think about how to establish legitimate structures of political authority with which to govern themselves? It is one thing when you tell the members of a group who form the great majority of a state's subjects—Englishmen, say—to take for granted the state's boundaries in their deliberations about what the people should do. It is quite another when you tell that to the members of the other groups I have just mentioned. To tell them that they must simply cast their lot with whatever group that history has served up to them seems manifestly unfair. Why should the dance of history that provided some people with communities stop just when *they* get a turn to express themselves on the floor? One does not have to believe, with Herder and Mazzini, that nations are natural divisions of the human race in order to express impatience with such a demand.[23] One need only share their perfectly reasonable insistence

22. Hamilton, Jay, and Madison, *The Federalist Papers*, no. 1.

23. "Natural divisions, the spontaneous tendencies of the peoples will replace the arbitrary divisions sanctioned by bad governments. The countries of the People will rise,

on the arbitrariness or artificiality of the historical divisions among states.

Resignation to the contingencies of history does not fit well at all with the rhetoric of popular sovereignty. Yet, in effect, that is what many liberal democratic theorists seem to demand from peoples uncomfortable with the shape of their communities: that they should accept whatever potential injustices history has served up to them with the boundaries of states so that we can all get on with the task of establishing liberal democratic forms of government. The fact that this advice almost invariably comes from people who are quite comfortable and unexposed within the given boundaries of states, people who are happy with the partners they were given when the music stopped playing at the dance of history, makes it particularly hard to accept.

Thus while the new popular sovereignty doctrine is not designed to help us determine the legitimacy of a particular community's control over a particular territory, it definitely opens the door to this question. And in doing so it raises a question that it cannot itself answer. Who belongs to the people in 1848 Venice, 1955 Algeria, or 1999 Quebec? Inhabitants of Venice, Algeria, or Quebec or all of the Austrians and Italians, Frenchmen and Arabs, Anglophones and Francophones who share the boundaries of the larger states to which they belonged at the time? We cannot simply say to those who put forward competing claims to territory in the name of different peoples, "let the people decide," since it is precisely which people should be associated with which territory that is at issue. Does letting the people decide disputes like those surrounding demands for Quebecois independence require a referendum among all the citizens within the boundaries of the province of Quebec or among all the citizens within the boundaries ruled by the federal government of Canada? You cannot answer such questions without, in effect, taking sides in the issue that you want to put before the people.[24]

You need to assume the existence of boundaries between peoples before you can exercise the principle of popular sovereignty. Therefore, you cannot use popular sovereignty to determine where the boundaries be-

---

defined by the voice of the free, upon the ruins of the countries of Kings and privileged castes." Mazzini, *The Duties of Man*, 52.

24. See, e.g., Whelan, "Democratic Theory and the Boundary Problem," 13, and Canovan, *Nationhood and Political Theory*, 17–18.

tween peoples should lie. Popular sovereignty can help guide us in determining our political arrangements. It cannot help us decide how to determine the shape of our collective selves. But by arguing that this collective self, the people, precedes and survives the state, it opens up the question of how to determine our collective selves and their control of states and territory. Where there is little concern or discomfort with the given boundaries of the state, this question will probably not surface. But where there is some controversy or discomfort, the inconsistency between these two ways of talking about self-determination is bound to come out. For while popular sovereignty rests on the assumption that the state is the creature of the people, to be dissolved and reconstituted as the people will, the people only receives limits of its identity from the boundaries of the state. It is little wonder then that those who are uncomfortable with the boundaries that history has delivered to them start looking to other visions of community as the source of state sovereignty. The modern doctrine of popular sovereignty does not single out national communities and encourage them to take control of their own affairs. But it does justify the delegitimation of state boundaries without giving any useful guidance—other than resignation—to those who are dissatisfied with the way in which they currently divide up political and cultural communities.

For while the new understanding of popular sovereignty effectively delegitimates foreign rule, it provides a subjectively arbitrary definition of the peoples who have the right to rule themselves. The people, according to popular sovereignty doctrine, is a group of individuals who share a politically defined territory and the institutions of government that operate within them. That makes the boundaries between one people and another depend upon the history of force, fraud, and convenience that has shaped the formation of states, rather than on any subjective ties of mutual concern and loyalty. By delegitimating foreign rule without giving us any principled alternative to national community as a way of justly dividing ourselves into different political communities the new principle of popular sovereignty politicizes these ties, especially among those who share some sense of national heritage.

If this account of the political impact of new understanding of popular sovereignty is accurate, then we should expect nationalism to emerge wherever such commitments are held by people who also share some sense of belonging to a national community. The course of nationalism's march through the modern world tends to confirm this hypothesis. For nationalism first appears in early modern France, England, and Holland, where the new understanding of popular sovereignty was first developed. And it then spreads along a path that is defined by the high points in the dissemination of this understanding of popular sovereignty: the North and South American wars of independence, the French Revolution, the 1848 revolutions, and the breakup of Eastern European, colonial, and Soviet empires.

The two conditions that first gave rise to nationalism in early modern Europe, a sense of national loyalty and a commitment to the new understanding of popular sovereignty as a condition of political legitimacy, are now shared around the world. The sense of connection to a national community has persisted and spread throughout the modern world, for a variety of reasons that students of nationalism have ably laid out. And the principle of popular sovereignty has effectively displaced its rivals—the last of which, the derivation of authority from the superior knowledge and commitments of the Marxist-Leninist vanguard party, crumbled with the collapse of Soviet communism—as a source of political legitimacy. Today, almost every regime, no matter how undemocratic, claims to derive its legitimacy in some way from the people it rules. Sufficient conditions for the emergence of nationalism are now in place throughout the modern world. Other factors surely swell this nationalist tide. But we can easily account for it without invoking them once we recognize the way in which commitments to the new understanding of popular sovereignty politicizes national loyalties.

Nations without Nationalism?

If I am right about the connection between popular sovereignty and nationalism, then nationalism may be a lot harder to separate from liberal democratic politics than its critics realize. Nationalism threatens liberal democratic political principles and practices primarily by the way in which it connects political rights and privileges to relatively exclusive understandings of intergenerational community. As a result, severing the connection between political and cultural community has been a major goal of those who try to reconcile liberalism and nationalism.

They pursue that goal in two different ways: by trying to refocus national loyalties on purely political objects or by trying to refocus them on purely cultural objects. In other words, they seek to undo one or the other of the two processes described in this chapter: the nationalization of political community or the politicization of national community. The first strategy, which is pursued by defenders of civic nationalism, aims at purifying national loyalties of the cultural particularism that accompanies national life in most modern political communities. The second strategy, in contrast, aims at purifying cultural particularism of the temptation to seek political power to which it has succumbed in the age of nationalism. I argued in chapter 1 that the first strategy, the celebration of civic nationalism, has merely replaced old myths about nationalism with new ones. This chapter suggests that the second strategy, the celebration of a purely cultural nationalism, faces similar difficulties.

The argument that politics corrupts the intrinsically cultural bonds of national community is an old one, stretching back at least to Herder's defense of cultural nationalism. It was popular among Austro-Hungarian pluralists like Otto Bauer and has been given new life in Yael Tamir's recent book, *Liberal Nationalism.* Rebecca West presents a particularly eloquent version of this argument in *Black Lamb, Grey Falcon*, her extraordinary account of her travels in Yugoslavia during the 1930s. It comes near the end of that long celebration of Yugoslavia's cultural diversity, when West finally reaches Kosovo and its shrines to Serbian nationalism. Deeply moved by the way in which some boys recite the legend of Serbian self-sacrifice here on Kosovo's "field of blackbirds," she is inspired to defend cultural nationalism against its critics.

> The little boys looked noble and devout as they recited. Here was the nationalism which the intellectuals of my age agreed to consider a vice and the origin of the world's misfortunes. I cannot imagine why. Every human being is of sublime value, because his experience, which must be in some measure unique, gives him a unique view of reality, and the sum of such views should go far to giving us the complete picture of reality, which the human race must attain if it is ever to comprehend its destiny. Therefore every human being must be encouraged to cultivate his consciousness to the fullest degree. It follows that every nation, being an association of human beings who have been drawn together by common experience, has also its own unique view of reality, which must contribute to our deliverance. . . . Here certainly I could look without any reservation on the scene, on the two little boys darkening their

brows in imitation of the heroes as they spoke the stern verse. . . . This was as unlikely to beget any ill as the wild roses and meadowsweets we had gathered by the road.[25]

After the violence unleashed by the recent attempt to keep Kosovo Serbian, these words are weighted with a terrible irony. Little boys "darkening their brows" in imitation of Serbian national heroes cannot help but suggest to us something considerably more sinister than the gathering of roadside flowers. Nevertheless, West's argument is not at all unreasonable. How can we deny that there is great value in the diverse ways in which people have come to express themselves and hand those forms of expression down to their children? Would not a world in which we lost touch with these forms of expression be immeasurably poorer? Why not try to recover and protect the life-affirming creativity of cultural nationalism from the life-threatening temptations of political nationalism?

Such is the goal that Yael Tamir, among others, pursues in her attempt to purge nationalism of its illiberal tendencies. Nations, she declares, should be understood as communities that allow for shared and voluntary forms of cultural expression. Nationalism, she suggests, is the form that such expression takes, although it has unfortunately been confused with the pursuit and exercise of political power. She concludes that if we can return to the original cultural understanding of nations and nationalism, then we can truly reconcile nationalism and liberalism.[26] Others share this conclusion, but speak instead of a return to "nations without nationalism,"[27] since, like myself, they identify nationalism with the political self-assertion of nations.

The viability of such a solution to the problems that nationalism creates for liberal democratic politics depends on just what it is that has led to the politicization of national community in the modern world. If the political self-assertion of national communities is a passing phenomenon based on values and practices that we are ready to discard, then this may indeed be a promising path for liberal democrats to follow. If, instead, it has developed because of features of modern life and politics that we

25. West, *Black Lamb, Grey Falcon*, 843.

26. Tamir, *Liberal Nationalism*, 57–58. I discuss the strengths and weaknesses of Tamir's argument more generally in "Reconciling Liberalism and Nationalism," 170–75.

27. Kristeva, *Nations without Nationalism*; Gottlieb, *Nations against States*.

now hold dear and/or indispensable, then it is not. In this chapter I have tried to show that the latter is true and thus that purifying nationalism of its taste for political power is no more plausible a project than the civic nationalists' efforts at purifying political nationalism of its taste for cultural particularism. For the key to the politicization of national loyalties lies in a notion that most liberal democrats continue to hold dear as a component of a decent political order: the idea of popular sovereignty.

PART 2

Introduction to Part 2

Part 2 turns to normative and practical issues, building on the concepts of community, nationhood, and nationalism developed in part 1. It focuses, in particular, on what I call the moral problem with nationalism, by which I mean the way in which nationalism seems to challenge or undermine moral restraints that we are ordinarily disposed to respect.[1]

The suspicion that there is something morally questionable about nationalism is widely shared. But nationalism's critics have found it difficult to articulate their sense of its moral limitations without challenging moral sentiments and convictions—feelings of communal loyalty and beliefs about popular sovereignty—that few of us seem ready to abandon in other contexts. As a result, many of them feel compelled to issue surprisingly radical challenges to received opinion in order to sustain their critiques of nationalism. And, conversely, defenders of popular sovereignty and communal loyalties often feel compelled to absolve nationalism of responsibility for the growth of communal conflict in modern political life in order to sustain these widely shared political commitments and moral sentiments.

The following chapters argue that there is indeed a moral problem with nationalism. But they suggest that misunderstandings of the moral psychology of community have led many of nationalism's critics to over-

1. My focus in part 2 is therefore considerably narrower than that of books, like Moore's *The Ethics of Nationalism* or McKim and McMahan's collection *The Morality of Nationalism*, that explore the whole range of moral issues raised by the prominence of nations and nationalism in modern political life.

state that problem and attack the very notion of communal loyalty or social friendship. Part 2, therefore, begins by stepping back once again from species to genus, from nation to community. Part 1 began by trying to correct the most familiar misconceptions of community, arguing that community is a generic component of human society, rather than a past or future alternative to distinctively modern forms of association. Part 2 begins by considering the moral value of community, as reformulated in part 1, and then moves on to national community, looking especially at the extent of its compatibility with liberal ideals and institutions. Only after defending the moral value of both community and national loyalty does it turn, in chapter 9, to nationalism and its moral limitations.

Nationalism, it is important to remember, represents something more than an especially strong attachment to one's nation and its members. As such, it draws on a much more complex moral psychology than national loyalty. It derives its special strength, as we have seen, from the mutual reinforcement of feelings of communal loyalty and beliefs about political legitimacy, rather than from an especially strong sense of connection to a particular community. The moral problem with nationalism, I shall argue, develops out of the intensification of communal hostility inspired by this convergence of sentiment and conviction, rather than from the intrinsic limitations of either communal loyalty or popular sovereignty. Once we recognize that this is the case, it becomes much easier to condemn nationalism's corrosive effects on our moral standards without condemning our disposition to form contingent communities like the nation. And, conversely, it becomes much easier to acknowledge the moral value of these communities without denying the contribution that nationalism has made to the growth of communal violence in the modern world.

The last three chapters of part 2 explore different ways of addressing nationalism's moral shortcomings. If you want to solve the moral problem with nationalism, then there are two ways of going about it: find the means of correcting nationalism's moral limitations or of eliminating its influence on modern politics. Get nationalism right or get rid of it. Chapter 10 considers the most popular means of normalizing nationalism: the establishment of a general right to national self-determination, a standard that we can use to determine both the validity and the limits of competing nationalist claims. Chapter 11, in contrast, looks at the most popular means of eliminating nationalism's influence on our lives:

the promotion of cosmopolitanism, with its broader view of the scope of communal loyalties and political principles.

As we shall see, however, each of these solutions to the moral problem with nationalism has its own difficulties. The establishment of a right to national self-determination cannot provide a standard with which to regulate nationalism, since it offers us no guidance in sorting out the conflicting claims that nations make in calling specific territories their "own." It thus intensifies the sense of entitlement that nationalists bring to their disputes with each other, while leaving us without a common standard against which to measure their competing claims. And cosmopolitanism fails to deliver on its promise of eliminating the political influence of nationalism because most of today's humbler, pluralist cosmopolitans are not really prepared, like their Stoic predecessors, to devalue partial communal loyalties and political organizations. They thereby leave the seeds of nationalism undisturbed. For it is the devaluing of partial loyalties and organizations, not the mere recognition of the existence of broader ties and principles, that allows cosmopolitanism to challenge nationalism's place in modern political life.

The final chapter suggests that if we cannot solve the moral problem with nationalism without abandoning feelings and principles that we have good reasons to respect, we might do better to think of this problem as something to be treated, rather than solved. Like Madison in his famous argument about factions in *Federalist* no. 10, I argue that if nationalism is a by-product of something we deeply value, we should focus on finding ways of minimizing its negative effects on our lives, rather than searching for ways of eliminating its causes. I try to show, in particular, how broadening our understanding of injustice can help us defuse some of the intensity of nationalists' hostility to those who oppose them. Nationalism, I conclude, may encourage the darker side of democratic politics. But we can deal with it better than we have up to now once we recognize the real character of its moral limitations.

Such a conclusion certainly falls short of the goals of more ambitious normative accounts of nationalism. But it should not be taken as a call to bow before the amoral—let alone immoral—realities of social and political life. For, as we shall see, nationalism draws its strength from a combination of morally valuable motivations. In order to deal effectively with the problems it creates for us we need to make peace with our own moral complexity, rather than with the limitations of a morally shabby world.

CHAPTER SEVEN

The Moral Value of Contingent Communities

Nations, I have argued, are best understood as intergenerational communities, groups of individuals whose shared cultural heritage marks them out as objects of special concern and loyalty. As such, they are also contingent communities. Nationality itself, let alone the particular nation to which one belongs, is far from a necessary or natural quality of human life. One's national allegiance, indeed, whether one has any sense of nationality at all, depends largely upon when and where one happens to have been born and raised.

It is the nation's contingency that makes it morally questionable in the eyes of many of its critics. How can you justify showing special concern and loyalty to a group of people who have done nothing to merit that concern, especially when it probably means that you will be expected to show more hostility than is merited to people who do not belong to that group? Our division among nations is morally arbitrary, since it reflects neither our assertion of moral purpose into the world nor our natural and unavoidable division into species. No wonder then that so many people complain about the "moral shabbiness" of our attachment to these communities.[1]

The nation's defenders often answer such complaints by challenging the description of national community as morally arbitrary. Chapter 1 considered and rejected one version of this argument: the denial of the contingency of national boundaries by supporters of what I have described as the myths of civic and ethnic nationalism. I argued there that

1. Dunn, *Western Political Theory in the Face of the Future*, 57–59.

we cannot portray national boundaries as the product of moral choice or natural necessity without seriously misrepresenting modern history and moral psychology.

Other defenders of the nation accept the moral arbitrariness of national boundaries, but point to a generally accepted moral good that nations serve. Will Kymlicka, for example, uses such an argument to persuade liberals that we need the cultural ties provided by national communities in order to develop the capacities for moral autonomy that they celebrate.[2] David Miller tries to convince social democrats that without the sense of mutual concern provided by national communities the egalitarian vision of social justice that they favor may be out of reach.[3] And Avishai Margalit and Joseph Raz try to convince all of us that we need something like the nation's "encompassing community" as a condition of moral and psychological development.[4] The moral significance of national community in these arguments rests on the moral goals that the nation helps us reach, rather than in the particular boundaries that distinguish one nation from another.

This more indirect approach to the defense of national community seems more promising to me, though it has some problems of its own, as I shall suggest in the next chapter. Nevertheless, it leaves unanswered a more fundamental issue, one that we need to address in order to evaluate the impact of nations and nationalism on modern political life: the moral value or disvalue of community itself. How should we assess our propensity to imagine ourselves connected by ties of mutual concern and loyalty to people with whom we share things?

Most of us, I suggest, are ambivalent about how to answer this question. On the one hand, the social friendships that sustain communal ties inform much of our everyday morality, as is clear from our celebration of ties of love and loyalty. On the other hand, many of our most familiar social institutions are clearly designed to check the selfishness and injustice that we suspect lurks within most assertions of group loyalty. Indirect and instrumental defenses of community leave this moral ambivalence in place and thus fail to sort out our conflicting intuitions about the moral value of community. Is social friendship an irreplaceable moral resource or a set of vices wrapped in the cloak of virtue? A necessary

2. Kymlicka, *Multicultural Citizenship*, 75–84.

3. Miller, *On Nationality*, 51, 73–80.

4. Margalit and Raz, "National Self-Determination."

evil that helps us reach other worthy goals or an unnecessary relic of an earlier and less rational age? An intrinsically valuable good that carries certain inconveniences or a morally neutral phenomenon that takes its value from the goals and character of those who rely on it?

This chapter tries to answer these questions. It proceeds in three steps. It begins by focusing attention on the role that social friendship plays in our everyday moral lives, thereby seeking to correct the one-sided picture of social morality presented by most moral philosophers. It then defends the moral value of that role, arguing that social friendship extends and deepens our concern for the well-being of others, thereby adding a much needed infusion of goodwill to our everyday lives. Finally, it argues that social friendship retains this value even when it conflicts with demands of justice, not because it represents some superior standard of morality, but because of our need for moral checks on our often overconfident and divisive assertions about what we owe each other.

This chapter thus develops and defends a kind of moral pluralism, one that focuses on the value of different and incommensurable sources of social morality, rather than different and incommensurable moral goods.[5] I argue here that the tension between social friendship and justice is itself a moral good, not just an inconvenient fact of life. And in the following chapters I argue that the key moral problem with nationalism is not its reliance on contingent forms of group partisanship, but rather its erosion of the boundary between justice and social friendship that allows them to check and balance each other.

Friendship and Justice: The Two Faces of Social Morality

Chapter 2 suggested that the cement of social order is mixed from three distinct motives: calculations of self-interest, beliefs about norms of justice or mutual obligations, and feelings of social friendship or mutual concern and loyalty. Justice and social friendship seem to be the distinctly moral elements in this mixture, since they inspire the kind of other-regarding behavior commonly associated with morality. But they dispose us to do things for the sake of others in very different ways.

5. As in the most familiar version of moral pluralism, Isaiah Berlin's theory of value pluralism. See Berlin, *Vico and Herder*, 145, 175–76, "The Pursuit of the Ideal," 5–6, and "My Intellectual Path," 1–23.

Beliefs about justice move us to give people what they deserve, what we believe that they are owed given their distinctive qualities and efforts; feelings of social friendship, to do what we can for the people to whom we feel connected. The former moves us to do things for others by promoting the sense that we owe them things; the latter, by promoting special concern for their well-being. One sustains social order and cooperation by diffusing a sense of mutual obligation; the other, by diffusing a sense of mutual concern. Justice is measured by whether you perform a specific set of obligations to others; friendship, by how well you show your concern for another's well-being. The same effort—say, clearing the ice on the sidewalk in front of your house—could represent either an act of justice or an act of social friendship, depending on whether it was inspired by your sense of legal and civic obligation or by your concern for your neighbors' well-being. As an act of justice, it represents one of a set of social actions that we believe that we owe others; as an act of social friendship, it represents one of a set of actions that expresses our concern for people to whom we feel connected in some way.

Pushed to its logical extreme, each of these two modes of social morality can and has sustained its own independent moral ideal: Solomonic justice versus Christian love, for example. The former consults feelings of special concern and loyalty, such as a mother's love for her child, only to help determine who truly deserves to receive disputed social goods. The latter abstracts from desert in order to celebrate returning love to even the least deserving of our enemies. In everyday life, however, almost all of us rely on both of these two modes of moral behavior. In other words, we do things for others both because we feel *obliged* to give them what we think that they deserve and because we are disposed to show *special concern* for the well-being of some of them. Whether or not we are right to employ these two different ways of looking out for others, there can be little doubt that almost all of us do so.

One crucial difference between social friendship and justice is the degree of specificity of the other-regarding acts that they call for. Justice promotes social cooperation by specifying our obligations to each other—so much so that for many theories of justice it is far more important that we establish clear and recognizable standards of mutual obligation than risk confusing matters by searching for the best or most accurate standards. Social friendship, in contrast, promotes social cooperation by spreading more or less intensely felt concern for the well-being of those with whom we share things. In doing so, it "creates open-ended duties to support and help one's friends," duties that we are likely "to take for granted, only giving them conscious consideration when we find ourselves in a situation of moral conflict."[6] What we require or expect from those with whom we are connected in this way will vary with circumstances, including the condition of the giver of help as well as the receiver, since as a relationship of mutual concern friends do not expect or want each other to harm themselves in helping each other.

The frequent use of the parent-child relationship as the paradigm of partial loyalties can obscure this point. Although parents and children generally do share a sense of mutual concern, the asymmetry of their relationship, the utter dependence of infants and young children on others for their survival and development, leads us to demand that parents meet a minimal set of special obligations, obligations that are often written into law. In other words, the special relationship between parents and children generates a set of special obligations that we believe that the former owe to the latter. But national loyalties, like many other forms of group loyalty, are not built upon such asymmetrical relationships of dependence. The relationship between siblings is a much better model for these forms of social friendships, especially for that which binds members of a national community, which is why they so often call on the metaphor of brotherhood.[7] Brothers and sisters, we say, "should be there for each other"; they should be ready to show special concern for each other's needs. But there is no list of sibling obligations to match that which we construct for parents. What siblings are expected to do for each other will depend on what they can do for each other without unnecessarily harming themselves. And that will depend not only on the resources that they possess but also on the structure of their needs and character. Brothers—or mothers or sons, for that matter—who pay little attention to the physical and psychic costs that a family member pays in caring for them are, in effect, betraying their friendship.

Another crucial difference between these two modes of social morality is the way in which they generate and justify dispositions to do things for others. Norms of justice are generated by our claims to know what

6. Miller, *National Responsibility and Global Justice*, 35–36.

7. Unfortunately, English has no recognizable gender neutral term to use in place of brotherhood and fraternity. Occasionally, I have toyed with the coinage "sibillity" and tried to imagine its impact in slogans like "liberty, equality, and sibillity." I doubt very much, however, that it would catch on.

kind of treatment we owe each other. We derive such knowledge from a tremendous variety of sources: tradition, divine revelation, hypothetical reasoning, convention, consent, and self-examination, among others. But whatever the source, the norm is justified with reference to something we claim to have learned about the world of human relationships. With justice, the claim to know something about what we owe each other disposes us to do things for others.

Feelings of social friendship, in contrast, are generated by our selective focus on things that we share with each other. Knowledge of the world, of the fact that we share things with each other, is not sufficient to generate social friendship's feelings of mutual concern. These feelings reflect a subjective affirmation of a particular form of sharing, rather than conclusions that we draw from certain facts about the world. Why should we feel special concern for the people with whom we share one thing rather than another? The answer, as Montaigne emphasized in his famous essay on friendship, is irreducibly subjective: "because it was he, because it was I."[8] With social friendship, unlike justice, we begin with the disposition to do something for others and cite our knowledge of the world to *limit*, rather than generate and justify, this disposition. In other words, our assertions about the world *end* our disposition to do for others with social friendship, while they inspire it with our norms of justice. That disposition reaches its limit when it leads us to violate some fundamental obligation that we believe we owe to others or to hurt other groups with whom we also share feelings of mutual concern.

For example, the current unacceptability of race-based community stems from the reprehensible principles of justice and extreme forms of self-preference with which it is now associated, rather than from the intrinsic unacceptability of race as a focus for shared concern and loyalty. In other words, it is *racism*, the belief that some races deserve a superior position and that others are innately inferior, that disqualifies race as a focus for social friendship. If we have little tolerance for assertions of racial community—except as a defensive form of solidarity among subordinated groups[9]—it is because our rejection of claims about racial supremacy and our unwillingness to abandon a minimal common hu-

8. Montaigne, *Essays*, "Of Friendship," 139.

9. Even determined opponents of group identity often make an exception for defensive group identities, even when they involve race. See, e.g., Mayerfeld, "The Myth of Benign Group Identity," 561.

manity reins in whatever feelings of special concern and loyalty that we may develop toward people with whom we share racial characteristics.

Given the wide range of things that we share, it is not surprising that we have such a wide range of overlapping and cross-cutting forms of social friendship.[10] But with social friendship there is nothing like the pressure to iron out inconsistencies that we have with our sense of justice. With justice, the need for specific obligations, as well as the derivation of those obligations from our assertions about the world, pushes us to clean up the conflicts within our standards. With social friendship, in contrast, we seem relatively comfortable living with overlapping and inconsistent social ties, as long as we do not face stark situations where we have to choose between, say, family and nation, or nation and humanity. Rather than look for ways of ironing out these inconsistencies we tend to look for ways of avoiding the situations in which they arise. Philosophers' repeated pleas to render our social friendships consistent usually fall on deaf ears.

Treating national loyalty as a special obligation, as do many of the philosophers who participate in the current debate about its moral value,[11] misses these distinctive features of social friendship and recasts attachment to national communities as a claim about justice. Special obligations and social friendships represent two different ways in which societies distribute positive duties, like caring for others, which are too onerous or intrusive to be imposed as a general duty to all individuals.[12] On the one hand, societies impose such duties on people in special relationships of dependence, like parent/child, or on those who practice certain professions, such as medicine, teaching, or social work, that involve exercising concern for others. On the other hand, societies usually expect people who feel connected to each other to show special concern for each other's well-being. Special obligations force us to sort out the conflicting standards of justice that we follow so that we can judge whether, for example, a parent's obligations to a child or a doctor's to a patient override an obligation to see that criminals are caught and punished. Social

10. As Samuel Scheffler (*Boundaries and Allegiances*, 50–51) notes, the range of what he calls "associative duties" is extraordinarily broad; such duties can be inspired by "almost any group."

11. For examples, see Moore, *The Ethics of Nationalism*; Hurka, "The Justification of National Partiality"; Weinstock, "National Partiality"; and McMahan, "The Limits of National Partiality."

12. Shue, "Mediating Duties," 690.

friendships, in contrast, force us to weigh our feelings against our obligations, so that we can get a sense of how far we should go in aiding those, say, who have committed an injustice. In other words, special obligations add a complication to our understanding of justice, while social friendship supplements justice's menu of social obligations with a different and irreducibly subjective criterion for measuring our moral duties.

The opposition between general and particular obligations fails to capture the real moral dilemmas that we face when social friendship and justice make competing demands upon us. The law-abiding child of a mafia don is not faced with a conflict between a particular obligation to support her father and a general obligation to uphold the law.[13] She is confronted, instead, with a tension between her special concern for her father's well-being—say, when he is being pursued by the law—and her obligation to obey and support the rules that establish a relatively just social order. The moral question for her is how far that concern can be expressed before it involves her in an injustice herself, rather than whether her general obligations to social justice trump her particular obligations to her parents. Treating such issues as a matter of conflicting obligations misses the delicate balancing acts between the competing demands of justice and social friendship that are one of the most familiar products of everyday moral conflict.

The difference between treating communal loyalties as a form of social friendship or as a set of special obligations may not seem very great. But I suggest that is only because we are used to measuring social morality primarily in terms of claims about justice. In order to get a sense of the one-sidedness of this approach, consider what things would look like if we began justifying claims of mutual obligation or justice in terms of social friendship. We would then say that we do not owe anyone anything unless it could be shown that we have some felt connection to that person. Before we pay back a debt to our creditors, we would have to be persuaded of our special concern for their well-being. In other words, our obligations would extend only so far as our social friendships. One might be very inventive in stretching social friendships to show that we have connections in almost every direction, just as some defenders of na-

13. This is a familiar example for those who want to show that communal loyalties are not sufficient to establish particular obligations. See, e.g., Stilz, *Liberal Loyalties*, 18. See Miller, *National Responsibility and Global Justice*, 33–34, for a contrary interpretation of the example.

tionalism are inventive in identifying special obligations to the members of their nation. But justice would be reduced to social friendship nonetheless, "doing good to friends and harm to enemies," as Polemarchus defines it in Plato's *Republic*.[14]

As a special obligation, national loyalties raise a question about justice: does our relationship with members of our national communities oblige us to show them special concern and loyalty? As a form of social friendship, however, they raise a very different question: do we know anything about the character of national community in general and of our nation in particular that would disqualify them as a focus of special concern and loyalty? By treating national loyalty as a special obligation moral and political philosophers are, in effect, reducing social friendship to a subset of justice. One might conclude, in the end, that this is the right way to proceed, that social friendships need to pass before the bar of justice before we treat them as morally acceptable. But we should not simply *assume* that this is so, given how radically it challenges the way in which we currently organize our moral lives. By reducing social friendship to special obligations we obscure from view not only the possibility that there may be some moral value in maintaining two independent sources of social morality, but also many of the moral problems that nationalism creates precisely because of the way in which it coordinates assertions of social friendship and social justice.

The Moral Value of Social Friendship

Our disposition to form communities and develop ties of social friendship is morally valuable for a very simple reason: it increases the amount of goodwill toward others that we express in our lives. If our sense of justice disposes us to give people what we think that they deserve, rather than what would best suit our own needs, then our sense of community disposes us to express some degree of concern for the well-being of large numbers of people toward whose fate we would otherwise be indifferent or hostile. Of course, it does so in a somewhat disorderly and haphazard way, by planting a confusing patchwork of overlapping and often inconsistent social friendships. But there can be little doubt that we would express far less concern for the good of others if we lacked the inclination

14. Plato, *Republic*, 332.

to imagine ourselves connected to people with whom we share things. For social friendship inspires us with concern for the well-being of others without demanding either heroic acts of self-abnegation or questionable calculations about how it might ultimately serve our own interests. Our disposition to form social friendships extends goodwill well beyond the relatively narrow confines of personal affection and familiarity. As such, it is a unique and irreplaceable moral resource.

In recent years moral philosophers have begun to treat the partial relationships and associative duties generated by our social friendships with much more care and sympathy than was common in the past.[15] But most of them remain reluctant to describe these relationships as part of morality, a term that most of them have been trained to identify with impersonal obligations and our sense of justice.[16] Instead, they tend to treat partial relationships as a supplement to morality. Some, taking advantage of our inheritance of parallel Greek and Latin philosophic vocabularies, distinguish between ethics and morality and identify social friendship and other forms of partial concern with the former. Ethics, according to this argument, concerns all that goes into a good human life, while morality concerns what we owe others, regardless of our special connections to them.[17] Community and social friendship are valuable, from this point of view, for their contribution to a full and satisfying human life, rather than for their contribution to the good of others. As Kwame Anthony Appiah puts it, "the most powerful defense of partiality is the simplest: for human beings, relationships are an important good . . . and many (noninstrumental) relationships require partiality." When nations and other partial communities "matter ethically, they do so, in the first instance, for the same reason that football and opera matter: as things cared about by autonomous agents, whose autonomous desires we ought to acknowledge and take account of even if we cannot always accede to them."[18]

15. See, e.g., Scheffler, *Boundaries and Allegiances*; Wolf, "Morality and Partiality"; Margalit, *The Ethics of Memory*.

16. For example, Susan Wolf argues ("Morality and Partiality," 243) that the importance of friendship and partial relationships draws our attention to the limits of morality rather than the limits of the way in which we generally conceive of morality.

17. Appiah, *The Ethics of Identity*, xiii, 236; Margalit, *The Ethics of Memory*, 7–8. Similarly, Susan Wolf ("Morality and Partiality," 249) distinguishes between impartial moral standards and broader "guides to life."

18. Appiah, *The Ethics of Identity*, 236, 245.

While I agree that we do value social friendships as part of a full and flourishing human life, it seems to me that the long-standing association of morality with impartial standards and obligations keeps Appiah and many other moral philosophers from acknowledging the much simpler defense of partial communities that I have presented: that they increase the fund of that relatively scarce moral resource in our lives, goodwill toward others. Defending partial community solely in terms of its contribution to a rich human life individualizes and de-moralizes something that seems to involve, for good or ill, a moral relationship between human beings. It takes mutual concern for the well-being of others and turns it into a means of promoting our *own* well-being. As David Miller suggests, "we cannot treat friendship just as an emotional attachment . . . without changing its essential character, and losing part of what gives it value."[19] For we all have experience of the way in which social friendships dispose us to seek the good of others, even at the expense of our own. Whatever help they offer toward "easing the burdens of selfhood," by providing us with sympathetic companions and a sense of belonging to a larger whole,[20] they grow out of social relationships of mutual concern, rather than the needs of discrete individuals.

I suspect that the resistance to describing such dispositions as moral reflects the lingering influence of Kantian assumptions about the unreliability of our inclinations—even other-regarding inclinations—as a motive for moral choice. These Kantian objections to the moral value of community and social friendship can be summarized in two words: egoism and arbitrariness. On the one hand, social friendship's other-regarding behavior looks like an extension of the self and its satisfactions, rather than a genuine concern for the well-being of others. On the other hand, even when our sense of community does promote genuine concern for others, it seems to do so in such a subjective and arbitrary way that it becomes an obstacle, rather than a means, to moral order. I address the first of these objections in this section, arguing that it is based on a misunderstanding of the nature of communal ties. I address the second objection in the following section, arguing that moral arbitrariness actually adds to the moral value of social friendships when they are understood as a check and balance on the judgments we make about social justice.

Although Kant is the most influential proponent of these objections,

19. Miller, *National Responsibility and Global Justice*, 36.

20. Kateb, *Patriotism and Other Mistakes*, 4.

they are probably as old as philosophy itself. Plato, for example, raises them clearly in the *Republic*. Social friendship, he suggests there, swallows up justice. It inspires us to distribute good things to our friends and bad things to our enemies rather than to the individuals whose abilities and actions merit reward and punishment. It leads us to favor those to whom we happen to feel connected and express hostility toward those who by chance are not included among our friends. It is no accident that Plato puts the definition of justice as doing good to friends and harm to enemies in the mouth of a character whose name (Polemarchus) means something like "warlord" in Greek.[21]

Even the poets and philosophers who celebrate community and social friendship tend to talk about friends as second or collective selves, which raises serious doubts about whether social friendship involves a concern for the good of others. Indeed, if they are right, we might worry that special concern for members of our communities merely provides moralistic cover for the expression of a whole set of selfish vices: vanity, when we celebrate the achievements of the communities and individual members with whom we identify; cruelty, when we rejoice in the suffering of those who oppose our friends; and, most of all, injustice, when we disdain our obligations to those with whom we do not identify and show favoritism to those with whom we do.

The first of these vices is probably the most commonly associated with community and social friendship. Even community's greatest defenders, such as Jean-Jacques Rousseau, sometimes describe it as an expanded self, a "common me,"[22] and thus support the characterization of communal ties as a kind of "group narcissism" or "disguised self-worship."[23] But that is only because they make the mistake, discussed in chapter 2, of identifying community with communion: that is, they confuse a form of association that bridges our differences with one that dissolves our sense of individuality in a larger collective self. No doubt, there are occasions when some of us sacrifice ourselves for our comrades because of an intense experience that makes us lose our sense of individuality. But in most acts of communal sacrifice, large and small, we are quite aware that something of our own is being sacrificed for the sake of others.

21. Plato, *Republic*, 332.

22. Rousseau, *The Social Contract*, book 1, chap. 6, and "Discourse on Political Economy," 121.

23. Kateb, *Patriotism and Other Mistakes*, 9, 19.

As for the celebration of friends as "second selves" that is a metaphor designed precisely to draw attention to the selflessness of friendship. Friends do what they can for each other. They hold things in common, *as if* there were no boundary between the two selves. But without the awareness of such a boundary that our mutual concern bridges, there would be no such thing as either friendship or community. Both involve heterogeneity, as Aristotle argues against Plato's efforts to model the political community as closely as possible on that of a single self.[24] And, as a result, both involve other-regarding feelings that take us beyond ourselves. These feelings can degenerate into a form of egoism, as when parents treat their children as possessions or live vicariously through their children's experiences. But such egoism represents a pathology of community and social friendship, a decay of the sense of mutual concern for the good of others that establishes and maintains them.

The most worrisome forms of egoism associated with community and social friendship emerge when membership in communities is connected in some way to membership in organizations that coordinate our activities. In such cases, we do not merely identify and sympathize with the triumphs and tragedies of the members of our communities; we tend to treat them as our own achievements. Think of national sports teams. When we celebrate "our" victories and defeats in the Olympics or the World Cup, we do not generally lose our sense of individuality—except, perhaps, in the cases of mob violence that sometimes break out on these occasions. Instead, we treat a particular organization, in this case a team, as the representative of our national community. That gives us the feeling that we, a group of people connected by ties of mutual concern and loyalty, triumph or fail along with the organization that represents us. In other words, it is the establishment of representative organizations that turns pride in the achievements of community members into a form of shared egoism in which we trumpet such achievements as our own. For while we often take pride in the victories of our countrymen and -women when they compete as individuals, we rarely treat their victories as our own unless they are part of a team sent to represent us. Identification with the success of others to whom we are attached is not the same thing as claiming that success as our own. We may take pride and identify with the achievements of countrymen and -women who win Nobel Prizes, but we rarely treat them as our own victories—at least un-

24. Aristotle, *Politics*, 1261a–b. This passage is discussed in chapter 2 above.

til organizations to which we belong, such as universities and states, start portraying these scientists as members of our team.

Having denied that this kind of collective egoism is an intrinsic element of social friendships, I do not want to underestimate its importance. Far from it. For it is closely connected not just with national sports teams, but with nationalism, in which we associate community with an especially powerful form of political organization, the modern state. This kind of collective egoism thus has a crucial role to play in the treatment of nationalism that follows this chapter. My point here is merely that although communities encourage the growth of group identity, they do not necessarily encourage the growth of collective egoism. Group identity comes in a variety of forms. Communities encourage people to identify with the experiences of the people to whom they are connected by ties of mutual concern and loyalty, to treat them with special pride and sympathy. Another kind of group identity, in which people treat the actions of the group as forms of self-expression, requires organization as well as community, specifically the establishment of recognizable collective representatives.

A more potent objection to the moral value of community is its connection to hostility and even cruelty toward those with whom we share no sense of connection. What good is the goodwill that social friendship brings into the world if it inspires an equal, let alone greater, amount of bad will? Doing good to friends would not be so offensive an interpretation of justice if it were not accompanied by the recommendation that we also do harm to our enemies.

But is Plato right that the two necessarily go together? He is certainly right about the first half of Polemarchus's definition of justice. Without the inclination to do some good for friends, regardless of whether they have done anything to merit it, there is no such thing as friendship or community. But how much harm to others necessarily follows from our disposition to display special concern for the members of our communities? Does an inclination to do good to friends entail an inclination to take things away from people who deserve them simply because they are not your friends? It certainly seems so in wartime, the paradigmatic situation that forces us to distinguish between friend and enemy. Showing concern for our friends in battle requires us to show equal hostility for everyone on the other side, regardless of their individual merits. When our side, our friends, is threatened in war we waste no time on judgments about which members of the other side most deserve to be harmed. We shoot first and ask questions later, if ever.[25]

But just how much of our social life resembles the wartime world of friends and enemies? Not much, I would suggest. To begin with, most of our lives are not lived in the zero-sum environment of the battlefield. Away from the battlefield, there is a vast middle ground between friends and enemies, a ground occupied by people toward whom friends are inclined to show neither special concern nor hostility. After all, while enemy is the exact opposite of friend, that is, the person toward whose well-being we are negatively rather than positively disposed, it merely represents one of many ways of not being a friend. In addition, there are acquaintances, bystanders, strangers, aliens, and neutral parties, to name just a few. Showing special concern for the people to whom we are attached does not require that we ignore the merits of the individuals who occupy this middle ground. Instead, it erects beside the principle of justice that leads us to distribute goods according to individual merits a second source of moral guidance, our sentiments of social friendship.

Social friendship certainly involves exclusion. It draws a line around the people with whom we share things, a line at which we end the special solicitude that we show to our friends. But it does not necessarily create an equal amount of opposition and hostility. Every time it creates an "us," it creates an "other," a group who is not us; but it does not necessarily create a "them," that is, an enemy. How "others" turn into "thems" is a key question for any study of nations and nationalism. But it is not community itself that does the job. For this reason I conclude that community and social friendship do not inspire an equal and opposite amount of bad will to offset the good that they bring into the world.

The most powerful objection to the morality of social friendship focuses instead on the way in which it seems to give its blessing to various

25. Preferably, though, the discounting of concern for justice and friendship ties among enemies is relative, rather than absolute. Montaigne, e.g., treats the ability to temper one's hostility to a friend in an unjust enemy's camp, as a wonderful example of true moral character. His hero in this regard is Epaminondas, the liberator of the Greeks from Spartan tyranny. Epaminondas, Montaigne suggests, "wedded goodness and humanity to the roughest and most violent human actions." "Terrible with blood and iron" in a just cause, "he goes breaking and shattering a nation invincible against anyone but himself, and turns aside in the middle of such a melee on meeting his host and his friend" (*Essays*, "On the Useful and the Honorable," 609).

forms of injustice. Social friendship, it seems, turns favoritism into a virtue. Even if it does not oblige us to break rules and betray our obligations to others in order to help our friends, it does encourage us to help them find ways of getting more of the good things and less of the bad than even we, let alone outsiders, think that they deserve. That is why Plato sought in the *Republic* to get rid of the family and all other private forms of social friendship: they keep us from giving individuals precisely what we owe them, what they deserve in light of their manifest abilities.

No doubt, there are a variety of ways that we can tweak our conceptions of justice in order to soften this harsh confrontation with the demands of social friendship. After all, few of us today share Plato's single-mindedly meritocratic view of justice, let alone his belief that we are all endowed by nature with particular abilities that are manifest to the perceptive eyes of philosophically gifted rulers. Nevertheless, I believe that it is important to keep the basic tension between social friendship and justice in the foreground when thinking about social morality. Contemporary commentators usually take our approval of family ties as a given against which to measure the acceptability of other forms of social friendship, such as national loyalty.[26] But if, unlike Plato, we value special concern for family members, it is not simply because we have relaxed his stringently meritocratic standards of justice; it is also because we do not treat justice, the determination of what we owe each other, as the sole measure of social morality. When we help our children or our neighbors or our classmates prepare for their day in court, it is their well-being, not—or not just—their getting the judgment that they deserve, that motivates us. That need not lead to a manifest injustice, that is, their getting much more good or less harm than they deserve. But it often does, as when a parent's or friend's deep pockets pay for the high-priced legal counsel who helps get a criminal off, a practice that plainly points to a deep tension between justice and social friendship.

Does the inclination to help our friends and family in such circumstances amount to an extension of selfishness? It does when portrayed, as by Plato, as a preference for our *own* over the good, as if our social friendships extended one's self into other people in the same way that one's ownership of property extends it into the world of things. But helping friends in circumstances where friendship and justice come into con-

26. See, e.g., Moore, *The Ethics of Nationalism*, 28, and Hurka, "The Justification of National Partiality," 144.

flict is often very costly—literally and figuratively—to us, and usually in ways that do not escape our notice. What makes our helping friends in these circumstances seem morally questionable is the impression that our friends do not truly *deserve* our help, not doubts about the genuineness of our concern for their well-being. In other words, it is the arbitrariness of our preference for our friends who have done wrong, rather than its selfishness, that makes it seem morally questionable. That is the more fundamental problem with social friendship. It supports an alternative and seemingly arbitrary mode of social morality, one that is measured by our feelings of attachment rather than our considered judgments about what we owe each other. In the end, the moral value or disvalue of community and social friendship depends on how we judge the challenge posed to our sense of justice by the feelings of mutual concern and loyalty that they promote.

Moral Pluralism and the Trade-Off between Social Friendship and Social Justice

Complaints about the egoism fueling communal expressions of mutual concern reflect a misinterpretation of social friendship, a misinterpretation that, ironically, is promoted by many of community's friends as well as its enemies. Complaints about their moral arbitrariness are quite another matter. For communal loyalties are indeed arbitrary, at least in the sense that they rest on subjective and changeable feelings rather than any kind of judgment about what kind of treatment others deserve to receive from us. And national loyalties are doubly arbitrary in that they are created by the affirmation of a contingent form of sharing.

As a result, few moral philosophers seem ready to endorse such loyalties when they conflict with the demands of justice, no matter how valuable they find partial relationships. At best, they argue, feelings of social friendship should act as a "moral tiebreaker," a way of helping us decide to whom we should direct our concern when we are not morally obligated to help one person rather than another.[27] If two people are drowning and you can save only one, there is nothing wrong with choosing to save your friend, your classmate, or your countrywoman. The absence of an impartial moral obligation to aid one of these victims first leaves us

27. Margalit, *Ethics of Memory*, 87. Similarly, see Wolf, "Morality and Partiality," 247.

free to follow our feelings of friendship. "Common-sense morality," it is suggested, "does not require more."[28]

I disagree. Commonsense morality demands considerably more than permission to use partial loyalties as a "moral tiebreaker" and, I shall argue, so should we. Commonsense morality treats these loyalties as an independent and competing source of moral guidance, rather than as a supplement to justice. When these loyalties come into conflict with the demands of justice it sees a distinctly moral dilemma, rather than, as some have suggested, a contest between love and morality.[29] Such dilemmas involve conflicting moral motivations: a disposition to do good for some as opposed to a determination to give people what they deserve. When, like the protagonist of Spike Lee's movie, we try in such situations to do the right thing, we struggle to figure out how much weight to give each of these motives in our decisions, rather than to resist the temptation to let love triumph over morality. (In Lee's movie *Do the Right Thing*, this struggle climaxes in an act that expresses his character's loyalty toward members of the African American community, even if it makes his white employer suffer more than he probably deserves to suffer.)[30] This is not to suggest that our everyday morality demands that we conclude that there is nothing wrong with the actions of the mother who hides her criminal son from the police or the patriot who condones torture and murder when it serves the interests of the members of her national community.[31] It merely suggests that we tend to see justice and social friendship as two independent and often competing sources of moral guidance, and that we therefore often face situations that give us cause for moral regrets, since we must transgress the demands of one or the other.

Is it a good thing that we tend to rely on two independent and competing sources of social morality? Or is it something that we should correct, most likely in favor of justice and its standards of mutual obligation, as suggested by the majority of contemporary moral philosophers?

How you answer these questions depends largely on the degree of

28. Tan, *Justice without Borders*, 162.

29. Wolf, "Morality and Partiality," 254.

30. That expression of group loyalty, however, is inspired in large part by the persistent indifference to the injustices suffered by the members of his community, which begins to suggest the complexity of the relationship between friendship and justice in our moral conflicts.

31. As argued by Wolf, "Morality and Partiality," 254.

confidence you express in the judgments we make about our mutual obligations. If, like Kant, you think that the only unqualifiedly good thing in this world is a good—that is, a free and rational—will, then you will make sure that subjective feelings of concern for others support rather than challenge our judgments about our mutual obligations. But if, like myself, you believe that we have as much to fear from moral self-righteousness as we do from mindless solidarity, then you might welcome the arbitrariness of social friendship as a way of protecting ourselves from the harm caused by excessive confidence in our ability to discern what people deserve from each other.

Given the history of moral error and fanaticism, the range of shifting and often inhumane beliefs about what we owe each other and the social divisions that they cause, I believe that we should be very grateful that social friendship provides us with a set of feelings that can check and balance our reasoning about how to go about doing the right thing. As Montaigne suggests, "it is enough to harden one's shoulders" to one's duty; we should not seek to "harden our hearts as well."[32] We should never forget that it is a friend or a family member or a compatriot that some duty obliges us to harm, for our feelings may be a surer guide to doing the right thing than our sense of obligation—a point that seemed especially important to Montaigne in the midst of the horrors of the French religious wars. Avengers may relent in their determination to inflict even well-earned punishment by the discovery of something that they share with their victims.[33] And the relentless pursuer of class justice or religious orthodoxy may be slowed by appeals to our common nationality, if not our common humanity.

Social friendships encourage us to do what we can for different groups of others, regardless of whether we can justify doing so before some bar of reason. As long we have reason to have doubts about the adequacy of that bar, we should be very glad that we have another source of social morality, even a relatively arbitrary one. Eliminating its feelings of mutual concern or subordinating them to our judgments of social justice would cast aside a precious moral resource. Plato was right. There is a deep tension between justice and social friendship. But I be-

32. Montaigne, *Essays*, "On the Useful and the Honorable," 609.

33. My favorite example: Tolstoy's Andrei Bolkonsky, whose thirst for vengeance dissolves when he discovers that the man who wronged him has, like himself, been badly wounded at the battle of Borodino.

lieve, against Plato, that this tension itself is a moral good, the foundation of a valuable, if rarely noticed, form of moral pluralism.

The disadvantage of social friendship as a moral resource is clearly its exclusiveness. If you do not happen to share the thing that we have come to imagine as a source of connection between us, there is nothing you can do about it. You are bound to remain an outsider. With justice, in contrast, it is up to you to determine how you are going to be treated, for you can always choose to live up to the relevant standard of justice. But justice's inclusiveness on this score generates its own distinctive form of exclusion. For if you can always choose to live up to shared standards of justice, then you are more deserving of blame for not doing so than you are for characteristics that you have no ability to eliminate. As long as we remain divided or uncertain about what constitutes the basic standards of justice, relying on justice for social morality can therefore intensify, rather than eliminate, our divisions. That is why communities rent by sectarianism so often turn to unchosen commonalities, like national heritage or territorial loyalties, in order to diminish communal violence.

We rely on our sense of justice to restrain our feelings of social friendship in ways that seem relatively uncontroversial. First of all, we rely on the sense that we owe people things to correct the consequences of unrestrained partisanship, the inclination to give the people we like things without any regard to desert that is celebrated in expressions like "my country, right or wrong." We also rely on our sense of justice to correct the prejudices that partisanship often introduces into our judgments about desert, as when we come to be believe that our country is right simply because it is our own and their country is wrong simply because it is theirs. And we rely on it to help us determine the appropriate degree of concern to show the different groups of individuals to whom we feel connected, as when evidence of the wrongs done by one's own country reminds us of our feelings of concern for those foreigners with whom we share nothing but our common humanity.

Our reliance on feelings of social friendship to check and balance our sense of justice is less familiar and thus considerably more controversial. It may even seem counterintuitive, given the predominance of justice and obligation in contemporary moral philosophy. Nevertheless, when we look at everyday moral practice it becomes clear that social friendships are used to check and balance our sense of justice in ways that parallel the use of justice to constrain social friendship.

First of all, we rely on the various forms of social friendship that we share in order to modify the harshness of an unrestrained sense of justice, a harshness best expressed by the famous Latin tag, "*fiat iustitia, pereat mundus* (let justice reign, even if the world perishes)."[34] Unmoderated by some degree of concern for the well-being of those to whom we apply our judgments about desert, justice can be a truly terrible force, regardless of whether it is inspired by the pursuit of revenge or by a philosopher's love of wisdom. Even where judgments of desert are not questionable, as they often are, it is a force that cries out for some counterbalance based on concern for the well-being of others. For our sense of justice is inspired by the disposition to give people what they deserve, rather than what they need.[35]

Second, we rely on feelings of social friendship to correct the distortions that our sense of justice often introduces into our feelings of concern for others, as when revolutionaries or religious fanatics insist that only the fate of the righteous or right-thinking should concern us. In other words, although an unconstrained sense of justice sometimes discourages any consideration of the consequences for others of our efforts to give people what they deserve, it can also encourage extremely selective forms of concern—for example, by discouraging any sympathy for "the undeserving poor." Just as partisanship encourages us to conflate friendship with desert, so our sense of justice encourages us to conflate desert with friendship or concern for the well-being of others.

Finally, and perhaps least obviously, feelings of social friendship can sometimes help us correct our standards of justice. For many of the injustices that people suffer will only be apparent to those who are especially attentive to the things that affect the well-being of a particular group. What appears, for example, to be a relatively neutral administrative regulation—say, dealing with the ritual slaughter or hunting of animals—can have terribly disruptive effects on some minority communities' whole way of life. But these effects will only be apparent to those who devote special attention to the well-being of the people affected by

34. Kant's confidence in relying on our judgments of justice to set the world right is made manifest by his extraordinarily narrow interpretation of this phrase, which he construes as "let justice reign, even if all the rascals in the world should perish from it." See Kant, "Perpetual Peace," 126. From Kant's perspective, only the world's "rascals" have something to lose from justice's unlimited reign.

35. For this reason Appiah (*Ethics of Identity*, 220) speaks of the "ruthless cosmopolitanism" that follows from the single-minded pursuit of universal and impartial standards of justice.

them. Without this kind of special attention we are bound to commit all kinds of injustices without knowing it.[36]

Most moral philosophers recognize that positive duties, especially those that involve caring for others, cannot be distributed as generally and universally as negative duties. For the exercise of these duties almost always requires that special attention be paid particular individuals or groups in order to identify and satisfy their needs. Contingent forms of community and the social friendships that they inspire are among the many means we have come to rely on for the distribution of these duties. Their arbitrariness, the fact that their members have done nothing to deserve any special attention and their boundaries' lack of any special moral significance, makes it hard to accept this means of identifying the kind of concern that we should show each other. But if we are looking to check and balance the limitations of our judgments about each other's desert, arbitrariness is to a certain extent a positive feature in criteria for social friendship. For in that case it is essential that we do *not* use the very judgments of desert that we are trying to check and balance with our appeals to social friendship to determine which forms of social friendship we deem acceptable. When we make judgments about who deserves our concern or which relationships—like parent/child, doctor/patient, drowning man/anyone who passes by—are special in a way that creates obligations to express concern for a particular group of others, we inevitably draw on our sense of justice. In order to correct or balance our sense of justice, rather than merely soften or humanize it, social friendship has to be able to draw on feelings that are not dictated or constrained by our sense of justice itself. Arbitrary forms of community can thus improve our moral insight into what we need from each other.

Let me repeat that I am not suggesting that the ties of social friendship morally trump the impartial duties generated by our sense of justice, let alone that we do nothing wrong when we break the law to protect a family member or compatriot. I am arguing, instead, that social friendship provides us with an independent and indispensable source of moral guidance, one that we ignore at our peril. I am thus defending a form of moral pluralism, rather than moral particularism in itself.[37] Like

36. See Yack, "Multiculturalism and the Political Theorists," 116–17.

37. Carmen Pavel makes a similar claim about moral pluralism in her account of the relationship between nationalism and cosmopolitanism in "Cosmopolitanism, Nationalism and Moral Opportunity Costs," 2. "Both," she argues, "incorporate objective demands

Sophocles in his great tragedy *Antigone*, I am defending the moral value of relying on two independent and sometimes competing sources of social morality, rather than the priority of our partial loyalties to the demands of justice. Relying on two different sources of social morality in this way inevitably creates moral conflicts, as we find ourselves in situations in which we cannot do justice without hurting those that we are disposed to help. But, like Sophocles, I believe that we need to rein in our arrogant belief that we can impose a consistent moral order on the world and learn to accept that in seeking to do the right thing we often cannot help doing some wrong as well.[38]

---

of morality that are in permanent tension with one another. To get a more accurate picture of our moral responsibilities we need to keep the tension in mind without suppressing either partial view."

38. Needless to say, my association of Sophocles with this conclusion is based on my own interpretation of Antigone, an endlessly reinterpreted play. I see the play's tension between the human law of the city and the divine law of the hearth and family duty as a confrontation between the knowledge-based demands of justice and the subjective ties of social friendship. Sophocles, I believe, teaches that we need both, that each defeats itself without the other, even though they are bound to come into conflict with each other at important points in our lives.

CHAPTER EIGHT

National Loyalty and Liberal Principles

Establishing the moral value of social friendship answers some criticisms of the nation, especially those that focus on the moral shabbiness of contingent and undeserved expressions of social friendship. But it leaves open questions about whether this particular form of community, with its reliance on shared cultural heritage, is compatible with our moral and political commitments.

Such questions are especially pressing for liberals, since their commitment to individual freedom and political pluralism seems to sit uneasily with communal loyalties rooted in a shared inheritance. Some liberals complain that the nation's affirmation of shared cultural heritage undermines liberal commitments to individual rights and social pluralism within a nation. Others complain that liberalism's affirmation of consent and individual autonomy precludes the use of inherited social connections to determine who belongs to a particular community. But both groups of critics reach the same conclusion: expressions of national loyalty and commitments to liberal principles are mutually exclusive. Liberal democrats cannot combine them without sacrificing the true meaning of one or the other or both.

This chapter addresses each of these arguments in turn and argues that they rest on misrepresentations of the nature of national community and the scope of liberal commitments. It tries to show, in particular, that these complaints about the incompatibility of national loyalties and liberal principles miss national community's open-ended character and exaggerate liberal commitments to choice and consent as the foundation of human association. It then goes on to discuss ways in which national loyalties have contributed to the realization of liberal ideals and institutions.

Nevertheless, this chapter does not claim that liberals are obliged in some way to express loyalty to their nations. It argues that national loyalty is compatible with liberal principles, not that it is required by them. A liberal nation, I conclude, is a group of individuals who both express special concern and loyalty toward people with whom they share a cultural heritage and rely on relatively liberal principles of justice to organize their basic political institutions. There is no logical inconsistency in this combination of dispositions and therefore no pressing need for liberals to eliminate national ties. Indeed, there are some good reasons for putting them together, as I argue in the fourth section of the chapter. But it is a mistake to seek a form of nationhood in which one entails the other.

The Nations We Know and Love

Conservative defenders of the nation make some of the most powerful arguments against the compatibility of liberal principles and national community. Roger Scruton, for example, argues that liberal nationalists want to reap all the advantages of communal membership without paying any of its cost. "The real price of community," Scruton insists, is "sanctity, intolerance, exclusion, and a sense that life's meaning depends upon obedience."[1] No amount of fiddling with the concept of nationhood can change this stubborn fact: endorse national loyalty and you endorse the priority of communal membership, with all of the latter's irrationality and penchant for ancestor worship. Liberals who seek to bring national loyalty into line with their basic principles of justice are guilty of trying to have their cake and eat it too.

Samuel Huntington makes a similar point about liberalism and national community when he warns that the demise of the American nation can only be put off by accepting "the Anglo-Protestant culture, tradition, and values that for three and one half centuries have been embraced by Americans of all races, ethnicities, and religions, and that is the source of their liberty, unity, power, prosperity, and moral leadership as a force for good in the world." The survival of the American na-

1. Scruton, "In Defence of the Nation," 310.

tion, from this point of view, does not require the continued supremacy of the ethno-cultural groups that originally settled it. But it does require a renewed commitment to the "Anglo-Protestant culture" that they created. Only then will "America still be America long after the WASPish descendants of its founders have become a small and uninfluential minority."[2]

Many liberals fear national loyalties because they are inclined to agree with conservatives that national ties undermine individual autonomy and cultural pluralism by committing us to the preservation of a distinct "cultural essence over time."[3] The nation's liberal defenders often counter such fears by pointing us toward a distinctly liberal form of nationhood, one rooted in shared choice of principles and cultural affinities, rather than in shared cultural inheritance. But, as we have seen in part 1, their visions of nations as voluntary associations for the expression of shared taste and political principle both misrepresent actual liberal nations and ignore the sense of intergenerational connection that gives national community its distinctive strength and character. The question then is whether national community remains compatible with liberal principles once we acknowledge the sense of intergenerational connection that sustains national community.

I believe that it does. For the conservatives' relatively closed conception of nationhood is based on a subtle, but fundamental misunderstanding of the nature of national community. It mistakes the nation's cultural *heritage* community for a cultural community. In other words, it confuses the shared *reception* of a cultural heritage as a focus of mutual concern and loyalty with the shared *attachment* or *commitment* to some particular part of a shared cultural heritage. National community, according to this view, grows out of a shared commitment to a particular set of cultural tastes and values that we have received from our predecessors. But, as I suggested in chapter 3, you do need not to practice or even like much of the cultural heritage you share with others in order to share membership in a nation. You need merely express special concern and loyalty for the people who have, like you, received that inheritance from previous generations. The survival of nations thus does not require the assimilation of later generations of individuals to some original cultural substance. It depends, instead, on the continued affirmation of an in-

2. Huntington, *Who Are We?*, xvii.

3. Mueller, *Constitutional Patriotism*, 51.

herited lineage, of a singular and often inconsistent accumulation of cultural artifacts as a focus of mutual concern and loyalty. No doubt, vanity, pride, and political expediency lead many members of a nation to celebrate all or part of their distinctive cultural heritage, especially when national loyalty turns into nationalism. But the fact remains that the thing that connects members of a nation is a shared inheritance, rather than a shared commitment to a particular set of beliefs or practices.

Chapter 3 offered a defense of this understanding of nationhood. Here let me note merely that conservatives often betray their reliance on this more open-ended understanding of the nation even in the midst of their heated defense of a nation rooted in its original values. For example, even as Huntington pleads with Americans to revive their nation by renewing their commitment to "Anglo-Protestant culture, traditions, and values," he acknowledges that it is "the America I know and love" that he is trying to save from an untimely demise,[4] rather than America itself. The American nation, it seems, can survive the abandonment of its original Anglo-Protestant cultural commitments, just not in a form that Huntington finds very attractive. Liberal multiculturalism seems much more of a threat to *his* identification with America than to its continued existence as a nation.

We need to be careful here to distinguish between two ways of talking about national identity. One refers to the characteristics that allow us to identify a diverse and ever-changing group of individuals as a single community. The other refers to the particular characteristics that people identify with such groups. National identity in the first sense is singular and constant by definition, since it is designed to help us find continuity in the midst of difference and change. National identity in the second sense need not be, and almost never is, singular and constant. For the continued existence of a nation is quite compatible with competing and changing perceptions of its character. What vibrant national community lacks competing visions of the nation we should all know and love? Or remains the nation that all preceding generations knew and loved? Our anguished debates about national identity concern which part of our nation's heritage to emphasize and celebrate. It is precisely the intrinsic pluralism of a national heritage, its collection of inconsistent and oddly matched cultural artifacts and virtues, that makes such debates so lively.

When your vision of national identity refers to the character and com-

4. Huntington, *Who Are We?*, xvii.

mitments of a nation's earliest generations, it is tempting to claim that it constitutes the singular and constant cultural core without which there would be no nation to argue about.[5] But that would be a misrepresentation. For nations are not political organizations. They have no constitution, no set of fundamental rules and principles that serve to bring future generations into line with a particular way of ordering their lives. The first generations of a nation establish the beginning of a line of cultural inheritance, rather than a singular model against which to measure the nation's survival. They constrain later generations by the contingent and often inconsistent combinations of cultural artifacts that they bequeath to later generations, rather than by any coherent vision of a nation's character. The coherence and unity of the heritage that we receive from preceding generations is one of the central myths of ethnic and conservative nationalism.

If, as suggested by such myths, membership in a national community required allegiance to some original set of cultural practices and values, then it would challenge liberal principles of justice in at least three ways. First, it would impede basic liberal reforms of law and government, since it would require the defense of illiberal practices if they were part of the nation's original cultural core. Second, it would impose severe restrictions on individual autonomy, since it would require that individuals adapt their tastes and values to fit their cultural inheritance. Finally, it would severely curtail social diversity, let alone multiculturalism, because it would demand all groups make use of a common cultural core. But if I am right about the relatively open-ended character of the nation's cultural heritage community, then these liberal objections to national community can be answered without falling back on the myths of a purely voluntary and civic nation.

If it is shared cultural heritage rather than shared culture that makes a nation, then membership in a nation that has long relied on, say, patriarchal and racist cultural traditions is not incompatible with the introduction of liberal principles of social and political justice. Concern for the feelings of the people who resist such changes might temper and delay the implementation of such reforms. But it need not block serious social and political reform, since no particular element of our shared cultural

5 It is harder to make this claim if your vision emphasizes later developments since, in that case, you would have to acknowledge that, like the members of earlier generations, people can belong to the nation without endorsing your vision.

heritage is sacrosanct as the continuing basis of national community. The overthrow of traditional practices and values, as in the French Revolution, is a horrible disruption of intergenerational community for conservatives, since they look to past example as the authority that establishes the connections between the living and the dead. For the members of nations, however, it need not disrupt intergenerational community, since for them the past is prologue not precept. The French nation that survived the Revolution now passes on Jacobin as well as ancien régime examples and traditions in its cultural heritage. It may not be the French nation that conservatives—in Burke's time or our own—know and love. But it is the French nation all the same.

Second, if it is the sharing of a cultural heritage rather than a particular culture that defines a nation, then membership in a national community does not demand the sacrifice of the kind of individual autonomy that most liberals defend. For, in that case, national community demands the expression of feelings of special concern and loyalty to the people with whom you share such a heritage, rather than an individual's assimilation to any particular cultural tastes or values contained within it. No doubt, it will be especially hard for people who develop such feelings to follow their own judgment when their compatriots are celebrating parts of that heritage that they find wrong or distasteful. For they will likely be accused of disloyalty as well as wrongdoing or bad taste. But obedience to inherited tastes and values is not, pace Scruton, part of the price we pay for national community. With national community we inherit a set of friends rather than a set of commitments to particular tastes and values.

Finally, if I am right about the relatively open-ended character of national community, then it becomes compatible with new forms of cultural pluralism and even multiculturalism. For if no core cultural values and commitments define national community, then the cultural heritage that nations pass on to later generations is heterogeneous by its very nature. And that means that different groups can identify very different characteristics and values with the same national community. Surprisingly, national community seems to have a built-in source of cultural pluralism.

The Anglo-Protestant America that Huntington knows and loves is only one of a number of Americas that Americans now know and love. Americans can argue about which provides the stablest, strongest, and most inspiring vision of their community. But they *need not agree* on a common answer to this question in order to maintain that community. For the cultural heritage that brings them together hints at many different and inconsistent answers. And if that is true about America, it is even more true of older nations. Think, for example, of all of the conflicting visions of nationhood that, say, Germans or Japanese can derive from their cultural heritage. It is only the need to package and sell our competing visions of a nation that leads us to treat a national heritage as a coherent and consistent whole.

And if membership in nations does not demand a commitment to certain core cultural practices and values, then it is even compatible with certain forms of multiculturalism. Multiculturalists demand, among other things, recognition of the diversity of cultural communities that make up modern societies. They are both border guards and border crossers, since they seek both to shore up smaller cultural communities against the forces of assimilation and to encourage us to view the world from a variety of cultural perspectives.[6] Huntington, like many other conservatives—as well as quite a few liberals[7]—views multiculturalism as a mortal threat to national community because he believes that nationhood requires a commitment to a common cultural or political core. But if nationhood does not require such a commitment, it is not necessarily incompatible with a variety of cultural communities. A multicultural nation, from this point of view, would be a community that both shares a cultural heritage and includes within it a diverse range of cultural communities. As Will Kymlicka points out, that description increasingly fits the United States, Canada, France, and many other liberal democratic nations. Each provides room, within its own distinctive community, for an increasingly wide range of cultural subcommunities.[8]

This is not to suggest that we think of national community as multiculturalism's friend and ally. Nationalism helped destroy the forms of multiculturalism that existed in polyglot cities, like Prague or Constantinople, not just the empires that sustained them. Multiculturalism there rested on the separation and coexistence of different cultural communities, rather than on their cooperation as subcommunities within a larger shared community.[9] As such, it supported much deeper expressions of cultural difference than the forms of multiculturalism found in contem-

6. See Yack, "Multiculturalism and the Political Theorists," for this understanding of multiculturalism.

7. For example, Arthur Schlesinger in *The Disuniting of America* ,and Brian Barry in *Culture and Equality: An Egalitarian Critique of Multiculturalism*.

8. See Kymlicka, *Politics in the Vernacular*, 26.

9. On different regimes of cultural toleration, see Walzer, *On Toleration*.

porary liberal democracies. But the political separation of cultural communities had costs in disorder and arbitrariness that few of us would be willing to pay today. The consolidation of national communities destroyed this earlier form of multiculturalism. But the relatively open-ended character of national community allows for the introduction of a stabler, if less vibrant form in its place.

Defending Birthright Citizenship

Even if membership in national communities leaves liberals sufficient room for individual freedom and diversity, that does not answer concerns about the seemingly illiberal way in which nations distinguish between members and nonmembers. In a feudal system, some liberals complain, it may have "seemed natural that an individual's position within the social order and his political allegiance were both assigned by the circumstances of birth. But this, we are repeatedly told, is not the approach favored in our modern world of free and autonomous individuals who can direct their own life and realize their potential, if they so choose."[10] If liberalism is committed to "a radical critique of all ascriptive privileges,"[11] then it is hard to avoid the conclusion that the nation's reliance on the contingencies of birth to allocate membership "runs counter to the core principles of liberal and democratic theory."[12]

This version of the argument about the contradiction between liberal principles and national loyalties is presented most clearly by recent critics of the practice of birthright citizenship, such as Ayelet Shachar and Jacqueline Stevens. Shachar complains that "the acquisition of automatic (birthright) membership in the polity is the least defensible basis for distributing access to citizenship because it allocates rights and opportunities according to aspects of our situation that result from unchosen circumstances that are fully beyond our control."[13] And Stevens argues that "it is hard to imagine any single principle that so fails basic intuitions about justice than that which would confine one's life to an arbitrarily small circumference based on the nation-state within which

10. Shachar, *The Birthright Lottery*, 115.

11. Bader, "Citizenship and Exclusion," 214.

12. Shachar, *The Birthright Lottery*, 124.

13. Ibid.

one's place of birth happens to be located." For "a requirement of individual freedom is the ability to make contracts and not birth the basis of obligations, including citizenship."[14] Birthright citizenship, they conclude, "flies in the face of our standard liberal and democratic accounts of citizenship as reflecting the choice and consent of the governed."[15] It affirms social connections that liberals are quick to denounce as endorsements of ethnic nationalism or feudal privilege when affirmed by others. No truly liberal society would tolerate it.[16]

The strength of such arguments rests largely on the accuracy of what Shachar calls "our standard liberal and democratic accounts of citizenship." Critics of birthright citizenship demand that liberals bring their practice into line with "what we are repeatedly told . . . [about] the approach favored in our modern world of free and autonomous individuals."[17] But if what we are repeatedly told about that world is inaccurate, then it is our understanding of liberal principles that stands in need of correction, not the common practice of liberal societies.

I believe that this familiar picture of liberal commitments does indeed need to be corrected. For it wildly exaggerates the degree of independence from inherited social connections demanded by liberal principles. Liberal practice, I suggest, should be measured by what it *does* with the social connections that arise out of our involuntary entry into the world, rather than by how well it succeeds in *eliminating* their influence.

Feudal analogies loom large in the unmasking of liberals' supposed hypocrisy about birthright citizenship. If it is wrong, so the argument goes, to grant people special status merely because they took the trouble to be born the son of a duke or the daughter of a slave-owner, then it must also be wrong to grant the privileges of citizenship just because they happened to be born in a particular place or to particular parents. Birthright citizenship, from this perspective, "is the modern equivalent of feudal privilege—an inherited status that greatly enhances one's life chances."[18]

But liberals do not reject feudal privilege simply because they are

14. Stevens, *States without Nations*, 59.

15. Shachar, *The Birthright Lottery*, 13.

16. Hence Stevens's repeated reference (*States without Nations*, 27–28, 56) to "so-called" liberal society and liberal theorists in her book.

17. Shachar, *The Birthright Lottery*, 115.

18. Carens, "Aliens and Citizens," 230. Stevens (*States without Nations*, 19) ups the ante and compares the disabilities created by birthright citizenship to those borne by slaves.

committed to eliminating inherited connections that greatly enhance or diminish one's life chances. They reject it because of the particular ways in which it affects our life chances: by granting authority over us to people who did nothing to earn it but draw a lucky number in the birth lottery and by creating for them special status and privileges. In other words, it is inherited social hierarchy, rather than inherited social connection per se, that makes feudal privilege so unacceptable to liberals. Birthright citizenship does indeed hand out life-enhancing privileges to people who merely had the good fortune to be born in a particular place or to particular parents. But these privileges neither grant those people special political authority over others nor raise them to a higher level of status within a hierarchical legal order. That is why so few liberals feel compelled to seek their elimination.

Liberals are much more ambivalent about inherited advantages that do not line up so neatly with their commitments against caste and patriarchy. For example, the inheritance of property undoubtedly increases the impact of the contingencies of birth on an individual's chance for a healthy and happy life. But eliminating property inheritance in the name of equalizing life chances sits uneasily with other liberal goals, such as limited government and personal freedom—hence the severe disagreements among liberals about how to deal with the matter. Beyond the rejection of entailed property, where concerns about inherited wealth and personal freedom line up neatly,[19] there is no generally recognized liberal position on the matter. The absence of such a position reflects the variety of competing liberal goals that are affected by the inheritance of property, rather than a failure to live up to liberal principles.

Disagreements among liberal theorists about the legitimacy of birthright citizenship, unlike their disagreements about the inheritance of property, seem to have had little impact on political practice. For the granting of citizenship to those born to citizen parents and/or within the territory of a state is pretty much the norm among liberal democratic states. That makes these states seem inconsistent, even hypocritical, to those who assume that liberal principles commit us to the dissolution

19. Perhaps that is why Shachar, in her efforts to reconceptualize birthright citizenship as a property right, portrays it as an entailed right, something liberals are disposed against. Does that mean we should disentail this property right and allow people to choose to whom it should be passed on? Hardly. Certainly Shachar does not suggest that we should, which raises serious doubts about her efforts to rethink birthright citizenship as a property right.

of all inherited social connections. But once we drop that assumption, then the possibility arises that birthright citizenship might represent a relatively liberal way of responding to a basic feature of the human condition: our involuntary and helpless entry into a world that we did not make for ourselves.

Recent debates about paths to citizenship tend to focus, understandably, on how we deal with immigrants, people who come into association with a particular state by voluntarily crossing its borders. But crossing borders is not the only or even the primary way in which people come to be connected with particular state organizations. Most of us come to be connected with particular states because we entered involuntarily into life at a particular place and time, rather than by choosing to cross a border. Immigration and naturalization laws represent our response to one major source of population growth. Birthright citizenship is a response to the other: the production of new and helpless persons by the natural processes of birth.

Is it a liberal response to this problem? Stevens laughs at the very idea. If "liberals have decided that nepotism is bad for running a business, how can they justify using this system for selecting citizens who will run a country? Even pseudo-intelligence tests, ones that did no better than randomly select for those who were ostensibly qualified, would be more in keeping with liberal norms than those of birthright, as the exclusions would be based on at least a pretense of preferring individual merit over birth."[20] And Shachar complains that birthright "is the least defensible basis for distributing access to citizenship" because, "unlike consent, merit, achievement, residency, compensation, or need," it relies on "unchosen circumstances that are fully beyond our control."[21]

But it is precisely the point of birthright citizenship to address the impact of such circumstances. It is precisely because we did *not* get to choose when and where to be born that we expect liberal states to grant citizenship to those born on its territory and/or to citizen parents. In other words, we expect liberal states to go further than merely eliminating social hierarchies based on the contingencies of birth; we expect them to equalize the status of those whose conditions of birth subject them to the sway of a particular political society. Most liberals recognize

20. Stevens, *States without Nations*, 56.
21. Shachar, *The Birthright Lottery*, 124.

that there is something very wrong with creating a semipermanent class of guest workers, since their inferior legal status threatens the norms of legal equality that represent one of liberalism's proudest achievements.[22] Would it not be even worse to create such a class from among a group of people who had no choice at all about whether to be connected with a particular state, people who were in no position to know or consider the consequences of their moving into its territory? But that is what they would have to do, were they to make citizenship dependent on mastering some test of loyalty, conviction, knowledge, or intelligence.

In the end, even severe critics of birthright citizenship like Shachar do not seem to believe that birthright citizenship itself is an illegitimate practice. (Otherwise, why propose taxing it, as she does,[23] rather than getting rid of it, as we have gotten rid of other "feudal" privileges?) It is the *exclusion* of those who do not receive this privilege that offends their sense of justice, rather than the *inclusion* of birthright citizens. Treating people's birth within a state's territory or to citizen parents as a *sufficient* condition for citizenship in that state is not really problematic from a liberal perspective—as long we give them a right to abandon this privilege and we put limits on how long they can pass it on after they have left the state's territory. It is the treatment of the circumstances of birth as a *necessary* condition of citizenship that is problematic for liberals. For doing so would ensure that we view all immigrants as legal inferiors rather than as potential equals. How far we should go in opening borders and paths to citizenship will depend on many factors, the weighting of which is bound to create disagreements among liberals. But coming up with an acceptable answer to that question does not preclude liberals from addressing questions about how they should handle the other way in which we come to be associated with the authority of particular states: by taking the trouble to be born in a particular place and time. The general reliance of current liberal democracies on the practice of birthright citizenship reflects a plausible answer to those questions, rather than a remnant of feudal ideologies. It only seems otherwise because the most familiar pictures of liberal society seem to commit us to a quixotic struggle to emancipate us from the effects of the contingent circumstances of our birth.

22. See, e.g., Walzer, *Spheres of Justice*, chap. 1.

23. Shachar, *The Birthright Lottery*, 15.

A Liberal Obligation to the Nation?

In the first two sections of this chapter I have tried to show that national community is compatible with liberal principles of justice, not that it requires or is required by such principles. In doing so, I have tried to remove liberal objections to national community, rather than prove that liberals ought to express national loyalties or that nations need to take up liberal principles of justice. But many liberal defenders of national community are not satisfied with demonstrating that national loyalties and liberal principles are compatible. They want to prove that liberal commitments oblige us to express loyalty to our nations. In order to succeed in doing so, they need to show that there is something morally significant about our national heritage, and to do so without falling back on the myths of ethnic and civic nationalism. In other words, they need to show that even though every national heritage is a contingent and inconsistent collection of cultural artifacts, it still is capable of creating moral obligations for those who share it.

Recent liberal defenders of the nation have met this challenge in two different ways. Some have argued that what makes national community morally significant is the presence within its inheritance of distinctive moral projects and achievements. Others have argued that what gives it moral value is its contribution to the realization of other, clearly recognized moral and political goals. Dominique Schnapper's defense of the nation in *The Community of Citizens* provides an excellent example of the first argument; Will Kymlicka's theories about national culture and liberal autonomy, a well-known example of the second. This section considers each argument in turn.

Schnapper clearly identifies the nation with liberal democratic theory's concept of the people as constituent sovereign. "The nation," she argues, "is defined by its ambition to transcend by citizenship particular biological, historical, economic, social, religious or cultural attachments." It seeks to integrate "all the people into a community of citizens to legitimate the action of the state, which is its instrument, by that community."[24] But because she recognizes that nations are unified by their singular and contingent histories, not just by their principles, Schnapper is not willing to redefine nationhood as the mere sharing of liberal democratic commitments. Nor is she willing to follow Habermas's

24. Schnapper, *La communauté des citoyens*, 44.

suggestion that merely situating universal principles within "the shared horizon" of an intergenerational community is sufficient to generate the sense of community we associate with the nation.[25] She argues, instead, that what defines nationhood must be a genuine blending of the universal and the particular, of principle and passion.

Schnapper finds such a mixture in the idea of a shared "political project." All nations, as she understands them, seek to transform individuals and ethnic groups into communities of free and equal citizens. But each does so in its own peculiar way, developing a distinctive "political project, born out of its singular history."[26] The British take pride in their role in inventing the institutions of private liberty, not just in their shared principles or their rich cultural heritage. The Americans take pride in their role in the creation of the first democratic society, not just in the principles of the Constitution or the virtues of the Founding Fathers. And the French take pride in their invention of national community as a fraternal force of social integration, not just in the "Declaration of the Rights of Man and the Citizen" or the glories of French art and literature.[27] Schnapper's understanding of nationhood preserves the singular intergenerational community that gives it its special force while, at the same time, eliminating the moral arbitrariness that makes it hard for most liberal moralists to accept. Each nation, in her view, pursues a morally significant goal, one fully in line with liberal democratic principles. But it does so in a particular way that its members celebrate as their own special heritage. Nations endure, Schnapper suggests, only when accompanied by striking events that communicate and commemorate their singularity as movers of such shared projects.

There are, however, at least two serious problems with this creative reconstruction of nationhood. First of all, there are not enough distinctive political projects to go round. After the British have grabbed liberty, the Americans equality, and the French fraternity, what projects are left for the Slovenians, the Turks, or the Vietnamese? They can certainly take up and imitate past political projects, but that hardly gives them much of a sense of their singular character. The reason for the discrepancy between the number of political projects and the number of nations is simple: the former reflects the limited number of distinctive interpretations we can

25. Ibid., 77.
26. Ibid., 55–58.
27. Ibid., 58–65.

make of a small set of political principles, while the latter reflects the unlimited set of ways in which the contingencies of human history and association can be combined. What makes the French nation singular is not the kind of political projects its members pursue, since the members of other nations could easily imitate them. What makes it singular is the contingent and unrepeatable accumulation of cultural experience it receives and passes on to later generations. And so it is with every other nation.

It is understandable that Schnapper would want to eliminate the moral arbitrariness of the heritage that binds members of a national community. It would be much easier to justify our special concern and loyalty for them if we could say that we share something of special moral value with them. For then we could say that it is the pursuit of that good, not the chances of history and cultural inheritance that connect us to our compatriots.[28] But making something of moral significance the source of nationhood not only misrepresents nations as they are, it threatens to undermine the open-ended character of nationhood that makes it relatively compatible with liberal principles. Turn nations into vehicles for morally significant political projects and you stiffen their resistance to change and cultural diversity, since there is an abiding set of national commitments that they have to protect. And when it comes to a contest between principles of political morality and seemingly arbitrary customs of minority communities, such as the wearing of headscarves, we can be pretty sure which side is going to lose.[29]

It may seem like common sense that if you want to make nations more congenial to liberal democratic ideals and institutions, you should try to find some way of introducing commitments to them into your understanding of national community. But as long as nations are constituted by the morally arbitrary contingencies of history and cultural heritage, doing so may be self-defeating. Seeking to promote greater inclusion and tolerance, you will probably end up inflating some nations' sense of superior-

28. Thomas Hurka ("The Justification of National Partiality") makes such an argument explicitly, suggesting that we are obliged to express their special concern for our nation and its members, but only when our interaction produces some moral good. Less ambitious than Schnapper, he is willing to accept less monumental achievements, like Canada's provision of universal health insurance, as the basis for valuing a national heritage.

29. For accounts of why so many French liberal democrats are against the wearing of headscarves in public schools, see Bowen, *Why the French Don't Like Headscarves*, and B. Winter, *Hijab and Republic*. For a discussion of Schnapper's ambivalent position on this issue, see Laborde, *Critical Republicanism*, 175–76, 187–88, 203–4.

ity to others. The behavior of the three nations who express so much pride in what Schnapper describes as their "political projects," France, Great Britain, and America, tends to confirm that suspicion. Liberal ideals and institutions are better served when we keep our principles of justice separate from the contingencies that define our national communities.

Will Kymlicka takes the opposite approach to binding liberalism and national loyalties more tightly together. Like a number of others, he argues that we need national community in order to realize basic liberal principles, in his case, the commitment to individual autonomy. Kymlicka argues that meaningful choice, and hence the exercise of individual autonomy, "is dependent on the presence of a societal culture, defined by language and history," something that in the modern world they derive from their nations.[30] As a result, liberal principles give people a "legitimate interest" in "ensuring access" to their national culture.[31] Liberals therefore should not only support national loyalties, Kymlicka concludes that they should seek to protect their expression as a basic right.

The problem with this argument is the identification of the nation with a culture. For a culture is not the same thing as a cultural community, let alone a national community. A culture refers to distinctive practices, customs, and attitudes that people share. People can share and have shared cultures without feeling any special concern and loyalty for each other. Cultural communities, in contrast, are groups of people who express such feelings for people with whom they share some cultural practices and traditions, even though the cultural differences that separate such communities are often so minor that it would be absurd to attribute to them different cultures. And a nation is a group of people who express feelings of special concern and loyalty for individuals who share a cultural heritage, not a culture. Sometimes shared cultural practices conveniently mark the difference between nations. But often they do not. Indeed, as Margaret Moore notes, in many cases there is far less violence between nations that are divided by culture, as within Belgium and Canada, than there is between nations that possess relatively few cultural differences, as in Burundi, Ireland, or the former Yugoslavia.[32]

No doubt, it is hard to imagine meaningful forms of autonomy without access to culture. But blocking access to a cultural or national commu-

30. Kymlicka, *Multicultural Citizenship*, 8, 82–83.

31. Ibid., 107.

32. Moore, *Ethics of Nationalism*, 57.

nity does not necessarily block access to culture. Culture, or to be more accurate, *cultures* have surely provided people with meaningful contexts of choice even in periods when other forms of community took precedence over those grounded in cultural difference. That hardly suggests that it is a good thing to erect barriers to expressions of cultural or national loyalty. But it does suggest that liberals need not require such access in order to provide individuals with meaningful contexts of choice.

Moreover, by identifying nations with cultures and cultures with cultural communities, we unnecessarily elevate the significance of national differences, which hardens divisions between nations and makes them all that much more resistant to the kind of adaptation and integration that opens room within them for cultural pluralism and individual autonomy. We may need access to a culture as a context for meaningful choice, but there is no reason to say that we need access to a single culture. Some of the world's most interesting and independent people emerge from culturally divided backgrounds. If there is room within the nation's cultural heritage community for access to multiple cultures, it is probably something that liberals should encourage.

Once again, as with Schnapper's argument, the attraction of Kymlicka's position is that it relieves liberals of the need for justifying a morally arbitrary form of community. It lends national community moral significance, in this case by making it a necessary condition for individual autonomy. But, as I have argued in chapter 7, national communities do not need such significance to retain their moral value. For even morally arbitrary communities are morally valuable as checks against the limitations of our sense of justice. Besides, it is precisely the moral arbitrariness of national community, its reliance on morally insignificant contingencies to establish the shared lineages that connect different generations, that gives national community the open-endedness that makes it compatible with liberal principles of justice. Liberal efforts to correct the nation's moral arbitrariness are therefore bound to be self-defeating.

Advantages of National Community

Liberal principles and national loyalty may not entail each other. But attachments to national community have helped liberals achieve their goals in a number of ways: by dissolving attachments to explicitly illiberal forms of community; by reinforcing the sense of society's priority to—and independence from—the state; and by providing a sense of intergenerational community that promotes concern for future generations and sustains the constitutional protection of individual rights. Such attachments are neither the sole nor a costless means of achieving these ends, which is why I do not treat them as necessary conditions for the realization of liberal political goals. Nevertheless, they do provide means of supporting these ends that continue to be in use today, which means that their abandonment would have some cost for anyone interested in maintaining a liberal polity.

First of all, national loyalties have served an important negative function in liberal politics: undermining attachments to intrinsically hierarchical and exclusive forms of community. Patriarchy and religious sectarianism are the two main targets of early liberal thought, since they provide the rationale for absolute and arbitrary power. The former makes sharing in a set of hierarchical relationships the source of mutual concern and loyalty in politics; the latter, sharing religious beliefs and practices. Liberals have challenged these hierarchical and sectarian loyalties in two different ways. One is the imaginary dissolution of community into its component individuals that is so familiar from liberal theory's thought experiments about states of nature and other original positions. But they have also challenged these loyalties by emphasizing our attachment to more egalitarian and less sectarian communities, such as the nation. The first approach, the dissolution of community into its component individuals, has received the greatest attention from political theorists since it occupies such a prominent place in the work of social contract theorists such as Locke, Kant, and Rawls. But the second approach, the redirection of loyalty away from patriarchal lords and religious sects, plays just as important a role in liberal politics.

Patriarchy models political community on the traditional extended family, with its structural hierarchies between adults and children, men and women, and masters and servants. National community undermines patriarchy by focusing our attention on a more equally shared or categorical understanding of communal membership. As we have seen, "one is a member of a nation directly as an individual." National community "posits whole categories of people without reference to their internal differentiation or claims priority over all such internal differences."[33] That helps counter competing loyalties that make the state seem like the ser-

33. Calhoun, *Nationalism*, 39.

vant of our superiors rather than of the community as a whole. Accordingly, "it is no accident that the modern notion of nation arises in tandem with modern ideas of . . . the individual."[34] Shifting loyalty from a web of hierarchical communities to national community opens up considerable room for individual self-assertion.

Religious sectarians model political community as a community of shared principle. Ironically, they share this approach with defenders of the civic nationalist image of community who rank among their harshest critics. Civic nationalists emphasize choice of principle as the basis for political community because of its potential inclusiveness; since it is always within our power to choose a set of principles everyone can become a member of such a community. But if it is always in the power of individuals to become members of our community, then we have reason to blame them for failing to do so, as people did not hesitate to do during Europe's horrible civil wars of religion.

Images of national community undermine these sectarian loyalties by emphasizing a common cultural heritage to people who distrust the religious beliefs and rituals of their neighbors. National loyalties are well suited to such a task because they do not involve judgments of right and wrong or truth and falsehood. They tell us that we can work together with our neighbors because of something that we share, despite our different beliefs about what is right or wrong. The sharing of a cultural heritage does not challenge the truth of our beliefs, at least directly, in a way that even the profession of liberal principles does. As a result, appeals to national loyalties, though not always successful, were one of the ways in which European liberals aimed at defusing demands to use the state to impose religious belief and ritual.

The disadvantages of this use of national loyalties to secularize the state are fairly obvious, especially now. It only works well among relatively homogenous populations with well-defined political boundaries or where national loyalties are malleable enough to adapt voluntarily to these boundaries. For a long time liberals tended to assume both: the former, in their contractual theories of justification; the latter, in their theories of modernization.

Consider, for example, John Stuart Mill's famous chapter on nationality in *Representative Government.* Mill urges the consolidation of national identities, suggesting, for example, that the absorption of Bretons

34. Ibid., 44–45.

and Basques into France is both possible and beneficial for all parties. "Nobody can suppose," he declares, "that it is not more beneficial to a Breton, or a Basque of French Navarre, to be brought into the current of the ideas and feelings of a highly civilized and cultivated people, to be a member of the French nationality, . . . than to sulk on his own rocks, the half-savage relic of past times." "The same remark," he calmly adds, "applies to the Welshman or the Scottish Highlander, as members of the British nation."[35] The stickiness of national loyalties, their resistance to this kind of consolidation in an age of popular sovereignty, has made liberal reliance on national loyalties much more problematic than Mill expected it to be.

The second way in which liberals have relied on national community is as a means of substantiating the rather abstract image of the people on which their theories of limited government rely.[36] These theories provide two ways of achieving limited government without creating the kind of arbitrary and overlapping powers that characterized medieval political systems. First of all, they introduce various institutional mechanisms—separation of powers, bicameral legislatures, federalism, judicial review, and so on—designed to stretch out and complicate a polity's constitutional structure. Second, they argue that we should we reserve sovereignty for the group that establishes a government's authority and thereby deny it to any individual or group that exercises that authority. In other words, liberals defend limited and regular government by distinguishing between the unlimited constituent sovereignty of the people and the limited governmental sovereignty of the state and its institutions.[37] The state, according to this distinction, is a hierarchically organized structure of institutions and offices, each of which has specific and limited powers. Only the power to establish or constitute such a structure is unlimited, and that power is reserved for the people as a whole and denied to any individual or group that claims to represent them.

This conception of the people has three major features. First, there is its priority to or independence from the state. For liberals it is crucial that individuals do not derive their sense of belonging from the very po-

35. Mill, *Considerations on Representative Government*, 250. Mill makes an exception for the Irish, however, due to the "atrocious government" (252) to which they have been subjected by the British.

36. See Canovan, *Nationhood and Political Theory*, 107, for a similar argument.

37. On the theory of constituent sovereignty, see chapter 4 above and the studies cited there.

litical organization that they are supposed to constitute and monitor. A second feature that all of these images must share is the relatively equal status of its membership. Whatever other inequalities may distinguish the members of the people, whatever inequalities may be legitimated by the form of political authority that it establishes, as members of the people they are imagined as possessing equal status, since the very question that the people must decide is the legitimacy of different forms of social inequality. Finally, since the power to impose religious beliefs was one of the most significant governmental powers that liberals were seeking to limit, shared religious beliefs are ruled out as the connection that binds the members of the sovereign people.

Liberals have relied on a variety of images of group membership to accustom individuals to thinking of themselves as members of the people understood in this sense—civil society, the nation, the common people, and so on. Each has its advantages and drawbacks. Civil society, in which membership is imagined as a chain of interdependence and interaction, is easily imagined as prior to the state.[38] But it has no obvious boundaries, which makes it hard to associate with a particular state.[39] Besides, until it came under attack by communist states, civil society's image of a chain of interdependence rarely generated very strong feelings. Our sense of belonging to the common people, the plebs or the third estate, does, in contrast, regularly inspire such feelings. But in doing so it generates suspicion of difference and achievement that troubles liberals. Identifying the people with the group who share a set of political institutions and practices avoids these problems. But in doing so, it abandons the sense of a group that precedes and survives the state.

Imagining the sovereign people as a national community makes up for some of the problems with other ways of fleshing out images of the

38. Thomas Paine (*The Rights of Man*, 185), e.g., insists that the greater part of social order "existed prior to government, and would exist if the formality of government was abolished."

> The mutual dependence and reciprocal interest which man has upon man, and all the parts of a civilized community upon each other, create that great chain of connexion which holds it together. The landholder, the farmer, the manufacturer, the merchant, the tradesman, and every occupation, prospers by the aid which each receives from the other, and from the whole. Common interest regulates their concerns, and forms their law; and the laws which common usage ordains, have a greater influence than the laws of government. In fine society performs for itself almost everything which is ascribed to government.

39. That is one reason why it is so easy to imagine a "global" civil society.

people. National images of community are especially helpful in reinforcing the sense that we belong to a community that precedes and survives the state. The pieces of cultural heritage around which nations are imagined are often older than existing states, or at least appear to be older, so it is relatively easy to imagine nations as existing prior to the state. In doing so, national community fills an important gap in the liberal political imagination. But it clearly introduces problems of its own. So while images of national community counter the class and status exclusions of the populist image, they introduce their own sources of exclusion with differences based on cultural heritage. While it helps us, unlike civil society, to imagine the boundaries that separate one people from another, these boundaries often fit very badly with existing political boundaries. And while the image of national community helps us flesh out our sense of belonging to the prepolitical group that establishes and legitimates state authority, it does not solve the problems created by our attachment to such an image of group membership. Nevertheless, if we have become comfortable with this odd image of dual membership in state and prepolitical community, it is largely because we think of ourselves as members of national communities that precede the establishment of states.

Finally, national loyalties help liberals establish a sense of intergenerational continuity that it is hard to establish through their principles of justice. As Margaret Canovan notes:

> Polities that are going to survive, let alone be able to take action have to be able to maintain some degree of unity and stability in face not only of the competition from other polities but of entropy resulting from the plurality and mortality of human beings. In a world where new people, all with their axes to grind, are continually replacing one another, the problem of maintaining unity and stability has always been at the root of politics, and what is interesting for our purposes is that it has historically been harder to solve on democratic than on non-democratic terms. . . . the more democratic the state is to be, the more need there is for the people to have some bond of unity other than that provided by common subjection.[40]

The nation, Canovan suggests, provides such a bond. Since its members share a cultural heritage, a place in a lineage, they imagine themselves connected to past and future generations as well as to each other

40. Canovan, *Nationhood and Political Theory*, 22.

in the present. These connections are especially helpful in promoting the concern for the well-being of future generations that every polity needs. Liberal theorists have found it hard to define and justify obligations to future generations. If the issue has been far less problematic in liberal practice, it is because liberal politicians regularly invoke the sense of concern for our "heirs" that membership in a national community promotes. And, as we have seen, it promotes this sense of concern without grounding it in either biological descent or our subordination to the past.

The nation's intergenerational community also serves liberal ideals and institutions in another, less obvious way: by supporting the constitutional protection of individual rights. National community, I suggest, helps provide a sense of intergenerational continuity without which the practice of liberal constitutionalism would be very hard to maintain.

Keeping governmental powers restrained within the limits constituted by the people rather than the government itself is clearly one of the most important and distinctive features of the liberal philosophy of limited government. Tom Paine, as usual, presents the liberal "common sense" of the matter most clearly.

> A constitution is a thing *antecedent* to a government, and a government is only the creature of a constitution. The constitution of a country is not the act of its government, but of the people constituting a government. It is the body of elements, to which you can refer, and quote article by article; and which contains . . . everything that relates to the complete organization of a civil government, and the principles on which it shall act, and by which it shall be bound.[41]

The reasoning behind this kind of liberal constitutionalism is fairly straightforward. Since government is established by the people, its actions must be subordinate to the rules and principles that the people use to constitute it. Making the Constitution superior to governmental rulings is only to say, as Alexander Hamilton argues in *The Federalist*, that the creature is subordinate to its creator.[42]

But this reasoning poses a serious difficulty for liberal democrats, that is, for those who believe that governmental authority, not just the constitution of government, must reflect popular consent. Why should the people of the past take precedence over the people of the present,

41. Paine, *The Rights of Man*, 93, 207.

42. Hamilton, Jay, and Madison, *The Federalist Papers*, no. 78.

the people who authorized the Constitution over the people who at later times authorizes governments? Why should the express wish of the people of 1787 taken to be the express wish of the people of 1887 or 1987? This is the so-called countermajoritarian difficulty that has inspired so much ingenuity among American constitutional theorists. A people working within the framework of a popularly established constitution is much more constrained in taking matters into its own hands than the people who originally establish such a constitution. There may be many ways of softening this blow to democratic accountability, for example, by showing that constitutional rules provide a necessary or enabling condition for the possibility of democratic governance.[43] But you cannot completely remove it. Even as an enabling constraint, a limitation that makes it possible for democratic majorities to do things that they could not otherwise do,[44] constitutions still constrain. And one way that they do so is by privileging the acts of the people who establish constitutions over the acts of the people who follow them.

Such privileging of past over the present does not fit very well with the image of the people presented by popular sovereignty theory. "The earth," Jefferson famously argues, "belongs to the living and not to the dead." "Each new generation is as independent of the one preceding, as that was of all which had gone before. It has then, like them, a right to choose for itself the form of government it believes most productive of its own happiness," a right that should be exercised in regular constitutional conventions, meeting every ten or twenty years to revise and reconsider the fundamental laws of the state.[45] For "by the law of nature, one generation is to another as is one independent nation to another."[46] That is why Jefferson was so eager to eliminate the "magic supposed to be in the word constitution."[47] By Jefferson's logic "a constituent assembly in Philadelphia, apparently, can no more legislate for future Americans than for contemporary Chinese."[48] Americans have been able to

43. For example, see Ely, *Democracy and Distrust*, and Holmes, "Precommitment and the Paradox of Democracy."

44. On the concept of enabling constraints, see Yack, "Toward a Free Marketplace of Social Institutions," 1967–68, and Holmes, "Precommitment and the Paradox of Democracy," 215–16.

45. Jefferson, *Writings*, 1402.

46. Ibid., 962–63.

47. Ibid., 251.

48. Holmes, "Precommitment and the Paradox of Democracy," 204.

use the Constitution to protect individual freedoms only because so few of them have shared his belief that different generations of Americans are as "one independent nation to another."

There is a Burkean element to liberal constitutionalism in America, a tendency to ancestor worship that is immediately recognizable to anyone familiar with the practice of American constitutionalism.[49] Like Burke, most liberal constitutionalists are inclined to treat their liberties *as if* they could be found in their constitutional inheritance, so as to mask innovations as interpretations of received laws and principles.[50] Madison, for example, rejects Jefferson's proposal to have frequent and regular constitutional conventions because it would deprive the Constitution of the "veneration which time bestows on everything, and without which even the wisest and freest governments would not possess the requisite stability." "In a nation of philosophers," he adds, "this consideration ought to be disregarded." But "in every other nation, the most rational government will not find it a superfluous advantage to have the prejudices of the community on its side."[51] And even Paine, who shared Jefferson's belief that "the earth belongs to the living," believes that "a constitution is the property of a nation" passed from one generation to another. He merely denies that the nation ever has the right to renounce its ultimate sovereignty, its ultimate right to dissolve old forms and establish new forms of governments.[52]

The difference between Burkean and liberal understandings of constitutionalism parallels the difference between conservative and national understandings of intergenerational community. Burke, like most conservatives, treats our constitutional liberties "as an *entailed inheritance* derived from our forefathers, to be transmitted to our posterity."[53] In other words, he grounds these liberties in the kind of subordination to

49. For complaints about this problem, see, e.g., Lazare, *The Frozen Republic*.

50. As Burke notes (*Reflections*, 36), even though common lawyers were often wrong in treating British rights as an inheritance rather than the fruit of political innovations, this proves his position "the more strongly, because it demonstrates the powerful prepossession toward antiquity, with which the minds of all our lawyers and legislators, and of all the people whom they wish to influence, have been always filled." In other words, it is the inclination to discover the new in the old, not the fact of historical continuity, which Burke relies upon. See Canovan, *Nationhood and Political Theory*, 69–70, on this point.

51. Hamilton, Jay, and Madison, *The Federalist Papers*, no. 49, 314–15.

52. Paine, *The Rights of Man*, 213, 62–65.

53. Burke, *Reflections*, 37.

the will of past benefactors that prevents us from selling or breaking up entailed estates. Liberal constitutionalists, in contrast, tend to treat our constitutional constraints as self-subordination, rather than subordination to others. They analyze constitutional restraint as a problem of precommitment and *self*-restraint, a much less intractable problem than justifying the dead taking precedence over the living. But they can proceed in this way only if they imagine the people as a continuing, intergenerational community. An attachment to national community helps make that possible, without relying on the conservative notion of inheritance as entailment. It thereby promotes the relatively open-ended form of constitutionalism that liberals prefer.

The Limits of National Loyalty

I have tried in this chapter to ease some liberal concerns about national loyalties. In order to complete this effort, however, I need to discuss the limits of national loyalty, since one thing that makes liberals especially nervous about national loyalties is the lack of clear indications of where their demands on us end. Like every other form of social friendship, our attachment to a national community disposes us to feel special concern for a group of individuals rather than set out for us a prescribed set of obligations. That sometimes makes it hard to resist compatriots who demand unconditional loyalty from us, since it allows them to portray any hesitation in accepting our country, right or wrong, as proof that we are not really concerned about the fate of our countrymen and -women. I have tried to correct this impression throughout this book, noting that balancing competing loyalties and working out the tensions between feelings of social friendship and beliefs about justice constitute a large part of our everyday moral life. But because communal loyalty is so rarely treated as a central concern of moral philosophy,[54] its limits, let alone the limits of its national species, are poorly understood. So I shall conclude this chapter by outlining the different ways in which we reach the limits of national loyalty.

The most important limitation on national loyalty is simplest and the easiest to miss: its dependence on our approval. Like all other forms of communal loyalty our attachment to the nation rests on our subjective

54. For recent exceptions, see Fletcher, *Loyalty*, and Keller, *The Limits of Loyalty*.

affirmation of something that we share with others. That means that no one is obliged to feel special concern and loyalty for the people with whom they share some cultural heritage. You may be obliged by your participation in a political organization like a state to pledge to acknowledge its authority and foreswear allegiance to all foreign potentates. But you are not obliged to feel special concern for the members of a nation just because you happen to share something with them, if what you share with them means little to you.

The notion that we are obliged to feel special concern and loyalty for people with whom we happen to share things, whether it is our skin color, our language, our place of birth, or stories about our founding fathers, is based on a misunderstanding of community—as well as nationhood—that I have striven to correct in this book. At any given time, we are connected to others by far more forms of sharing than we can handle. Most of them go unacknowledged and ignored. Those who lecture us about our obligations to express certain forms of communal loyalty are in fact trying to get us to affirm one form of sharing over another—for example, our Russian over Ukrainian heritage, or our Pan-Serbian over Russian heritage, or our European or Asiatic heritage over all the others. Or they are trying to move us to affirm some completely different form of sharing as a focus of mutual concern or loyalty, such as religion or our humanity, since we are in no way obliged to affirm any of the various cultural heritages that we share with people. Of course, most of us do affirm shared cultural heritages as a focus of community, and do so without thinking much about it. But the first limit of national loyalty lies within us, in its subjective origins.

Once we have affirmed a shared cultural heritage as a focus of social friendship, then the primary limits on national loyalty are those described in chapter 7: our beliefs about justice and the other forms of sharing that we affirm at the same time as our identification with the nation. Even if you are persuaded to think of national ties as the highest form of loyalty, that does not mean that you should always sacrifice the good of friends or family or humanity for the good of nation. It only means that it is that the nation is the community that will most often command the subordination of your loyalties. For communal loyalties do not line up neatly, like steps in a chain of command with an unlimited power at the top, much to the annoyance of political propagandists. They are much more disorderly than that, pulling us in different directions with the different groups in whom they encourage us to take an interest. The inherent diversity of communal attachment thus acts to some degree as a check on national loyalty. Political propagandists can only get around that diversity by erecting a duty that demands the subordination of all other loyalties to one's loyalty to the nation. But such a duty is a principle of justice, a conviction that in fact constrains rather than fulfills our disposition to express feelings of communal loyalty.

As long as we do not adopt the principle that the good of the nation trumps all other moral concerns—the last thing you would imagine liberals to do—then beliefs about justice or our mutual obligations are available to support limits on the assertion of national loyalty. I have tried in the preceding chapter to show that reliance on our convictions about justice and feelings of social friendship to check and balance each other is a mundane and familiar part of our everyday moral life, rather than the dramatic confrontation that it is often portrayed to be. In this chapter I have tried to show that there is nothing in this particular form of community, one based on the affirmation of a shared cultural heritage, that is precluded by a commitment to basic liberal democratic principles of justice.

The tensions between justice and national loyalty tend to become dramatic when your beliefs about justice demand an action that could cause serious harm to your compatriots. Such situations arise most often in war. If your compatriots are fighting what you consider to be an unjust war, or fighting a war with manifestly unjust means, then you might begin by merely avoiding complicity in the wrongs your social friends are doing. But, in the end, you may find yourself in a position in which you have to contemplate doing harm to people whose well-being you are disposed to promote. In such a situation you may say, simply, that no balance between justice and national loyalty is possible, that the wrong is so great and heinous that you must take action to stop it, even if that means harming people to whom you are attached. Or you may decide, like many of the participants in the 1944 conspiracy to assassinate Hitler, that it is precisely your concern for the long-term well-being of the members of your community that compels you to take actions that cause them harm in the short term.[55] The first option limits national loyalty by rejecting its demands when it supports a particularly heinous form of injustice. The second option, in contrast, limits national loyalty by reinter-

55. This argument figures prominently among those, like Alisdair MacIntyre, in *Is Patriotism a Virtue?*, who seek to show that patriots need not be blind to the wrongs done by their countrymen and women.

preting it in the light of our beliefs about injustice. (After all, the reason that you are emphasizing the long-term good of the community is because the short-term advantage rests on such a horrible injustice.) Such reinterpretations of national loyalty are quite common in this kind of conflict, since they are much easier to sustain psychologically for people who have become accustomed to expressing concern for a particular group of individuals.

That brings us to the final limit on national loyalty, the one that most of the anti-Hitler conspirators found so hard to contemplate: the dissolution of the communal connection itself, the assertion that you cannot maintain any connection to people who have done and benefited from terrible wrongs. If the establishment of communal loyalties rests on subjective affirmation, then they can, in principle, be dissolved by its withdrawal. Yet, it is interesting to see how rarely this option is exercised, at least among members of nations who are not themselves the victims of the injustice.[56] To a certain extent the rarity of such withdrawal reflects moral complacency, an unwillingness to deal with the disdain and alienation that usually follows from the self-conscious dissolution of moral ties. But it also reflects a peculiar feature of national community, one that I have tried to emphasize in this chapter. The nation is not an intrinsically moral or purposive community. It does not bring together people who affirm a shared choice of goal or moral principle. As a result, terrible actions undertaken by its members do not necessarily define the community, which makes it easier to maintain one's connections to it, even when one is fully aware of and opposed to these actions. Those actions become part of a nation's heritage, just as the creation of a slave society is part of the American heritage. While you would probably have no trouble walking away from a community organized for the purpose of enslaving Africans or exterminating religious minorities, your ties to a nation that has done such things in the past are much harder to dissolve, since they are always open to revision and development. So though the ability to dissolve our connection to a national community remains an important limit on claims to national loyalty, it tends to be the least invoked in moral difficulties.

56. And, sometimes, even among victims of injustice, like Dreyfus, whose continued loyalty to the army and nation that framed him and disdained his religion struck Judith Shklar as nothing short of madness. See Shklar, "Obligation, Loyalty, Exile," 191.

CHAPTER NINE

The Moral Problem with Nationalism

Nationalism's Moral Complexity

Nationalism, I have argued in part 1, is best understood as a mixture of feelings of special concern and loyalty for the members of our nation with beliefs about the importance of national community in our lives. In its most powerful and influential form, it blends national loyalty with beliefs about the nation's right to have the final say in the political arrangements by which it is governed. Nationalists, according to this account, do not merely believe that nations should be sovereign; they seek sovereignty for the members of the national community to whom they feel connected. And they do not merely express special concern and loyalty for the members of that community; they seek to secure their well-being by gaining for their nation the political sovereignty that they believe it has coming to it.

The moral problem with nationalism, so understood, seems obvious for many people: its unapologetic endorsement of group partisanship. Nationalism, these critics complain, induces a kind of moral blindness that allows us to ignore the harm done to outsiders in pursuit of our own nation's well-being. At its best, it encourages morally shabby forms of favoritism and special pleading. At its worst, it unleashes a kind of tribalism, a reversion to a primitive condition in which we abandon the complex ties of mutual obligation that civilization has built up among different peoples.

It is not very difficult to counter the harshest of these tribalist or "dark gods" critiques of nationalism.[1] Nevertheless, it is hard to shake the suspicion that there is something morally questionable about nationalism—which may be why so many intelligent observers continue to invoke the language of tribalism,[2] despite repeated warnings against doing so from our most sophisticated students of the phenomenon. The expression of national loyalties may be quite compatible with commitments to basic liberal political principles. But it also seems to invite spectacularly illiberal actions, actions that violate the most minimal standards of justice and humanity. The hounding, expulsion, or outright massacre of the members of national minorities; unlimited, terror-filled campaigns for national liberation; all-out war over relatively minor territorial disputes between states—these are just some of the forms of communal violence that have accompanied the rise of nationalism to prominence in modern political life. There may not, as Rebecca West complains, be "the smallest reason for confounding nationalism, which is the desire of a people to be itself, with imperialism, which is the desire of a people to prevent other peoples from being themselves."[3] But, sadly, the desire of peoples to be and govern themselves has sometimes proved harsher to their neighbors than the imperialist's desire to rule over them.

It would simplify things immensely if we could assign the good things to one kind of nationalism and the bad to another. But, as we have seen in part I, this division of nationalism into morally valuable and abhorrent forms cannot be sustained without developing self-serving myths about it. Perhaps, instead, we should think of nationalism itself as morally neutral, as a way of mobilizing and coordinating the activities of individuals, rather than as a drive to achieve a morally valuable or questionable goal.[4] Understood in this way, nationalism derives its moral qualities from the causes and characters of its proponents. Nationalism doesn't kill people, nationalists do. In the hands of a Milosevic or a Hitler it is a terrible weapon; in the hands of a Churchill or a Gandhi, it is a very different matter.

Since advocates of virtually every cause and ideology except anar-

1. See Gellner, *Thought and Change*, 149–51.

2. For recent examples, see Sen, *Identity and Violence*, and Maalouf, *In the Name of Identity*.

3. West, *Black Lamb, Grey Falcon*, 843.

4. The direction of a "nationalist movement is determined by the people who join it, whoever they may be" (Wiebe, *Who We Are*, 5).

chism have relied on nationalism as a rallying cry, this way of resolving nationalism's moral ambiguity seems much more plausible than dichotomies between good and bad nationalisms. Nevertheless, it begs a crucial question: is there is anything especially problematic, from a moral point of view, in mobilizing human beings in this particular way?[5]

In this chapter I argue that there is indeed a moral problem with nationalism, quite apart from its exploitation by unscrupulous or fanatical political entrepreneurs. But I suggest that this problem is considerably subtler and more insidious than tribalism or extreme group partisanship. For the tribalist account of the nationalist's propensity to communal violence is grounded in an overly simple understanding of the moral psychology of nationalism. Far from encouraging the abandonment of any moral connections to members of other nations, nationalism owes much of its intensity to the existence of just such a connection: namely, the belief that outsiders are *obliged* to allow us, as members of a nation, to organize our own political lives. From this perspective, those who impede our nation's efforts to gain control of its political affairs strike us as *wrongdoers*, not just as competitors or enemies. As such, they are deemed to merit punishment as well as resistance, a combination of judgments that greatly deepens our hostility toward them.

This connection to nonmembers is, morally speaking, the primary difference between national loyalty and nationalism, at least in the political form in which the latter has spread throughout the modern world. Our sense of attachment to a national community establishes moral connections only among its members: the feelings of social friendship or mutual concern and loyalty that lead us to take a special interest in their well-being. Nationalism, in contrast, combines such connections among members of our nation with a sense of justice that connects us to nonmembers as well. Indeed, for political nationalists the very fact that *we* feel connected to each other as members of a national community imposes an obligation on *others* to allow us to take control of our political lives.[6]

It is this combination of beliefs about justice and feelings of communal loyalty that makes nationalism morally problematic. For it both deepens our hostility toward the members of rival communities and weakens the

5. Margaret Moore makes a similar point in *The Ethics of Nationalism*, 44.

6. Of course, such an obligation is very hard to justify, since it is hard to see why our feelings about each other should impose an obligation on a third party. See especially Brillmayer, "The Moral Significance of Nationalism."

moral restraints we ordinarily rely on to check such antipathies. Nationalism, you might say, not only loads the weapon of communal conflict, it disables the safety.

The pursuit of national sovereignty does not offend our sense of justice and humanity in the way that, say, the demand for racial hierarchy now does. Nor, I have argued, does the expression of special concern and loyalty to the members of our nation. But the combination of these two things does make us much more likely to harm others in ways that we would ordinarily condemn as unjust or inhumane. That is why I describe nationalism as morally problematic rather than morally wrong. Nationalism weakens our resistance to doing morally abhorrent things, even if it does not set us morally abhorrent goals to achieve.

If accurate, this account of the moral problem with nationalism has important practical implications. For it suggests that loosening nationalists' sense of connection to their nation neither cures nor inoculates us against the problem of nationalist violence. Those of us with no illusions about the natural or primordial origins of our nations are therefore much more susceptible to nationalism's corrosive effect on moral restraints than we like to think we are. We may have no difficulty rejecting demands for closed and homogenous nations, each a moral world unto itself. But as long as we believe that the members of other nations are obliged to grant our nation final say over our political arrangements, then we too will be influenced by the combination of indignation and communal loyalty that disposes nationalists to treat their opponents so harshly.

If you disapprove of national community, you are bound to disapprove of nationalism, since these beliefs about national sovereignty deepen and intensify the partial loyalties that make the nation morally objectionable to you in the first place. But even if, like myself, you find real moral value in the feelings of mutual concern and loyalty that sustain contingent communities like the nation, that does not necessarily mean that you will find similar moral value in nationalism. For the combination of national loyalties with beliefs about the nation's rights and obligations creates moral problems that each lack on their own.

You Don't Have to Be a Fanatic to Act Like One

Tribalism, the mutual hostility often ascribed to primitive human communities, is one obvious precedent for the intense group hatreds displayed in the worst nationalist conflicts. The fanaticism of religious and revolutionary sectarians is another. These historical precedents suggest that the unusual harshness of nationalists in these conflicts stems from a kind of moral blindness or one-sidedness. Fanatics believe so strongly in their principles that they are ready to let the whole world suffer and perish, including themselves, as long as truth and justice prevail. Tribalists, in contrast, ask only whether a course of action serves to benefit or harm the members of their community. They are so intensely concerned about the well-being of their community that they lose sight of any sense of obligation to outsiders. Violent nationalists, many assume, must suffer from a similar kind of moral blindness toward their rivals. How else to explain their indifference to the suffering that they cause?

But moral blindness or one-sidedness is not the only way of intensifying the antipathy we feel toward the members of other communities. If, as I have argued in chapter 7, beliefs about justice and feelings of social friendship can act as checks on each other's excesses when opposed, then it stands to reason that they will tend to intensify our feelings of hostility when they line up together against the members of opposing communities. When, for example, our beliefs about justice identify our enemies as wrongdoers, not just as people who pose a threat to members of our community, we generally express much deeper hostility toward them. For we then believe that our opponents deserve to suffer, not just that they have to be stopped from harming our friends and loved ones. That is one reason why religious and revolutionary wars tend to be so much more murderous than their counterparts: they encourage us to treat our enemies as something akin to murderers. These wars confront us with enemies who seem to be wrongdoers of the worst sort, blasphemers against the Lord or exploiters of the people, enemies we are therefore disposed to punish as well as fight. Two distinct moral judgments, one based on our sense of justice, the other on our sense of social friendship, combine to deepen our antipathy toward them:[7] that they have done something that merits punishment and that they threaten the well-being of the members of our community.

7. Since every battle is fought in the name of a cause—the recovery of occupied territory, the preemption of a future aggressor, etc.—it might seem that you get this combination of moral motivations in every war. But in sectarian wars these beliefs identify our enemies *themselves* as wrongdoers, as blasphemers and counterrevolutionaries, not just as the supporters of a just or unjust cause. That is what intensifies our antipathy toward them.

Even if, unlike fanatics, we are not disposed to pursue our vision of truth and justice at all costs, the combination of these judgments sometimes inspires us to act as if we do. Religious and revolutionary armies are not generally filled with Savonarolas and Saint-Justs. Yet their sense that their enemies merit punishment as well as resistance makes it hard for them to control themselves when they get their enemies in their power. In the end, it seems, you do not have to be a fanatic—or a tribalist—to act like one.

Although I have begun this section by invoking the extreme and relatively rare example of sectarian warfare, the intensification of hostility through the combination of moral motives is an everyday occurrence. Think how much more strongly you feel about people who cut in line in front of a friend or a family member than people who cut in line in front of the group of strangers next to you. Both have committed an injustice that merits correction. But the former has harmed people whose well-being is a matter of some concern to you as well. That makes you much more disposed to strike out against them or at least to call attention to their misdeed.

Such intensification of hostility to others tends to be especially pronounced when calculations of self-interest line up with beliefs about justice and feelings of social friendship against our rivals, as I shall suggest that they often do among nationalists. That is what I believe Marx had in mind when he spoke about the working class as an objective force for revolutionary change. He believed that class solidarity, self-interest, and an intense sense of the injustice to which they were subjected all lined up together to direct the proletariat against capitalism and the ruling class that benefited from it. A major reason why Marx's revolutionary vision failed was that most European workers displayed as much or more concern for the well-being of the members of their nations as for the members of their class.

The combination of these different motives not only tends to intensify our hostility toward others when they line up against them; it also undermines the moral resources we ordinarily rely on to restrain such feelings. Each of these motives, calculations of self-interest, beliefs about justice, and feelings of social friendship, restrains our behavior toward others in a distinctive way. Beliefs about justice fuel the sense that we owe things to other people. Feelings of social friendship, which most people extend to some degree to all other human beings, inspire some degree of concern for their well-being. And calculations of self-interest remind us of the long-run advantages of cooperation with others, as well as the more immediate dangers of striking out at them. After all, even when you join a mob attacking a relatively vulnerable individual, you take the risk that you may be the one person whom that individual succeeds in taking to the grave with him.

On its own, however, each of these motives for cooperation also identifies a group of others toward whom no consideration is due: the competitors who counter our long-term interests, the wrongdoers who violate our standards of justice, and the enemies who seek to harm our friends. That is why restraints on our behavior toward others break down when we become so intensely driven by one of these motives that we are unmoved by the other two. Fanatics see only the wrongdoer in the violator of their principles, not the potential partner in mutually beneficial projects or the member of their family, nation, or species. Tribalists see only the threat to their friends in their enemies, not the potential partner or the bearer of rights. And the tyrant, the con man, and the stock manipulator, to name a few exemplars of the single-minded pursuit of self-interest, see only the obstacle to be overcome, not the object of concern or obligation.

But when all of these motives are engaged against some rival, it becomes much more difficult to invoke them as sources of moral restraint, once again leading us to act like the fanatic or tribalist without really being one. Montaigne warned us that it was enough to stiffen our shoulders to our duty, that we should never harden our hearts to the point where we no longer feel distress when duty and friendship conflict.[8] But what if your heart is already deeply engaged in the matter, say, that it bleeds for the suffering of your friends and countrymen at the hands of the infidels or the counterrevolutionaries? Then it is going to be much harder to invoke some more general sense of humanity to restrain your desires to make your enemies suffer when they fall into your hands. Similarly, if you believe our enemies are wrongdoers as well as the cause of your community's suffering, it will be much harder to invoke some sense of justice to protect them from your anger at what they have done to people you care about. And if it seems to be in our interest to see them suffer as well, then the last source of restraint is blocked.

In order to see how the demands of self-interest, social friendship, and justice might line up together to weaken our self-restraint in dealing

8. Montaigne, *Essays*, "On the Useful and the Honorable," 609.

with those who oppose us, it is worth considering a timely and controversial example: the recent drift toward allowing the torture of prisoners captured by Americans in their so-called Global War on Terror. Restraints on the use of torture draw on all three of the motives discussed in this section. Self-interest suggests that the practice be banned so that you will not be subjected to torture yourself if you ever have the misfortune to become a prisoner. Beliefs about justice suggest that such behavior is a violation of a prisoner's rights. And our sense of humanity, our feelings of social friendship for other human beings in general, abhors the willful cruelty that the practice of torture introduces.

Why then did these long-standing restraints against the torture of prisoners break down among Americans holding captives from recent wars in Afghanistan and Iraq? One reason, I suggest, is that Americans saw their captives as great wrongdoers, not just enemies. For if ever there were a war in which our enemies were perceived as murderers, then the Global War on Terror is it.[9]

The Geneva Convention codifies the rules for the treatment of prisoners of war, members of the enemy forces that oppose us in battle. But terrorists do not just oppose us; they fight us in ways that break all civilized rules of engagement, ways that make them seem like murderers, not just enemies. As such, we are disposed to punish them, to impose suffering on them that goes beyond that which merely neutralizes them as enemies. Conversely, because we perceive them as our enemies as well as murderers, we are disposed to hurt them in ways—assassination, bombing, and so on—that we ordinarily deny ourselves when treating people accused of crimes.[10] Clearly, this combination of perceptions greatly deepens our inclination to do them harm. But it also makes it harder to call on other moral motives to check this inclination, since both our sense of justice and our sense of friendship are already engaged in our perception of terrorist prisoners. How can these prisoners, of all people, claim the privileges of the Geneva Convention when they reject all civilized rules of warfare? How can they appeal to our sense of human-

9. So much so, that there is considerable confusion about what kind of prisoners they represent: accused criminals awaiting judgment and punishment or prisoners of war kept from harming us for the duration of hostilities.

10. We tend to feel the same way about domestic prisoners whom we charge with subversion. They not only commit an injustice meriting punishment, such as the destruction of life or property, but also rise in opposition to us, thereby encouraging us to fight them in ways we deny ourselves to ordinary criminals.

ity when they practice indiscriminate violence against our compatriots? Add to this picture the pressing interest that Americans had in gaining information from these prisoners and it is easy to see how resistance to the practice of torture might weaken and crumble, from prison guards to the White House.

Note that in this scenario, it is a weakening of the resistance to cruel treatment of others, rather than a direct assault on our commitments against it, that leads to the acceptance of torture. The barriers to the torture of prisoners were not washed away in an outburst of fanatical self-righteousness or xenophobic tribalism. They were undermined, instead, by the interaction of calculations of interest, beliefs about justice, and feelings of communal loyalty. Nationalism, I shall argue, works in a similar way to undermine our resistance to cruelty toward the members of neighboring and competing national communities.

The Moral Psychology of Nationalist Cruelty

The question is asked again and again by the victims of ethnic cleansing: how can people who have long been our neighbors, schoolmates, and customers treat us with such cruelty? It is as if, these victims complain, our tormentors carry two distinct images of the world in their brains: one in which we are partners in a whole range of cooperative and even friendly activities and the other in which we are like beasts against whom nothing is forbidden.[11] Participation in these cooperative activities suggests that the perpetrators of ethnic cleansing cannot be so fanatically devoted to their national community that they deem the very presence of their victims offensive and dangerous. Why then with the rise and spread of nationalism do they so often come to act as if they do?

The previous section suggests an answer to this question, one that does not require us to ascribe a schizophrenic view of the world to the practitioners of ethnic cleansing. The spread of nationalism does not cancel a first, more cooperative image of our neighbors, thereby releasing the primitive xenophobe we all carry around deep inside us. Instead, it disposes to us to act more harshly toward them because it regularly puts us into situations where calculations of interest, feelings of social friendship, and beliefs about justice all line up against the members of

11. Lieberman, *Terrible Fate*, xiii.

rival nations, situations that tend to intensify our feelings of hostility toward our rivals and undermine the moral restraints we usually rely on to control such feelings.

Let us begin with the way in which the spread of nationalism changes our interests in the mistreatment of the members of rival nations. The rise of nationalism is often said to lift the lid on a boiling pot of age-old communal hatreds. The delegitimation of foreign and imperial rule, it is said, eliminates the outside overseers who keep the members of rival nations from going at each other's throats. This view seems hard to accept when a clear line between rival nations, let alone their mutual hostility, often takes shape only in the wake of nationalist agitation. How, for example, can we blame postwar violence between Lithuanians and Poles on the age-old hatred between them when even the Polish national epic, Mickiewiscz's *Pan Tadeusz*, begins by invoking "Lithuania, my fatherland?"[12]

But although the rise of nationalism does not simply release communal antipathies from the institutions that have constrained them, it does give us a new and powerful reason to fear, compete with, and act harshly toward the members of other nations with whom we find ourselves sharing political boundaries. For the rise and spread of nationalism introduces a new and supremely important good for nations to seek: actual and symbolic sovereignty over a given territory. Even if we were not particularly interested in this good and what it can do for us, we are bound to fear what the other communities with whom we share territory might do with it and therefore oppose their efforts to achieve it.

Prior to the rise of nationalism, more than one nation could treat the same territory as its own, since that sense of connection to territory did not require exclusive ownership or control.[13] The rise of nationalism, with its demand for national sovereignty, changes that, making the mixing of national populations, something that imperial rulers treat as the norm, highly problematic. Minority nationals within a given territory now have good reason to look at the members of the majority nation as imperialists, seeking to rule over them. Members of the majority nation now have good reason to look at minorities as obstacles to their efforts to take control of their collective lives, especially when these minorities can call on the aid of powerful friends abroad in homeland and expa-

12. Snyder, *The Reconstruction of Nations*, 29.

13. See chapter 5 and 6 above.

triate communities. Both groups thereby gain a powerful interest, quite apart from any judgment about the intrinsic value of cultural homogeneity, in redrawing political borders and moving populations to create more nationally uniform political units. National minorities have an interest in creating new territorial boundaries in which they can act as majorities. And national majorities have an interest in dispersing or eliminating the powerful minorities that obstruct their efforts to exercise actual and symbolic sovereignty over their territories.

The rise of nationalism thus gives nations who share political units an interest in initiating the range of practices that we have come to describe as ethnic cleansing. The association of ethnic cleansing with its most horrific example, the Nazi campaign of genocide against the Jews—with its racist ideology and its fanatical drive to complete the job even if it took resources away from their fight for survival—has made ethnic cleansing seem much more irrational than it is. But once the rise of nationalism introduces a competition for national sovereignty the practice of ethnic cleansing becomes eminently rational, since, despite its general vilification, its effects are rarely reversed. That probably explains why it has been so commonplace, especially in the wake of the collapse of the empires that controlled Eastern and Central Europe.[14] Whether it is in the end a rational policy to pursue, given all of one's goals and all of the potential long-term costs, is another issue. Like all such disruptive practices, the removal of rival populations involves a serious risk to its initiators. And it involves serious losses, from the possible future fruits of cooperation with your rivals that you are sacrificing. My point is merely that the rise of nationalism gives us a new interest in treating the members of other nations with whom we share political territories in ways that are unusually harsh and cruel: their removal, violent or not, from the places where they have long lived.

But life puts us into many situations in which we have a strong interest in treating others cruelly. What makes this situation special is that, as with Americans' recent flirtation with torture, our sense of concern for others and our sense of justice, which we usually rely on to restrain such interests, line up against our rivals as well.

As nationalists, we seek sovereignty for the members of our national community. It is their well-being that is threatened by the rival nations

14. See Lieberman, *Terrible Fate*, and Mann, *The Dark Side of Democracy*, for excellent accounts of just how widespread the practice has been in the last two hundred years.

that impede our efforts to take control of our political affairs. We fear what will happen to them, not just ourselves, and that both intensifies our antipathy toward people who block our interest and makes it harder to sympathize with their suffering, since our sympathies are already deeply engaged by the actual and potential suffering of our compatriots. The harsh action that we might never undertake merely to advance our own interests, we are often quite ready to perform when it also protects the well-being of those to whom we feel connected. That is one reason that most of us are so much readier to kill in war than as separate individuals.

That our hostility toward people who threaten our interests might be intensified when we imagine that the same people threaten the well-being of members of our community probably seems obvious. But it is hard to see as long as we think of community as the subordination to or submergence in the group. For in that case we see the influence of community only in those extraordinary moments when we are ready to sacrifice self-interest for the good of others. We thereby miss the everyday experience of communal life, in which our mutual concern for each other's well-being coincides with and reinforces other, more self-serving motives. The history of nationalist conflicts, no doubt, records many moments of self-sacrifice, even self-conscious martyrdom. But it is driven by situations in which our sympathy for the plight of our countrymen and -women lines up with and reinforces our own interests in harsh treatment of our rivals.

Of course, this combination of friendship and interest would not be very powerful unless we felt a relatively strong attachment to the members of our national community, something that is by no means the norm in human history. But the rise of nationalism, as I have argued in chapter 5, greatly increases the importance of national community and the feelings of loyalty it inspires. It does so primarily by making nations responsible for taking control of the most powerful of modern political organizations, the state. Your national heritage, its myths and heroes and folk songs, may leave you cold, compared to many more interesting things you find that you share with others. But if you—or simply most people around you—believe that people who share such a heritage should be able to take charge of their own political lives, then you are bound to take the connections that it establishes much more seriously and feel more concern for the ups and downs of the people who share them.

Moreover, the rise and spread of nationalism not only increases the importance of national community as an object of special concern and loyalty, it tremendously raises the stakes of communal competition for nations and thus the sense of what our compatriots might suffer as well as gain from it. The winners in the competition enjoy the advantages of political sovereignty: general recognition by the international community, the ability to preserve and enhance a national cultural heritage, and access to the powerful organizational tools of the modern state. The losers, in contrast, not only fail to gain these goods. They find themselves in a situation in which their very existence as a community is threatened. For in a world of nation-states, the stateless nation is in a very precarious position indeed. Ask any Kurd or Palestinian. So the threat to the well-being of community members in nationalist conflicts is often perceived as a threat to the very existence of the community, not just to the material well-being of the members of community, but to the contingent line of cultural heritage that connects them to each other. This threat of communal death significantly raises the stakes and the level of hostility in many nationalist conflicts, especially those between small and vulnerable national communities.[15] For it leads us to strike out against our rivals not just for the sake of self-interest, not just out of concern for the well-being of compatriots, but out of concern for the very survival of our connections to our compatriots.

So the rise of nationalism makes it far more likely that we treat the members of other national groups who live among us as both threats to our own interests and to the well-being of people whose happiness concerns us. But combinations of self-interest and feelings of communal loyalty are rather common. What makes nationalism an especially explosive force is that it lines up with beliefs about justice against the members of rival nations as well. For nationalism, as it has spread throughout the modern world, rests on a belief that nations should be allowed to have the final say in the arrangement of their political affairs. People who impede these efforts to establish national sovereignty do not just oppose us and threaten our loved ones; they fail to meet their obligations. And that means, like our opponents in a sectarian war, we tend to see them as wrongdoers who deserve to be punished, not just as enemies whose threat to our friends and our interests need to be resisted. The national-

15. Bibo, "The Distress of East European Small States," 22–23.

ist principle of political legitimacy thus both intensifies our hostility to the members of rival nations and makes it harder to call on our sense of justice to restrain our interest in treating them harshly.

The rise of nationalism creates new and very serious conflicts of interest between the members of neighboring nations. But, at the same time, it disposes us to treat our rivals' pursuit of these interests as illegitimate, as a kind of conspiracy against our community and its efforts to achieve national sovereignty. Nationalist minorities tend to see the national majorities within a given territory as imperialists, as pursuers of an illegitimate domination over them. Nationalist majorities tend to see resistance to their efforts to exercise control over political life in their territories as subversion, as a conspiracy to undermine their legitimate efforts to take control of their political life. It is this delegitimation of opposition to national sovereignty, not some atavistic distaste for social heterogeneity, that makes it so hard for them to cooperate with their rivals. Even in the worst, most genocidal cases of ethnic cleansing, the victims are always hounded as conspirators and subverters of the national will, people who, like the Jews or Armenians, are thought capable of making up for their lack of numbers with their riches and international connections.

In addition, the delegitimation of opposition to our nation's sovereignty breathes new life and energy into all of the "age-old" recriminations and suspicions between nations, the stories of past indignities, invasions, and betrayals that we learn about as part of our cultural heritage. For these charges now provide the most vivid confirmation of the bad will and unjust intentions of our nation's rivals. The spread of nationalism does not lift the lid on passions generated by these age-old complaints. But it does connect old grudges to a general principle of justice that can turn them into passionate points of contention.

Putting it all together, the spread of nationalism puts us in situations where it would seem to serve our interests to remove the members of rival communities from their territories by one means or another. It intensifies our attachment to our national communities and gives us new reason to fear for their survival. And, most important, it introduces a principle of political legitimacy that makes organized opposition to our efforts to gain political sovereignty over "our" territory seem like an unjust and conspiratorial act. In such situations, our sense of justice and our sense of concern for others, motives that we ordinarily rely on to restrain especially cruel acts of self-interest, deepen and reinforce our inclinations to strike out at our rivals. Nationalist commitments do not, in themselves, justify the forcible removal of the members of rival nations from places where they have long lived. But they do seriously weaken the moral restraints on such actions by portraying them as wrongdoers and threats to people we care about, rather than just as competitors or rivals.

Although I have focused on conflicts within existing polities, nationalism's combination of beliefs about political legitimacy and feelings of group loyalty intensifies communal hostility and weakens moral restraints on cruelty across political borders as well. For it is not at all unreasonable to think that powerful forces beyond our borders, not just within, work to undermine our nation's ability to exercise control over its political arrangements. When we think that this is the case, we view our enemies, like participants in sectarian wars, as wrongdoers as well as threats to our compatriots. Not every international conflict or rivalry between nationalists will be intensified in this way. But those that involve national communities that are relatively insecure in their sovereignty or have a particularly expansive sense of the meaning of sovereignty are strongly affected by this dynamic. New nation-states, like the small Balkan states before World War I, get into such intense disputes with their neighbors because they see them not only as rivals and threats, but as wrongdoers out to subvert their newly won sovereignty. Locally powerful nation-states, like the United States issuing the Monroe Doctrine announcing the illegitimacy of foreign interference in the Americas, begin to see opposition to their interests as illegitimate efforts to thwart national sovereignty. And nation-states that are both powerful and insecure, like imperial and, especially, Nazi Germany, begin to treat all efforts to oppose them as conspiracies to destroy their nation's ability to take control of their own affairs.

Once again, my point is that you do not have to be a fanatic or a narrow-minded tribalist in order to begin to act like one. In other words, you do not have to have particularly intense commitments to one's national community or fanatical convictions about the wrongs done by its rivals in order to develop intense hostility to them. When your nation's rivals' opposition to the members of your community is perceived as illegitimate, the combination of your sense of community and your sense of justice will deepen your feelings of hostility toward them and weaken your resistance to acting on those feelings.

One often sees such intensification of hostility among members of the relatively new nation-states that are challenged and constrained by the

Western states from which they only recently liberated themselves. Indignation against what is perceived as illegitimate interference in the lives of their communities often combines among them with deep concerns about the material misery and social humiliation of their compatriots to produce especially intense feelings of hostility. For example, radical Arab nationalists may sometimes employ terrorism, even self-destructive terrorism. But it is not necessarily fanaticism, an uncompromising commitment to an ideology that sets out God's chosen order for the world, that inspires them to do so. For the fanatic's intense hostility to their enemies can and has been reproduced by the combination of indignation and communal loyalty. The result, hostility so intense that it can inspire indiscriminate terrorism against unarmed civilians, may be the same. But the different motivations call for different responses.[16]

This section's account of nationalism's moral limitations has a number of advantages. First of all, it helps us explain the ordinariness of the practitioners of nationalist violence. Given the horrors associated with this practice, we want to think of its perpetrators as monsters whose moral deformities would make them stand out in a crowd, single-minded fanatics shouting apocalyptic slogans or narrow-minded xenophobes incensed by the very sight of foreigners. Instead, we get, as ethnic cleansing's victims complain, ordinary people who had, at least before they turned to violence, seemed content to play, work, and make deals with the people they came to victimize. Unlike fanatics or tribalists, they do not seem blind or indifferent to the ties of interest, justice, and even friendship that they share with their victims. But they find themselves in a situation where all of these motives seemed to line up against their rivals, greatly diminishing the value and salience of such ties. Many, no doubt, know they are doing wrong when they strike out at their rivals, but they seem able to set that thought aside given their sense that their victims are wrongdoers and that their actions protect the well-being of their compatriots, not just their own self-interest.

Second, this account helps explain the relative suddenness of the communal violence associated with the rise of nationalism. When national communities with a history of extensive cooperation suddenly turn on

16. Of course, these motivations are not mutually exclusive. Someone can be driven to engage in terrorism both by religious fanaticism and nationalist passions. My point is merely that two different paths can lead to the same result, thereby encouraging us on occasions to confuse the violent nationalist with the religious fanatic and vice versa.

each other, it is natural to assume that they must have long been nursing intense grudges or disdain for each other. But when, as is often the case, an objective search of the recent past finds little evidence of such sentiments, we are left asking ourselves how such intense communal passions could arise, so to speak, out of nothing. Looking at the way in which the combination of interest, friendship, and justice intensify communal feelings can help us answer such questions. For it shows us that intense feelings can be generated out of relatively weak beliefs or communal attachments when changing circumstances bring all three into line with each other.

Finally, this account helps us see why nationalists are ready to fight such intense and violent battles over what seem like such minor causes or cultural differences. Beliefs about the illegitimacy of organized opposition to our nation's attempts to take control of its political life turn relatively minor causes—say, a dispute about the possession of some small border town or province—into a major issue, a conspiracy to undermine our nation's sovereignty. And they turn small differences in cultural heritage into the source of major disputes, when the members of the communities distinguished by these differences are perceived as wrongdoers who are attempting to subvert our control of our political lives. Nationalists, no doubt, engage in a great deal of what Michael Ignatieff, following Freud, calls the "narcissism of minor differences,"[17] the wild exaggeration of the antiquity, the uniqueness, and significance of the things that distinguish their nation from others. That sometimes makes them seem ready, like Swift's Lilliputians, to kill their neighbors over something as trivial as which end of the egg one should break.[18] But it is the right of people who feel connected by such differences to take charge of their political arrangements that gets nationalists so agitated, not these minor cultural differences themselves.

Of course, one might wonder why people would defend such a right unless they were deeply, perhaps irrationally, attached to the relatively minor differences that distinguish, say, Ukrainian from Russian communities. But you do not have to be very deeply attached to one's Ukrainian cultural heritage to fear what will happen to people who share it under

17. Ignatieff, "Nationalism and the Narcissism of Minor Differences."

18. Or, to update the example, like Gary Shteyngart's Svanis and Svevos, in his recent novel *Absurdistan*, who kill each other over which way to slant the footrest in their crucifixes.

a government controlled by Russians. Even John Stuart Mill, who ridiculed those nationalists who "sulk on the rocks" of their distinctive inheritance, makes exceptions for nations that have, like the Irish, suffered "atrocious" treatment at the hands of their "more civilized" neighbors.[19] Even if you do not get excited about protecting your national heritage, you are quite likely to get excited about protecting the people who share it with you in a world in which nations are claiming sovereignty over the machinery of government.

Irony Is No Solution

Nationalism is morally problematic because it disposes people to harm their communal rivals in ways that, absent its influence, they would condemn as unjust or inhumane or both. Nationalism does not teach us that we can do no wrong when we act in service of the nation or that we should be indifferent to the suffering of those who oppose the members of our community. But it does dispose us to act as if we did believe these things by lining up calculations of interest, feelings of communal loyalty, and beliefs about political legitimacy against the members of rival nations. In doing so, it makes many ordinary members of a nation much more willing to go along with the relatively few individuals among them—the fanatics, the xenophobes, and the self-seeking political entrepreneurs—who do not recognize any moral restraints on our treatment of the members of other nations.

Nationalism, I am suggesting, has a subtly insidious effect on our moral judgment. Rather than directly challenge moral restraints on our treatment of others, it corrodes and weakens them. That makes nationalism morally problematic, something to be handled with caution, rather than morally wrong. We cannot and should not avoid all situations in life where interest, friendship, and justice all line up in the same direction. After all, doing the right thing is occasionally the best thing that we can do for ourselves and the people we love. But we need to be aware of the way in which this coincidence of motivations intensifies our hostility to those who oppose us and undermines the moral checks and balances that we usually rely on to restrain such feelings.

If this analysis is correct, spreading awareness of the contingent and

19. Mill, *Considerations on Representative Government*, 252.

constructed character of nationhood is not likely to have much of an impact on nationalist violence. For it suggests that the passions that spur this violence do not generally come from a "singular" and morally blinding identification with one's nation.[20] Nationalism's critics, especially its liberal critics, often assume that "ethnic cleansers are motivated by essentialist views about blood and belonging." But as Timothy Snyder notes, in his incisive study of ethnic violence in postwar Eastern Europe, closer analysis reveals that "most employ a sophisticated constructivist view of nationality." "Irony" about national origins, he rightly concludes, should be "a way to ask questions, not a substitute for answers."[21]

Liberals have challenged nationalism with many of the tools they employed in their battle against religious fanaticism and the communal violence that it inspired: arguments for greater toleration of difference; historical criticism that undermines the intensity of communal attachments by revealing the contingent and contradictory nature of founding beliefs and documents; and encouragement of our self-interest in material improvement as a restraint on the intense passions that pose a threat to others. But these tools have proved much less effective in combating the communal violence inspired by nationalism than that inspired by religious convictions because the former is inspired by a mix of moral motivations, rather than the one-sided devotion to a view of the truth inspired by the latter. (Besides, states cannot possibly be neutral with regard to cultural heritage in the way they can try to be with regard to religion, if only because they must make use of cultural artifacts such as language to organize our political lives.)[22] If hatred of cultural difference is not the problem, then toleration of others is not the solution. If it is the combination of a belief about the *injustice* of a nation's rivals with feelings of communal loyalty that gets nationalists most agitated, then a more ironic or pluralistic view of the sources of national identity is unlikely to make them less violent. And if it is the seeming coincidence of self-interest with friendship and justice that intensifies their hostility against the members of rival nations, then an emphasis on material interests is unlikely to make them more cooperative.

Finally, if irony and toleration of cultural difference is no solution to

20. Sen, *Identity and Violence*, xiv.

21. Snyder, *The Reconstruction of Nations*, 11–12.

22. See Kymlicka, "Misunderstanding Nationalism," and *Politics in the Vernacular*, 23–25.

the moral problem with nationalism, then it is no protection against it either. That means that nationalism is *our* moral problem, not just the problem of those others who hold unreasonable beliefs about the natural or primordial origins of their nation. For even if we recognize the contingent and constructed character of national community, that does not make us, as nationalists, less likely to see organized resistance to its efforts to take control of its own affairs as illegitimate. Even if we emphasize our nation's recent political or civic heritage, rather than some mythical line of descent disappearing in the mists of the distant past, we are still affected by the combination of calculations of interest, feelings of communal loyalty, and beliefs about political legitimacy that increases hostility to our rivals and undermines self-restraint. Liberal nationalists, people who emphasize toleration of cultural differences and the contingent origin of nations, have a few more resources to call on in resisting the impact of nationalism's combination of moral motivations. But they too, like the French at the beginning of the revolutionary wars or the Americans during the Cold War's red scares or the internment of Japanese Americans in World War II, have been ready to strike out harshly at others when they have felt their control of their political lives threatened by foreign groups.

Liberal nationalism is not a contradiction in terms, since, as I have argued, nationalism neither demands nor fully justifies these illiberal actions. But it always involves some tension, given the way in which nationalism disposes us against the members of rival nations. Liberals cannot inoculate themselves against the moral problem with nationalism by adopting a more reasonable understanding of nationhood or a greater appreciation of cultural difference. If they choose to endorse nationalism, then they need to be aware of the need to fight nationalism's corrosive effect on their own moral judgments, not just on the judgments of their more illiberal and irrational rivals.

CHAPTER TEN

What's Wrong with National Rights to Self-Determination

As I have already suggested, there are two ways of solving the moral problem with nationalism: improve nationalism or eliminate it, bring nationalism into line with ordinary moral standards or remove it as a political force in our lives. These two alternatives mark the boundaries within which most moral debates about nationalism take place. At one end of the spectrum are those who believe that nationalism can be normalized; at the other, those who believe that we need to find ways of ending its influence on us.

There are, in turn, two ways of normalizing nationalism: identify and promote a form of nationalism that is morally respectable or find some regulative framework that allows nationalism to flourish, but only within morally acceptable limits. Earlier chapters addressed and rejected attempts to distinguish intrinsically good forms of nationalism from their morally problematic counterparts. This chapter considers the most popular means of regulating nationalism: the establishment of a general right to national self-determination.

The recognition of such a right, it is hoped, would normalize nationalism by satisfying nationalist demands in a way that would keep them from violating our moral standards. For defenders of national self-determination rights, like defenders of individual rights of expression and association, use their principle to constrain as well as justify freedoms. They hope to derive from these rights a principled standard with which to regulate the inflated demands for control that nationalists are disposed to make. Like the rights to free speech and association, the right to national self-determination reaches its limit when it interferes with its legitimate exercise by others. Its goal is the peaceful ideal that Mazzini celebrated, a world in which all nations join hands in respecting each other's right to determine its own affairs.[1]

The high-water mark of this approach to addressing the moral problem with nationalism was probably Woodrow Wilson's celebration of national self-determination at the end of World War I. "Nations must be respected," Wilson declared. "Self-determination is not just a phrase. It is an imperative principle of action."[2] The difficulties in applying this approach at Versailles certainly dampened enthusiasm for the principle of national self-determination. But it retains a considerable presence in contemporary political discourse, not least through the influence of the right to self-determination that the United Nations grants to "peoples" in numerous declarations. As a result, attitudes toward the right to national self-determination are often ambivalent. On the one hand, many liberal democrats talk as if it follows in some obvious way from their basic moral commitments, since, as John Stuart Mill wrote, "one hardly knows what any division of the human race should be free to do if not to determine with which of the various collective bodies of human beings they choose to associate themselves."[3] On the other hand, bitter experience with the application of this right has convinced many of them that it represents "one of the last, most difficult, and most precarious of the freedoms to which human beings may lay claim."[4] The revival of normative theorizing about nationalism has, accordingly, led to both a new wave of arguments in favor of the right to national self-determination and renewed skepticism about its practical value.[5]

Perhaps then we should think of the right to national self-determination as one of those attractive principles that has unfortunate consequences when applied to a complex and imperfect world.[6] "That every

1. Mazzini's vision is well elaborated in the recently published collection of his writings, appropriately titled *A Cosmopolitanism of Nations*.

2. Woodrow Wilson, quoted in Moynihan, *Pandemonium*, 78.

3. Mill, *Considerations on Representative Government*, 250.

4. Emerson, *From Nation to Empire*, 218.

5. See, e.g., Binder, "The Case for Self-Determination"; Philpott, "In Defense of Self-Determination"; Margalit and Raz, "National Self-Determination"; and Nielsen, "Liberal Nationalism and Secession." For some incisive criticisms of the recent wave of liberal theories of national self-determination, see Horowitz, "Self-Determination."

6. Wilson himself seemed to come to that conclusion in his confession that when he proclaimed "that all nations had a right to self-determination" he did so "without the

'nation' should have its own state . . . *is defensible in theory.* In practice it has produced war, terrorism and what we have now learned to call 'ethnic cleansing.'"[7] Good in theory, bad—sometimes horrendous—in practice. It would not be the first time we would have to settle for such a conclusion.

But I do not believe that we should do so in this case. The dictum "good in theory, bad in practice" often represents little more than an excuse for theoretical laziness, a convenient way of blaming the world for our own failure to identify the problems with superficially attractive theories.[8] In this chapter I argue that there is something seriously wrong with the right to national self-determination itself, not just with the consequences of its application to an imperfect world. I suggest that even if you think of national self-determination as a *good* thing, it makes no sense to treat it as a *right.*[9] Furthermore, I try to show that once we recognize this problem it becomes much easier to make sense of the otherwise confusing role that the assertion of collective self-determination rights has played in modern politics.

In the current intellectual environment—the near hegemony of what Judith Shklar called "the liberalism of rights" as opposed to "the liberalism of fear"[10]—asking whether something is the *right* thing to do is often treated as the same as asking whether we *have a right* to do it. But this narrowing of our perspective on justice, however useful it may be for some issues, has not served us very well when it comes to nationalism.[11] For, in practice, it leads to much more intense and intransigent claims as nationalists come to view their opponents as denying them their rights

knowledge that nationalities existed" in such profusion and complex circumstances. "You do not know," Wilson continued, "the anxieties that I have experienced as a result of many millions of people having their hopes raised by what I have said." Quoted in Cobban, *The Nation-State and National Self-Determination*, 64–65.

7. William Pfaff, quoted in Dahbour, *Illusion of the Peoples*, 3. Interestingly, Guyora Binder ("The Case for Self-Determination," 224) suggests that until very recently most scholars were inclined to draw the opposite conclusion, that however "potent" the right to national self-determination may be "in practice," it is "quite disreputable in theory."

8. As Jeremy Bentham complains in his indispensable *Handbook of Political Fallacies*, 198–201. Alfred Cobban (*The Nation-State and National Self-Determination*, vii) draws the same conclusion.

9. David Miller draws a similar conclusion in "Secession and the Principle of Nationality," 65, and *On Nationality*, chap. 4.

10. Shklar, "The Liberalism of Fear," 3–20

11. See Beiner, "National Self-Determination," 163.

rather than asserting competing claims. And, in theory, it leads to an impoverished understanding of the normative issues that nationalism raises.

National Self-Determination as a Fundamental Right

The assertion of a general right to national self-determination is liberalism's most provocative contribution to nationalist politics. Needless to say, national leaders did not wait to get the go-ahead from liberal theorists before claiming rights to land and recognition. But the notion that we can and should measure all such claims against a standard derived from a fundamental human right is a distinctly liberal idea. It takes the liberal conception of respect for basic rights as a necessary condition of political legitimacy and applies it to the way in which we divide territories and populations. Just as earlier conceptions of human rights delegitimate any regime that fails to secure for its members certain basic individual freedoms, so the right to national self-determination delegitimates any division of population and territory that prevents national communities from exercising their freedom to direct their own affairs. In doing so, it proclaims a right to revolution,[12] not against any particular form of government, but against the extension of a state's authority over particular populations and territories. Liberal political theorists advance natural or human rights as a baseline against which to measure the competing rights to political privilege and authority that history has handed down to us. The right to national self-determination is advanced to provide us with a standard against which to measure the competing claims to communal territory and recognition that we have inherited from the past.

Of course, self-determination can refer to many things. But there can be little doubt that it is the desire for some form of self-government that is at stake in most debates about the right to national self-determination. When people insist that nations have a right to self-determination they are, for the most part, demanding that nations (or their members) should be granted the opportunity to organize and control their own political affairs.[13] And they are saying that we must no longer leave the distri-

12. See Emerson, *From Empire to Nation*, 298.

13. Whether or not they can exercise this right as a division of a larger political community is not of any importance to the issue examined in this chapter. Nor is the much dis-

bution of the world's territory and populations to chance, convenience, and the exercise of force, that our sense of belonging to national communities must take precedence over the morally arbitrary contingencies that have up to now shaped the boundaries of political units. Rights are commonly understood as freedoms that others are under an obligation to respect.[14] The assertion of a fundamental right to national self-determination maintains that the existence of a particular form of communal connection, that which binds the members of a nation, obliges us to get out of the way of their efforts to establish and manage their own forms of political organization in their own territory.

A nation, it is important to remember, is a community rather than an organization. Its members are bound by their feelings of mutual concern and loyalty, rather than by any system of rules and obligations that coordinate their actions and authorize collective agents to represent them. The right to national self-determination thus proclaims the right of a particular kind of community to organize itself in a particular political way. One kind of we, a group bound by feelings of social friendship, demands the right to organize or take control of another kind of we, the one established by the especially powerful form of political organization we call the modern state. The standards by which the right to national self-determination measures and corrects current divisions of population and territory are therefore subjective in nature: the feelings of social friendship that constitute particular national communities and the associations with particular territories that mark these territories as their own.

Some theorists have tried to limit national self-determination rights by directing them toward the management of shared cultural interests, rather than self-government.[15] They argue that we should respect a nation's right to preserve and enhance its own cultural heritage, rather than its right to extend its authority over territory by means of a state's institutions. Such an approach to collective self-determination was not unusual in the past, especially under the multinational empires that were once so

---

cussed question of whether this right should be thought of as a collective right of the national community or the individual right of its members.

14. As Joseph Raz puts it (*The Morality of Freedom*, 166), "X has a right if and only if X can have rights and . . . an aspect of X's well being (his interest) is a sufficient reason for holding some other person(s) under an obligation" to allow X to pursue that interest.

15. See, e.g., the arguments of Yael Tamir in "The Right to National Self-Determination," and *Liberal Nationalism*, chaps. 2–3.

common. But it is very hard to reproduce in a world of sovereign states and peoples. For that world begins with an assumption that the authority of the state, and the people who empower it, extends evenly throughout a given territory,[16] which makes demands for cultural autonomy within a state almost impossible to grant. The proponents of the cultural interpretation of national self-determination therefore usually end up either settling for rights of cultural expression—what Will Kymlicka calls "multicultural" as opposed to "self-government" rights[17]—or demanding some control of the state as a means of exercising their cultural autonomy.[18] By asserting a right to self-determination nations usually end up contending for the right "to control a portion of the earth's surface,"[19] for self-government in our world is impotent without control of territory.[20]

The right to national self-determination, as ordinarily understood, thus consists of two distinct rights: a right to form or shape a political organization and the right to control a portion of the earth's surface. In other words, national self-determination, unlike the self-determination of individuals, is a process by which nations determine both the shape and the decisions of their collective political selves. As such, it includes under one heading two very different kinds of actions: the *formation* and the *direction* of collective selves. The former raises questions about association, about the groups with which we share the burdens and privileges of a political community. The latter raises questions about the exercise of government, about how we take control of our common affairs. Granting a colonial nation its own political unit might satisfy its demand for the former, but as long as it remains politically subordinate to an imperial authority, it has not been granted the right to national self-determination. Granting the members of a nation the right to participate in running its affairs within the political units in which they find themselves might satisfy the demand for the latter, but as long as it is denied the opportunity

16. See, e.g., Morris, *An Essay on the Modern State*, 36. "In the modern world, governance is territorial," based on the distinction that the modern state draws between what is internal and what is external.

17. Kymlicka, *Multicultural Citizenship*, 27–35.

18. See Shalit, "National Self-Determination: Political, Not Cultural."

19. Nielsen, "Liberal Nationalism and Secession," 105.

20. As Margaret Moore notes, if you think of collective self-government as a moral good, then you must treat control of territory as a good as well. See Moore, *The Ethics of Nationalism*, chap. 7.

to form its own political community, it has still been denied the right to national self-determination. As a general or first-order right, the right to national self-determination rejects claims to land or association that prevent nations from organizing themselves politically or extending the authority of that organization throughout their own territory.

The Problem with National Self-Determination Rights

What's wrong then with national rights to national self-determination? For one thing they are very difficult to implement. They tend to destabilize already fragile regimes; to intensify and harden the claims that groups make upon each other by transforming them into inalienable rights; to force us to undertake cruel population transfers to relocate nations in their "own" territories; and to make promises that we cannot live up to, since we lack an adequate supply of states to meet the demands of existing nations, let alone potential ones. In short, they seem to stir up as at least as much conflict as they resolve. But the problem with the right to national self-determination goes beyond the discomfort and dangers that accompany our efforts to apply it as a standard for the division of the world's populations and territories. For, in the end, the right to national self-determination fails to provide us with any such standard at all.

That may seem like a very strange complaint to make. After all, the most familiar definition of nationalism, as the ideology that demands that the boundaries of states be brought into line with the boundaries of nations, seems to provide us with just such a standard. But what exactly are the boundaries of nations? The question is more difficult to answer than it may seem at first.

When invoking this understanding of nationalism most people talk as if the boundaries of nations refer to one set of lines on a map that can be used to correct others. But nations are distinguished from each other by something much more subjective than lines on a map. True, they almost always display a strong connection with particular places, places where their members live or once lived or that figure prominently in the stories that their members tell about themselves. But these places are sites of national triumphs and tragedies, past or present greatness, rather than divisions of territory, neatly separated by physical boundaries. The clearly defined territories that nations often claim—for example, the province of

Kosovo rather than its celebrated battlefields and monasteries, the province of Quebec rather than the areas associated with the original *habitants* and their Francophone descendants—get their physical boundaries from the administrative borders of states and empires, rather than from the aspirations of nations. The boundary that defines the province of Quebec is therefore no more national in character than the boundary that defines the Canadian polity—as many native representatives will remind you when they discuss their opposition to Quebec's independence.

States are territorial organizations, spatial containers defined by the borders that mark the point at which their authority ends. Nations, in contrast, are intergenerational communities with strong subjective ties to particular places. They may aspire to organize themselves as states, thereby turning themselves into neatly bounded containers of co-nationals. But it is as subjectively bound communities that they assert their right to do so, not as territorial organizations. Recognizing this right therefore obliges us to get out of the way of efforts to bring the divisions of populations and territories into line with the feelings of social friendship that bind members of nations to each other and to specific territories, rather than efforts to correct one set of lines on a map with another.

This difference in character between the boundaries of nations and the boundaries of states is the source of many of the worst problems that accompany attempts to grant nations their right to determine themselves. For the location of a nation's own territory often does not match the places where most members of that nation reside. And the places where most of them reside are often shared with members of other nations. So rather than simply redrawing maps in ways that would replace one set of spatial containers with a less arbitrarily drawn set of spatial containers, the implementation of the right to national self-determination requires the separation and sorting of subjectively connected populations to bring them into line with their sense of connection to particular places.

But this difference between national and state boundaries does not just make it difficult to implement national self-determination rights; it raises serious questions about their very existence as a standard with which to correct arbitrary divisions of populations and territory. For if it is the subjective association with people and places that these rights demand we use to correct the boundaries of states, then it is entirely possible, even likely, that particular populations and/or places will be associated with more than one nation. In that case, nations could not exercise their own right to self-determination without violating the rights of other nations. Rather than provide us with a standard for assessing competing claims to populations and territories, the right to national self-determination would then merely shift the grounds on which communal conflicts are fought—meanwhile arming the combatants with the confidence and self-righteousness that comes from asserting what they take to be a fundamental right.

In fact, conditions in which multiple nations have strong connections to the same people or places are the norm rather than the exception. That is to be expected if nations are communities bound by ties of social friendship, rather than organizations coordinating the activities of its members. For it is the demands of political organizations like the modern state that compel us to draw sharp territorial lines around those whom we count as members of our group, not the demands of social friendship.

It is not difficult at all to share some sense of mutual concern and loyalty with the members of more than one nation as long as circumstances do not put them directly in conflict. Indeed, multiple national identities, one often nested in another—Ukrainian, Russian, Slav; Palestinian, Jordanian, Arab; Scots, Welsh, Briton—are commonplace. The assertion of a right to national self-determination forces us to choose among these multiple connections so that we can more effectively organize nations politically. As a result, rather than grant nations the right to organize and direct their own political affairs, it grants them the opportunity to compete for that right. And the communities that win are usually those that excel at nation-building, a process that, as Walker Connor reminds us, inevitably involves a great deal of "nation-destroying."[21]

In order to correct the arbitrary division of populations associated with the current borders of states, the right to national self-determination claims to identify the groups, the nations, which we should allow to organize their own political institutions. But if these communities tend to overlap each other in their sense of connection, not just in their place of residence, then this right does not tell us which population groups must be allowed to form their own political associations. It points instead to a political problem: how to connect the plural and overlapping pattern of communal loyalties with a form of political organization, the modern state, which relies on singular structures of authority. Some will solve this problem by engaging in nation-building, a process that, to a great extent, adapts national communities to the structures of state. Others will try to

21. Connor, *Ethnonationalism*, 28–66.

build "plurinational" states,[22] a process that, in effect, adapts state organizations to the pluralistic structure of communal loyalties. The right to national self-determination, however, offers us no guidance on which path to choose and therefore provides no standard against which to measure the division of populations in the world.

The lack of such a standard is even more acute when it comes to using the right to national self-determination to correct the division of territories. States demand an exclusive understanding of what constitutes their own territory. Since the extent of their territory is defined by the line at which their monopoly on legitimate authority ends, only one state can call any particular territory its own. Multiple states can claim a particular territory, but in doing so they seek the exclusive authority within it that would make that territory theirs and theirs alone. Nations, as we have seen, do not share this exclusive understanding of what constitutes their own territory. Since it is a set of subjective associations that connects nations to particular places—the experience of past or present occupation; memories of a homeland; great cultural, religious, or military achievements; great national tragedies; lost empires and independent states—more than one nation can treat the same territory as its own.

But how can nations be said to possess the right to take exclusive control of their territories when multiple nations have good reason to treat the same territory as their own? As in the case of the division of populations, the assertion of this right merely shifts the argument from competing stories about how to define the boundaries of states to competing stories about how to define the boundaries of nations.[23] Such a shift in argument may be welcome in some cases, since many national claims to territory are much more justly asserted than claims based on a history of conquest or royal marriage contracts. But it does not establish anything like a general right to national self-determination because it offers no standard against which to measure these claims when they conflict with each other, as they so often do. When two national communities—Israeli Jews and Palestinian Arabs, for example—have a special attachment to

22. See, e.g., Keating, *Plurinational Democracy*.

23. That is why, as Lea Brillmayer notes, nationalists typically advance two different kinds of argument: one to establish the coherence and distinctiveness of their national community, the other to establish their community's claim to the territory that they seek to govern. See Brillmayer, "Secession and Self-Determination," 189.

the same land, how do you decide which has the right to determine itself there? The group that was there first? The group that was there most recently? For the longest time? The group for whom the land is most holy? Most familiar? The right to national self-determination provides us with no standard against which to measure these arguments; it just increases the indignation and intransigence with which they are advanced.

The right to national self-determination presents itself as a first-order right, a principle that we can rely on to establish minimally acceptable criteria for a legitimate division of the world into different political communities. In reality, it merely gives its blessing to a host of competing arguments about second-order rights, rights derived from claims about homelands, long-standing residency, unjust occupation, unfair treatment, and so on.[24] Perhaps that is why the most serious studies of nationalism and territorial rights usually end up shifting at some point from the language of basic rights to the language of competing claims.[25] No doubt, some of these claims will be juster and more persuasive than others. But in order to assess them properly, we must reject what Rogers Brubaker calls the "architectonic illusion" about nationalism, the notion "that nationalist conflicts are susceptible of fundamental resolution through national self-determination." "Chronic contestedness is . . . part of the very nature of nationalist politics." The search for a standard that would normalize nationalism is therefore "misguided in principle," as well dangerous in practice.[26]

24. See the strong arguments on this point in Moore "The Territorial Dimension of Self-Determination," and *The Ethics of Nationalism*, 20, 176–201.

25. A good example is Tamar Meisels's recent book *Territorial Rights*, an unusually careful and insightful analysis of the justifications offered for claims to territory. Although the book, like the title, begins by focusing on general rights to territory, her conclusions lead her again and again to replace that language with language about arguments and claims. For example, she concludes that a nation's historical connections to territory should be taken seriously as a moral argument, but "they do not amount to rights," since "they do not constitute sufficient reason for holding others to be under the relevant duties" (38). Similarly, with arguments based on historical injustice, the efficiency of land use, and the establishment of settlements (42, 63, 93), these arguments establish morally significant claims to our attention, but nothing approaching territorial rights. Indeed, as I shall elaborate in chapter 12, it is precisely the recognition of the moral significance of these claims that fall short of generating generic rights that makes Meisels's book so helpful to the study of these normative issues.

26. Brubaker, "Myths and Misconceptions in the Study of Nationalism," 279–80.

Popular Sovereignty and the Antinomy of Collective Self-Determination

If the idea of a first-order right to national self-determination is so deeply flawed, why do so many liberal democrats keep coming back to it, even after the disappointments of previous attempts to put it into practice? One reason is that it seems to rest on two rights that almost all of them recognize as components of a legitimate political order: the right of free association and the right to popular sovereignty. The first seems to support a nation's right to form its own political organization; the second, its right to use that organization to extend its authority throughout its own territory.

The easiest way of justifying the right of nations to form or shape their own political organizations is to invoke the right of individuals to choose with whom they wish to associate. That is clearly what Mill has in mind when he asserts that "one hardly knows what any division of the human race should be free to do if not to determine with which of the various collective bodies of human beings they choose to associate themselves."[27] And that is the principle that recent defenders of the right to national self-determination most frequently invoke, though they acknowledge that the nation is just one of many groups entitled to invoke it.[28] From this point of view, it is not at all difficult to identify the standard raised by the right to national self-determination: nations—or any other communities that care to do so—must be given the opportunity to form their own sovereign political organizations. The difficult thing is to figure out whether we can afford the consequences of granting such a right.

But this point of view only makes sense if the right to national self-determination represents nothing more than the right to divide up populations in a particular way. If it also represents a right to divide up territory among the populations of the world, it is much more difficult to defend. It is relatively easy to identify a standard to govern the division of populations since in that case we are only talking about the connections that link people to each other and we can thus look to their choices and feelings for guidance. "Let them have their political community," we

27. Mill, *Considerations on Representative Government*, 250.

28. See, e.g., Philpott, "In Defense of Self-Determination," and Wellman, *A Theory of Secession*.

can say to ourselves, since that's their own business, a question about the people with whom they feel connected or choose to associate. It is much harder, however, to identify a standard to govern the division of territories among people, if only because such a standard must justify the connection of a particular group of people to a particular territory, that is, to something that is not exclusively theirs in the way that their choices and feelings can be portrayed to be. "Let them have their own land" is thus much harder to accept than "let them have their own political association," since it involves dividing and granting a particular group of people something that could be—and usually is—ours or another group's in a way that their feelings and choices could never be. In the end, we cannot simply grant "a prima facie right to self-determination" to "any group within a defined territory,"[29] because the definition of territory, that is, its division into bounded units, is no less an issue for national self-determination than the division of populations into political communities.

What justifies the claim that nations have the right to use their political organizations to assert their authority over the territories that they call their own? Some have argued that our interest in preserving and enhancing the nation's intergenerational cultural community gives its members a strong claim to exercising some degree of control over a nation's territory.[30] In an unusually sustained version of this argument, Avery Kolers speaks of the "plenitude" or richness of "ethnogeographic" connections with territory as a justification for claims to control particular parts of the world—though, like the right of association, this argument does not apply only to nations.[31] But however persuasive such arguments might be, they merely add to the repertoire of arguments that nations might use in claiming particular territories as their own; no one would think of them as the basis of a first-order right against which to measure all the claims that different groups make to exercise authority over particular territories. So how has it come to seem plausible to think of national self-determination as the expression of such a right?

The answer, I believe, is that the right to national-self-determination has come to be identified with the right to popular sovereignty. Popular

29. Philpott, "In Defense of Self-Determination," 353.

30. See, e.g., Gans, *The Limits of Nationalism*, chaps. 3–4.

31. Kolers, *Land, Conflict, and Justice*, 5, 82, 100–38. Kolers (5) suggests that "a territorial right exists if and only if an ethnogeographic community demonstrably achieves plenitude in a juridical territory."

sovereignty, the right of peoples to form and disband political organizations that control the territory that they occupy, is indeed a first-order right, one by which most of us determine the minimal conditions of a government's legitimacy. When you identify peoples with nations it is easy to conclude that the latter possess the right to organize themselves in ways that establish their control over their own territory.[32] The right of association seems to oblige us to allow the members of nations the right to build their own political house, the right of popular sovereignty to allow them to master what goes on within it.

There is, however, a serious problem with establishing a general right to national self-determination by combining popular sovereignty rights to control territories with rights of association: the assertion of each of these two rights undermines the assertion of the other when it comes to dividing us up into separate political communities. The right to form national states is a right to bring the political division of the world's population into line with the sense of mutual connection shared by members of nations. The right granted by the principle of popular sovereignty to peoples is, in contrast, a right of a given population, the people who permanently reside within the boundaries of a given state, to act as the ultimate source of the political authority that operates within those boundaries. The former *challenges* what it portrays as the arbitrariness of the given distribution of populations and territories among states and provides us with a minimal condition for a more legitimate division of the political world. The latter *assumes* a given distribution of populations and territories among states and provides us with a minimal condition for the legitimate exercise of political authority within them. Assert one right and you effectively undermine the other.

Nationalists and defenders of popular sovereignty both seek to be masters in their own house. But for defenders of popular sovereignty the house they seek to master is the politically bounded territory within which they happen to reside, while for nationalists it is the place or places that loom large in the cultural heritage that binds the members of their community. You can consistently grant all peoples the right to control their own territory, but only so long as you employ popular sovereignty's subjectively arbitrary definition of a people and its territory.

32. Indeed, Hugh Seton-Watson (*Nations and States*, 445) suggests that nationalist ideology is nothing more than "the application to national community of the Enlightenment doctrine of popular sovereignty."

For this right is derived from the basic hypothetical of popular sovereignty: if there is a state, then its authority over a territory must be derived in some way from those who permanently reside within its borders, whoever they may be. Alternatively, you can correct for the subjective arbitrariness of these communal divisions by insisting that groups have a right to form political communities made up of individuals with whom they share some important sense of mutual connection—but only if you are willing to give up the idea of a general standard against which to measure competing claims of national communities to control particular patches of territory. For this right is derived from principles of free association that dissolve the connections between particular groups and particular places established by the principle of popular sovereignty.

In other words, the establishment of a general standard according to which we can assign collective rights to control particular territories rests on the acceptance of the relatively *arbitrary* division of political communities created by the history of state formation. And the establishment of a general standard according to which we can assign groups rights to form political communities rests on the acceptance of relatively *subjective* standards against which to measure their claims to particular territories. You can grant groups the right to dissolve the given boundaries of states to form their own political communities. Or you can grant them the right to control the territory within the given boundaries of the states within which they reside. But you cannot do both together. You cannot give groups the right to challenge and correct both communal and territorial divisions. Such is the antinomy of collective self-determination.

The right to national self-determination promises to resolve this antinomy by offering, in the nation, a community that can guide the division of both population and territory. But, as we have seen, this promise is never kept. For national self-determination rights do not provide us with a standard to determine which subjectively connected community possesses the right to control a particular territory; they direct us instead to the competing claims that nations have made to mark out some particular territory as their own. The general association of the nation with the people of popular sovereignty theory merely conceals the absence of such a standard.

Given the important contribution that beliefs about popular sovereignty have made to the emergence of nationalism, not to mention our tendency to use the terms people and nation interchangeably, it is not surprising that popular sovereignty rights are so often confused with national self-determination rights.[33] But it is very unfortunate because it gives many of us the impression that we have a plausible way of defining and defending a general standard against which to measure the rights to particular territories that nations claim.

Popular Sovereignty and Foreign Rule

There is another reason that liberal democrats keep coming back to the right to national self-determination, despite its manifest theoretical and practical limitations: their sense that it follows from their rejection of foreign rule. If we treat foreign rule as illegitimate, does that not suggest that we recognize the right of subjectively connected groups of individuals, like the members of nations, to take charge of their own political affairs? Not necessarily. The delegitimation of foreign rule, and with it the dismantling of empires, can and should be derived from the increasing acceptance of the constituent sovereignty of the people, rather than from a commitment to national self-determination rights.

As we have seen in chapter 6, the principle of popular sovereignty declares foreign rule illegitimate, not just aristocratic and patriarchal political principles of authority. But foreign rule in this context refers to the source of a ruler's authority rather than the shape of his or her affiliations. Political authority, according to this principle, must be derived from and exercised by members of the people who are to be subjected to it, however they may feel about each other and outsiders. Some may share a stronger sense of mutual concern and loyalty with groups of people in other states than with many members of their own people. But that does not make those permanent residents of other states any less foreign to them, from a political perspective; for those groups have no share at all in the right to establish and disestablish political authority that is reserved for the permanent residents of a polity.

This indictment of foreign rule may seem undemanding, since it merely requires that regimes declare themselves to be the voice or representatives of those whom they govern. Yet it effectively delegitimates all forms of imperial rule, perhaps the commonest form of government in human history. For while imperialism is often justified by the benefits that others are seen to gain from the extension of imperial authority

33. See chapters 4 and 6 above.

over them, it does not, by definition, rest in any way on their approval. As a result, the forms of imperial rule that flourished well into the twentieth century became increasingly difficult to maintain as commitments to popular sovereignty began to spread to every corner of the world. One after the other, the great empires fell, the continental empires after World War I, the colonial empires after World War II, and the Soviet Empire with the collapse of communism.

But no matter how effective it may have been in delegitimating imperial rule, this understanding of foreignness does nothing to establish national self-determination rights. Popular sovereignty merely requires that a state derive its authority from the people who inhabit it. It says nothing about the composition of the people or to what degree they need to identify with each other. As a result, it treats French rule over the Algerians or British rule over the Quebecois as illegitimate, but it says nothing about the legitimacy of the incorporation of the Algerians into the French people or the Quebecois into a Canadian or even British people. It declares foreign rule to be illegitimate but operates with a subjectively arbitrary understanding of foreignness.

It might seem that the right to self-determination that the United Nations ascribes to peoples requires a much more robust and subjective understanding of the distinction between ourselves and foreigners, that it obliges us to allow people who share a strong sense of communal loyalty to take charge of their own political affairs. After all, Wilsonian rhetoric about national self-determination provided much of the inspiration for this declaration of fundamental rights. But that initial understanding of collective self-determination was quickly scaled back in the face of the resistance of existing states to dismemberment, the resistance of colonial empires to dissolution, and finally the unwillingness of the new states that emerged from those empires to allow the issue of borders to become a source of state conflict and weakness.[34] As a result, United Nations proclamations grant the right of self-determination to peoples, rather than nations.

A common interpretation of the UN commitments to collective self-determination rights complains that they represent a hypocritically—or, for some, wisely—truncated application of the right to national self-determination, one designed to legitimate the self-assertion of colo-

34. See Sureda, *The Evolution of the Right of Self-Determination*, and Cassese, *The Self-Determination of Peoples.*

nial nations against European rulers, but deny most other nations the same opportunity.[35] I would suggest, however, an alternative interpretation of these rights. While they may have been inspired by Wilsonian rhetoric about the right to national self-determination, the legal rights to collective self-determination now recognized and practiced by the international community do not represent a half-hearted and inconsistent application of that principle. They represent, instead, a relatively consistent application of the principle of popular sovereignty, a principle that, as noted in the preceding section, declares foreign rule to be illegitimate without granting nations the right to dismember states and form their own political communities. In other words, the right to self-determination that the international community now grants to peoples represents the right of the whole body of each state's permanent residents to act as the ultimate source of the authority that the state exercises over its territory and population. Such a right rules out most explicit forms of imperialism, especially the kind of imperialism the European powers exercised in Asia and Africa, which openly acknowledged its claim to rule over alien and inferior peoples. But it does not rule out—nor does it expressly approve—the incorporation of smaller groups into larger peoples. The result is a principle that declares, for example, French rule over Morocco or British rule over India to be illegitimate, but leaves open the question of the legitimacy of the incorporation of the Baltic states into the former Soviet Union or the Basque and Catalonian regions into Spain. Such a principle obviously leaves us without a standard to adjudicate many of our most troubling communal conflicts, since these conflicts so often revolve around claims that a smaller people should be thought of as part of a larger one, rather than that one people should be subordinate to another. But it does provide us with a standard that is both consistent in itself and one that has been applied with considerable consistency since the dissolution of Europe's colonial empires after World War II.

I would suggest that the international community currently recognizes a right to rebel against foreign rule, understood as the explicit assertion of a right to rule over alien peoples, rather than anything like a national right to self-determination, let alone a national right to secede from multinational states. This is not to suggest that there is anything

35. See especially Binder, "In Defense of Self-Determination," 235–40.

like an internationally recognized right to keep existing states intact.[36] There is considerable sympathy for national groups that find themselves trapped within larger political communities, especially when they have only been recently incorporated into the larger community.[37] Moreover, the principle of popular sovereignty grants rights to peoples rather than states, so it does not grant states a right to do what is necessary to keep their borders intact. What I am suggesting, instead, is that the international community ascribes no general rights to either states or nations when it comes to the question of redrawing political boundaries. It deals with such issues in a more ad hoc way, considering the justice of competing claims, the consequences of change, and the interests of the parties affected. That may be frustrating, since the worst injustices often involve the forced incorporation of one community into another, for example, the Magyarization of Slavs, rather than Austro-Hungarian rule over them. But it is not hypocritical. It merely recognizes that we do not have access to a general right with which to determine the justice of competing national aspirations to self-determination, even if we do have access to such a right with which to measure and reject the legitimacy of explicit forms of imperialism.

Conclusion

The concept of human rights has provided a relatively stable and happy ground upon which to erect a minimal standard for legitimate government, a baseline against which to measure competing claims to power and privilege. It cannot, however, do the same for competing claims about how to draw up the boundaries that divide territory and population among states. Insisting on the existence of such a right merely deepens the intensity with which we assert these claims against each other.

Nevertheless, rejecting the right to national self-determination does

36. In other words, while the right to national self-determination is opposed by those who want to maintain the territorial integrity of states, territorial integrity is not treated as a right of states, at least with regard to internal threats. See Mayall, "Sovereignty, Nationalism, and Self-Determination."

37. That explains why there is so much more sympathy for separatists who come from recently incorporated political units, like the Baltic republics of the former Soviet Union, than for those who come from long incorporated political units, like Quebec.

not mean that we are obliged to respect existing boundaries between states as legitimate or just. It just means that we do not have access to a general principle that can correct the contingent and morally arbitrary division of the earth among its peoples. We have every reason to continue to make judgments about the justice or injustice of these divisions. But these judgments should be more or less judgments that reflect a variety of competing and inconsistent factors, rather than the either-or judgments inspired by principles that distinguish legitimate from illegitimate ways of ordering our political lives.

CHAPTER ELEVEN

Cosmopolitan Humility and Its Price

If nationalism is the problem, then cosmopolitanism, the celebration of figurative or literal world citizenship, seems like an obvious place to look for the solution. But cosmopolitanism, at least in its traditional form, exacts a high price for its services: estrangement from the great mass of people who still invest their partial connections with so much moral significance.

The first self-styled cosmopolitans, Diogenes and his Stoic followers, were happy to pay that price. They looked to nature's eternal order, the *cosmos*, as their true home, rather than the unstable communities built by human beings. By describing themselves as citizens of the world, the Stoics proudly proclaimed their independence from the irrational beliefs and practices that sustain ordinary human communities. All human beings are members of their cosmopolis, regardless of the accidents of birth that assign them to a particular nation, state, or social status. But few possess the strength of mind and character needed to recognize and be guided by its rules. As a result, the Stoic celebration of cosmopolitan citizenship has the ironic effect of dividing the human race into two camps: the few sages, a community of the wise, who can actually live as citizens of the world and the vast majority of people who cannot.[1]

Few contemporary cosmopolitans are ready to pay such a high price for the establishment of a universal community. As pluralists, they are uncomfortable with talk of a natural moral order. As egalitarians, they are disinclined to dismiss the ways in which most people conduct their

1. Schofield, *The Stoic Idea of the City*, 64–65, 91–92, 95, 103; Vogt, *Law, Reason and the Cosmic City*, 4, 65, 111.

lives. And, as democrats, they are far more concerned about organizing effective means of popular oversight and representation. Contemporary cosmopolitans seek to lower the barriers that divide us against each other, rather than the barriers that keep the best of us from taking up our shared place in the natural order of things. A cosmopolitan community that separates us into active and passive citizens of the world is not much use to them.

Most contemporary cosmopolitans therefore favor a much humbler, "more inclusive" understanding of cosmopolitanism.[2] And they often advance ideals—"rooted cosmopolitanism," "cosmopolitan patriotism," "embedded cosmopolitanism," not to mention "cosmopolitan nationalism"[3]—that would have made little sense to Diogenes and the Stoics. These new cosmopolitans are inclined to distinguish between "a universal will to find common ground and a cosmopolitan will to engage human diversity."[4] Even Martha Nussbaum, who enthusiastically invokes the original Greek understanding of cosmopolitanism, acknowledges the value of particular attachments and clothes her ancient subjects with some of her own sympathy for the value of partial communities.[5]

This new "both/and" understanding of cosmopolitanism[6] certainly makes for a more attractive ideal in a world inhabited by pluralists and egalitarians. The question is whether cosmopolitanism still solves our moral problems with nationalism in this humbler, more inclusive form. Traditional cosmopolitanism tackles nationalism head on by challenging one or both of its sources: feelings of national loyalty and beliefs about the sovereignty of peoples over states and the bounded territories that they govern. If the new conceptions of cosmopolitanism no longer de-

2. A. Anderson, "Cosmopolitanism, Universalism, and the Divided Legacies of Modernity," 265–89, 267.

3. See Appiah, "Cosmopolitan Patriots"; M. Cohen, "Rooted Cosmopolitanism"; Erskine, *Embedded Cosmopolitanism*; and, for "cosmopolitan nationalism," Beck, *Cosmopolitan Vision*, 9.

4. Hollinger, "Not Universalists, Not Pluralists," 239.

5. Nussbaum, "Patriotism and Cosmopolitanism," 6–7. As a result, Diogenes, perhaps the most famous misanthrope in Western history, comes off as a great lover of humanity in Nussbaum's account (15). For the difficulties that Stoics had reconciling Diogenes's "obvious contempt" for human beings with their exalted vision of the cosmopolitan community, see Stade, "Cosmos and Polis, Past and Present," 283–84.

6. Fine, *Cosmopolitanism*, 16.

mand that we transcend our attachments to particular nations and states, if they celebrate communal pluralism rather than world citizenship and global governance rather than a global state, how can they still solve our moral problems with nationalism?

They could do so quite well if the moral problem with nationalism were merely a kind of moral blindness, the denial of moral concerns or obligations that go beyond the nation's boundaries. In that case, the new cosmopolitanisms would undermine nationalism by compelling nationalists to recognize the variety of overlapping communities in which they participate, including the one that encompasses all of humanity. But, as I have argued in chapter 9, it is not a lack of any sense of moral connection to outsiders that makes nationalism morally problematic. Few nationalists think that the lives of nonnationals count for nothing. Very few indeed would be willing to send a trolley car barreling into a crowd of foreigners simply to spare their compatriots the inconvenience of waiting for it to pass. What makes nationalism so problematic, I have argued, is the way in which it lines up communal loyalty with our beliefs about the obligations of outsiders, rather than a blinding loyalty to our compatriots. Reminding us of the range and variety of our communal connections does nothing, in itself, to eliminate nationalism's corrosive effect on our moral standards.

In order to work effectively against nationalism the new conceptions of cosmopolitanism need to do more than merely demonstrate the compatibility of national and cosmopolitan attachments. They need to demonstrate that the former should be subordinated to the latter, but without disdaining our partial attachments, as the Stoics did. This chapter looks at their efforts to do so and finds them lacking. Cosmopolitan humility, I conclude, does not come for free. The price of traditional cosmopolitanism is a certain degree of distance from the kind of life that most human beings live. The price of cosmopolitan humility, I suggest, is the persistence of many of the moral problems, including those associated with nationalism, that are generated by partial communal loyalties.[7] The communal pluralism of both/and conceptions of cosmopolitanism more accurately reflects the patchwork of social friendships within which we

7. Recognizing this development, some advocates of the new cosmopolitanism have begun to wonder whether we need an even "newer" conception, one that would go beyond merely endorsing "heterogeneity." See Robbins, "Cosmopolitanism: New and Newer," 48.

live our lives. But it leaves in place the forces that make nationalism such a problem in modern political life.

The Many Faces of Modern Cosmopolitanism

Chapter 2 pointed to three basic motives for social cooperation: feelings of social friendship, beliefs about justice, and calculations of self-interest. Each of these motives provides contemporary cosmopolitans with a focus for arguments in favor of the priority of cosmopolitan social connections to national ones. The first of these arguments complains about contingent and morally arbitrary boundaries that undermine our sense of connection to humanity as a whole. The second insists that our shared beliefs in the equal moral worth of human beings obliges us to expand the scope of our principles of distributive justice to include them all, not just those with whom we share communal loyalties or political obligations. The third, more a prudential than a moral argument, figures prominently in recent defenses of cosmopolitan democracy. It claims that since the rapidly changing conditions of modern social life have undermined the nation-state as an effective means of democratic self-government, we now have a powerful interest in developing cosmopolitan forms of political organization that can better address the increasing array of problems that currently elude our control.

The rest of the chapter addresses each of these arguments in turn. Before doing so, however, we need to consider the different ways in which the term cosmopolitanism is currently used. For although its usage is nowhere near as confusing as that of the terms nation and nationalism, it has picked up a number of different meanings over the years, all of which have come into play with the emergence of cosmopolitanism as a focus for moral and political aspirations.

As suggested by its Greek roots, cosmopolitanism originally referred to a sense of loyalty and obligation that extends beyond one's city (*polis*) to the broader, more natural order of the world or, more accurately, the universe (*cosmos*). That meaning persists to this day, although contemporary cosmopolitans tend to replace nature's order with less transcendent understandings of cosmopolitan community. Meanwhile, a second meaning of the term has become much more common in ordinary speech. It refers to the character of those who move comfortably across the boundaries that separate cultural and political communities. Cosmopolitans, in this sense, need not extend their loyalties or obligations beyond their cities or nations. They are distinguished, instead, by the ease—even the pleasure—with which they engage with the members of different and often unfamiliar communities.

More recently, a third meaning has come to the fore in the work of anthropologists and sociologists, who, it has been suggested, have finally "prised the study of cosmopolitanism away from the previous monopoly of philosophers."[8] It refers to a particular condition of social existence, a structure of social relations that require the regular crossing of cultural and political boundaries, rather than to the beliefs or character of those who do the crossing. Such conditions are not new; one need only recall the capital cities of great multinational empires, such as Rome or Vienna or Istanbul, for older examples. But they have become far more widespread, so the argument goes, with the development of the new forms of communication and commerce associated with the process of globalization, which leads some commentators to proclaim the arrival of a new cosmopolitan era in human history.[9]

Arguments for cosmopolitan democracy rely heavily on this third meaning of cosmopolitanism. Arguments for cosmopolitan community and justice tend to rely, in contrast, on the first two meanings. Indeed, one might say that a major goal of the more inclusive approach to cosmopolitanism is to find a way of integrating the first and second meanings of the term.

These two ways of characterizing cosmopolitanism are not mutually exclusive. Nothing prevents the same person from both emphasizing the importance of some common feature of humanity and taking great delight in the diversity of human cultures and beliefs. But they certainly do not entail each other. A cultural cosmopolitan may savor her familiarity with extraordinarily different ways of life without feeling any special connection to the people who live them. Conversely, a cosmopolitan philosopher like Diogenes may imagine himself a citizen of the world without expressing much interest in what goes on beyond his tub in the Athenian marketplace. In both cases, cosmopolitanism involves a commitment or inclination to cross the boundaries that ordinarily separate

8. Holton, *Cosmopolitanisms*, 2, 207.

9. See especially Beck, *Cosmopolitan Vision*, discussed below.

human groups. But in the second case border crossing is effected by focusing on commonalities, while in the first it is effected by developing some familiarity and comfort with communal differences. Cosmopolitans of both types are happy to declare that nothing human is alien to them. But for one type that is because they celebrate the common ground that supports all forms of human life; for the other, it is because they see some value in all of the different products of human striving.

These days, the most familiar representative of the more universalist conception of cosmopolitanism is probably Immanuel Kant. No less committed than the Stoics to a vision of universal moral community, Kant was as famously provincial as Diogenes—though he shared little of the latter's misanthropy.[10] Kant, however, made cosmopolitanism much more attractive to modern egalitarians by democratizing the Stoic understanding of our humanity. For he insisted that it is the goodwill of the ordinary moral person, rather than the refined intelligence of the philosopher, that exemplifies our humanity. By doing so, he brought the realization of our shared capacity for moral reason within reach of people with no special training or intellectual virtues.[11]

The more pluralistic ideal of cosmopolitanism has no equally familiar representative, though Kant's sometime friend and rival, Johann Gottfried Herder, would be a good choice for the role. Herder believed that our humanity is manifested in the inconsistent and ever-unfolding collection of capacities and virtues produced by different human cultures.[12] From this point of view, Kant and most of the great figures of the Enlightenment were guilty of a kind of provincial arrogance, since they took their own century's attachment to a particular understanding of rational calculation and autonomy to represent the foundation of our species' humanity. For Herder, the real cosmopolitan must be open to all of the partial virtues perfected by different ages and cultures, the sublimity of the biblical patriarchs and the spirituality of the Catholic Middle

10. On the similarity between Kant and the Stoics, see Nussbaum, "Kant and Stoic Cosmopolitanism."

11. As Pauline Kleingeld notes ("Six Versions of Cosmopolitanism," 509), leading figures of the German Enlightenment, such as the philosopher Wieland, were quite comfortable distinguishing between the "true" citizens of the world, the sages, from the mere "world-dwellers" with whom they share the cosmopolitan community. The stratified conception of the Stoic cosmopolis was therefore very much alive in Kant's time.

12. This is the subject of Herder's magnum opus, *Ideas*.

Ages no less than the particular forms of rationality developed in the Age of Enlightenment.[13]

Today's more inclusive visions of cosmopolitanism try to combine the virtues of universalist and pluralist understandings of the ideal. In particular, they try to integrate the former's moral clarity and egalitarianism with the latter's openness and appreciation for cultural difference.[14] The question, of course, is how one can consistently combine these two different ways of crossing the barriers between human beings. Although these two forms of cosmopolitanism are not mutually exclusive, they certainly cannot be combined in the forms bequeathed us by Kant and Herder. You cannot say both that our humanity is defined by the moral law within each human being and by the collection of partial and inconsistent virtues produced by different ages and cultures. Kant and Herder thus provide us with convenient end points for the spectrum of compromises on which the new cosmopolitans want to locate themselves.

The construction of such compromises is not, in itself, all that difficult. What is difficult is constructing compromises between moral universalism and cultural pluralism that effectively address the moral problem with nationalism. Here, I suggest, is where the new cosmopolitanism tends to fall short. As Samuel Scheffler notes, most of the arguments made by moderate cosmopolitans seek to demonstrate why the recognition of ethical and cultural particularism does not block our access to more universal standards, a point that it is fairly easy to establish.[15] The difficult point for these cosmopolitans is to explain why these universal standards should take precedence over those generated by more local and partial communities, and to do so without falling back into the kind

13. Isaiah Berlin (in *Vico and Herder*) has rightfully corrected the false impression of Herder as an irrationalist. Nevertheless, Herder was merciless in his ridicule of Enlightenment philosophers' naive pretensions to superiority, especially in his early essay, *Another Philosophy of History*.

14. Most advocates of this combination approach it from the universalist direction, seeking to soften the rejection of cultural particularity associated with most universalist conceptions of cosmopolitanism. Some, however, approach it from the opposite direction, seeking to soften what they have begun to perceive of as an overly strident emphasis on difference. See A. Anderson, "Cosmopolitanism, Universalism, and the Divided Legacies of Modernity," 267–68. Anderson focuses here on social critics like Homi Bhabha and Judith Butler.

15. Scheffler, *Boundaries and Allegiances*, 117.

of disdain for ordinary communal life that they were trying to escape in the first place.

Taking Communal Pluralism Seriously

Most cosmopolitans today argue that the boundaries that separate nations are "morally arbitrary," rather than morally wrong.[16] In other words, they insist that while there is nothing wrong with grouping human beings in this way, such divisions must be subordinate to groupings based on factors, such as our shared humanity, which are not arbitrary from a moral point of view. "People should not be penalized because of the vagaries of happenstance, and their fortunes should not be set by factors like nationality and citizenship."[17] Although these partial ties have considerable value, people "must acknowledge these [ties] as morally contingent and that their most important duties are to humanity as a whole and its overall developmental requirements."[18]

> The accident of where one is born is just that, an accident; any human being might have been born in any nation. Recognizing this, . . . we should not allow differences of nationality or class or ethnic membership or even gender to erect barriers between us and our fellow human beings. We should recognize humanity wherever it occurs, and give its fundamental ingredients, reason and moral capacity, our first allegiance and respect.[19]

Such complaints about our reliance on the contingency of national boundaries loom large in cosmopolitan rhetoric. But it is often unclear just what distinguishes a morally arbitrary way of grouping human beings from one that is not. As David Miller notes, cosmopolitans tend to equivocate between two ways of understanding moral arbitrariness in their arguments against national loyalties. According to the first, it is their contingency or accidental character that marks some shared qualities as morally arbitrary. We deserve no special reward or penalty, it

16. Nussbaum, "Patriotism and Cosmopolitanism," 14; Appiah, "Cosmopolitans and Patriots," 27; Tan, *Justice without Borders*, 27–28, 159–60; Mollendorf, *Cosmopolitan Justice*, 55–56, 79.

17. Caney, "Cosmopolitan Justice and Equalizing Opportunities," 125.

18. Held, "Principles of Cosmopolitan Order," 10.

19. Nussbaum, "Patriotism and Cosmopolitanism, 7.

is suggested, for qualities that we possess just because we happened to take the trouble to be born in a particular place or time. According to the second, it is their irrelevance to the distribution of particular goods that marks some distinctions as morally arbitrary. It is suggested that we gain no claim to a larger share of a good, such as admission to an elite college, by our possession of qualities that are irrelevant to its distribution, such as beautiful eyes or great height.[20] National boundaries are certainly morally arbitrary in the first sense, since they treat a contingency, a shared cultural inheritance, as a focus for special concern and loyalty. That they are morally arbitrary in the second sense is not nearly so clear.

It might seem, at first glance, as if anything that is morally arbitrary in the first sense must be morally arbitrary in the second, that qualities for which we are not ourselves responsible have no place in determining how we distribute goods. After all, we regularly deny that claims that the good fortune to be born to wealthy and upper-class parents, or the relative misfortune to be born to poor and lower-status parents, should have anything to do with the distribution of a whole range of goods, from political authority to admission to publicly funded schools. But in doing so we are actually making two distinct judgments, one about the source of the distinctions and the other about its relevance to the distribution of the good. "The mere observation that national boundaries are morally arbitrary—hardly controversial if what it means is just that nobody deserves to be born in one country rather than another—does not take us very far" in making the second of these two judgments.[21] That becomes clear when we consider inherited qualities, like the unequal needs of the handicapped, which we all consider highly relevant to the distribution of goods.[22] It is important, therefore, to distinguish between these two ways of talking about moral arbitrariness. Miller is right that the failure to do so has made arguments in favor of cosmopolitan understandings of justice seem much stronger than they really are.[23]

I would suggest, however, that there is another reason for this confusion about the meaning of moral arbitrariness: the concept is being invoked to support two distinct arguments in favor of a cosmopolitan

20. Miller, *National Responsibility and Global Justice*, 32–33

21. Scheffler, "Cosmopolitanism, Justice and Institutions," 70.

22. Miller, *National Responsibility and Global Justice*, 33.

23. Ibid., 33–34.

moral perspective. The first focuses on community and the extension of our sense of mutual concern and loyalty to all of humanity. The second focuses on justice and the extension of the scope of our mutual obligations to include all of humanity. The argument about justice has received far more sustained attention from moral philosophers. But the argument about community and mutual concern is more widely invoked today, especially in cosmopolitan rhetoric. It therefore merits much further attention. Its relative neglect, I suspect, is due to its reliance on two concepts that tend to make contemporary moral philosophers uncomfortable: social friendship and nature. The former, as we have seen, is rarely treated as a moral phenomenon by contemporary philosophers; the latter has been the subject of so much misuse that most philosophers try to keep it out of any moral inquiry.

The repeated complaints about the contingent or accidental quality of national boundaries—"the accident of where one is born is just that, an accident; any human being might have been born in any nation"[24]—clearly implies a contrast with groupings that are natural or necessary, not just with those that reflect our own moral choices. Why, they ask, should we be willing to ignore our common humanity, our shared characteristics as a species, for the sake of connections that come and go, connections that so easily could have been otherwise? Contingency, I have suggested, gains its meaning from contrasts with human choice and purpose, on one side, and natural necessity, on the other.[25] When contrasted with chosen qualities, it is the lack of purposiveness, something shared with natural necessities, that marks a quality as contingent. When contrasted with natural qualities, it is the lack of necessity, something shared with chosen differences, that marks a quality as contingent. Cosmopolitan complaints about the moral arbitrariness of national divisions invoke both senses of contingency, condemning—or, at least, subordinating—them as qualities that possess neither purpose nor necessity.

Without recognition of this contrast between natural and contingent qualities it is hard to understand why nationalism's critics think it so important that we be convinced that national communities are imagined, invented, or constructed. They do so, I believe, because they see themselves as exposing the illusions and ignoble lies that misrepresent national differences as natural—hence necessary and inevitable—divisions

24. Nussbaum, "Patriotism and Cosmopolitanism," 7

25. See the penultimate section of the book's introduction.

among human beings. They want to make it perfectly clear that nature does not divide humanity into separate species, that the differences that distinguish the members of different races and nations are almost entirely the product of historical accident or human imposition. Do not be fooled by nationalist myth-makers, they tell us: nature unites humanity, no matter how much the history of force, fraud, and misfortune has divided us.

What is so important about this message? Why should it matter so much that we not mistake national differences for natural ones? Perhaps because despite years of complaint about the naturalistic fallacy, people still seem inclined to connect the natural with the good. At the very least, enough people still seem to make that connection to justify a concerted effort to unmask the contingent character of national boundaries, rather than simply remind us of the fallacy of identifying the natural with the good.

But I believe that this connection between the natural and the good shapes the moral vision of many cosmopolitans, not just the nationalists whose myths they try to expose. After all, they are not merely arguing that national boundaries have less moral significance than generally thought because they are contingent, rather than natural. They are arguing that national loyalties should be subordinated to cosmopolitan loyalties because of the former's contingency. The moral arbitrariness that subordinates national community to humanity in these arguments cannot refer merely to the fact that we have inherited them, rather than produced them by our moral choices. For we inherit our humanity no less—in fact, even more directly—than our nationality. It is their contingency, the fact that they could easily have been otherwise, that subordinates national communities in these arguments, which suggests that it is the natural necessity of humanity that establishes its moral priority. Cosmopolitans who make this argument are urging us to make sure that a sense of mutual connection based on what we share as a species should not be undermined by connections that reflect neither natural necessity nor moral purpose.

The legacy of Stoic cosmopolitanism supports them in doing so. The Stoics, as we have seen, had no difficulty answering questions about why contingent and conventional boundaries should be subordinated to their natural counterparts. For they viewed nature as a moral order, not just as a set of shared dispositions and faculties. In affirming our shared nature as the focus of mutual concern and loyalty they were affirming our place within an ordered whole and our subjection to its laws. Few contemporary cosmopolitans still invoke the Stoic vision of a cosmos governed by natural laws. But many, I believe, still draw on its association of nature with moral order in their complaints about the moral arbitrariness of national communities.

Once we identify and abandon this unspoken reliance on teleological conceptions of nature, it becomes clear that we need to go beyond assertions about the contingency of national boundaries in order to portray them as morally irrelevant. As we shall see, the most familiar and well developed of these arguments focus on justice rather than community, more specifically on the obligations said to follow from our shared belief in moral equality. National boundaries are morally arbitrary, according to these arguments, because they do not provide us with an appropriate ground for departures from a basic norm of equality, rather than because they represent contingent divisions of something that we all share by nature.

But that does not mean that nature has no role to play in our understanding of human community. It merely means that it cannot be used to establish the moral priority of cosmopolitan to national forms of community. The fact remains, however, that nature gives us a form of sharing whose affirmation points to a human community and a universal expression of mutual concern and loyalty. The observed differences among races and nationalities cannot erase that common core of our humanity. Things could easily have been otherwise, since any number of evolutionary scenarios could have produced a world with a variety of distinct hominid species.[26] But it has not. Nature unites rather than divides. It just does not give us, in itself, a moral reason for prioritizing natural over contingent divisions in imagining community. The contingency of national boundaries thus points to communal pluralism rather than cosmopolitanism, to the variety of forms of sharing that we affirm as foci for mutual concern and loyalty, rather than to the moral priority of what we share as human beings to what we share in other ways.

In the end, there is a kind of moral arbitrariness in all expressions of human community, not just those built on contingent forms of sharing. For the ties that connect human communities do not reflect moral judgments about the qualities of the people to whom we extend special con-

26. Imagine how different our arguments about equality would be if we had to face questions about the status of, say, Neanderthals versus *Homo sapiens*.

cern and loyalty. They reflect, instead, a disposition to imagine different things that we share with others—natural, chosen, or contingent—as sources of mutual connection. It is the sharing of things among human beings that generates the special feelings of mutual concern and loyalty that define human communities, not the special qualities possessed by those who do the sharing. To take human community and communal pluralism seriously, you need to acknowledge the role that morally arbitrary dividing lines play in our moral lives. Kwame Anthony Appiah is simply wrong when he declares that to the extent our partial communities "matter ethically, they do so, in the first instance, for the same reason that football and opera matter."[27] They matter morally because people ordinarily rely on the feelings generated by these communities to shape the degree of concern that they direct toward others.

Cosmopolitan Justice

As noted, cosmopolitans these days rely much more frequently on arguments about social justice than arguments about social friendship in order to convince us to broaden our sense of social connection. These arguments about the priority and universality of our obligations of justice usually build on the premise that free and equal rational beings like ourselves form a single moral community, since all such beings owe each other certain basic forms of respect and consideration. The model of moral community here is Kant's famous "kingdom of ends," the imagined condition in which all individuals treat each other as ends in themselves, rather than merely as means to their own ends.[28] Our obligations of justice are rooted, so the argument goes, in the duties established by our membership in such a community, hence their universality and their priority to any partial obligations established by social friendships and other special relationships.

It is important, in passing, to note that the term community is being used in these arguments in a different sense than that used in this book. It does not refer to a group of individuals who are *disposed* to treat people with whom they share things as objects of special concern and loyalty. It refers, instead, to a group of individuals who are *obliged* by what

27. Appiah, *The Ethics of Identity*, 236, 245.

28. Kant, *Fundamental Principles of Metaphysics of Morals*, 50–51.

they share to treat each other with special respect and dignity. In this understanding of moral community the very fact of sharing something, in this case our character as free and equal rational individuals, itself creates a moral community, regardless of how we may feel about the matter. In my understanding of community, in contrast, communal ties rest on a subjective disposition to treat some form of sharing as a source of mutual concern and loyalty; the mere sharing of a trait is not sufficient in itself to create a community.

This distinction is important because it supports the objection to arguments about the priority of cosmopolitan justice raised at the end of chapter 7, where I defended our reliance on social friendship ties as a means with which to check and balance the excesses of our sense of justice. Such an objection might not carry much weight with earlier, far less humble cosmopolitans, like the Stoics, who believed that they had identified the higher natural laws that govern the cosmos, or like Kant, who believed that he had established the metaphysical foundations of morals and justice in our irrefutable capacity for contra-causal freedom. But for those of us less confident in our ability to determine the metaphysics of morals, it should give some pause. For it is precisely their reluctance to make such claims about their access to a higher moral order that has compelled so many cosmopolitans to step back from the Stoics' dismissive attitude toward partial moral relationships. Should they not be interested in making sure that our assertions about justice are checked and balanced by other moral motives?

Indeed, it seems a little odd that the move among contemporary cosmopolitans to extend the reach of principles of justice is occurring at precisely the time when confidence in our ability to ground domestic justice in rational and universal principles has been waning. The evolution of Rawls's theory of justice provides a striking example of this development. What started in 1971 as a theory about the principles of justice that all rational individuals would choose, were they constrained to reason impartially, became by the 1980s a theory about the principles of justice that would be chosen by individuals comfortably participating in a "democratic public culture."[29] There are many reasons for this diminished confidence in our ability to reason our way to universally valid principles of justice: communitarian concerns about moral context

29. Compare Rawls, *A Theory of Justice* to, especially, Rawls, "Justice, Political, not Metaphysical."

and the social constitution of individuals; pragmatist concerns about the practical motives sustaining arguments; Foucauldian concerns about the imposition of models of reasoning in the guise of discovering them; liberal concerns about moral pluralism. The list runs very long. But they all point in the direction of diminished confidence in our ability to identify rational and universal principles of justice.

Yet when we move beyond the confines of domestic justice there is little sign of the caution that most moral philosophers now exercise when talking about the sources of justice. Rawlsian visions of justice that can only be retailed at home with all kinds of supporting assumptions about social and political context are now being offered wholesale to humanity at large. Philosophers are discovering natural duties of justice that bring us together as a universal moral community that they never dreamed of talking about when debating the sources of domestic justice. What is going on here?

It seems to me that the argument's shift in focus, from the content to the scope of our claims about justice, has encouraged some cosmopolitans to speak as if they are reasoning their way to universal moral standards, when they are merely demonstrating our openness to such standards. As already noted, the largest part of the cosmopolitans' efforts in moral philosophy has been devoted to demolishing the obstacles that communitarians and moral relativists have placed in the way of reasoning about extra-communal standards of morality and justice.[30] Such efforts are often successful, paving the way for arguments, claims, and counterclaims about the content and status of universal principles of justice. But the removal of the barriers to making arguments about extra-communal standards seems to have been treated or experienced by many cosmopolitans as if it liberated them from the constraints on moral reasoning that most of them accept when arguing about justice within the domestic sphere. In this way, otherwise humble cosmopolitans begin to lose their humility.

Nevertheless, contemporary cosmopolitans usually seek the most minimal and uncontroversial moral premises upon which to build their arguments to broaden the scope of our justice obligations. Many believe that they have found such a premise in the idea of equal moral worth of all human beings, the characteristic that Kant ascribes to the members

30. Scheffler, *Boundaries and Allegiances*, 117.

of his universal moral community.[31] The question is how much you can get out of this weak or relatively uncontroversial cosmopolitan premise, in particular how close it brings you to strong cosmopolitan conclusions about the scope of our principles of distributive justice or our obligation to give equal weight to the interests of everyone affected by our actions.[32] It is clear—and quite noteworthy—that the once highly controversial principle of equal moral worth is now so widely accepted these days that it is often mistaken for a platitude. It is far less clear, however, what conclusions about justice follow from our acceptance of this principle. Does the honoring of special obligations to the members of an organization like the nation-state amount to an unjustifiable departure from the standards of justice entailed by our commitment to equal moral worth? That will depend on many things, the most important of which is probably your understanding of the relationship between justice and morality.

The assertion of equal moral worth is compatible with many ways of constructing our justice obligations that do not require the establishment of cosmopolitan principles of distributive justice. One might argue, for example, that as members of a universal moral community of free and equal rational individuals we are obliged to establish systems of law and justice, capped by sovereign authorities, which allow us to maximize our external freedom in our interactions with each other. Such systems of justice may need to be limited in scope in order to maximize their effectiveness in facilitating our freedom of interaction, in which case we will also need additional forms of justice to deal with relationships that go beyond this limit: a law of nations to deal with relations between these different sovereign systems of justice and some basic rules of cosmopolitan right to deal with the interactions between individuals who cross their boundaries. In these circumstances, the set of obligations derived from our membership in a universal moral community would not be co-extensive with the various sets of obligations derived from the different settings in which we practice justice.

In fact, just such an argument was made by none other than Immanuel Kant,[33] whom we could call as a rebuttal witness against some of the

31. See, e.g., Tan, *Justice without Borders*, 1, 94, and Pogge, "Cosmopolitanism and Sovereignty," 169–70.

32. Miller, *National Responsibility and Global Justice*, 27–28.

33. In the first part of his *Metaphysics of Morals*, which has been translated under the title of "The Doctrine of Right," as well as under the title of *The Metaphysical Elements of*

claims about cosmopolitan justice that are now being made in his name. Kant himself would never have endorsed the idea that "cosmopolitanism, according to the Kantian tradition, depends on the existence of a universal moral law, and an idea that it is possible to create or move toward a world society where this moral law becomes the basis of international law and world political organization."[34] The law that binds us as members of a universal moral community is not realizable in the rules and principles of a juridical condition, according to Kant. For the latter governs only the external manifestation of our will—what we do, rather than why we do it. It governs by means of sticks and carrots, coercive pushes and seductive pulls, rather than by means of the exercise of our moral freedom. And in its most important setting, the state, it rests on the foundation of a common authority, a sovereign will, that moral individuals are obliged to obey as part of their obligation to establish a juridical condition. In short, heteronomy is the rule with the practice of justice, not moral autonomy, which rules in the kingdom of ends.

Unlike the Stoics, Kant clearly distinguishes between the obligations that we all share as members of his universal moral community and the obligations against which we measure the political and legal institutions of civil society. A society that lacks such institutions need not be harsh and unjust. But it is "without justice"[35] no matter how well behaved its members may be. In the kingdom of ends, we govern ourselves according to the moral law, just as Stoic sages govern themselves according to the natural law. But in civil society or the juridical condition we are obliged to follow additional rules—including obedience to the rule established by sovereign authorities—that allow us to maximize our external freedom in our interactions with each other. The relationship between these two sets of duties is not between the higher, intrinsically correct standard of duty and its approximation in positive law, as it is with the Stoics. It is, instead, the relationship between one set of moral duties that we are obliged to follow as free and rational creatures and another, different set of duties that the first set of duties obliges us to construct for ourselves.[36] Our membership in a universal moral community obliges us to establish

Justice. The second part of this work, "Public Law," is divided into three sections: "Municipal Law," "The Law of Nations," and "Cosmopolitan Justice."

34. Thompson, "Communal Identity and World Citizenship,"190.

35. Kant, *The Metaphysical Elements of Justice*, 76.

36. "If you are so situated to be unavoidably side by side with others, you ought to abandon the state of nature and enter, with all others, a juridical state of affairs." Ibid., 71.

civil societies and the duties of justice that they make possible, according to Kant. It does not oblige us to establish duties of justice that match the breadth of our moral duties as members of the kingdom of ends. Kant's followers can only make it seem as if it does so by exaggerating the significance that he attached to the concept of cosmopolitan right.[37]

Establishing the existence or possibility of a universal moral community among all free and equal rational beings does not, in itself, answer questions about the nature and breadth of the obligations of justice that connect us to each other. It all depends upon how you conceive the relationship between morality and justice. If even someone so certain of our membership in a universal moral community and so concerned about establishing the conditions of perpetual peace as Kant resists universalizing our justice obligations, then that should give us pause when we encounter claims about how that membership entails an equally universal understanding of justice.[38]

Kant concludes that the most effective means of rendering justice is by establishing a number of sovereign systems of "municipal justice," supplemented by the "law of nations" and "cosmopolitan right" to deal with the gaps between these systems. Others might disagree with this judgment, perhaps because they disagree with his description of world government as a "soulless despotism" that "falls into anarchy after stifling the seeds of the good."[39] But the judgment that Kant makes about the breadth of our justice obligations is determined by arguments about the effectiveness of organizing our systems of justice in one manner or another, not by reference to the universality of our moral obligations. If one shares Kant's concern with effectively organizing our social interactions with each other, as most current cosmopolitans clearly do, then you have to go beyond judgments about the nature of moral community in order to broaden the scope of our obligations of justice.

For if we seek justice as an effective means of organizing social cooperation, not just as a way of measuring the quality of our obligations, then the social connections that sustain political organizations will not be irrelevant to our judgments about justice, however contingent they

37. As effectively demonstrated by Jeremy Waldron in "Cosmopolitan Norms," 87–92.

38. To put it another way: Kant was a moral cosmopolitan and he certainly looked to cosmopolitan forms of political organization to promote perpetual peace. But he did not defend an especially cosmopolitan understanding of justice. For a similar argument, see Canto-Sperber, "The Normative Foundations of Cosmopolitanism."

39. Kant, "Perpetual Peace," 113.

may be. Justice, as Rawls famously argues, measures the virtues of the basic structure of a society, the system of institutions and practices we construct to organize a fair system of cooperation. Where no such structure exists, nor any pressing need to create one, his principles of justice have no application—which is why he rejected the cosmopolitan interpretation of his *Theory of Justice* advanced by many of his students.[40] Shared assumptions about our equal moral worth cannot, in themselves, establish the priority of our more universal obligations of justice. They need further support from observations about the nature and effectiveness of the various means by which we currently construct systems of cooperation. For that we turn to social and political cosmopolitans and their arguments for cosmopolitan democracy.

Cosmopolitan Democracy and the Cosmopolitan Condition

Most defenders of the increasingly popular ideal of cosmopolitan democracy are drawn to arguments in favor of cosmopolitan justice and community. But they rest their case primarily on their interpretation of the changing conditions of modern social life and the new challenges that those conditions pose for us. They insist that a cosmopolitan reorganization of our political institutions is both necessary and desirable, regardless of how we feel about community or what we believe about justice. Moral cosmopolitans demand that we transform the world to bring it into line with the norms implicit in our commitments to humanity and equality. Cosmopolitan democrats, in contrast, urge us to bring our outdated moral and political ideals into line with our increasingly cosmopolitan conditions of existence. Face the facts, they tell us. The world is changing and we cannot effectively address its problems unless we are ready to change along with it. It is the people who think that they can impose obsolete visions of state sovereignty and national autonomy on a world that has left them behind that are being unrealistic, not the cosmopolitans.[41]

Like the other cosmopolitans considered in this chapter, most advo-

40. Scheffler, "Cosmopolitanism, Justice and Institutions," 69–71.

41. The shift in cosmopolitan arguments from reformation to adaptation to worldly realities is noted as well by Craig Calhoun in "Belonging in the Cosmopolitan Imaginary," 534.

cates of cosmopolitan democracy eschew the arrogant visions that inspired their predecessors. They call for global governance rather than a global state. Their goal is to remove the obstacles that keep us from working together to address problems that cross national and regional boundaries, not to subordinate local political organizations to their cosmopolitan counterparts. State sovereignty is indeed the major object of their criticism, but only because its claim to exclusive authority within particular territories keeps us from matching the boundaries of our political organizations to the scale of our different political problems, not because it prevents us from integrating all such claims into a single, worldwide structure of sovereignty.[42] Cosmopolitan democrats therefore see themselves as pluralists, rather than as straightforward universalists. They too call for a kind of "both/and" cosmopolitanism.

The popularity of such claims about the emergence of cosmopolitan conditions clearly reflects the extraordinary degree of attention directed at the phenomenon of globalization. But it is also inspired by the collapse of Soviet communism and the end of the Cold War. For these events not only eliminated the most formidable obstacles to the processes of globalization, they also ended what might be described as a civil war within the "party of humanity" envisioned by Enlightenment cosmopolitans, the ideological division among progressive intellectuals about how best to control and harness natural forces to ease the human condition. No wonder then that some intellectuals are inclined to invoke the fall of the Berlin Wall as the symbol of the emergence of the "new cosmopolitanism."[43]

Of course, there is considerable irony in this characterization of the end of the collapse of Soviet communism, since it was the losing side in the Enlightenment civil war that sang the *Internationale* and explicitly opposed nationalism. The winning side—our side—defended the nation-state and the right of peoples to self-determination. After all, the most obvious and immediate political consequence of the fall of the Berlin Wall was national, not cosmopolitan, in character: the political reunification of Germany. This suggests that we should exercise some caution in identifying globalization with cosmopolitanism. The forces of global-

42. See Held, *Democracy and the Global Order*, for the most influential version of this argument. See also the collection of articles that Held edited with Daniele Archibugi and Martin Kohler, *Re-Imagining Political Community*.

43. Fine, *Cosmopolitanism*, 1.

ization certainly played a role in tearing down the barriers that divided the sides in the Cold War. But they have yet to prove themselves as powerful against the nation-state and the principles of political legitimacy that sustain it.

Like most cosmopolitan arguments, claims about our newfound cosmopolitan condition waver between relatively banal and relatively extreme forms.[44] The banal form merely draws our attention to the way in which new forms of commerce, technology, and communication have drawn more people into increasingly cosmopolitan conditions of existence. The more extreme form, defended most energetically by Ulrich Beck in a stream of monographs and manifestos,[45] insists that these new social forces have propelled us all into a new and unprecedented cosmopolitan way of life—obviously, a much more controversial claim. In other words, this argument wavers between using the cosmopolitan condition to describe an interesting feature of current social existence and using it to define a new epoch in human history.

The argument also appears in a more moderate version, one that suggests that we need to adapt our political institutions to the new cosmopolitan realities if we want them to meet the goals we set for them. This version of the cosmopolitan condition argument, which figures prominently in David Held's defense of cosmopolitan democracy, differs from the more extreme version in a subtle, but important way. In the more extreme version, our social and political institutions have already been undermined by our new cosmopolitan condition. The nation-state and the world it brought into being are pale shadows of what they were at the height of their power. In the more moderate version of the argument, democratic nation-states lack or block the capacity to meet the demands that we place on them, even if they are not in a state of collapse. One version of the argument focuses our attention on a description of the collapse of state sovereignty; the other, on the gap between our goals and the current capacities of democratic nation-states.

In the most extreme version of this argument, Ulrich Beck insists that cosmopolitans need no longer fear being ridiculed for their impracticality. Today, he suggests, it is the so-called realists who are being unreal-

44. Scheffler (*Boundaries and Allegiances*, chap. 7) applies this distinction to what he calls the cultural and ethical conceptions of cosmopolitanism. It seems to apply as well to what we might call the sociological conception.

45. See especially Beck, *Cosmopolitan Vision*.

istic, since they ignore "the important fact . . . that the human condition has itself become cosmopolitan," that cosmopolitanism has become the defining feature of a new era, in which "national differences and borders are dissolving."[46] "Everyday life has become cosmopolitan in banal ways, yet the insidious force of nationalism continues to haunt people's minds," especially the minds of intellectuals. For even though the "national phase of modernity" has ended, many students of social and political life continue to practice a "zombie science" based on obsolete national divisions.[47]

The enthusiasm with which Beck proclaims the arrival of the new cosmopolitan era makes him an easy target of criticism. But even though few writers proclaim the new cosmopolitan era with anything like Beck's confidence, many still move casually from assertions about the emergence of new forms of social connection to assertions about the epoch-making transformation of the human condition. This move adds considerable "rhetorical force" to moral arguments for cosmopolitanism, since it suggests that "cosmopolitanism is now such a natural part of everyday life that it is an inevitable given."[48] For this reason, Beck's rather extreme assertions about our cosmopolitan condition merit closer scrutiny.

Beck claims that the recent changes in our conditions of life are so great as to constitute a new epoch, a "second modernity" defined by its cosmopolitanism, just as the "first modernity" was defined by its reliance on the nation-state.[49] Like all such constructions of contrasts between epochs, Beck's tends to exaggerate change and underplay continuity. For example, it tends to discount or ignore the many examples of cosmopolitan conditions of life that occur before the emergence of his new cosmopolitan epoch.[50] But in one case his exaggeration of discontinuity seems fatal to his argument: the place of state sovereignty in modern political life. It is certainly true that his "first modernity" is the era in which state sovereignty is explicitly endorsed as a norm, so much so that it is often termed the Westphalian age in honor of the treaty with which that norm is identified. And it is also true that some of the attri-

46. Ibid., 2.

47. Ibid., 19, 112.

48. Holton, *Cosmopolitanisms*, 50, 63.

49. Beck, *Cosmopolitan Vision*, 2, 19.

50. For which, see Holton, *Cosmopolitanisms*, 64–77.

butes of state sovereignty that were once taken for granted are now being undermined by the forces of globalization. But it is no less true that the Westphalian era also saw tremendous limits on state sovereignty, limits created by imperialism, revolutionary warfare, and counterrevolutionary actions. The taming of these forces in our world represents an advance for state sovereignty, one that has to be balanced against what it has lost due to globalization.

I therefore agree with those students of international politics who suggest that what we have seen in recent years is a change in the rules of the sovereignty game, the establishment of new limitations on the external sovereignty of states and the removal of some old ones, rather than anything like the end of state sovereignty.[51] The fact that the United Nations, the most important international political organization, generally defends both state and popular sovereignty should be enough to make this point clear. Why then do so many commentators feel comfortable with jumping, like Beck, from assertions about the emergence of new limitations on state sovereignty to proclamations of its disappearance?

The sense that we are experiencing the end of state sovereignty rests, I believe, on an optical illusion that has been irresistible for many of sovereignty's critics. When they look back on the period in which state sovereignty came to be recognized as an international norm, what stands out is the assertion of a norm restricting external interference in the internal affairs of states, rather than the limiting conditions built into the norm or all of the flagrant violations of the principle. When you view the past in this way, new constraints on the external sovereignty stand out and suggest its collapse as a norm, even though you are living in an age that has delegitimated some of the most blatant violations of this norm, such as the pursuit of empire in Asia and Africa.

Social theorists, like Beck, are particularly prone to this kind of optical illusion since they are trained to define societies in terms of the distinctive forms of social cohesion that animate them. This selective focus on the most distinctive features of any particular form of social order, and abstraction from the less distinctive features that they share with other societies, allows them to compare and contrast, say, gemeinschaft and gesellschaft, tradition and modernity, or Durkheim's mechanical and organic solidarity. It also tempts them to construct a vision of his-

51. See Jackson, *Quasi States: Sovereignty, International Relations and the Third World.*

tory as a succession of ideal types of social order, which makes the appearance of new forms of social connection seem like harbingers of completely new ways of life.[52]

This kind of optical illusion plays an especially striking role in recent debates about modernity and postmodernism, or so I have argued in my book *The Fetishism of Modernities.* If you conceive of modernity as a coherent and integrated condition in which all aspects of life are informed by rationalism and individual self-assertion, then the high value postmodernists place on irony, uncertainty, and multiple perspectives seem to indicate the arrival of a new social condition. But why in the world should anyone treat the modern condition as an integrated and coherent whole, least of all postmodernists, a group of thinkers whose most famous assertion is their resistance to the grand metanarratives that conceal the inconsistencies of the world in which we live?[53]

Something similar, I suggest, is happening among those who claim that state sovereignty is disappearing in our new cosmopolitan condition.[54] As Robert Fine suggests in his relatively sympathetic critique of Beck, "the sense of epochal change that plays so large a part in social theory can itself be misleading if it simply makes a cult of novelty."[55] The novelty of the constraints on state sovereignty and national autonomy emerging today are used to define our new, intrinsically cosmopolitan epoch, but can only do so because of an absurd exaggeration of their extent and power in the preceding Westphalian epoch. Understood in this way, the Westphalian era, like the vision of modernity supplanted by postmodernity, is a never-was, rather than a has-been. The new limitations on state sovereignty and national autonomy do not spell the end of these social institutions because they never existed in the form that is said now to be disappearing from our world.[56]

52. This tendency of social theorists to treat their ideal types of social order as the guide to historical development has seriously impeded the study of nationalism, since it has disposed us to treat it as an anomaly, a modern form of organization that seems to rely on premodern communal sources of connection.

53. Yack, *The Fetishism of Modernities*, introduction, chap. 3.

54. Indeed, before Beck began describing our era as a "cosmopolitan age" he was announcing just as confidently the coming of a very different kind of "second modernity." Beck, *Risk Society*, and Beck et al., *Reflexive Modernization*. See also Yack, *The Fetishism of Modernities*, 137–41.

55. Fine, *Cosmopolitanism*, 8.

56. See Nakano, "A Critique of Held's Cosmopolitan Democracy," 34–35.

The Value of Internal Sovereignty

The more moderate version of the cosmopolitan condition argument does not rely on this optical illusion to make its point. It treats national sovereignty as an ineffective means of dealing with the problems created for us by new cosmopolitan conditions, rather than as a spent force. These conditions, so the argument goes, demand much more flexible forms of political organization, forms that take their boundaries from the range of people affected by particular issues and problems.[57] State sovereignty has become an obstacle to effective political organization, according to this argument, since it makes it difficult for us to work together to address problems at their appropriate level. Moreover, if I am right that commitments to national sovereignty provide the catalyst that turns national loyalty into nationalism, then removing this obstacle to more effective government would strike a powerful blow against nationalism as well.

Let us assume, for purposes of argument, that assertions of state and popular sovereignty do indeed impede more effective ways of addressing our current problems. Before endorsing the cosmopolitan democrats' conclusion, we would still need to identify the costs of ending our reliance on such assertions and ask ourselves whether they are worth paying. In what follows, I suggest that cosmopolitan democrats underestimate these costs because they do not look closely enough into the ways in which modern liberal democracies employ commitments to the sovereignty of states and peoples.

For many, the price of abandoning state sovereignty seems simple and clear: the threat of anarchy, the danger that without a single hierarchically ordered structure of sovereign authority we can never be sure whose word makes law. But this argument is easy to counter. For while Hobbes and other defenders of sovereignty may want us to believe that no sovereign means no government, that is clearly untrue. Sovereign authority, as conceived by Bodin and Hobbes, is designed to replace the kind of multiple, overlapping, and competing centers of authority that were the norm for most premodern societies.[58] We have become so used to thinking of domestic authority as singular in character that we may

57. Held, *Democracy and Global Order*, 236.

58. See Bull, *The Anarchical Society*; Quaritsch, *Souveranität*; and Spruyt, *The Sovereign State and Its Competitors.*

be inclined to agree with Hobbes and describe a web of multiple and overlapping authorities as little more than anarchy. But in doing so we are subscribing to a controversial understanding of government, one that places great emphasis on the value of certainty about what counts as lawful, rather than to anything like a morally neutral understanding of the concept.

My concerns about the cost of abandoning the concept of internal sovereignty lie, instead, much closer to the hearts of liberal democrats. For it seems to me that cosmopolitan democrats ignore or severely underestimate the contributions made by internal sovereignty to eminently liberal democratic goals such as limited government, public accountability, and the rule of law. Such a claim might sound extremely paradoxical, since the concept of internal sovereignty is generally identified with claims to unlimited and, therefore, arbitrary authority. But that familiar picture fails to take into account the way in which the concept has developed from its origins in the ambitions of absolutist monarchs and their defenders. In order to correct that picture and judge its value for liberal democrats, we need to step back for a moment from the argument about cosmopolitan democracy and take a closer look at how the concept of sovereignty has evolved in modern politics.

Most recent debates about the concept have focused on what is usually referred to as external sovereignty, the right that states claim to be free of each other's intervention in their internal affairs. But judging from everyday usage, the concept of internal sovereignty seems to inspire as much or more confusion. It is getting harder and harder these days to find anyone willing to endorse the proposition that there is or should be a "final and absolute authority in the political community,"[59] still the commonest definition of the concept. Nevertheless, most people seem quite comfortable talking about the sovereignty of states, peoples, and nations. Moreover, they seem inclined to talk about the sovereignty of both states and peoples, despite the insistence of Hobbes and other theorists of sovereignty that two sovereigns in one state add up to no sovereigns.

No doubt, much of this ambivalence about sovereignty arises from our use of a single term to characterize both the structure of political authority within a state and rights that states assert against each other. And further confusion is created by the way in which sovereignty, like

59. Hinsley, *Sovereignty*, 1.

all influential concepts, has attracted new meanings over time.[60] But even when we take into account and correct these sources of confusion a riddle remains about our attitudes toward state sovereignty. We seem quite comfortable asserting and defending something whose most familiar meaning is abhorrent to most of us.

I suggest that the source of this ambivalence about state sovereignty lies in our failure to distinguish clearly between two distinct attributes of internal sovereignty, attributes that modern liberal democracies have managed to pry apart. Legal autonomy, the idea of an absolute or legally unlimited power at the peak of any structure of political authority, is the more familiar and controversial of the two. Singularity, the idea that there can or should be one and only one structure of coercive authority governing a political community, is far less familiar, but is so widely accepted that most people find it hard to imagine political society without it.[61] Both attributes of sovereignty point to a form of authority. But autonomy involves the subordination of limited to unlimited authority while singularity involves the subordination of a territory and its inhabitants to a single structure of legal authority. In one case, sovereignty points to *unlimited* legal authority; in the other, to *exclusive* legal authority.

Legal autonomy is the attribute we have in mind when we talk about the sovereignty of rulers, parliaments, or peoples. Its classic formulation is Jean Bodin's definition of sovereignty as "the most high, absolute and perpetual power over citizens and subjects in a commonwealth."[62] Singularity is the attribute we have in mind when we talk about the sovereignty of the state. Its classic formulation is Weber's definition of the state as the bearer of "the monopoly of the legitimate use of force."[63]

Both autonomy and singularity promote the concentration of power and political authority. But they do so in different ways. One concentrates authority by removing limits on the exercise of power by particular actors and institutions; the other, by removing rivals to an institutional structure's monopoly on coercive authority.[64] Both involve a kind of finality, a term generally associated with sovereignty. But one involves

60. See Bartelson, *A Genealogy of Sovereignty*.

61. Indeed, this is one of the areas in which cosmopolitan democrats believe they have to work to broaden the political imagination of modern citizens.

62. Bodin, *Six Books of a Commonweale*, 84.

63. Weber, *Economy and Society*, 54.

64. Of course, a singular structure can be made quite complicated through the use of familiar institutional devices such as federalism, the separation of powers, and the creation

the finality that comes with having the last say in a line of authoritative judgments, while the other involves the finality that comes from making compelling judgments that cannot be made anywhere else.

The difference between autonomy and singularity amounts then to the difference between supremacy and monopoly. Legally autonomous rulers share authority with lesser officials and institutions, all of whom are subordinate to their unlimited authority. The sovereign state, in contrast, does not share coercive authority with any other institution or actor. If any institution or actor legitimately exercises coercive authority, then it is, by definition, part of such a state, part of the sovereign, rather than subordinate to the sovereign as lesser officials are subordinate to sovereign rulers. The sovereignty of the state thus refers to its singular or monopolistic exercise of authority over a territory, rather than its position at the top of an ascending hierarchy of powers.

What most of us recoil from today, I suggest, is the combination of autonomy and singularity demanded by absolutist monarchs and totalitarian states. In other words, what we reject is the idea of an *unlimited* power at the top of a *singular* structure of political authority, which is the way in which sovereignty was originally conceived and defended by Bodin and Hobbes. Autonomy and singularity both concentrate power in ways that inspire reasonable fears of oppression. Autonomous sovereigns are frightening for the obvious reason that no act, no matter how terrible, is beyond their legally constituted power. Singular sovereigns are frightening, in contrast, because of the lack of rivals to turn to when one rejects what that they have done. You may establish legal limits to the state's power, but when you have eliminated any rival centers of coercive authority, such as the private armies of local notables or the separate courts and sanctuaries of the Catholic Church, then you have no place to turn for protection when the state's actors and institutions line up against you.[65] But it is the combination of autonomy and singularity that confronts us with a truly terrifying concentration of power—just as Hobbes intended it to do. For when you combine autonomy and singularity, you establish an unlimited power that has at its disposal a monopoly of coercive authority. And by doing so, you eliminate both kinds of

of bicameral legislatures. The key to singularity is that all such institutions form a single structure of authority in which none is completely independent.

65. This is the source of Montesquieu's and Tocqueville's concern about the disappearance of so-called intermediary powers.

checks to political authority: the rival centers of authority that can resist the actions of a legally unlimited ruler as well as the legal limits that can constrain the authority of rulers and institutions who lack such rivals. It is not surprising then that the assertion of sovereignty by early modern rulers and their defenders inspired a countermovement for limited government, a countermovement that gave birth to the liberal democratic state.

Nevertheless, it is a mistake to see that countermovement as a wholesale rejection of the modern concept of sovereignty, let alone a return to the medieval preference for plural and competing centers of authority. John Locke, for example, was clearly disturbed by the idea of vesting an absolute and unlimited power in any ruler or institution. Hence his famous retort to Hobbes: men are not "so foolish that they take care to avoid what mischiefs may be done them by polecats or foxes, but are content, nay, think it safety, to be devoured by lions."[66] But Locke never rejected the idea of a singular structure of authority as a necessary condition of good government. As a result, he tried to develop ways of taming the lion of singular legislative authority rather than establish rival centers of authority guarded by a crew of polecats and foxes.

After all, it would be relatively easy to combine popular sovereignty as Locke understands it with a system of divided and competing centers of legislative authority. For, as we have seen, one way of ensuring limited government is to make sure that there are completely independent sources of authority within a territory so that you have some place to run when the government turns against you. If you can turn to church courts or military tribunals or the power of a local notable after having lost in the king's courts, then there are clearly powerful limits on the authority of government. But Locke, and, I believe, most contemporary liberal democrats, reject this approach to limited government. For absolutism is not the only way in which arbitrariness enters into politics. When competing centers of authority are independent of each other, then our fate rests on a test of strength between their occupants, rather than on the application of general rules to like cases. Independent centers of authority may provide us with a refuge from the agents of the state, but they render us dependent on the goodwill of the notables, these polecats and foxes, whose strength sustains them.

Locke, like later defenders of the constituent sovereignty of the peo-

66. Locke, *Two Treatises*, 2:§93.

ple, tames internal sovereignty by dividing its two key attributes, autonomy and singularity. He vests the final, unlimited authority claimed by sovereign rulers in the people, but the people understood as the prepolitical community of all citizens and subjects that constitutes and deconstitutes government, rather than as a majority of citizens that sits atop a community's structure of legislative authority. And he vests the monopoly of coercive authority in a single structure of political institutions, rather than create different and competing centers of legislative authority. But he envisions this singular structure of authority as ultimately accountable to the people who establish it and retain the right to disestablish it. As a result, Locke introduces two different "supreme" powers into his system of government: one focused on the singular structure of legislative authority; the other focused on the people's power to constitute and deconstitute legislative authority.[67]

This division of the attributes of sovereignty between the state and the people is widely shared today, which helps explain why we seem so comfortable talking about the sovereignty of both peoples and states. Most of us resist the notion that the will of the people should be subjected to final or unrevisable limits, even if we insist that only supermajorities should be allowed to revise constitutional restraints on it. But this concentration of power in the people does not seem so frightening as long as the people—or the nation—is imagined as exercising its power indirectly through the establishment and disestablishment of forms of government, rather than through the direction of the machinery of government against individuals and groups. Most of us resist the idea that there should be many completely independent centers of political authority, (as opposed to the separation of powers within a single complex structure of authority). But the idea of a single hierarchical structure of political authority does not seem so menacing as long as the state is perceived as a system of mutually limiting powers, rather than the tool of some unlimited power sitting at its head. We still fear any conception of sovereignty that unites autonomy and singularity in one sovereign actor or body of actors; but the separation of these two attributes of sovereignty has made us comfortable with the concept.

By separating sovereignty's attributes in this way modern liberal democracies have managed to establish singular structures of authority

67. See Beer, *To Make a Nation*, as well as the discussion of constituent sovereignty in chapter 4 above.

without absolutism or, to say much the same thing, to practice limited government without establishing independent and competing centers of authority. Hobbes argued, in effect, that a polity needs a final and unlimited power in order to maintain a singular structure of coercive authority. But the separation of the constituent sovereignty of the people and the governmental sovereignty of the state allows liberal democracies to defy the logic of Hobbes's argument. They do indeed rely on an unlimited power to recognize the beginning and end of the structure of state authority. But that unlimited power is the power to establish and disestablish the limited powers exercised by various offices and officers of the state, rather than a constituted power to exercise the state's monopoly on coercive authority. And no matter how much liberal democracies rely on the play of ambition against ambition to keep officials from exceeding the limits of their authority, those limits are established by the officials' position within the state's singular structure of authority, rather than by the strength of will exercised by representatives of independent and competing centers of authority. The combination of state and popular sovereignty thus helps liberal democracies combat the arbitrariness and lack of accountability created by divided government as well as that created by absolutism.

Cosmopolitan democrats seem to have missed this contribution to liberal democratic ideals, perhaps because most of them have missed the way in which the concept of internal sovereignty has evolved from its origins in the assertions of absolutists. Of course, we could seek to reproduce this combination of state and popular sovereignty at a broader, more cosmopolitan level, with the human race serving as the people and a universal federal state maintaining a singular, worldwide structure of authority. But, as pluralists and democrats, most contemporary cosmopolitans are not interested in this kind of expansion of the scope of sovereignty. Understandably leery of world states and sovereigns, they seek to replace state sovereignty with a more flexible approach to political organization, rather than reconfigure it to match a more cosmopolitan popular sovereign. Indeed, many see the idea of independent and overlapping centers of authority as a better means of limiting governmental power, not just as a more effective way of addressing our problems in a cosmopolitan age. This approach, however, leaves untouched the problem of arbitrariness that led early liberals like Locke to reject this idea as a means of instituting limited government. It is hard to imagine the return of anything like the arbitrariness of absolutism with the institution of cosmopolitan democracy as most of its contemporary supporters imagine it. But the return of the arbitrariness that preceded absolutism, the arbitrariness created when the limits of coercive power depend on tests of will rather than legal and constitutional rules, seems far more likely. For, as William Scheuerman has noted, cosmopolitan democrats seem to be unconcerned with the ways in which their proposals introduce arbitrariness and undermine rule of law ideals.[68]

Of course, we might discover someday an alternative means of protecting against this kind of arbitrariness without invoking the peculiar combination of state and popular sovereignty upon which liberal democracies currently rely to do the job. Perhaps the European Union will develop such means as it proceeds with its experiment in transnational government.[69] But we do not have such means at our disposal now, which suggests that the abandonment of internal sovereignty comes at a far greater cost than suggested by today's cosmopolitan democrats. These critics of nationalism and state sovereignty are, understandably, unwilling to pay the price of an older and more arrogant vision of cosmopolitan political organization, with its frightening images of a world state and a world sovereign. But, like the other cosmopolitans considered in this chapter, they seem unaware of the moral and political price of their cosmopolitan humility.

Conclusion

My aim in this chapter has not been to disparage cosmopolitan attitudes and institutions. The broadening of our sympathies, the expansion of our

68. Scheuerman, "Cosmopolitan Democracy and the Rule of Law," 449–54. This is part of a broader critique that Scheuerman makes of the idea of "global governance without global government," the idea that you can decouple popular sovereignty from state sovereignty and still effectively represent the populace and maintain democratic accountability. See Scheuerman, "Global Governance without Global Government?"

69. But the European Union has certainly not discovered these alternatives yet, as Held sometimes seems to imply. As Scheuerman ("Cosmopolitan Democracy and the Rule of Law," 449) notes, "although there is no question that a great deal can be learned from the EU about this matter, Held's appeal to the EU experience only begs the question at hand. Even those enthusiastic about the emerging EU legal system would likely deem it presumptuous to suggest that EU law in its present incarnation represents a full satisfactory embodiment of traditional rule of law virtues." On the "elision" of the difference between European and "cosmopolitan" levels of organization, see Calhoun, *Nations Matter*, 16.

sense of justice, and the construction of transnational social and political organizations can all improve our lives in important ways. My purpose, instead, is to show that the relatively moderate forms of cosmopolitanism that are most attractive to us today do not provide us with a means of eliminating the moral problems that nationalism creates for us.

So much the worse for moderation, some might conclude. If the price of cosmopolitan humility is so high, then perhaps we need to recover some of the boldness, even the arrogance, of earlier cosmopolitans. Such a conclusion is certainly tempting in the face of the arguments presented in this chapter. But we should resist it. Cosmopolitan humility is a product of the intrinsic limitations of older forms of cosmopolitanism, not just of a desire to spare the feelings of ordinary people. For traditional cosmopolitans rarely seem more provincial than in the accounts of the universal forms of moral order and reasoning that they derive from our common humanity. Disdaining partial attachments as sources of moral insight both narrows their understanding of humanity and blinds them to their own reliance on partial viewpoints and loyalties. The result is a form of cosmopolitanism that often "enacts the very parochialism it decries."[70] "Both/and" cosmopolitanism may sometimes seem like an attempt to have one's cake and eat it too. But its deeper source is the recognition that "it is an error to hope that we can ever achieve a truly cosmopolitan vision of the cosmopolis."[71]

70. Mehta, "Cosmopolitanism and the Circle of Reason," 629–30. Mehta provides a particularly striking example in his discussion of Jürgen Habermas's claim that "to gain distance from one's own traditions and broaden limited perspectives is the advantage of Occidental rationalism." The quote is taken from Habermas, "Remarks on Legitimation," 162.

71. Pagden, "Cosmopolitanism, and the Legacy of European Imperialism," 20.

CHAPTER TWELVE

Learning to Live with Nationalism

If we can neither get nationalism right nor get rid of it—at least without abandoning things we have good reason to value—then we need to learn how to make the best of the moral difficulties it creates for us. Moderate the effects, rather than remove the cause: Madison's advice about how to handle the problem of faction seems appropriate for addressing the moral problem with nationalism as well.[1] For the rise of nationalism, like the growth of factions, is a by-product of the way in which we have established and legitimated popular government in the modern world. In order to eliminate the moral problem with nationalism we would have to eliminate the commitment to popular sovereignty that has pushed national loyalties in the direction of nationalism. If we want to maintain that commitment, then we need to learn more about how to live with and control nationalism, rather than search in vain for means of correcting or eliminating its influence on our lives.[2]

Of course, it would take another book—and a considerably more knowledgeable author—to answer this call in a thorough and persuasive way. Fortunately, nationalism's students are doing some of their best work in this particular area these days. Social scientists and political theorists have begun to recapture the variety of ways in which states can act to defuse intercommunal conflicts, from asymmetrical forms of federal-

1. Hamilton, Jay, and Madison, *The Federalist Papers*, no. 10.

2. Will Kymlicka ("Liberal Nationalism and Cosmopolitan Justice") makes a similar point in response to those who fret about the European Union's inability to create a larger political community in place of its component nation-states. Their obsession with transcending nationalism obscures their success in defusing the problems that it ordinarily creates.

ism to the creation of multicultural rights. In doing so, they have helped us broaden the menu of options for dealing with these conflicts beyond the stark choice between secession and assimilation.

My modest contribution to this project has been mostly diagnostic, rather than prescriptive or preventive. I have tried to show that it is the delegitimation of opposition to our pursuit of national sovereignty that makes nationalism so morally problematic, rather than its mere endorsement of partial communal loyalties. In other words, it is the encouragement of the belief that our communal rivals are wrongdoers, not just others or opponents, that tends to undermine ordinary moral restraints among nationalists, rather than the sanctification of collective selfishness.

The final chapter of the book follows up on this diagnosis of nationalism's moral limitations by asking what can be done to defuse this sense of the illegitimacy of opposition to one's pursuit of national self-determination. You counter fanaticism by encouraging a sense of humanity and compassion. You counter barbarism by encouraging an attachment to the norms and benefits of civilization. But if, as I have argued, nationalism is the product of a mixture of ordinary moral motives, rather than an expression of the one-sided moral blindness of the fanatic or the barbarian, then a different and subtler approach is needed.

The obvious first step is to get people to stop thinking and talking about national self-determination as a basic right. But such an effort needs to be accompanied by the recognition of the new sources of injustice created by the spread of the principle of popular sovereignty if it is going to have any chance of moderating nationalist passions. Unfortunately, the increasingly popular identification of injustice with the violation of rights makes it difficult to take both of these steps together, since it suggests that where there is no right to something, there is no wrong done in withholding it. But if we are interested in learning how to live more comfortably with nationalism, then we need to begin developing ways of doing so. For denying or ignoring the wrongs that accompany the triumph of popular sovereignty sparks resentments just as deep as the illusion that every national community has a right to control its own piece of the earth.

Before proceeding, let me emphasize that my focus here, as throughout the book, remains on the moral psychology of community. I am asking about what we can do to defuse the intensity of our reactions against those with whom we compete in intercommunal conflicts, rather than what we can do to resolve or minimize those conflicts themselves. In other words, I am looking at ways of thinking about the forms of injustice that fuel nationalist conflicts, rather than what we are obligated to do about them. Such concerns may seem a little abstract or metaethical to those who, rightly, insist on the urgency of addressing questions about how to resolve and adjudicate current controversies. But as long as such conflicts persist, we have good practical reasons for seeking answers to my more limited questions as well—especially if some of the most familiar answers tend to enflame passions that they were designed to defuse. Learning how to live with nationalism requires the refinement and broadening of our moral imagination, not just of our menu of moral obligations and institutional remedies.

No Right, but Many Wrongs

Most attempts to moderate nationalist passions proceed as if a narrow-minded love of one's own were the primary moral problem with nationalism. They tend, accordingly, to focus on broadening and diversifying our feelings of communal loyalty. Such efforts are certainly welcome and, I believe, much less antithetical to nationalist sensibilities than they are ordinarily assumed to be. But they are unlikely to make much headway in defusing nationalist passions if they have misunderstood their source. The Serbs who say that they cannot stand "breathing the same air as Croats"[3] are not expressing an inability to deal with difference. After all, they would probably have no difficulty sharing a meal—let alone their oxygen—with an American or Swede or any of a number of "others" whose differences go way beyond those found among their Croat neighbors. It is indignation at the wrongs that they ascribe to Croats that fuels their passion, not the relatively minor cultural differences that distinguish them from their neighbors.

The great moral problem created by the spread of nationalism is that it promotes the belief that we are entitled to pursue national self-determination without interference from our neighbors and then regularly puts us in situations in which some of our neighbors are bound to contest that right. No doubt, we can find situations in which distaste for cultural difference becomes so intense that it inspires people to think of their

3. Semelin, *Purify and Destroy*, 29.

communal rivals as unjust, depraved, or inhuman. But the rise of nationalism eliminates the need for such an intense reaction against cultural difference. For it turns the inclination of outsiders to oppose our efforts to gain control of our political fate into a manifestation of unjust or depraved character. Mere concern about the impact of our actions on their compatriots' well-being comes to be seen, in itself, as something dishonest and subversive. In this way, even the smallest differences can support intense conflicts—not because we narcissistically obsess about the relatively small points of distinction between us and our rivals,[4] but because our beliefs about national self-determination encourage us to identify these minor differences with the line between right and wrong.

Our first task then, if we are looking to moderate nationalist passions, is to try to counter this association of intercommunal rivalry with injustice. The place to start, as already noted, is to try to get people to stop thinking and talking about national self-determination as a fundamental right. Theoretically, the concept itself is incoherent, as argued in chapter 10. Practically, its impact is devastating. For it promises the members of national communities something it cannot deliver: a space in which they can pursue self-determination free from the interference of others.

And this remains the case even with much narrower understandings of collective self-determination rights, such as the "remedial right to secession" recently defended by Allen Buchanan.[5] Buchanan argues that states, and the peoples sovereign over them, legitimately exercise authority over particular configurations of territory only so long as they meet basic, but fairly low standards of respect for human rights. When they fail to meet these minimal standards they lose that claim to authority, a conclusion accepted by all those who recognize a right to rebel against despotic and totalitarian states. Similarly, Buchanan insists that when states repeatedly and systematically violate the rights of the members of geographically concentrated groups, they lose their claim to exercise authority legitimately in the latter's territory. Nations have no right to secede in order to protect their distinctive way of life, let alone their wealth or their slaves, according to this argument. But "when the only alterna-

4. Ibid., 27–33. See also Ignatieff, *Warrior's Honor*, 53, and "Nationalism and the Narcissism of Minor Differences."

5. In Buchanan, *Justice, Legitimacy, and Self-Determination*, chap. 8. Buchanan offers there a revised and more systematic version of the argument he first presented in *Secession: The Morality of Political Divorce.*

tive to continuing to suffer these injustices is secession," Buchanan insists that "the right of the victims to defend themselves voids the state's claim to the territory and this makes it morally permissible for them to join together to secede."[6]

The problem with this defense of relatively narrow collective self-determination rights is that while it establishes fairly solid grounds for voiding a state's authority, it does nothing to establish a seceding group's right to control any particular configuration of territory. That leaves us with a right to rebel against a despotic regime, but not a right to secede. For, as Buchanan emphasizes, "to make a case that a group has a right to secede one must show that the group's claim to the territory in question is valid."[7] If two different groups—say, the Kurds and the Shia under Hussein's dictatorship—are justified in rebelling against the Iraqi state, which gets to draw the boundaries of its successor? If one group, like the Shia in Iraq, has a more expansive vision of its territory, a vision that leaves little room for its rivals' state, how do we determine who gets to exercise the right to secede? Buchanan's remedial right to secession cannot answer such questions because, like all other defenses of collective self-determination rights, it does not provide us with the grounds upon which groups can make valid claims to control particular configurations of territory.

So our task would seem to be simple: root out the sense that nations bear a right that trumps other claims in disputes about the drawing of borders and the distributions of populations. Such a task would be extremely difficult to complete, since this right not only occupies a familiar place in everyday political rhetoric, it is closely linked to the principle of popular sovereignty, the most widely recognized principle of political legitimacy in modern political life.

But let us suppose, for the moment, that we could overcome these difficulties and succeed in eliminating appeals to a fundamental or first-order right to national self-determination. What should we then say to those who continue to complain about the obstruction of their efforts to take control of the organization of their nation's political life, as well as about the unfairness of their being denied something that other national

6. Buchanan, *Justice, Legitimacy, and Self-Determination*, 354.

7. Ibid., 337. Indeed, Buchanan italicizes the following sentence: *"Unless a theory can provide a plausible account of the validity of the claim to territory by those to whom it ascribes the right to secede, it fails."*

communities have achieved and are inclined to celebrate? What should we say, for example, to the Kurds who complain about the unfairness of their situation, blocked from bringing together into their own state a people strewn across the borders of a number of different states that have mistreated them?

We could say, I suppose, that you are the victim of misfortune, rather than injustice. While you may have been dealt a bad hand, the members of national communities who were dealt—or more skillfully played—a better hand are under no obligation to allow you to challenge the way states are currently organized in your part of the world. Of course, we would have to add that to the extent that members of your community are being denied their basic rights of speech, association, emigration, voting, and so on, they are indeed victims of injustice. You would be wronged, we could say, if you were denied membership in the people who represent the sovereign master of the territory in which you reside. But the conditions that impede your efforts to establish your nation's sovereignty are not unfair or unjust. There is no wrong done you if the house you master is not the one that you believe to be your own. You have a right to master the house you happen to occupy with others, not the one with which you sense some special connection.

We could say all this, but our pleas would almost certainly be rejected. Indeed, speaking in this way would most likely enflame rather than defuse the sense of grievance felt by the members of nations disadvantaged by the way in which political boundaries have been drawn. For this message is bound to smack of hypocrisy and complacency, coming, as it almost invariably does, from people who have done well in the political lottery and therefore find it easy to connect their cultural heritage community and their state. As Avner de Shalit suggests, its deliverers are bound to sound like parents who devour the last scoop of ice cream and then tell their children that they should be happy to accept fruit or nuts for dessert because there is no more ice cream in the house. In doing so, they are quick "to dismiss the demand for national self-determination, . . . claiming that we already have too many states in this world. But they can afford that assertion because they have already enjoyed, or benefited from, having a state" and they have little interest in determining exactly what it would cost to go back to the store for more.[8] The spread of the new constitutive conception of popular sovereignty has led, I have ar-

8. Shalit, "National Self-Determination," 918.

gued, to the nationalization of our sense of political community and the politicization of our sense of national community. We can hardly expect that those made most vulnerable by this new condition would be willing to stop talking about the injustice or unfairness of the situation in which they find themselves.[9]

Yet is that not exactly what we are obliged to do once we reject the concept of a right to national self-determination? Not at all. After all, "entities inhabit our moral world other than full fledged rights."[10] There may be no right to national self-determination, but there are still many ways in which we may wrong those who seek it. The widespread identification of injustice itself with a denial of a right betrays an impoverishment of our understanding of justice, in which a particular means of delivering justice, rights, has come to stand for the concept as a whole. Denying the members of nations the right to come together to govern their "own" territories does not require that we ignore the wrongs they may suffer from the ways in which populations and territories have been divided.

We do not need to be able to identify a violated right in order to identify a wrong. As J. R. Lucas suggests, complaints of injustice arise from the sense that we have been "done down" by others, that others have harmed us in ways that we did not have coming to us.[11] One way of doing us down is to give us less than what we perceive as our fair share of some distribution, less than the portion to which we believe we have a right. Another is to block the exercise of a freedom that we expect regimes to respect as conditions of their legitimacy. But there are other ways of doing us down. For example, even if we are not at all certain what our fair share of some good might be, we are quite certain that we are done down when we get the short end of the stick from people who are hostile, indifferent, or obviously self-interested—the situation so often faced by those who claim to have been wronged by the way in which territories and populations have been divided.

The boundaries that divide states and populations often do significant harm to the members of many communities. And they were created, for the most part, by actors who were hostile or indifferent to the interests of many of the various communities within them. How can we expect

9. See Meisels, *Territorial Rights*, 2, for a similar argument.

10. Ibid., 38.

11. Lucas, *On Justice*, 5–8. See also Shklar, *The Faces of Injustice*, 36–37, 83.

the members of such communities to treat them as the products of bad luck rather than injustice? Since in almost every dispute both sides can find some reason to complain about how they have been wronged by the way in which territories and populations have been divided in the past, complaints about historical injustice cannot generate rights to collective self-determination. But these complaints deserve a respectful hearing. To treat historical injustices as mere misfortunes because no nation has a right to national self-determination represents another way of doing the members of a nation down

The triumph of popular sovereignty, as we have seen, does not provide us with a means of correcting the wrongs done to different communities by the ways in which territory and population have been divided. Indeed, in some ways it heightens the significance of these wrongs, since they now enhance or impede our efforts at taking control of our political lives, rather than merely answer questions about which lord should rule over us. When the principle of popular sovereignty comes to be recognized, some people find themselves members of majority nations at the center of already powerful states, others conspicuous minorities at the peripheries of collapsing empires. It finds some communities well positioned to take effective control over their political fate, others newly vulnerable to the majorities who dominate the sovereign peoples within which they now discover themselves. Only those who have benefited from the history of force, fraud, and diplomacy that has created current political boundaries could describe the latter group as mere victims of misfortune.

Let us return to the predicament in which the Kurds find themselves. Are the Kurds, spread so vulnerably across the borders of frequently hostile states, the victims of injustice or misfortune? Leave aside for the moment all of the undeniable wrongs that they have suffered at the hands of despots like Hussein, wrongs that led to the establishment of the quasi-autonomy that many of them now enjoy under an American protectorate. Apart from the wrongs that they have suffered at the hands of their recent rulers, is there any reason to think that their current division represents an injustice rather than a particularly unfortunate draw from the historical deck?[12]

12. As Judith Shklar has argued (*The Faces of Injustice*, 1–5, 81–2), it is much harder to distinguish between the harms caused by injustice and misfortune than is ordinarily supposed, even in cases where the line between them seems obvious, as in the aftermath of a

To begin with, it is hard to deny that the Kurds were done down by the way in which the state of Iraq, newly forged after World War I from three former provinces of the Ottoman Empire, was imposed on them by the British. This was not a misfortune, a contingent combination of unlucky circumstances. It was a choice made by one imperial power about what to do with the political debris of another, a choice that surely increased the vulnerability of Kurds to the Arab majorities around them.

But even apart from the injustices of past decisions, consider the situation as it is now. The American military may have overthrown Hussein's regime in Iraq, but its government remains committed to the political integrity of the Iraqi state. That has meant that while they have provided protection and a certain degree of autonomy for the Kurds in northern Iraq, they have prevented the Kurds from seeking to secede and establish an independent Kurdish state—let alone making any move toward integrating Kurdish populations and territory beyond the borders of Iraq. They can offer many reasons for doing so. For example, they argue that Kurdish independence cannot be allowed because it would destabilize the region, since it would be met with force by regional powers like Turkey who fear its impact on their own Kurdish minorities. Regional warfare, as well as the expansion to the north of ongoing civil conflicts in Iraq, is not in anyone's interest, so the argument goes, least of all the Kurds. Better to build a sturdy house to master than to burn down your house in an attempt to establish your right to call it your own. Hence the current situation with de facto Kurdish autonomy in the north of Iraq while preserving the de jure integrity of the Iraqi state.

This argument against national self-determination, like others in similar situations, is a serious one. If there is no fundamental right to national self-determination, then it would be wrong for us to ignore the potential disruptions that might be caused by seeking it in an unstable part of the world. But in making such judgments we need to remember that third parties in such situations are almost always disposed to exaggerate the dangers of disturbing settled boundaries and institutions. After all, even assuming that they have no stake in protecting or undermining

hurricane or earthquake. This is because the occurrence of a natural disaster often leads us to address concerns about neglect, hostility, and self-interest that we rarely consider in the ordinary course of affairs—hence the frequent discovery that the victims of misfortune were in fact victims of injustice, as when we discover that people in power were ignoring complaints about the inadequacy of their preparations for emergencies.

the power of a particular state, third parties are likely to have a greater interest in keeping things quiet than in trying to get things right.[13] That does not necessarily mean that they are wrong to resist nationalist demands or that the nationalists are right in their assessment of future consequences. But it does mean that the nationalists in such cases have good reason to worry about the complacency and self-interest of those who tell them that they obstruct the nationalists' pursuit of self-determination for the nationalists' own good. For even a purportedly factual calculation of the costs of action or inaction can conceal a kind of injustice to the seekers of national self-determination.

Commentators often describe intractable intercommunal conflicts as clashes of competing rights. I believe that we would do better to characterize them as clashes of wrongs, conflicts in which the parties invoke the wrongs that they have suffered—not necessarily at each other's hands—to justify their claims to territory and autonomy. The clash of rights, after all, is a highly ambiguous expression. On the one hand, by acknowledging that competing groups can plausibly assert rights to the same territory, it seems to recognize the legitimacy of competing claims to control a territory. On the other hand, by invoking rights, it continues to suggest the illegitimacy of opposing the exercise of these claims. When we characterize intercommunal conflicts as clashes of rights we are more or less acknowledging that while the opposing sides may each have good reasons to think that they have been wronged, neither possesses a right to the result they seek. But our habit of treating injustice as the violation of rights keeps us from saying so.

No right, but many wrongs. We need to become more comfortable with thinking and talking about intercommunal conflict and competition in this way if we are interested in defusing some of the hostility that nationalists display against their opponents. That is why I believe that we need to challenge and correct the liberal habit of identifying injustice with the violation of rights when considering issues of collective self-determination. For this relatively limited vision of justice and injustice creates for us an unnecessary choice between two evils: dismissing claims that nations can be wronged by political divisions of territory and population or endorsing rights to collective self-determination that are bound to increase intercommunal hostility, no matter how narrowly they are construed.

13. See Bradshaw, *Bloody Nations*, 2, and Shalit, "National Self-Determination, 918–19.

The clash of competing assertions of the right to national self-determination is much more explosive than the clashes between different rights with which we are familiar from the daily life of liberal democracies. When, for example, the right to free speech and the right to protection from violence come into conflict with each other, the assertion of one right does not delegitimate the assertion of the other. These conflicts point, instead, to the tension between two of our basic commitments. We deal with such tensions by balancing these two commitments in some way, so that we will not have to sacrifice one for the sake of the other. The clash of rights to national self-determination, in contrast, involves two competing assertions of the same principle. Those who resist our assertion of that principle do not ask us to balance one shared commitment against another; they simply demand that others get out of their way. We might want to hedge and say that both sides believe in the right to national self-determination and look for some compromise that allows each some share of it. But in that case, we should stop calling national self-determination a right and begin treating it as a political goal, a guiding principle or a moral aspiration.

Becoming comfortable with the notion that there are no rights, but many wrongs when it comes to national self-determination would not provide us with a standard against which to measure competing nationalist claims. Indeed, it would probably increase the tedious back and forth of historical grievances. But what sounds tedious to an outsider is often a matter of life and death to the insider. It is a sign of respect, as well as an acknowledgment of our own cognitive limitations, to take such claims seriously. Failure to do so is another way of doing someone down. Besides, when wrongs clash we can, at least in principle, acknowledge that our rivals may have suffered an injustice without thereby delegitimating our own claims. Conceiving of nationalist conflicts in this way therefore opens room for compromise that quickly disappears when we think of them as contests over who gets to invoke a right to collective self-determination.

What's So Special about Nations?

But what is so special about nations that we should take their claims to political self-determination so much more seriously than those made by, say, religious or economic communities? Nothing, declares Buchanan.

"Singling out nations for self-government is a form of discrimination."[14] Lea Brillmayer, for one, agrees with him, arguing that the morally compelling component of nationalist claims always depends on the secondary arguments that they make, arguments about recent conquests, long-standing occupations, historical injustices, and the like. The persuasiveness of these claims, she suggests, owes nothing to the assertion that these claims are being made in the name of a particular kind of community.[15]

Since I have argued in chapter 10 that the right to national self-determination gives us no way to measure competing claims to control a particular piece of territory, I have to acknowledge that Brillmayer and Buchanan have a point. Even those who recognize a right to national self-determination rely on these secondary arguments in judging competing claims. But even so, it should be clear that the fact these claims are being made in the name of nations leads us to entertain them much more seriously than those made by other groups. In doing so, are we just responding to political expediency, the ability of nationalist groups to cause trouble, or do we have morally compelling reasons for paying more attention to national claims to political self-determination? Or to put it negatively, do we have a morally compelling reason for thinking that the failure to do so amounts to a kind of injustice?

I have argued throughout this book that there is nothing about the nation in itself that lends it any special moral status. It is not a natural form of community, let alone the natural foundation of political organization. As a contingent community rooted in shared cultural heritage, it is not formed to pursue a particular purpose, let alone a particular moral purpose. It is not the bearer of particular political projects nor is it a necessary foundation for the achievement of individual autonomy. Yet considered within the context in which it has risen to such political prominence, the triumph of the modern conception of popular sovereignty, I believe that the nation possesses qualities that give it a special claim on our attention. It has, as it were, the standing to make claims, rather than the right to override the claims of other groups.[16]

The first of these qualities is the capacity to help mobilize populations

14. Buchanan, "What Is So Special about Nations?," 295.

15. See Brillmayer, "The Moral Significance of Nationalism."

16. Avery Kolers (*Land, Conflict, and Justice*, 46) makes a similar suggestion about standing in response to Buchanan's argument in "What Is So Special about Nations?"

and generate collective power, the capacity to inspire and ease the coordination of the activities of large numbers of human beings. As Margaret Canovan has suggested, nationalism functions like a battery: a cheap and mobile source of collective energy for an extraordinary range of causes.[17] All modern regimes, liberal democracies included, have drawn on this source of energy because it requires so much less repression than most other means of mobilizing and coordinating collective efforts. This energy is not some intrinsic quality of the nation as a focus for communal loyalty, a quality that opens us up to especially deep or primitive passions. It is rather the quality that the nation possesses as a focus for communal loyalty for individuals who have come to believe that the people who inhabit a territory have the right to constitute and de-constitute its political institutions. For people committed to this principle of political legitimacy, I have argued, the mutual reinforcement of feelings of social friendship and convictions about political legitimacy gives nationalism the capacity to work up powerful passions without the effort that it would ordinarily take to promote either especially deep convictions or communal loyalties.[18] In other words, the nation is not born a special community. It becomes special within the context of a political principle that currently grounds our institutions and that most of us are loath to abandon.

This special quality of nations has a moral claim on our attention for two reasons, one negative, the other positive. Negatively, this capacity to generate cheap collective energy tremendously increases the vulnerability of small or relatively peaceful national communities, both within and across the borders of nationalizing states. Without access to it, it becomes very difficult for such communities to defend themselves. Nationalism may be responsible for some of the twentieth century's most horrific acts of violence; but, as was the case in World War II, it also provided much of the energy that has allowed us to defeat their perpetrators.[19] If we have constructed a political world that exposes communities to this new capacity to mobilize collective force, then how can we ignore the pleas of exposed national communities to gain access to it as

17. Canovan, *Nationhood and Political Theory*, 73–74.

18. See chapter 6 above.

19. As Brendan O'Leary points out, nationalism played a crucial role in mobilizing the forces that eventually defeated the totalitarian regimes responsible for the twentieth century's most horrible examples of mass murder. See O'Leary, "Ernest Gellner's Diagnosis of Nationalism," 87n85.

well, especially when we make such liberal use of it ourselves? No doubt, nationalism is a powerful weapon for the strong, waiting to be exploited by fanatics and political entrepreneurs alike. But because it is much less costly than most other forms of political mobilization, it is also one of the favorite weapons of the weak.[20] Modern political conditions tremendously increase both the vulnerability and the political value of national communities. They compel us, I would suggest, to give special consideration to claims of national self-determination before rejecting them.

The nation's special capacity to generate collective power in modern political conditions also gives it a more positive moral claim on our attention. The coordination of individual actions to generate collective forms of power is difficult and most often costly. Access to a capacity to generate collective power relatively cheaply is thus an extraordinarily valuable resource to any group of individuals. Leaving aside self-protection, this resource opens up the possibility of forms of public action and improvement that would be difficult to imagine without it. Assertions of national self-determination thus have a special claim on our attention because of what they can help a group of people do in modern political conditions, not just because of the special risks to which these conditions may expose them.

The second quality of national communities that lends them a special claim on our attention is the way in which they help a group represent its needs and interests. This capacity looms very large in nationalist rhetoric.[21] Time and again defenders of national self-determination complain about how minority status within a larger polity prevents the proper representation of the needs of the members of their community, even in a well-functioning liberal democracy. The problem is not that the voices of the minority nation are silenced in the larger polity's representative bodies. It is rather that in the larger setting they disappear into a larger stream of voices that drains away the special insight that we might have gained into its conditions and desires by hearing them respond to each other in their own assembly. National community, Catherine Frost suggests, provides us with a "shared frame of reference" that helps bring the

20. As Craig Calhoun reminds us in *Nations Matter*, 36. See also S. Cohen, *Politics without a Past*, 3–4. Cohen suggests that the loss of a sense of our place in history's flow can leave us speechless, like Winston Smith in *Nineteen Eighty-Four*, when we try to organize opposition to powerful institutions.

21. See especially Frost, *Morality and Nationalism*. See also Moore, *The Ethics of Nationalism*, 87–88.

representation of a group into focus.[22] To represent people well you need to give them more than the mere opportunity to express their needs and interests in a center of power; you need to give them a setting in which they can make sense of and refine each other's claims. Without something like the sense of belonging to an ongoing, intergenerational community that national loyalties provide, representation tends to degenerate into the mere declaration and accumulation of needs and interests.

But even if Frost is correct in her general point about representation, and I believe that she is, we need to ask what makes the nation so special as a representational "frame of reference"? Why should we assume that the loss of this particular frame of reference should be such a blow to the prospects of adequate representation? Certainly, there are other frames of reference, larger and smaller, to which people have access in their representative assemblies. Why should we privilege the nation in this way?

Once again, the answer to these questions lies in the political setting created by the triumph of the principle of popular sovereignty, rather than in the intrinsic qualities of the nation. It is the nation's affinity to the people of popular sovereignty thinking that makes it an especially apt frame of reference for modern political representation. In other circumstances, under other principles of political legitimacy, the invocation of a prepolitical community like the nation would make little sense as the frame of reference within which to consider a political community's needs. But, as I noted in chapters 4 and 8, the invocation of the constituent sovereignty of the people gives national community a political resonance it lacks in other circumstances. Moreover, the association of the people with the nation gives the latter a historical depth that it can never attain on its own. For it helps us imagine the group that constitutes legitimate political authority as extending forward and backward in time, as the receivers of the legacies from the past and the protectors of those who come after us in the future, something that makes it an especially effective frame of reference for the representation of its members' needs and interests. And it does so, as we have seen in chapter 8, without relying on any substantive commitments or cultural practices as a necessary condition of membership, which allows room for a great variety of competing perspectives to be represented within the national frame.

22. Frost, *Morality and Nationalism*, 103. Frost concludes that "the moral worth of nations arises in its role as a shared frame of reference that enables representation" (7).

The Dark Side of Democracy?

If nationalism is an unintended by-product of the way in which popular sovereignty has been established in the modern world, then learning how to live with nationalism seems to be a required subject for friends of democracy. Does that mean that we should treat nationalism as "the dark side of democracy," as Michael Mann suggests?[23] I think so, but only if we properly qualify each word in his provocative description—including the word "the."

To begin with, nationalism, as Mann recognizes,[24] is not a by-product of democracy per se, but rather of the particular way in which we tend to construct democracy in modern states. As noted in chapter 6, it is the constitutive or indirect understanding of popular sovereignty, with its emphasis on consent of the people as the source of the political legitimacy of rulers and institutions, that opens the door to nationalism. More direct forms of democracy, with their emphasis on taking turns in positions of power, promote greater partisanship as well as greater involvement in politics. They thereby deflect attention away from shared cultural heritage as the focus of political community. Indeed, the appeal to national loyalties has been one of the most effective means of controlling the factionalism that was long treated as democracy's greatest defect. Because we are so familiar with the exploitation of nationalism to stifle dissent and enhance the power of established elites and ambitious political entrepreneurs, we tend to discount the sincerity of such appeals. But they have played a powerful role in both raising the status of the ordinary people, since they share equally with elites their membership in national communities, and in motivating elites to respect and even make sacrifices for the interests they share with ordinary people.[25]

So the cultivation of national loyalties encouraged by our new, constitutive understanding of popular sovereignty has helped us solve—or at least temper—an old problem with democratic government. But in doing so it has helped create a new and unexpected set of problems. Critics of nation-state democracy are therefore correct in insisting that democ-

23. Mann, *The Dark Side of Democracy.*

24. Ibid., chaps. 1–3.

25. Liah Greenfeld's *Nationalism* does an excellent job of highlighting and explaining the former.

racy and nationalism need not go together. The more civic or republican modes of democracy characteristic of ancient city-states have already demonstrated the point; the more cosmopolitan forms of democracy advocated by so many contemporary theorists are designed to confirm it. But even when we bracket the tremendous obstacles to producing or reproducing these different forms of democracy in present circumstances, there are good reasons to doubt that these alternative conceptions of democracy can solve our moral problem with nationalism. For, as I argued in chapter 1, while republican patriotism differs from nationalism in many ways, it shares its tendency to intensify hostility toward outsiders. And, as I argued in chapter 11, the pluralism of contemporary cosmopolitans keeps them from challenging national loyalties in a way that would prevent the growth of nationalism in modern democracies.

Second, nationalism represents *a* dark side of modern democracy, not *the* dark side. In other words, it is one of a number of dark or problematic by-products of our commitment to democratic forms of government. Factionalism, one of the oldest complaints against democracy, has already been mentioned. Free people to express and organize themselves and the emergence of factions is inevitable. For, in Madison's famous words, freedom is to faction as "air is to fire."[26] And since, as Hume notes, "the human mind . . . is wonderfully fortified by a unanimity of sentiments, so is it shocked and disturbed by any contrariety,"[27] the opportunity to organize factions tends to intensify conflict, a point confirmed by the murderous histories of republican and religious civil wars. We may not talk much anymore about factionalism as a dark side of democracy—except for the low hum of complaints about partisanship—but only because so much effort has been devoted to teaching us how to live with and moderate the problems that it creates for us.

Another dark side of democracy, one that shares much with nationalism, is populist resentment, the combination of sentiments and convictions that exaggerates the character and judgment of ordinary people and denigrates the character and judgment of elites of all sorts. Demagogues and popular dictators are experts in the exploitation of these resentments; fascist parties are their most dangerous products. Like nationalism and factionalism, populism is a by-product of something of

26. Hamilton, Jay, and Madison, *Federalist Papers*, no. 10.

27. Hume, "Of Parties in General," 60–61.

great value to democratic societies: the correction of our tendency to attribute special worth and status to the lives of those with special knowledge, ability, wealth, or power. Equality of worth and status is something that has to be asserted and reasserted. It cannot simply be assumed, especially in complex and stratified societies like our own. But its assertion inevitably stirs up populist passions.

Like factionalism, the growth of populist resentments has been held against democracy as long as this form of government has been discussed. The normalization of democracy in the modern world thus required that we learn how to live with and moderate populism's impact on democratic politics. If Madison is the canonical reference for learning how to live with factionalism, Tocqueville is the name that we most associate with cultivating the tools within democracy to constrain populist resentment.[28] One reason that there is no comparable canonical reference for learning how to live with the moral problems that nationalism creates for democratic societies is that this particular dark side of democracy, unlike factionalism and populism, is relatively new. Indeed, it represents, in part, the product of an effort to address these older complaints about democracy.

Finally, there is nationalism's "darkness" to qualify. To call nationalism a dark side of modern democracy is not to suggest it unleashes irrational or instinctive passions, the inner beast or savage that civilized humanity has tried so hard to constrain. On the contrary, nationalism draws on motives, feelings of communal loyalty and convictions about political legitimacy, that are the stuff of everyday moral life in civilized society. The moral problem with nationalism is that it combines these everyday motives in a way that tends to intensify hostility to rivals and weaken the moral constraints that we ordinarily rely on to control such hostility. As a result, it corrodes moral judgment rather than sets us off in pursuit of evil or inhuman goals.

That said, we should not ignore just how dark this dark side of democracy can be, even if it does not unleash the savage passions bottled up within civilized people. Like factionalism and populism, nationalism has a high body count. We need to recognize that our political commitments promote the growth of a force that is capable of inspiring extraordinary

28. As with factionalism, there is good reason to fear that we have learned their lessons all too well and are now exaggerating populism's dangers.

and unexpected forms of communal violence. Such intercommunal violence may be the exception, rather than the rule.[29] But given the dispositions we have been considering, it remains a real possibility in a surprisingly wide range of circumstances, including the life of relatively stable liberal democracies like our own. The defense of democracy in the past required an effort to figure out how to live with and moderate the evils of factionalism and populist resentment. Today it requires a search for better ways of living with and moderating nationalism's corrosive effect on our moral standards.

29. As ably demonstrated by James Frearon and David Laitin in "Explaining Interethnic Cooperation." See also Laitin, *Nations, States, and Violence.*

Conclusion

We cannot choose when or where or to whom we are born. That might not matter very much for solitary creatures who emerge into life fully grown, like Athena from the head of Zeus. But for social animals like ourselves, creatures who are born helpless and take an unusually long time to mature, the contingencies of birth cut deep. They shape both the development of our faculties and the way in which we relate to others. Long before we possess the means of directing our lives, we find ourselves connected to a wide range of people with whom we never chose to associate.

What we make of these connections depends in large part on how we imagine and organize our lives together. For a long time human beings were inclined to exaggerate their significance: to treat them as natural barriers to association, as if they marked the boundaries between species; to invest them with great moral significance, as if the virtues of honored patriarchs and matriarchs were passed on to their descendants; and, worst of all, to erect upon them rigid systems of social hierarchy, as if our parentage should determine the nature and extent of the legal privileges to which we are entitled. No wonder then that so many modern political ideals are advanced as means of relieving us of the weight of the circumstances of our birth. Or that so many social theorists identify distinctly modern societies with the rejection of inherited community.

It is this identification of modern society and morals with individual choice that makes the rise of nationalism seem so incongruous to modern philosophers and social theorists. A relatively old form of intergenerational community, the nation, has apparently risen to unprecedented political importance in precisely the era that was supposed to curtail its influence. In other words, one of the most powerful new forces in modern society, nationalism, does not seem to be behaving in distinctly modern ways. Either nationalism is something other than it seems or there is something wrong with our understanding of community and modern society.

Most theoretical studies of nationalism pursue the first of these two solutions to the puzzle posed by nationalism's unexpected rise to prominence in modern politics. They bring nationalism back into line with the conceptual frameworks that support most theories of modern society by explaining away either nationalism's novelty or its reliance on inherited community. This book has pursued the second solution. By revising the concepts of community and modern society that make nationalism seem like such an anomaly in the modern world, it has tried to bring our conceptual frameworks back into line with the social phenomena that have raised doubts about them. In doing so, it has tried to build on nationalism's roots in the way in which we imagine the contingencies of birth without falling back on the myths of common descent and kinship that have exaggerated their significance in the past.

The key to that effort has been my construction of a more flexible and mundane understanding of community, one that conceives of community as a basic building block of human association, rather than as the negation of the relatively individualistic forms of association developed by modern societies. The understandings of community bequeathed us by the classic social theories of the nineteenth and twentieth centuries treat community as a residual category, a concept defined by its lack of features associated with distinctly modern societies.[1] That has led, I believe, to an exaggerated sense of its closedness, holism, and reliance on blood ties, which, in turn, guarantees that any form of community that flourishes in modern conditions will seem like an anomaly. Repetitive debates between primordialists and modernists, between scholars who think that nationalism represents the triumph of the old over the new and those who think the opposite, are inevitable as long as we continue to conceive of community in terms of its opposition to distinctly modern forms of association.

My alternative understanding of community attempts to move the

1. I discuss the concept of residual categories in *The Fetishism of Modernities* (56–57), focusing specifically on the concepts of antiquity and traditional society and their definition in terms of their lack of "modernity."

concept beyond these projections of past or future alternatives to modern forms of association. It treats community, instead, as a flexible form of social cooperation that plays a significant role in every society and historical period. Community, in my account, rests on the development of feelings of mutual concern and loyalty among people who share things, feelings that vary in intensity and exclusiveness according to the forms of sharing affirmed at different times and places. Viewing community in this way allows us to explore its interaction with motives and institutions usually associated with distinctly modern forms of association. This is a great advantage in the study of nationalism because, as we have seen, nationalism's rise to prominence challenges us to figure out why an older form of intergenerational community should have taken on such unprecedented political importance in the modern era. The more familiar understandings of community prompt us to ask whether nationalism serves or overwhelms distinctively modern forms of association. My understanding allows us to focus on the points of contact between new and old forms of association that might change the way in which we appropriate national ties.

The most important of these points of contact, I have argued, is the new conception of popular sovereignty that has become the predominant principle of political legitimacy in our world. The spread of commitments to this principle, I have tried to show, has tended to nationalize our understanding of political community and politicize our understanding of nationality. That helps explain both the unexpected emergence of nationalism as a force in modern politics and the moral problems nationalism creates for us. For if nationalism is, in large part, a product of our commitment to the principle of popular sovereignty, then it is going to be far more difficult to eliminate from our lives than most people seem to think.

Not that I am suggesting that nationalism, nations, or any other form of intergenerational community will always play a prominent role in our lives. It took a very specific set of historical conditions to raise communities based on shared cultural inheritance to their current political importance. These conditions have proved far stabler than many have expected, hence nationalism's defiance of so many predictions of its imminent demise. But just because theorists have embarrassed themselves in the past with their claims to have seen the owl of Minerva taking flight over nationalism's grave, that does not mean that these conditions will last forever—or even past the next few generations.

What will abide in our lives, I believe, is our disposition to form communities, to develop ties of mutual concern and loyalty among people with whom we share things. Even if we do end up developing more cosmopolitan forms of political organization in the future, that disposition will continue to shape the way in which we work together with others, most likely in unexpected ways. This book has argued that in order to make sense of nationalism and the problems that it creates for us we need to recognize that these feelings of social friendship play just as important a role in our social lives as calculations of self-interest and beliefs about justice. That role will not end with the passing of nationalism, whenever it takes place; it will just take different forms. So if we want to be better prepared for future developments in the history of human association than we were for the nation's unexpected rise to prominence in an individualistic age, then we need to become much more familiar with the moral psychology of community and its impact on our lives.

Bibliography

Alter, Peter. *Nationalism*. London: Edward Arnold, 1989.

Anderson, Amanda. "Cosmopolitanism, Universalism, and the Divided Legacies of Modernity." In *Cosmopolitics, Thinking and Feeling beyond the Nation*, edited by B. Robbins, 265–89. Minneapolis: University of Minnesota Press, 1998.

Anderson, Benedict. *Imagined Communities*. London: Verso, 1991.

Appiah, Kwame Anthony. *Cosmopolitanism: Ethics in a World of Strangers*. New York: Norton, 2006.

——. "Cosmopolitans and Patriots." In Nussbaum et al., *For Love of Country*, 21–29.

——. *The Ethics of Identity*. Princeton, NJ: Princeton University Press, 2005.

Archibugi, Daniele, David Held, and Martin Kholer, eds. *Imagining Political Community: Studies in Cosmopolitan Democracy*. Stanford, CA: Stanford University Press, 1998.

Arieli, Yeoshua. *Individualism and Nationalism in American Ideology*. Cambridge, MA: Harvard University Press, 1964.

Aristotle. *Complete Works*. Edited by Jonathan Barnes. 2 vols. Princeton, NJ: Princeton University Press, 1984.

——. *Eudemian Ethics*. In Aristotle, *Complete Works*, 2:1922–81.

——. *Motion of Animals*. In Aristotle, *Complete Works*, 1:1087–96.

——. *Nicomachean Ethics*. In Aristotle, *Complete Works*, 2:1729–1861.

——. *Politics*. In Aristotle, *Complete Works*, 2:1986–2129.

Armstrong, John. *Nations before Nationalism*. Chapel Hill: University of North Carolina Press, 1982.

Ascheron, Neal. *Stone Voices: The Search for Scotland*. New York: Hill and Wang, 2002.

Axelrod, Robert, and William Hamilton. "The Evolution of Cooperation in Biological Systems." In *The Evolution of Cooperation*, edited by R. Axelrod, 85–105. New York: Basic Books, 1989.

Bader, Veit. "Citizenship and Exclusion." *Political Theory* 23 (1995): 211–46.

Barnard, F. M. *Self-Direction and Political Legitimacy*. Oxford: Clarendon Press, 1988.

Barrès, Maurice. *Scènes et doctrines du nationalisme*. Paris: Emile Paul, 1902.

Barry, Brian. *Culture and Equality: An Egalitarian Critique of Multiculturalism*. Cambridge, MA: Harvard University Press, 2001.

Bartelson, Jens. *A Genealogy of Sovereignty*. Cambridge: Cambridge University Press, 1995.

——. *Visions of World Community*. Cambridge: Cambridge University Press, 2009.

Barth, Frederick, ed. *Ethnic Groups and Boundaries*. London: Allen & Unwin, 1969.

Baumeister, Roy. *The Cultural Animal*. Oxford: Oxford University Press, 2005.

Béaud, Olivier. *La puissance de l'état*. Paris: PUF, 1994.

Beck, Ulrich. *Cosmopolitan Vision*. Cambridge: Polity Press, 2006.

——. *Risk Society: Towards a New Modernity*. London: Sage, 1992.

Beck, Ulrich, et al., eds. *Reflexive Modernization*. Stanford, CA: Stanford University Press, 1994.

Beer, Samuel. *To Make a Nation*. Cambridge, MA: Harvard University Press, 1993.

Beiner, Ron. "Introduction: Nationalism's Challenge to Political Philosophy." In Beiner, *Theorizing Nationalism*, 1–25.

——. "National Self-Determination: Some Cautionary Remarks concerning the Rhetoric of Rights." In Moore, *National Self-Determination and Secession*, 158–80.

——, ed. *Theorizing Citizenship*. Albany: SUNY Press, 1995.

——, ed. *Theorizing Nationalism*. Albany: SUNY Press, 1998.

Beissinger, Mark. "Nations That Bark and Nations That Bite." In J. A. Hall, *The State of the Nation*, 169–90.

Bell, David. *The Cult of the Nation in France*. Cambridge, MA: Harvard University Press, 2001.

Ben Menahem, Yemima. "Historical Contingency." *Ratio* 10 (1997): 99–107.

Benda, Julien. *The Treason of the Intellectuals*. New York: Norton, 1969.

Bentham, Jeremy. *Handbook of Political Fallacies*. Baltimore: Johns Hopkins University Press, 1952.

Berlin, Isaiah. *Liberty*. Oxford: Oxford University Press, 2002.

——. "My Intellectual Path." In his *The Power of Ideas*, 1–23. Princeton, NJ: Princeton University Press, 2000.

——. "Nationalism: Past Neglect and Present Power." In his *Against the Current*. New York: Penguin, 1982.

——. "The Pursuit of the Ideal." In his *The Crooked Timber of Humanity*, 1–19. New York: Knopf, 1991.

——. *Vico and Herder.* New York: Viking, 1976.

Bhabha, Homi, ed. *Nation and Narration.* London: Routledge, 1990.

Bibo, Istvan. "The Distress of East European Small States." In his *Democracy, Revolution, Self-Determination: Selected Writings*, 13–88. Highland Lakes, NJ: Atlantic Research and Publications, 1991.

Billig, Michael. *Banal Nationalism.* New York: Sage, 1995.

Binder, Guyora. "The Case for Self-Determination." *Stanford Journal of International Law* 29 (1993): 223–70.

Bix, Herbert. *Hirohito and the Making of Modern Japan.* New York: Harper Collins, 2000.

Bodin, Jean. *Six Books of a Commonweale.* New York: Arno, 1979.

Booth, W. J. "Communities of Memory: On Identity, Memory, and Debt." *American Political Science Review* 93 (1999): 249–63.

Bowen, John. *Why the French Don't Like Headscarves.* Princeton, NJ: Princeton University Press, 2007.

Bradshaw, Cherry. *Bloody Nations: Moral Dilemmas for Nations, States, and International Relations.* Aldershot: Ashgate, 2009.

Breuilly, John. *Nationalism and the State.* Chicago: University of Chicago Press, 1991.

——. "Nationalism and the State." In *Nationality, Patriotism, and Nationalism in Liberal Democratic Societies*, edited by R. Michener. St. Paul, MN: Paragon, 1993. 19–48.

Brewer, Marilyn. "The Psychology of Prejudice: Ingroup Loyalty or Outgroup Hate." *Journal of Social Issues* 55 (1994): 429–44.

Brillmayer, Lea. "The Moral Significance of Nationalism." *University of Notre Dame Law Review* 71 (1995): 7–34.

——. "Secession and Self-Determination: A Territorial Interpretation." *Yale Journal of International Law* 16 (1991): 177–204.

Brubaker, Rogers. *Citizenship and Nationhood in France and Germany.* Cambridge, MA: Harvard University Press, 1992.

——. *Ethnicity without Groups.* Cambridge, MA: Harvard University Press, 2004.

——. "Myths and Misconceptions in the Study of Nationalism." In J. A. Hall, *The State of the Nation*, 272–306.

——. *Nationalism Reframed.* Cambridge: Cambridge University Press, 1996.

Buchanan, Allen. *Justice, Legitimacy, and Self-Determination: Moral Foundations of International Law.* Oxford: Oxford University Press, 2007.

——. *Secession: The Morality of Political Divorce.* Boulder, CO: Westview, 1991.

——. "Theories of Secession," *Philosophy and Public Affairs* 26 (1997): 31–61.

——. "What Is So Special about Nations?" In *Rethinking Nationalism*, edited by J. Coutone et al., 283–309. Calgary: University of Calgary Press, 1998.

Bull, Hedley. *The Anarchical Society.* New York: Oxford University Press, 1977.

Burke, Edmund. *Reflections on the Revolution in France.* Indianapolis: Hackett, 1987.

Calhoun, Craig. "Belonging in the Cosmopolitan Imaginary." *Ethnicities* 3 (2003): 531–53.

——. *Nationalism.* Minneapolis: University of Minnesota Press, 1997.

——. *Nations Matter: Culture, History, and the Cosmopolitan Dream.* London: Routledge, 2007.

Caney, Simon. "Cosmopolitan Justice and Equalizing Opportunities." In *Global Justice*, ed. T. Pogge. Oxford: Basil Blackwell, 2001.

Canovan, Margaret. *Nationhood and Political Theory.* Cheltenham: Edward Elgar, 1996.

——. *The People.* Oxford: Polity, 2005.

Canto-Sperber, Monique. "The Normative Foundations of Cosmopolitanism." *Aristotelian Society* (2008): 265–81.

Carens, Joseph. "Aliens and Citizens." In Beiner, *Theorizing Citizenship*, 232–54.

Cassese, Antonio. *The Self-Determination of Peoples: A Legal Reappraisal.* Cambridge: Cambridge University Press, 1995.

Catlin, G. E. G. "The Meaning of Community." In *Community*, edited by C. Friedrich, 114–34. New York: Liberal Arts Press, 1959.

Cobban, Alfred. *The Nation-State and National Self-Determination.* New York: Thomas Crowell Company, 1969.

Cohen, Mitchell. "Rooted Cosmopolitanism." *Dissent* 39 (1992): 453–77.

Cohen, Shari. *Politics without a Past: The Absence of History in Post-Communist Nationalism.* Durham, NC: Duke University Press, 1999.

Colley, Linda. *Britons: The Making of a Nation.* New Haven, CT: Yale University Press, 1992.

Connor, Walker. *Ethnonationalism.* Princeton, NJ: Princeton University Press, 1995.

Dahbour, Omar. *Illusion of the Peoples: A Critique of National Self-Determination.* Lanham, MD: Lexington, 2003.

Dawkins, Richard. *The Selfish Gene.* Oxford: Oxford University Press, 1989.

Denitch, Bogdan. *Ethnic Nationalism: The Tragic Death of Yugoslavia.* Minneapolis: University of Minnesota, 1994.

Devine, T. M. *A History of the Scottish Nation.* London: Penguin, 2000.

Diderot, Denis, et al. *L'Encyclopédie.* Neufchâtel: Faulche & Compans, 1765.

Dietz, Mary. "Patriotism." In *Political Innovation and Conceptual Change*, edited by T. Ball, 177–93. Cambridge: Cambridge University Press, 1989.

Dower, John. *Embracing Defeat: Japan in the Wake of World War II.* New York: Norton, 1999.

Duara, Prasenit. *Rescuing History from the Nation: Questioning Narratives of Modern China*. Chicago: University of Chicago Press, 1995.

Dumont, Louis. *German Ideology: From France to Germany and Back*. Chicago: University of Chicago Press, 1994.

Dunn, John. *Western Political Theory in the Face of the Future*. Cambridge: Cambridge University Press, 1993.

Elster, Jon. *The Cement of Society: A Study of Social Order*. Cambridge: Cambridge University Press, 1989.

Ely, John. *Democracy and Distrust*. Cambridge, MA: Harvard University Press, 1980.

Emerson, Rupert. *From Empire to Nation*. Cambridge, MA: Harvard University Press, 1960.

Eriksen, T. H. *Ethnicity and Nationalism*. London: Pluto, 2002.

Erskine, Toni. *Embedded Cosmopolitanism*. Oxford: Oxford University Press, 2008.

Fehrenbach, Elizabeth. "Nation." *Handbuch der Politisch-Soziale Grundbegriffe in Frankreich 1680–1782* 7 (1986): 75–107.

Fine, Robert. *Cosmopolitanism*. New York: Routledge, 2007.

Finley, Moses. "The Ancient Greeks and their Nation." In his *The Use and Abuse of History*, 120–33. New York: Viking, 1975.

Fletcher, George. *Loyalty: An Essay on the Morality of Relationships*. New York: Oxford University Press, 1993.

Forster, E. M. *Two Cheers for Democracy*. Harmondsworth: Penguin, 1985.

Forsyth, Murray. "Thomas Hobbes and the Constituent Power of the People." *Political Studies* 29 (1981): 191–203.

Foster, R. F. *Modern Ireland*. London: Penguin, 1988.

Fraisse, J. C. *Philia: La notion de l'amitié dans la philosophie de l'antique*. Paris: PUF, 1974.

Francis, Emmerich. *Ethnos und Demos: Soziologische Beiträge zur Volkstheorie*, Berlin: Duncker & Humblot, 1965.

Frank, Jason. *Constituent Moments: Enacting the People in Post-Revolutionary America*. Durham, NC: Duke University Press, 2009.

Franklin, Julian. *John Locke and the Theory of Sovereignty*. Cambridge: Cambridge University Press, 1978.

Frearon, James, and David Laitin. "Explaining Interethnic Cooperation." *American Political Science Review* 90 (1996): 715–35.

Frost, Catherine. *Morality and Nationalism*. New York: Routledge, 2006.

Furet, Francois. *Interpreting the French Revolution*. Cambridge: Cambridge University Press, 1981.

Galston, William. "Realism in Political Theory." *European Journal of Political Theory* 9 (2010): 385–411.

Gans, Chaim. *The Limits of Nationalism*. Cambridge: Cambridge University Press, 2002.

Gellner, Ernest. *Nations and Nationalism*. Ithaca, NY: Cornell University Press, 1983.

——. *Thought and Change*. London: Weidenfeld and Nicholson, 1964.

Gentile, Emilio. *The Sacralization of Politics in Fascist Italy*. Cambridge, MA: Harvard University Press, 1996.

Gilbert, Paul. *Philosophy of Nationalism*. Boulder, CO: Westview, 1998.

Goodin, Robert. "Conventions and Conversion, or Why Is Nationalism Sometimes So Nasty?" In McKim and McMahan, *The Morality of Nationalism*, 88–99.

Gottlieb, Gideon. *Nations against States*. New York: Council on Foreign Relations, 1993.

Greenfeld, Liah. *Nationalism: Five Roads to Modernity*. Cambridge, MA: Harvard University Press, 1992.

Grosby, Steven. *Biblical Ideas of Nationality*. Winona Lakes, IN: Eisenbrauns, 2002.

——. *Nationalism: A Very Short Introduction*. Oxford: Oxford University Press, 2005.

——. "Nationalism and Social Theory: The Distinction between Community and Society." In *Routledge International Handbook of Contemporary Social and Political Theory*, edited by G. Delanty and S. P. Turner, 280–89. London: Routledge, 2011.

——. "The Verdict of History: The Inexpungeable Tie of Primordiality." *Ethnic and Racial Studies* 17 (1994): 164–71.

Habermas, Jürgen. *Between Facts and Norms*. Cambridge, MA: MIT Press, 1996.

——. "Citizenship and National Identity." In Beiner, *Theorizing Citizenship*, 255–82.

——. "The European Nation-State: On the Past and Future of Sovereignty." In his *The Inclusion of the Other*. Cambridge: MIT Press, 1998.

——. *The New Conservatism*. Cambridge, MA: MIT Press, 1989.

——. "Remarks on Legitimation." *Philosophy and Social Criticism* 24 (1998): 157–71.

Hall, John A. "Nationalisms, Classified and Explained." In his *Coercion and Consent: Studies on the Modern State*, 124–48. Cambridge: Polity, 1994.

——, ed. *The State of the Nation: Ernest Gellner and the Theory of Nationalism*. Cambridge: Cambridge University Press, 1998.

Hall, Jonathan M. *Ethnic Identity in Greek Antiquity*. Cambridge: Cambridge University Press, 1997.

——. *Hellenicity*. Chicago: University of Chicago Press, 2002.

Hamilton, Alexander, John Jay, and James Madison. *The Federalist Papers*. New York; Mentor, 1981.

Hardin, Russell. *One for All: The Logic of Group Conflict.* Princeton, NJ: Princeton University Press, 1995.

Hechter, Michael. *Containing Nationalism.* Oxford: Oxford University Press, 1999.

Hegel, G. W. F. *Philosophy of Right.* Oxford: Oxford University Press, 1967.

Held, David. *Democracy and the Global Order: From the Modern State to Cosmopolitan Governance.* Stanford, CA: Stanford University Press, 1995.

———. "Principles of Cosmopolitan Order." In *The Political Philosophy of Cosmopolitanism*, edited by G. Brock and H. Brighouse. Cambridge: Cambridge University Press, 2005.

Herbst, Jeffrey. *State and Power in Africa.* Princeton, NJ: Princeton University Press, 2000.

Herder, J. G. *Another Philosophy of History.* Indianapolis: Hackett, 2004.

———. *Ideas: Outlines of a Philosophy of History of Man.* New York: Bergmann, 1966.

Hertz, Frederick. *Nationality in History and Politics.* London: Routledge & Kegan Paul, 1944.

Hinsley, F. H. *Sovereignty.* Cambridge: Cambridge University Press, 1986.

Hobbes, Thomas. *Leviathan.* London: Penguin, 1968.

———. *De Cive.* Oxford: Clarendon, 1983.

Hobsbawm, Eric. *Nations and Nationalism since 1780.* Cambridge: Cambridge University Press, 1989.

———. "Some Reflections on 'The Break-Up of Britain.'" *New Left Review* 105 (1977): 3–24.

Hobsbawm, Eric, and Terence Ranger, eds. *The Invention of Tradition.* Cambridge: Cambridge University Press, 2005.

Hollinger, David. "Not Universalists, Not Pluralists: The New Cosmopolitans Find Their Own Way." *Constellations* 8 (2001): 236–48.

———. *Postethnic America.* New York: Basic Books, 1995.

Holmes, Stephen. "Precommitment and the Paradox of Democracy." In *Constitutionalism and Democracy*, edited by J. Elster, 195–240. Cambridge: Cambridge University Press, 1988.

———. "The Secret History of Self-Interest." In his *Passions and Constraints*, 42–68. Chicago: University of Chicago Press, 1995.

Holton, Robert. *Cosmopolitanisms.* New York: Palgrave, 2009.

Hont, Istvan. "Permanent Crisis of a Divided Mankind: The Contemporary Crisis of the Nation-State in Historical Perspective." *Political Studies* 42 (1994): 166–231.

Horowitz, Donald. *Ethnic Groups in Conflict.* Berkeley: University of California Press, 1985.

———. "Self-Determination: Politics, Philosophy, and Law." In *Ethnicity and Group Rights: Nomos* 39, edited by W. Kymlicka and I. Shapiro. New York: New York University Press, 1996.

Hume, David. "Of Parties in General." In his *Essays: Moral, Political and Literary*, 54–63. Indianapolis: Liberty Fund, 1987.

Huntington, Samuel. *Who Are We? The Challenges to America's National Identity*. Cambridge, MA: Harvard University Press, 2004.

Hurka, Thomas. "The Justification of National Partiality." In McKim and McMahon, *The Morality of Nationalism*, 139–57.

Hutchinson, John. *The Dynamics of Cultural Nationalism*. London: Allen & Unwin, 1987.

Ignatieff, Michael. *Blood and Belonging: Journeys into the New Nationalism*. New York: Noonday, 1995.

———. "Nationalism and the Narcissism of Minor Differences." In Beiner, *Theorizing Nationalism*.

———. *The Warrior's Honor: Ethnic War and the Modern Conscience*. New York: Henry Holt, 1998.

Isaacs, Harold. "Basic Group Identity." In *Ethnicity: Theory and Experience*, edited by N. Glazer and P. Moynihan. Cambridge, MA: Harvard University Press, 1975.

———. *Idols of the Tribe*. Cambridge, MA: Harvard University Press, 1975.

Jackson, Robert. *Quasi States: Sovereignty, International Relations and the Third World*. Cambridge: Cambridge University Press, 1990.

Jefferson, Thomas. *Writings*. New York: Library of America, 1984.

Kamenka, Eugene, ed. *Nationalism: The Nature and Evolution of an Idea*. London: Edward Arnold: 1976.

Kant, Immanuel. *Fundamental Principles of Metaphysics of Morals*. Indianapolis: Bobbs-Merrill, 1949.

———. *The Metaphysical Elements of Justice*. Indianapolis: Bobbs-Merrill, 1965.

———. *The Metaphysics of Morals*. Cambridge: Cambridge University Press, 1991.

———. "Perpetual Peace." In his *On History*, 85–136. Indianapolis: Bobbs-Merrill, 1977.

Kateb, George. *Patriotism and Other Mistakes*. New Haven, CT: Yale University Press, 2006.

Keating, Michael. *Plurinational Democracy: Stateless Nations in a Post-Sovereignty Era*. New York: Oxford University Press, 2001.

Kedourie, Elie. *Nationalism*. New York: Praeger, 1960.

Keller, Simon. *The Limits of Loyalty*. Cambridge: Cambridge University Press, 2007.

Kleingeld, Pauline. "Six Versions of Cosmopolitanism in Late Eighteenth Century Germany." *Journal of the History of Ideas* 60 (1999): 505–24.

Kohn, Hans. *The Idea of Nationalism*. New York: Macmillan, 1951.

Kolers, Avery. *Land, Conflict, and Justice: A Political Theory of Territory*. Cambridge: Cambridge University Press, 2009.

Koonz, Claudia. *The Nazi Conscience*. Cambridge, MA: Harvard University Press, 2003.

Kristeva, Julian. *Nations without Nationalism*. New York: Columbia University Press, 1993.

Kymlicka, Will. *Liberalism, Community, and Culture*. Oxford: Clarendon, 1989.

——. "Liberal Nationalism and Cosmopolitan Justice." In Post, *Another Cosmopolitanism*, 128–44.

——. "Misunderstanding Nationalism." *Dissent* (Winter 1995): 130–37.

——. *Multicultural Citizenship*. Oxford: Oxford University Press, 1995.

——. *Politics in the Vernacular*. Oxford: Oxford University Press, 2001.

——. "Sources of Nationalism," in McKim and McMahon, *The Morality of Nationalism*, 56–65.

Laborde, Cecile. *Critical Republicanism: The Hijab Controversy and Political Philosophy*. Oxford: Oxford University Press, 2008.

Laitin, David. *Nations, States, and Violence*. Oxford: Oxford University Press, 2007.

Lawson, George. *Political Sacra et Civilis*. Cambridge: Cambridge University Press, 1992.

Lazare, Daniele. *The Frozen Republic*. New York: Harcourt Brace & Company, 1996

Lebovics, Herman. *True France: The Wars over Cultural Identity, 1900–45*. Ithaca, NY: Cornell University Press, 1992.

Lieberman, Benjamin. *Terrible Fate: Ethnic Cleansing in the Making of Modern Europe*. Chicago: Ivan Dee, 2006.

Locke, John. *Two Treatises of Government*. Cambridge: Cambridge University Press, 1960.

Long, A. A. "The Concept of Cosmopolitanism in Greek and Roman Thought." *Daedalus* (2008): 50–58.

Lucas, J. R. *On Justice*. Oxford: Clarendon, 1980

Maalouf, Amin. *In the Name of Identity*. New York: Arcade, 1996.

MacIntyre, Alisdair. *Is Patriotism a Virtue? Lindley Lecture*. Lawrence: University Press of Kansas, 1984.

MacNeil, W. H. *Polyethnicity and National Unity*. Toronto: University of Toronto Press, 1986

Maistre, Joseph de. "On the Sovereignty of the People." In his *Against Rousseau*, edited by R. Lebrun, 45–194. Montreal: McGill-Queens University Press, 1996.

Mann, Michael. *The Dark Side of Democracy: Explaining Ethnic Cleansing*. Cambridge: Cambridge University Press, 2005.

——. *Fascists*. Cambridge: Cambridge University Press, 2004.

Margalit, Avishai. *The Ethics of Memory*. Cambridge, MA: Harvard University Press, 2002.

Margalit Avishai, and Joseph Raz. "National Self-Determination." *Journal of Philosophy* 87 (1990): 439–61.

Markell, Patchen. "Making Affect Safe for Democracy." *Political Theory* 28 (2000): 38–63.

Marx, Anthony. *Faith in Nation: Exclusionary Origins of Nationalism.* Oxford: Oxford University Press, 2003.

Mayall, James. "Sovereignty, Nationalism, and Self-Determination." *Political Studies* 47 (1999): 474–502.

Mayerfeld, Jamie. "The Myth of Benign Group Identity." *Polity* 30 (1998): 555–78.

Mazzini, Giuseppe. *A Cosmopolitanism of Nations.* Princeton, NJ: Princeton University Press, 2009.

———. *The Duties of Man.* London: Dent, 1907.

McKim, Robert, and J. McMahan, eds. *The Morality of Nationalism.* Oxford: Oxford University Press, 1997.

McMahan, Jeff. "The Limits of National Partiality." In McKim and McMahan, *The Morality of Nationalism*, 107–38.

Mehta, Pratap. "Cosmopolitanism and the Circle of Reason." *Political Theory* 28 (2000): 619–39.

Meinecke, Friedrich. *Cosmopolitanism and the National State.* Princeton, NJ: Princeton University Press, 1970.

Meisels, Tamar. *Territorial Rights.* Dordrecht: Springer, 2005.

Mendel, David. *The Rise and Fall of Jewish Nationalism: Jewish and Christian Ethnicity in Ancient Palestine.* Grand Rapids, MI: Eerdman's, 1992.

Mill, John Stuart. *Considerations on Representative Government.* Indianapolis: Bobbs-Merrill, 1958.

Miller, David. *National Responsibility and Global Justice.* Oxford: Oxford University Press, 2007.

———. *On Nationality.* Oxford: Oxford University Press, 1995.

———. "Secession and the Principle of Nationality." In Moore, *National Self-Determination and Secession*, 62–78.

Mollendorf, Darrel. *Cosmopolitan Justice.* Boulder, CO: Westview, 2002.

Montaigne, Michel de. *Essays.* Translated by Donald Frame. Stanford, CA: Stanford University Press, 1965.

Montesquieu, C. S. de. *Mes pensées.* In his *Oeuvres Complètes.* 2 Vols. Paris: Pleiade, 1951.

Moore, Margaret. *The Ethics of Nationalism.* Oxford: Oxford University Press, 1998.

———, ed. *National Self-Determination and Secession.* Oxford: Oxford University Press, 1998.

———. "The Territorial Dimension of Self-Determination." In Moore, *National Self-Determination and Secession*, 134–57.

Morgan, Edmond. *Inventing the People*. New York: Norton, 1988.

Morris, Christopher. *An Essay on the Modern State*. Cambridge: Cambridge University Press, 1998.

Mosse, George. *Confronting the Nation: Jewish and Western Nationalism*. Hanover, NH: Brandeis University Press, 1993.

Mostov, Julie. *Power, Process, and Popular Sovereignty*. Philadelphia: Temple University Press, 1992.

Moynihan, Patrick. *Pandemonium: Ethnicity in International Politics*. Oxford: Oxford University Press, 1993.

Mueller, Jan-Warner. *Constitutional Patriotism*. Princeton, NJ: Princeton University Press, 2007.

Musil, Robert. "'Nation' as Ideal and Reality." In his *Precision and Soul*, 101–15. Chicago: University of Chicago Press, 1995.

Nakano, Takeshi. "A Critique of Held's Cosmopolitan Democracy." *Contemporary Political Theory*, 5 (2006): 33–51.

Nässtrom, Sofia. "The Legitimacy of the People." *Political Theory* 35 (2007): 624–58.

Nathanson, Stephen. "Nationalism and the Limits of Global Humanism." In McKim and McMahan, *The Morality of Nationalism*, 176–87.

Nielsen, Kai. "Liberal Nationalism and Secession." In Moore, *National Self-Determination and Secession*, 103–33.

Nora, Pierre. "Nation." In *Critical Dictionary of the French Revolution*, edited by F. Furet and M. Ozouf , 742–53. Cambridge, MA: Harvard University Press, 1989.

Norman, Wayne. *Negotiating Nationalism*. Oxford: Oxford University Press, 2006.

Nussbaum, Martha. "Kant and Stoic Cosmopolitanism." *Journal of Political Philosophy* 5 (1997): 1–25.

——. "Patriotism and Cosmopolitanism." In Nussbaum et al., *For Love of Country*, 3–17.

Nussbaum, Martha, et al. *For Love of Country: Debating the Limits of Patriotism*. Boston: Beacon, 1996.

O'Leary, Brendan. "Ernest Gellner's Diagnoses of Nationalism." In J. A. Hall, *The State of the Nation*, 40–88.

Pagden, Anthony. "Cosmopolitanism, and the Legacy of European Imperialism." *Constellations* 7 (2000): 3–22.

Paine, Thomas. *The Rights of Man*. Harmondsworth: Penguin, 1969.

Parekh, Bikhu. "The Incoherence of Nationalism." In Beiner, *Theorizing Nationalism*, 295–325.

——. "The 'New Right' and the Politics of Nationhood." In *The New Right: Image and Reality*, edited by N. Deakin. London: Runnymede Trust, 1986.

——. *Rethinking Multiculturalism*. Cambridge, MA: Harvard University Press, 2000.

Pasquino, Pasquale. "The Constitutional Republicanism of Emmanuel Sieyes." In *The Invention of Modern Republicanism*, edited by B. Fontana, 107–47. Cambridge: Cambridge University Press, 1994.

——. *Sieyes et l'invention de la constitution en France*. Paris: Odile Jacob, 1998.

Pavel, Carmen. "Cosmopolitanism, Nationalism and Moral Opportunity Costs." *Polity* 41 (2009): 489–513.

Philpott, Daniel. "In Defense of Self-Determination." *Ethics* 105 (1995): 352–85.

Plamenatz, John. *On Alien Rule and Self-Government*. London: Longmans, 1960.

——. "Two Types of Nationalism." In Kamenka, *Nationalism*.

Plato. *Republic*. New York: Basic Books, 1989.

Pogge, Thomas. "Cosmopolitanism and Sovereignty." In *World Poverty and Human Rights*, edited by T. Pogge. Cambridge: Polity, 2002.

Poole, Ross. *Nation and Identity*. London: Routledge, 1999.

Post, Robert, ed. *Another Cosmopolitanism*. Oxford: Oxford University Press, 2006.

Quaritsch, Helmut. *Souveranität: Entstehung und Entwicklung des Begriffs in Frankreich und Deutschland vom 13. Jahrhundert*. Berlin: Duncker & Humblot, 1986.

Rabinow-Edling, Susanna. *Slavophile Thought and the Politics of Cultural Nationalism*. Albany: SUNY Press, 2005.

Rabkin, Jeremy. "Grotius, Vattel, and Locke: An Older View of Natality and Nationalism." *Review of Politics* (1997): 293–322.

Rawls, John. "Justice as Fairness: Political, Not Metaphysical." *Philosophy and Public Affairs* 15 (1985): 223–51.

——. *A Theory of Justice*. Cambridge, MA: Harvard University Press, 1971.

Raz, Joseph. *The Morality of Freedom*. Oxford: Clarendon, 1986.

Renan, Ernst. "What Is a Nation?" In Bhabha, *Nation and Narration*, 9–22.

Reynolds, Susan. *Kingdoms and Communities in Western Europe (900–1300)*. Oxford: Clarendon, 1984.

Ridley, Matt. *The Origins of Virtue*. New York: Viking, 1997.

Robbins, Bruce. "Cosmopolitanism: New and Newer." *Boundary* 2 (2007): 47–60.

Roshwald, Aviel. *The Endurance of Nationalism: Ancient Roots and Modern Dilemmas*. Cambridge: Cambridge University Press, 2006

Rousseau, Jean-Jacques. "Discourse on Political Economy." In his *Basic Political Writings*, 111–38.

——. *The Social Contract*. In his *Basic Political Writings*, 141–227.

Sayer, Derek. *The Coasts of Bohemia*. Princeton, NJ: Princeton University Press, 1998.

Scheffler, Samuel. *Boundaries and Allegiances*. Oxford: Oxford University Press, 2001.

———. "Cosmopolitanism, Justice and Institutions." *Daedalus* (2008): 68–77.

Schelereth, Thomas. *Cosmopolitan Ideal in Enlightenment Thought*. Notre Dame, IN: University of Notre Dame Press, 1977.

Scheuerman, William. "Cosmopolitan Democracy and the Rule of Law." *Ratio Juris* (2002): 439–57.

———. "Global Governance without Global Government?" *Political Theory* 36 (2008): 133–51.

Schlesinger, Arthur. *The Disuniting of America*. New York: Norton, 1992.

Schmalenbach, Hans. "Communion—a Sociological Category." In *Hans Schmalenbach on Society and Experience*, edited and translated by Günther Lüschen and Gregory P. Stone. Chicago: University of Chicago Press, 1977.

Schnapper, Dominique. *La communauté des citoyens: Sur l'idée moderne de la nation*. Paris: Gallimard, 1994.

Schofield, Malcolm. *The Stoic Idea of the City*. Cambridge: Cambridge University Press, 1991.

Scruton, Roger. "In Defence of the Nation." In his *The Philosopher on Dover Beach*, 299–337. Manchester: Carcanet, 1990.

Semelin, Jacques. *Purify and Destroy: The Political Uses of Massacre and Genocide*. New York: Columbia University Press, 2009.

Sen, Amartya. *Identity and Violence: The Illusion of Destiny*. New York: Norton, 2006.

Seton-Watson, Hugh. *Nations and States*. London: Methuen, 1977.

Shachar, Ayelet. *The Birthright Lottery*. Princeton, NJ: Princeton University Press, 2009.

Shalit, Avner de. "National Self-Determination: Political, Not Cultural." *Political Studies* 44 (1996): 906–20.

Shklar, Judith. *The Faces of Injustice*. New Haven, CT: Yale University Press, 1989.

———. "The Liberalism of Fear." In her *Political Thought and Political Thinkers*, 3–20. Chicago: University of Chicago Press, 1998.

———. "Obligation, Loyalty, Exile." *Political Theory* 21 (1993): 181–97.

Shteyngart, Gary. *Absurdistan*. New York: Random House, 2006.

Shuck, Peter, and Rogers Smith. *Citizenship without Consent*. New Haven, CT: Yale University Press, 1987.

Shue, Henry. "Mediating Duties." *Ethics* 98 (1988): 687–704.

Sieyès, E. J. "Contre la ré-totale." In Pasquino, *Sieyes et l'invention de la constitution en France*.

——. *Écrits Politiques*. Paris: Editions des archives contemporaines, 1985.

——. *What Is the Third Estate?* New York: Praeger, 1964.

Singer, B. C. J. "Cultural versus Contractual Nations: Rethinking their Opposition." *History and Theory* 35 (1996): 309–37.

Smith, Anthony. *The Antiquity of Nations*. London: Polity, 2004.

——. *The Ethnic Origins of Nations*. Oxford: Basil Blackwell, 1986.

——. *National Identity*. New York: Penguin, 1991.

——. *Nationalism and Modernism*. London: Routledge, 1998.

——. *Theories of Nationalism*. New York: Harper and Row, 1971.

Smith, Rogers. "Citizenship and the Politics of People-Building." *International Journal of Citizenship Studies* 5 (2001): 73–96

——. *Civic Ideals*. New Haven, CT: Yale University Press, 1998.

——. *Stories of Peoplehood*. Cambridge: Cambridge University Press, 2003.

Snyder, Timothy. *The Reconstruction of Nations*. New Haven, CT: Yale University Press, 2003.

Sober, Eliot, and D. S. Wilson. *Unto Others: The Evolutionary Psychology of Unselfish Behavior*. Cambridge, MA: Harvard University Press, 1998.

Spencer, P., and H. Wollman. "Good and Bad Nationalisms: A Critique of Dualism." *Journal of Political Ideologies* 3 (1998): 187–96.

Spinner-Halev, Jeff. "Democracy, Solidarity, and Post-Nationalism." *Political Studies* 56 (2008): 604–28.

Spruyt, Hendrik. *The Sovereign State and Its Competitors*. Princeton, NJ: Princeton University Press, 1994.

Stade, Ronald. "Cosmos and Polis, Past and Present." *Theory, Culture and Society* 24 (2007): 283–85.

Stern, Paul. "Why Do People Sacrifice for Their Nation?" In *Perspectives on Nationalism and War*, edited by J. Comaroff and P. Stern, 99–122. Langhorne, PA: Gordon and Breach, 1995.

Stevens, Jacqueline. *Reproducing the State*. Princeton, NJ: Princeton University Press, 1999.

——. *States without Nations: Citizenship for Mortals*. New York: Columbia University Press, 2009.

Stilz, Anna. *Liberal Loyalties*. Princeton, NJ: Princeton University Press, 2009.

Stokes, Gale. "Cognition and the Function of Nationalism." *Journal of Interdisciplinary History* 4 (1974): 525–42.

Sureda, A. R. *The Evolution of the Right of Self-Determination: A Study of United Nations Practice*. Leiden: A. W. Sijthoff, 1973.

Tambiah, Damien. "Ethnic Conflict in the World Today." *American Ethnologist* 16 (1989): 335–49.

Tamir, Yael. *Liberal Nationalism*. Princeton, NJ: Princeton University Press, 1993.

——. "The Right to National Self-Determination." *Social Research* 58 (1991): 565–90.

——. "Theoretical Difficulties in the Study of Nationalism." In Beiner, *Theorizing Nationalism.*

Tan, Kok-Chor. *Justice without Borders: Cosmopolitanism, Nationalism, and Patriotism.* Cambridge: Cambridge University Press, 2004.

Thom, Martin. "Tribes within Nations." In Bhabha, *Nation and Narration*, 23–43.

Thompson, Janna. "Communal Identity and World Citizenship." In *Re-Imagining Political Community*, edited by D. Archibugi and D. Held, 179–97. Stanford, CA: Stanford University Press, 1998.

Tönnies, Ferdinand. *Community and Society.* New York: Harper, 1963.

Trevor-Roper, Hugh. "The Highland Tradition in Scotland." In *The Invention of Tradition*, edited by E. Hobsbawm and T. Ranger. Cambridge: Cambridge University Press, 1995.

Vincent, Andrew. *Nationalism and Particularity.* Cambridge: Cambridge University Press, 2000.

Viroli, Maurizio. *For Love of Country: An Essay on Patriotism and Nationalism.* Oxford: Oxford University Press, 1995.

——. "Reply to Xenos and Yack." *Critical Review* (1998): 1–9.

Vogt, K. M. *Law, Reason, and the Cosmic City: Political Philosophy in the Early Stoa.* Oxford: Oxford University Press, 2008.

Waal, Franz de. *Good-Natured: The Origins of Right and Wrong in Humans and Other Animals.* Cambridge, MA: Harvard University Press, 1996.

Waldron, Jeremy. "Cosmopolitan Norms." In Post, *Another Cosmopolitanism*, 83–101.

Walker, Brian. "Social Movements as Nationalisms, or The Very Idea of a Queer Nation." In *Rethinking Nationalism*, edited by J. Couture et al., 505–49. Calgary: University of Calgary Press, 1998.

Walzer, Michael. "The New Tribalism: Notes on a Difficult Problem." In Beiner, *Theorizing Nationalism*, 205–18.

——. *Spheres of Justice.* New York: Basic, 1983.

——. *On Toleration.* New Haven, CT: Yale University Press, 1997.

——. *What It Means to Be an American.* New York: Marsilio, 1992.

Weber, Eugen. *Peasants into Frenchmen.* Stanford, CA: Stanford University Press, 1976.

Weber, Max. *Economy and Society.* Berkeley: University of California Press,

Weinstock, Daniel. "National Partiality: Confronting the Intuitions." *Monist* 82 (1999): 516–41.

Wellman, Christopher. *A Theory of Secession: The Case for Political Self-Determination.* Cambridge: Cambridge University Press, 2005.

West, Rebecca. *Black Lamb, Grey Falcon.* London: Penguin, 1988.

Whelan, Frederick. "Democratic Theory and the Boundary Problem." In *Nomos* XXV: *Liberal Democracy*, edited by J. R. Pennock and J. W. Chapman, 13–47. New York: NYU Press, 1983.

Wiebe, Robert. *Who We Are: A History of Popular Nationalism*. Princeton, NJ: Princeton University Press, 2002.

Williams, Bernard. *In the Beginning Was the Deed: Realism and Moralism in Political Argument*. Cambridge: Cambridge University Press, 2005.

Winter, Bronwyn. *Hijab and Republic: Uncovering the French Headscarf Debate*. Syracuse, NY: Syracuse University Press, 2008.

Wolf, Susan. "Morality and Partiality." *Philosophic Perspectives* 6 (1992): 243–59.

Wolin, Sheldon. "Norm and Form." In *Athenian Political Thought and Democracy and the Reconstruction of American Democracy*, edited by Peter Euben et al., 29–58. Ithaca, NY: Cornell University Press, 1994.

Woodward, C. van. *The Old World's New World*. Oxford: Oxford University Press, 1990.

Wright, Robert. *The Moral Animal*. New York: Vintage, 1994.

Yack, Bernard. "Can Patriotism Save Us from Nationalism? Rejoinder to Viroli." *Critical Review* 12 (1998): 203–206.

———. "Democracy and the Love of Truth." In *Democracy and Truth*, edited by J. Elkins and A. Norris. Philadelphia: University of Pennsylvania Press, 2012.

———. *The Fetishism of Modernities*. Notre Dame, IN: University of Notre Dame Press, 1997.

———. "Does Liberal Practice 'Live Down' to Liberal Theory? Liberalism and Its Communitarian Critics." In *Community in America*, edited by C. Reynolds, 147–69. Berkeley: University of California Press, 1988.

———. "Multiculturalism and the Political Theorists." *European Journal of Political Theory* 1 (2002): 107–18.

———. "The Myth of the Civic Nation." In Beiner, *Theorizing Nationalism*, 147–69.

———. *The Problems of a Political Animal*. Berkeley: University of California Press, 1993.

———. "Reconciling Nationalism and Liberal Individualism." *Political Theory* 23 (1995): 165–82.

———. "Toward a Free Marketplace of Social Institutions." *Harvard Law Review* 101 (June 1988): 1961–77.

Yeats, W. B. *Explorations*. London: Macmillan, 1962.

Young, Crawford. *The African Colonial State in Comparative Perspective*. New Haven, CT: Yale University Press, 1994.

Zerubavel, Eviatar. *Time Maps: Collective Memory and the Shape of the Past*. Chicago: University of Chicago Press, 2003.

Zubaida, Sami. "Nations, Old and New." *Ethnic and Racial Studies* 12 (1989): 329–39.

Index

www.ingramcontent.com/pod-product-compliance
Lightning Source LLC
Chambersburg PA
CBHW022136020426
42334CB00015B/915
9780226944678